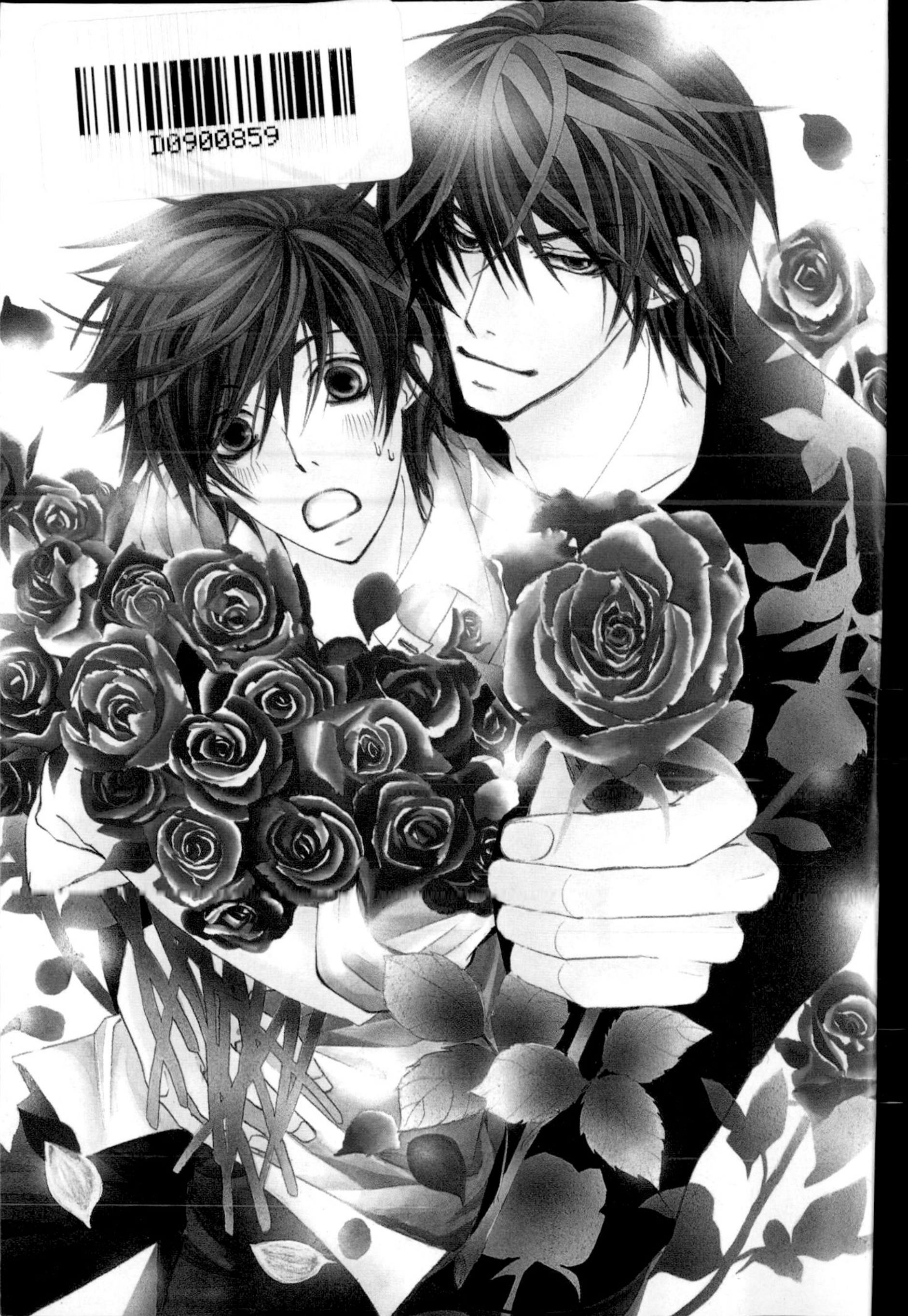

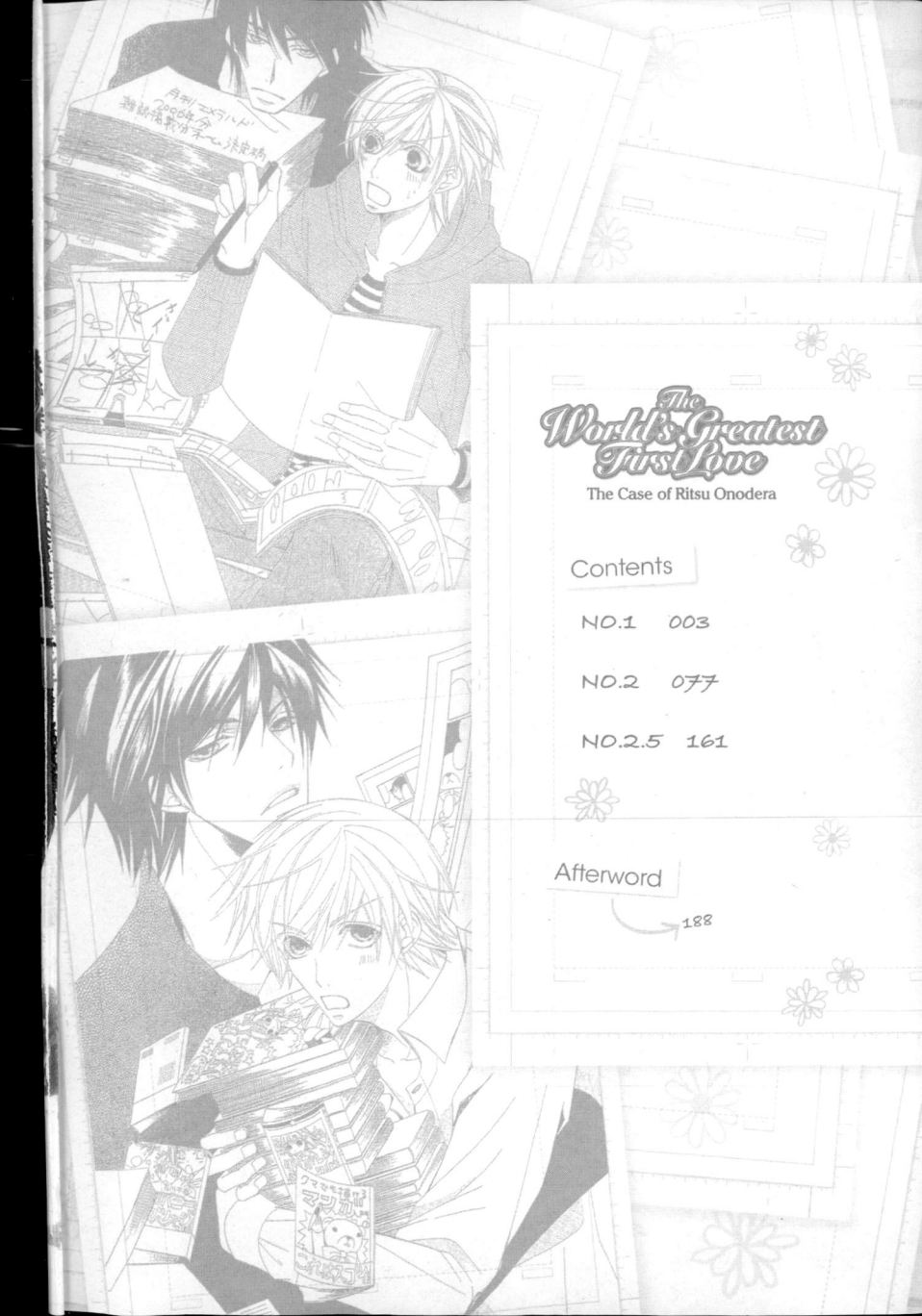

The World's Greatest First Love
The Case of Ritsu Onodera

Contents

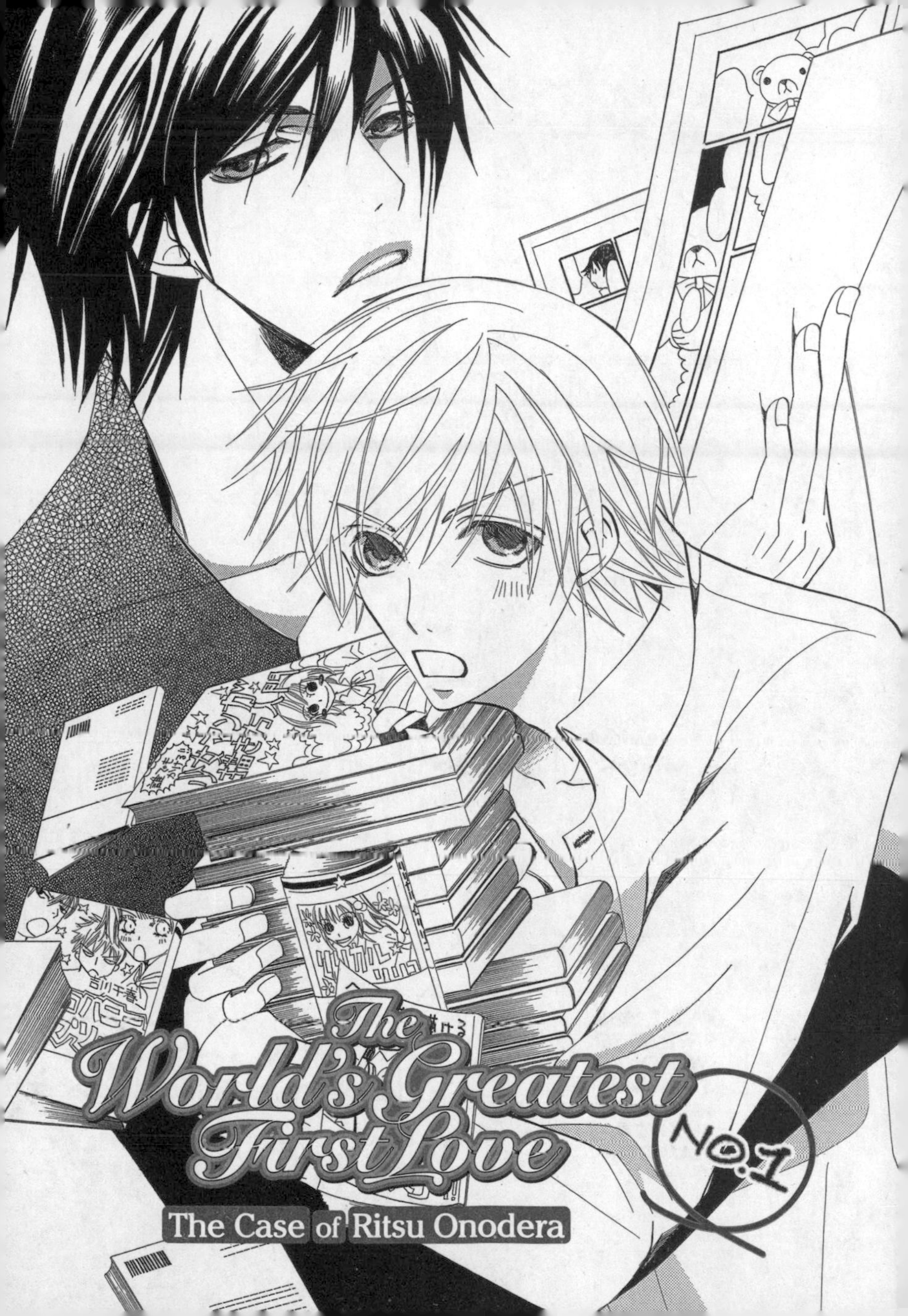
The World's Greatest First Love
NO.1
The Case of Ritsu Onodera

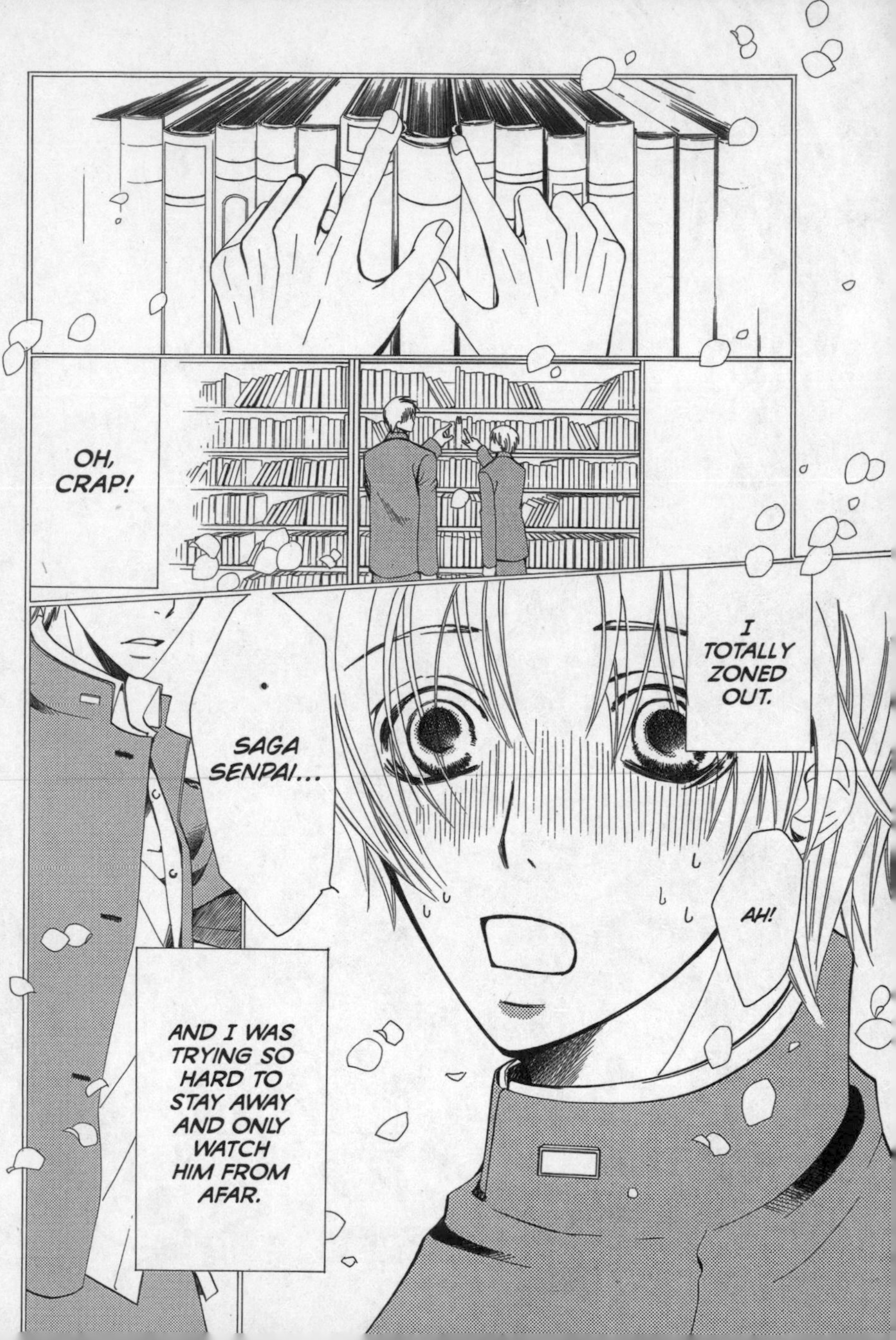
OH, CRAP!
I TOTALLY ZONED OUT.
AH!
SAGA SENPAI...
AND I WAS TRYING SO HARD TO STAY AWAY AND ONLY WATCH HIM FROM AFAR.

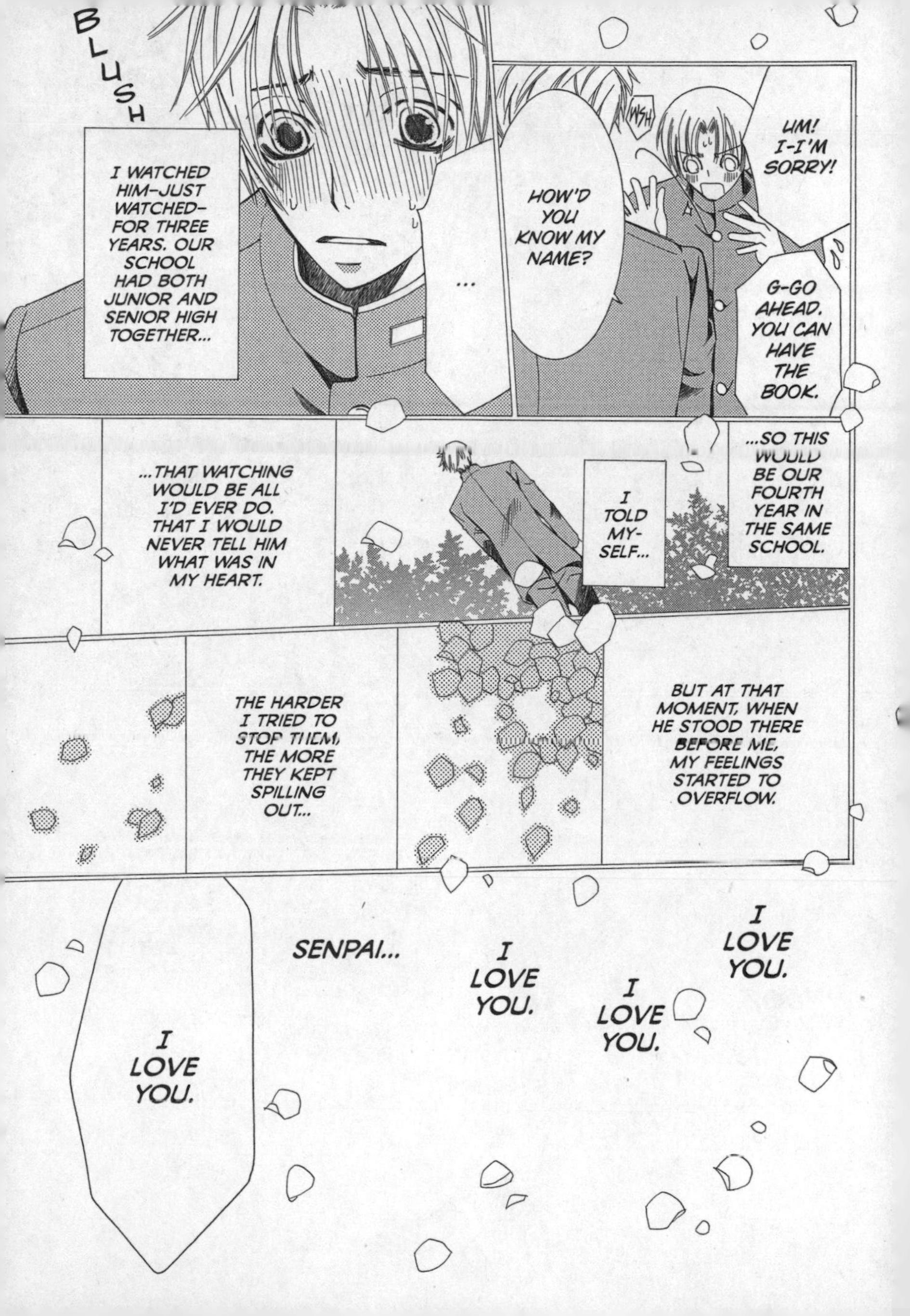
WSH
UM! I-I'M SORRY!
G-GO AHEAD. YOU CAN HAVE THE BOOK.
HOW'D YOU KNOW MY NAME?
...
BLUSH
I WATCHED HIM–JUST WATCHED–FOR THREE YEARS. OUR SCHOOL HAD BOTH JUNIOR AND SENIOR HIGH TOGETHER...
...SO THIS WOULD BE OUR FOURTH YEAR IN THE SAME SCHOOL.
I TOLD MYSELF...
...THAT WATCHING WOULD BE ALL I'D EVER DO. THAT I WOULD NEVER TELL HIM WHAT WAS IN MY HEART.
BUT AT THAT MOMENT, WHEN HE STOOD THERE BEFORE ME, MY FEELINGS STARTED TO OVERFLOW.
THE HARDER I TRIED TO STOP THEM, THE MORE THEY KEPT SPILLING OUT...
I LOVE YOU.
I LOVE YOU.
I LOVE YOU.
SENPAI...
I LOVE YOU.

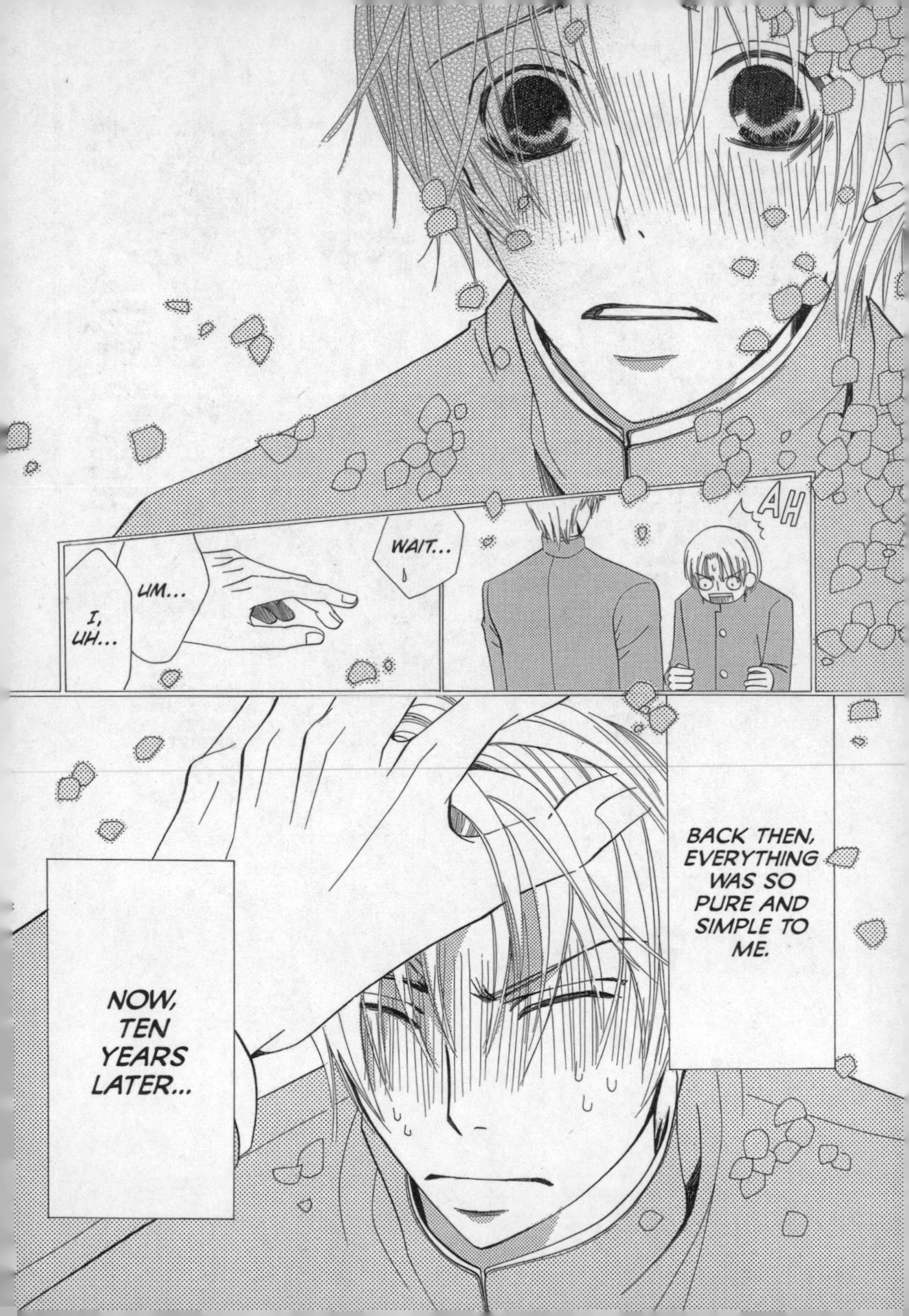
AH
WAIT...
UM...
I, UH...
BACK THEN, EVERYTHING WAS SO PURE AND SIMPLE TO ME.
NOW, TEN YEARS LATER...

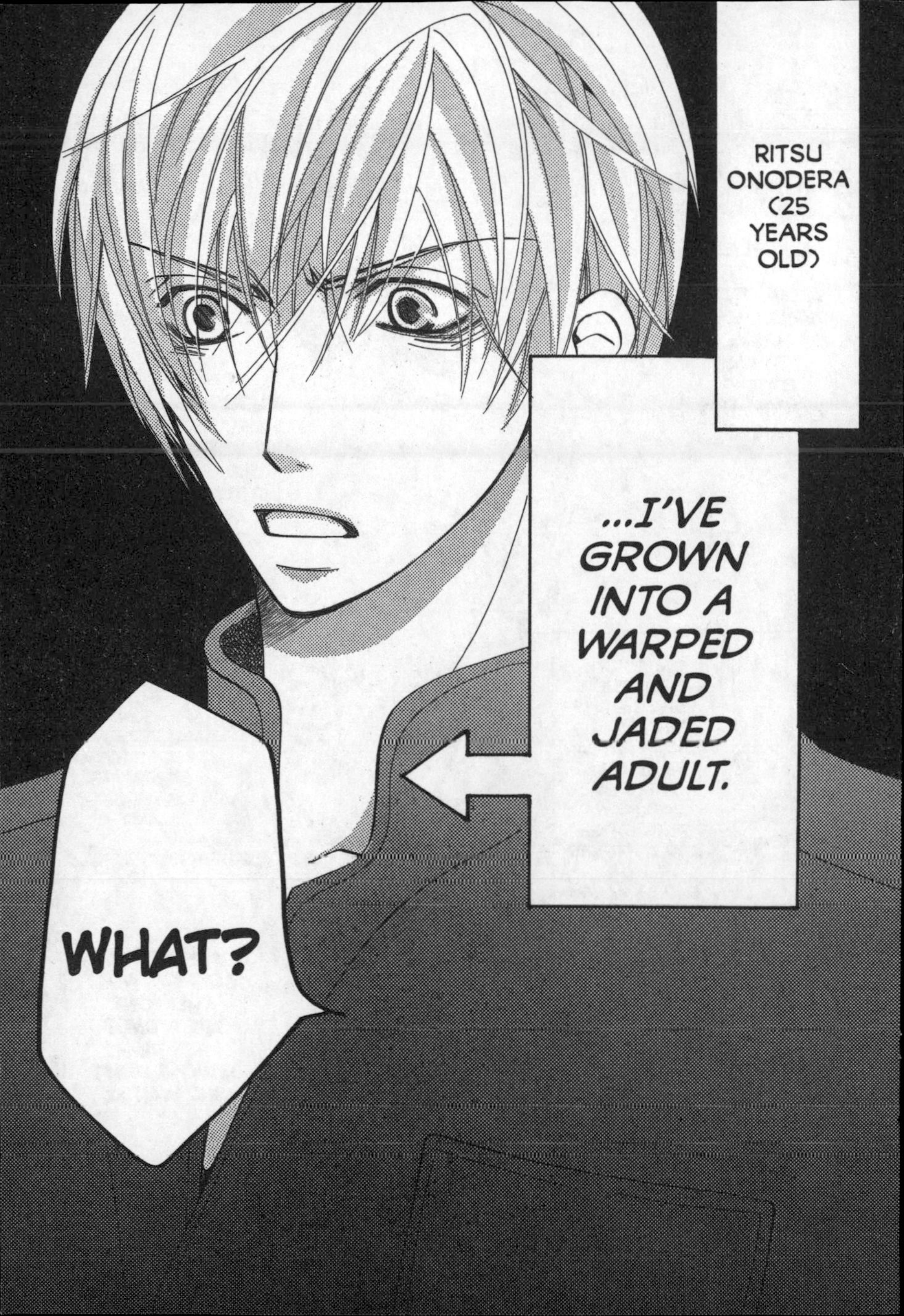
RITSU ONODERA (25 YEARS OLD)
...I'VE GROWN INTO A WARPED AND JADED ADULT.
WHAT?

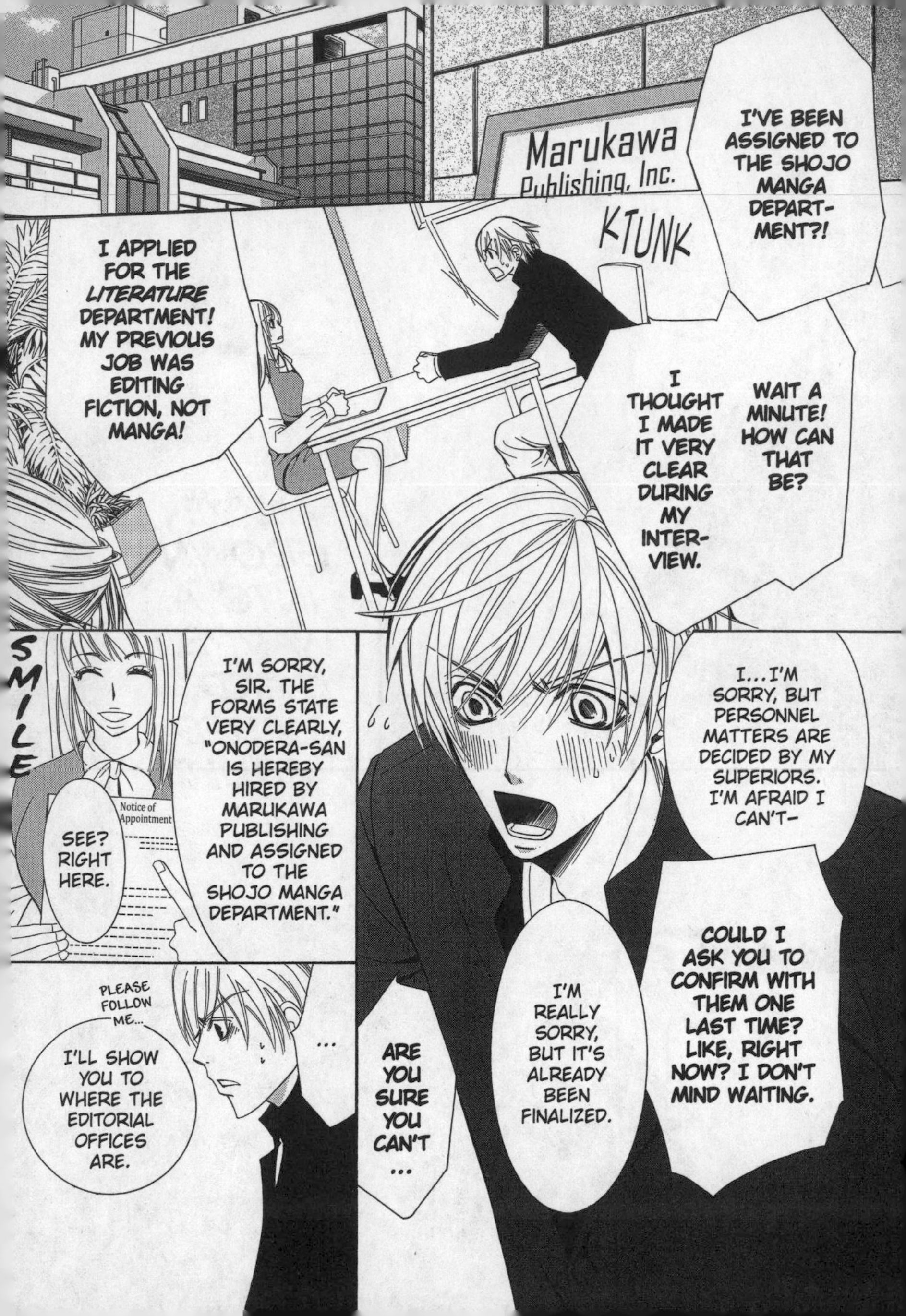
Marukawa Publishing, Inc.
I'VE BEEN ASSIGNED TO THE SHOJO MANGA DEPARTMENT?!
KTUNK
WAIT A MINUTE! HOW CAN THAT BE?
I THOUGHT I MADE IT VERY CLEAR DURING MY INTERVIEW.
I APPLIED FOR THE *LITERATURE* DEPARTMENT! MY PREVIOUS JOB WAS EDITING FICTION, NOT MANGA!
I...I'M SORRY, BUT PERSONNEL MATTERS ARE DECIDED BY MY SUPERIORS. I'M AFRAID I CAN'T-
COULD I ASK YOU TO CONFIRM WITH THEM ONE LAST TIME? LIKE, RIGHT NOW? I DON'T MIND WAITING.
I'M REALLY SORRY, BUT IT'S ALREADY BEEN FINALIZED.
ARE YOU SURE YOU CAN'T ...
I'M SORRY, SIR. THE FORMS STATE VERY CLEARLY, "ONODERA-SAN IS HEREBY HIRED BY MARUKAWA PUBLISHING AND ASSIGNED TO THE SHOJO MANGA DEPARTMENT."
SMILE
Notice of Appointment
SEE? RIGHT HERE.
...
PLEASE FOLLOW ME...
I'LL SHOW YOU TO WHERE THE EDITORIAL OFFICES ARE.

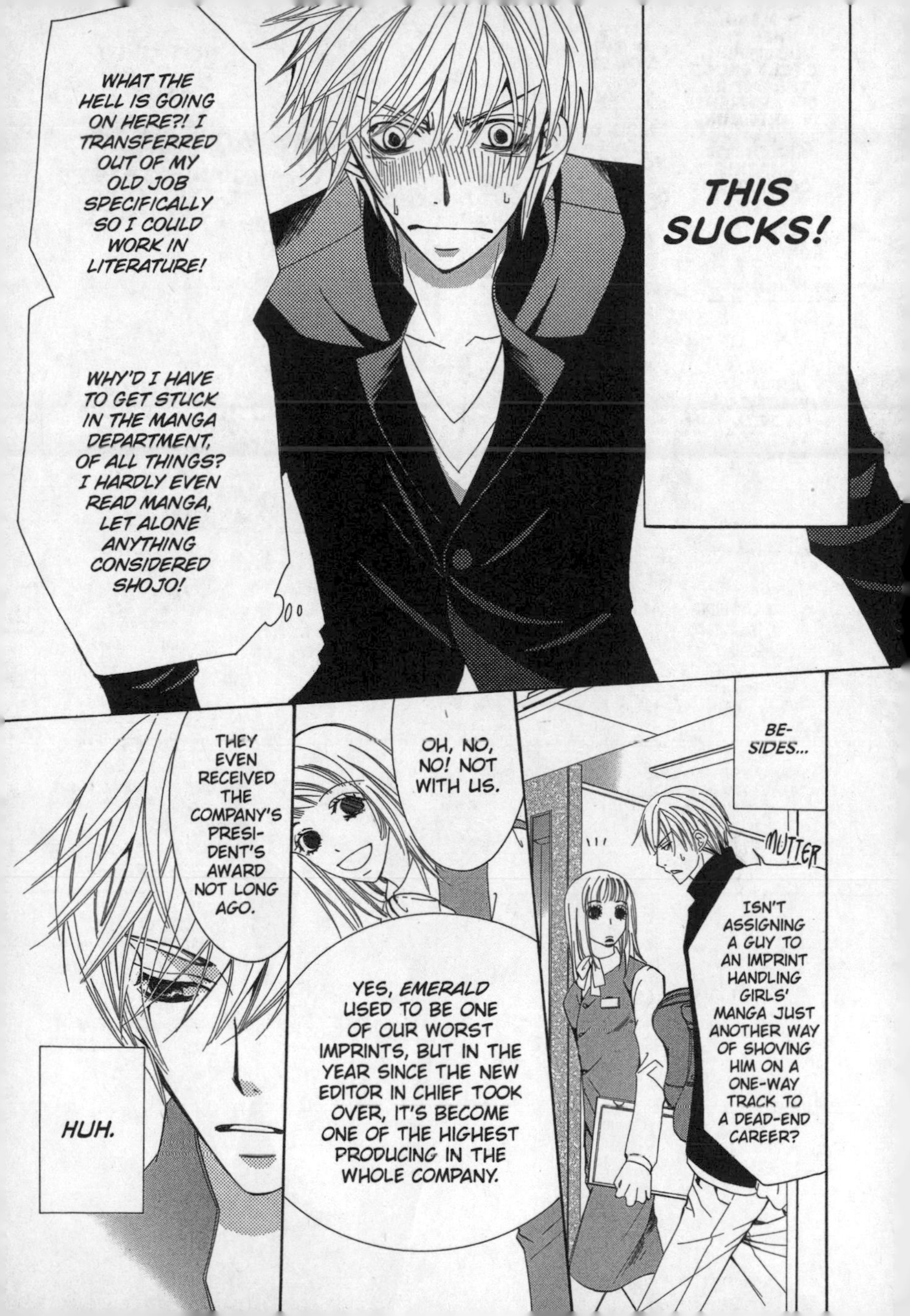
THIS SUCKS!
WHAT THE HELL IS GOING ON HERE?! I TRANSFERRED OUT OF MY OLD JOB SPECIFICALLY SO I COULD WORK IN LITERATURE!
WHY'D I HAVE TO GET STUCK IN THE MANGA DEPARTMENT, OF ALL THINGS? I HARDLY EVEN READ MANGA, LET ALONE ANYTHING CONSIDERED SHOJO!
BE-SIDES...
MUTTER
ISN'T ASSIGNING A GUY TO AN IMPRINT HANDLING GIRLS' MANGA JUST ANOTHER WAY OF SHOVING HIM ON A ONE-WAY TRACK TO A DEAD-END CAREER?
OH, NO, NO! NOT WITH US.
YES, *EMERALD* USED TO BE ONE OF OUR WORST IMPRINTS, BUT IN THE YEAR SINCE THE NEW EDITOR IN CHIEF TOOK OVER, IT'S BECOME ONE OF THE HIGHEST PRODUCING IN THE WHOLE COMPANY.
THEY EVEN RECEIVED THE COMPANY'S PRESI-DENT'S AWARD NOT LONG AGO.
HUH.

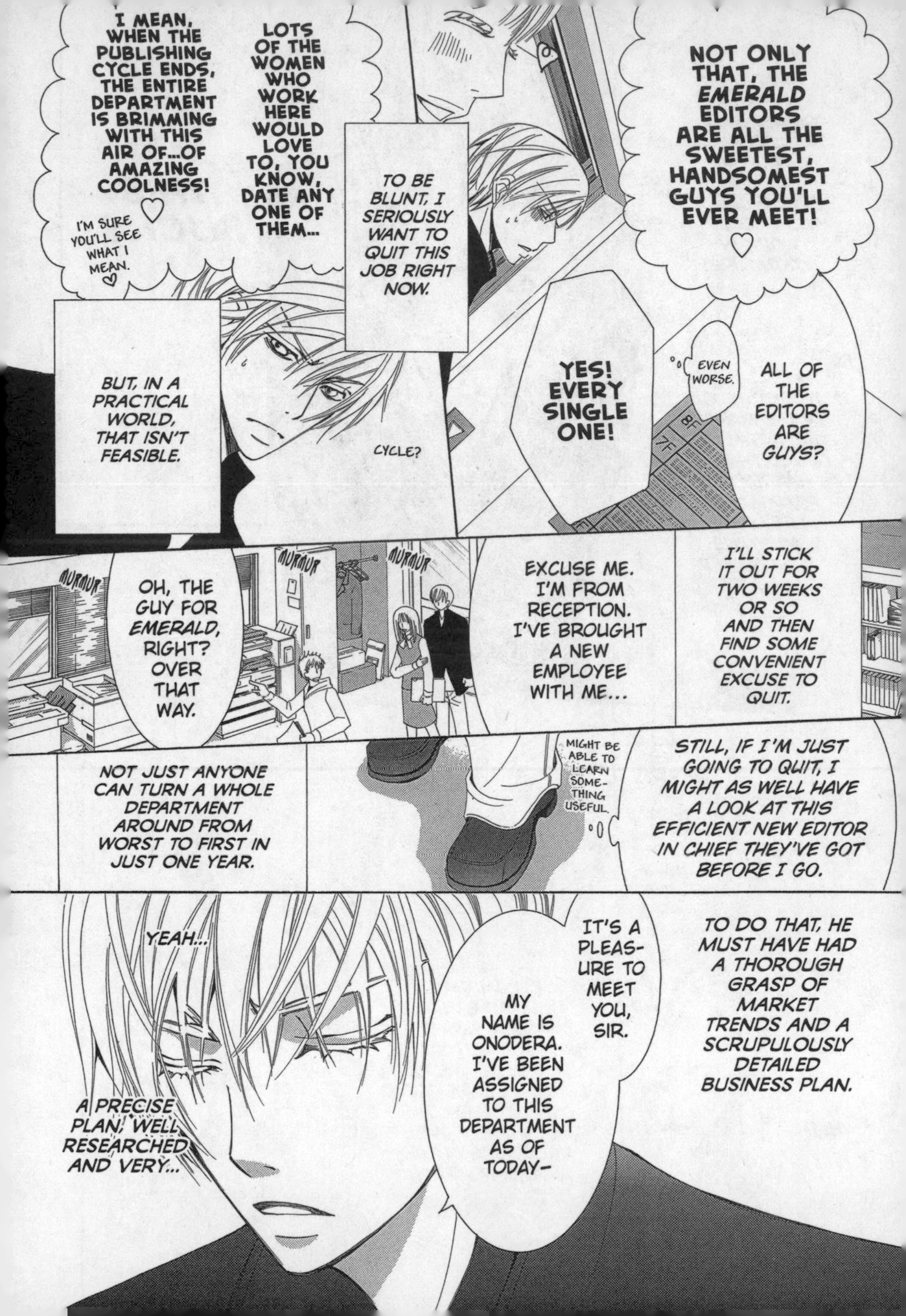
ALL OF THE EDITORS ARE GUYS?
EVEN WORSE.
YES! EVERY SINGLE ONE!
NOT ONLY THAT, THE EMERALD EDITORS ARE ALL THE SWEETEST, HANDSOMEST GUYS YOU'LL EVER MEET! ♡
TO BE BLUNT, I SERIOUSLY WANT TO QUIT THIS JOB RIGHT NOW.
LOTS OF THE WOMEN WHO WORK HERE WOULD LOVE TO, YOU KNOW, DATE ANY ONE OF THEM...
I MEAN, WHEN THE PUBLISHING CYCLE ENDS, THE ENTIRE DEPARTMENT IS BRIMMING WITH THIS AIR OF...OF AMAZING COOLNESS! ♡
I'M SURE YOU'LL SEE WHAT I MEAN. ♡
CYCLE?
BUT, IN A PRACTICAL WORLD, THAT ISN'T FEASIBLE.
I'LL STICK IT OUT FOR TWO WEEKS OR SO AND THEN FIND SOME CONVENIENT EXCUSE TO QUIT.
EXCUSE ME. I'M FROM RECEPTION. I'VE BROUGHT A NEW EMPLOYEE WITH ME...
MURMUR
MURMUR
OH, THE GUY FOR EMERALD, RIGHT? OVER THAT WAY.
MURMUR
STILL, IF I'M JUST GOING TO QUIT, I MIGHT AS WELL HAVE A LOOK AT THIS EFFICIENT NEW EDITOR IN CHIEF THEY'VE GOT BEFORE I GO.
MIGHT BE ABLE TO LEARN SOME-THING USEFUL.
NOT JUST ANYONE CAN TURN A WHOLE DEPARTMENT AROUND FROM WORST TO FIRST IN JUST ONE YEAR.
TO DO THAT, HE MUST HAVE HAD A THOROUGH GRASP OF MARKET TRENDS AND A SCRUPULOUSLY DETAILED BUSINESS PLAN.
A PRECISE PLAN, WELL RESEARCHED AND VERY...
IT'S A PLEAS-URE TO MEET YOU, SIR.
MY NAME IS ONODERA. I'VE BEEN ASSIGNED TO THIS DEPARTMENT AS OF TODAY-
YEAH...

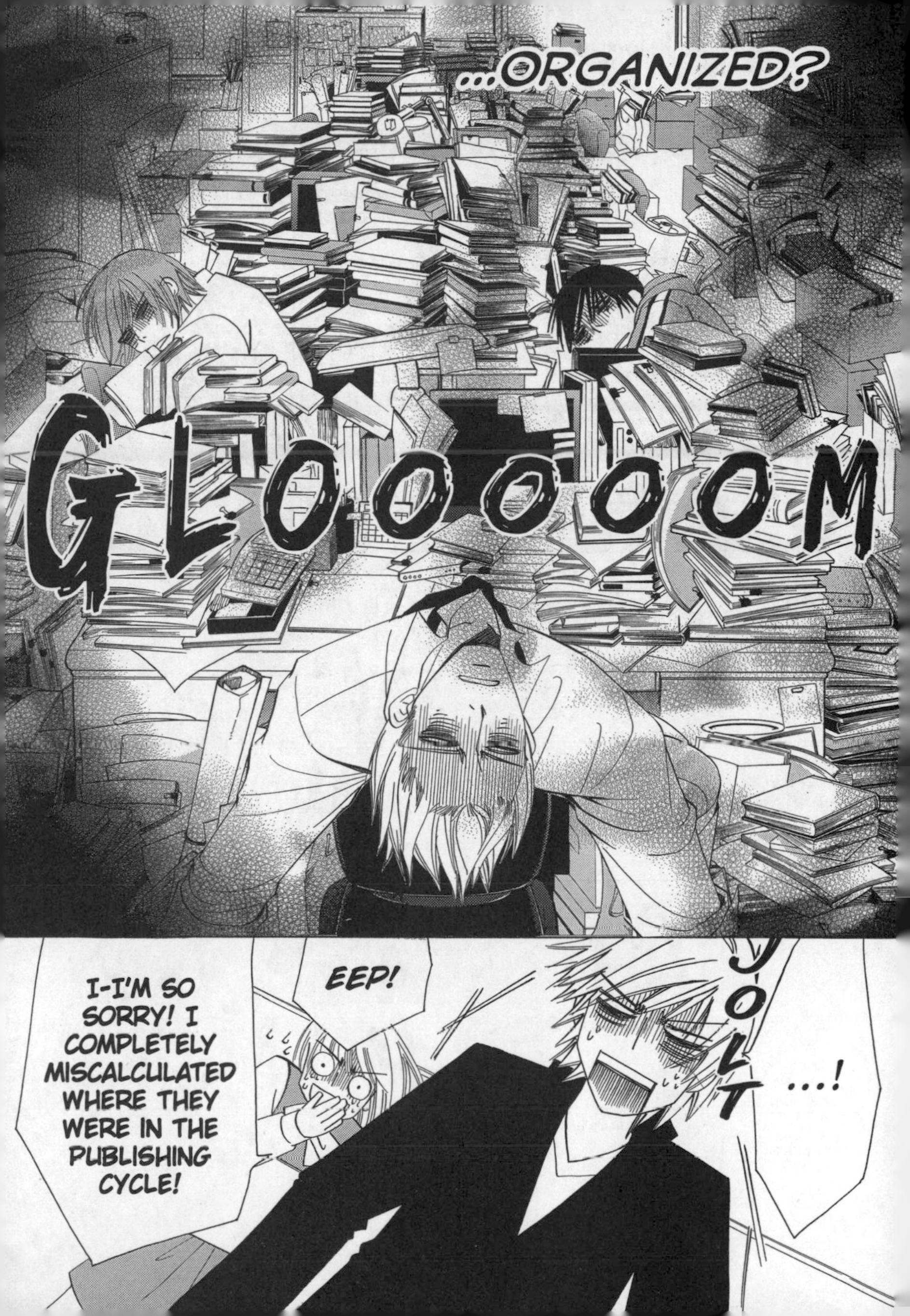
...ORGANIZED?
GLOOOOOOM
JOLT
...!
EEP!
I-I'M SO SORRY! I COMPLETELY MISCALCULATED WHERE THEY WERE IN THE PUBLISHING CYCLE!

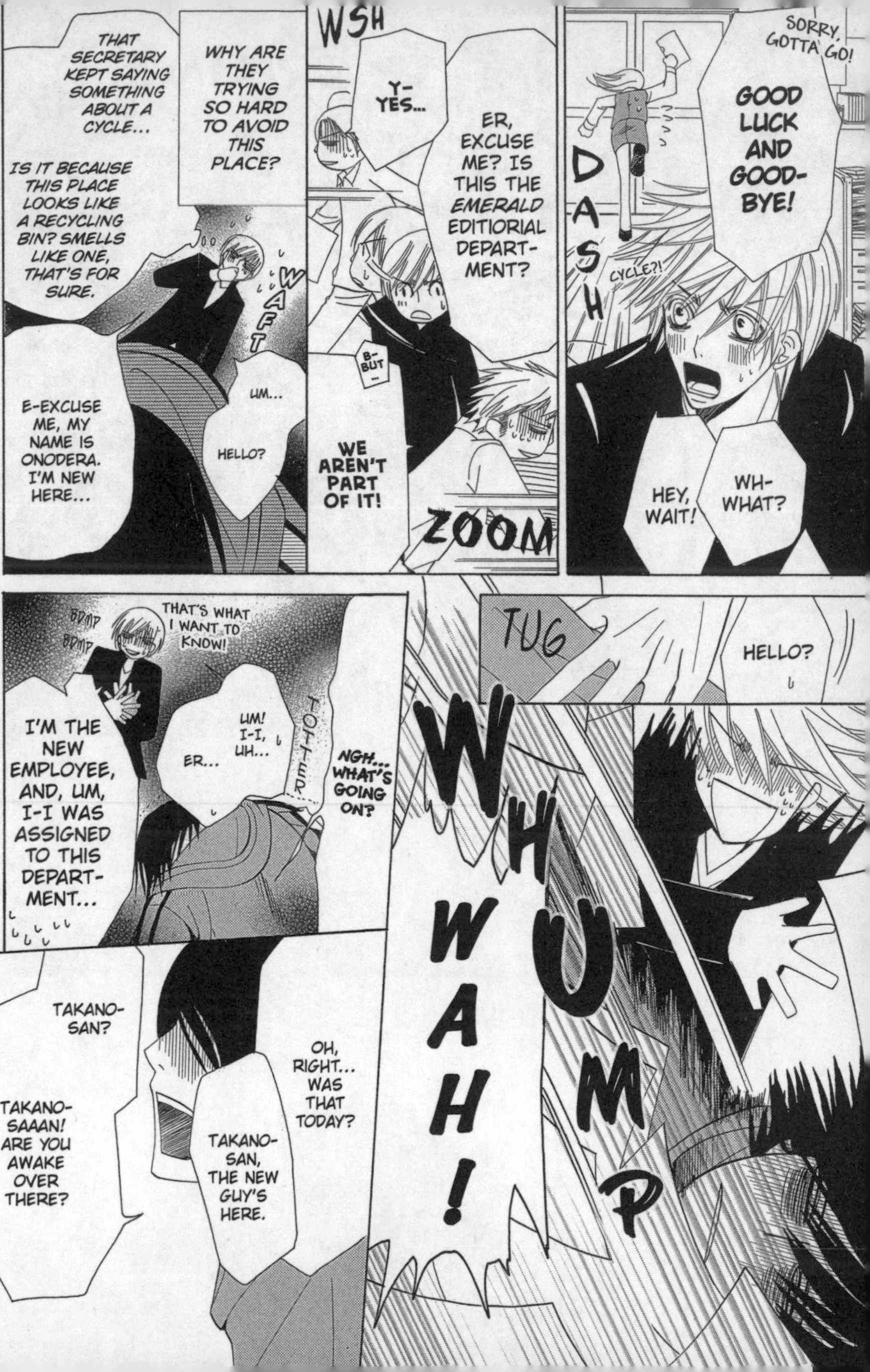
SORRY, GOTTA GO!
GOOD LUCK AND GOOD-BYE!
DASH
CYCLE?!
WH-WHAT?
HEY, WAIT!
WSH
Y-YES...
ER, EXCUSE ME? IS THIS THE EMERALD EDITIORIAL DEPARTMENT?
B-BUT...
WE AREN'T PART OF IT!
ZOOM
WHY ARE THEY TRYING SO HARD TO AVOID THIS PLACE?
THAT SECRETARY KEPT SAYING SOMETHING ABOUT A CYCLE...
IS IT BECAUSE THIS PLACE LOOKS LIKE A RECYCLING BIN? SMELLS LIKE ONE, THAT'S FOR SURE.
WAFT
UM...
HELLO?
E-EXCUSE ME, MY NAME IS ONODERA. I'M NEW HERE...
TUG
HELLO?
WHUMP
WAH!
THAT'S WHAT I WANT TO KNOW!
BDMP BDMP
UM! I-I, UH...
ER...
I'M THE NEW EMPLOYEE, AND, UM, I-I WAS ASSIGNED TO THIS DEPARTMENT...
TOTTER
NGH... WHAT'S GOING ON?
OH, RIGHT... WAS THAT TODAY?
TAKANO-SAN, THE NEW GUY'S HERE.
TAKANO-SAN?
TAKANO-SAAAN! ARE YOU AWAKE OVER THERE?

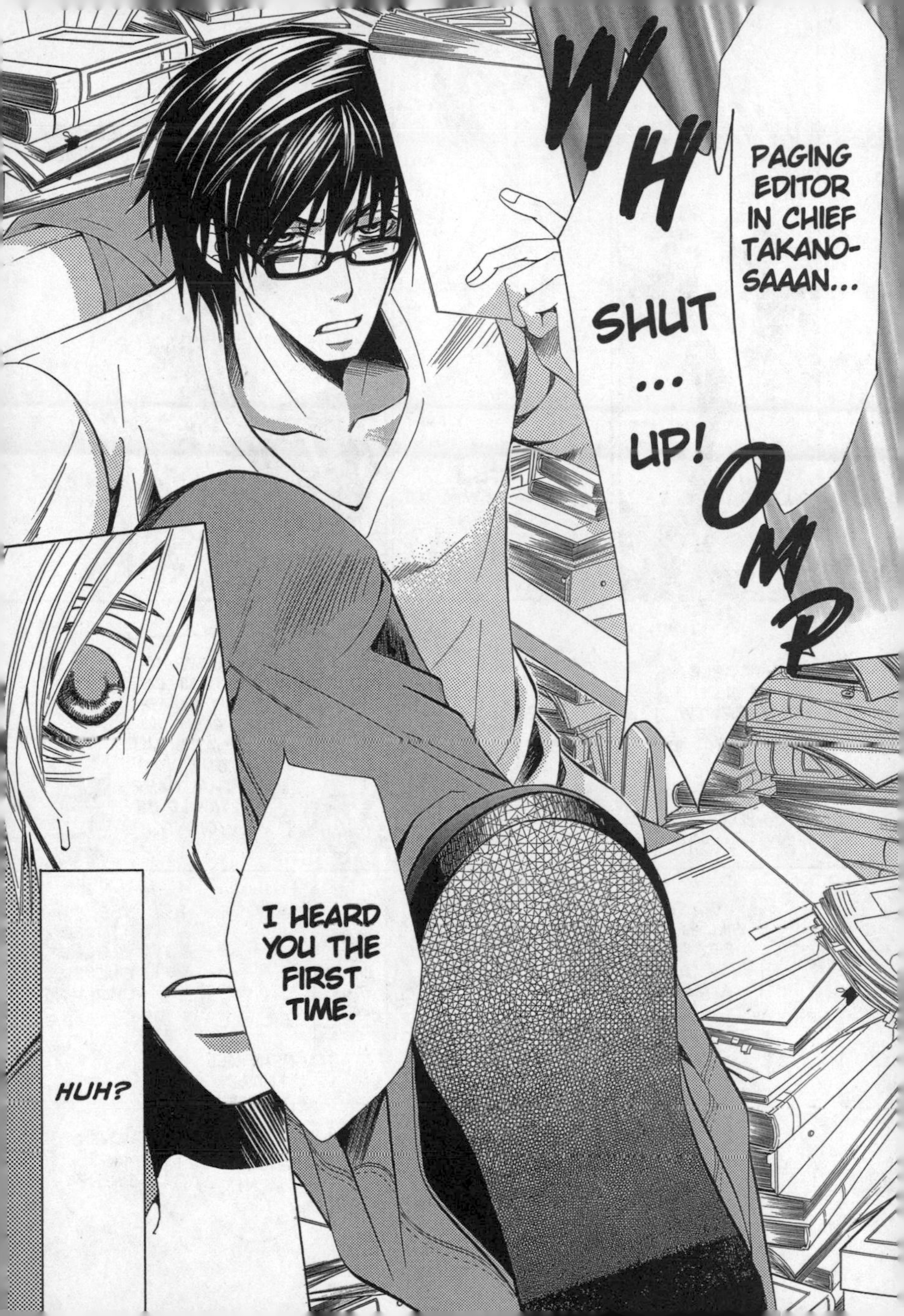
PAGING EDITOR IN CHIEF TAKANO-SAAAN...
SHUT ... UP!
WH
OMP
I HEARD YOU THE FIRST TIME.
HUH?

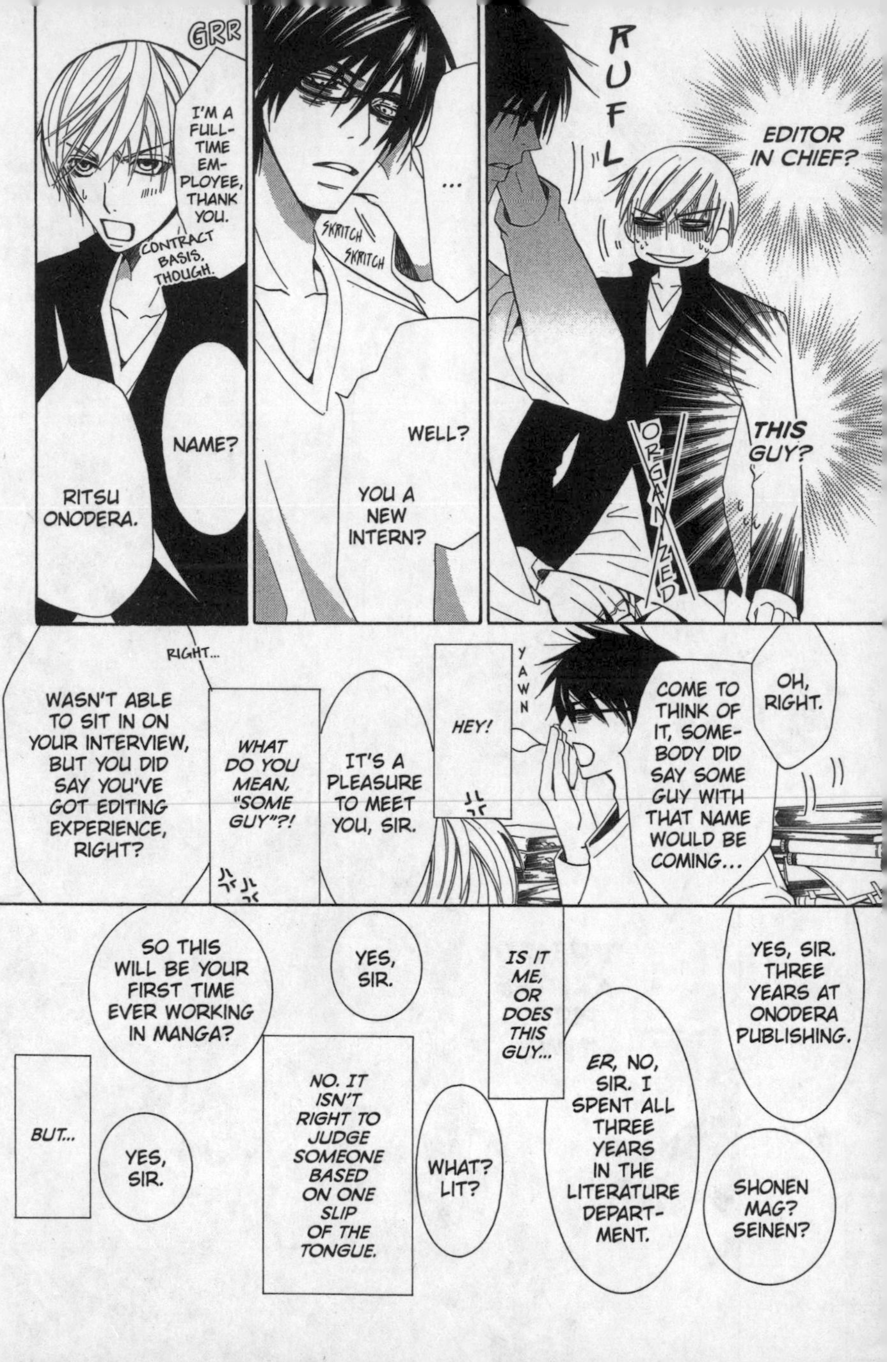
RUFL
EDITOR IN CHIEF?
THIS GUY?
ORGANIZED
...
SKRITCH SKRITCH
WELL?
YOU A NEW INTERN?
GRR
I'M A FULL-TIME EMPLOYEE, THANK YOU.
CONTRACT BASIS, THOUGH.
NAME?
RITSU ONODERA.
OH, RIGHT.
COME TO THINK OF IT, SOMEBODY DID SAY SOME GUY WITH THAT NAME WOULD BE COMING...
YAWN
HEY!
IT'S A PLEASURE TO MEET YOU, SIR.
WHAT DO YOU MEAN, "SOME GUY"?!
RIGHT...
WASN'T ABLE TO SIT IN ON YOUR INTERVIEW, BUT YOU DID SAY YOU'VE GOT EDITING EXPERIENCE, RIGHT?
YES, SIR. THREE YEARS AT ONODERA PUBLISHING.
SHONEN MAG? SEINEN?
ER, NO, SIR. I SPENT ALL THREE YEARS IN THE LITERATURE DEPARTMENT.
IS IT ME, OR DOES THIS GUY...
WHAT? LIT?
NO. IT ISN'T RIGHT TO JUDGE SOMEONE BASED ON ONE SLIP OF THE TONGUE.
YES, SIR.
SO THIS WILL BE YOUR FIRST TIME EVER WORKING IN MANGA?
YES, SIR.
BUT...

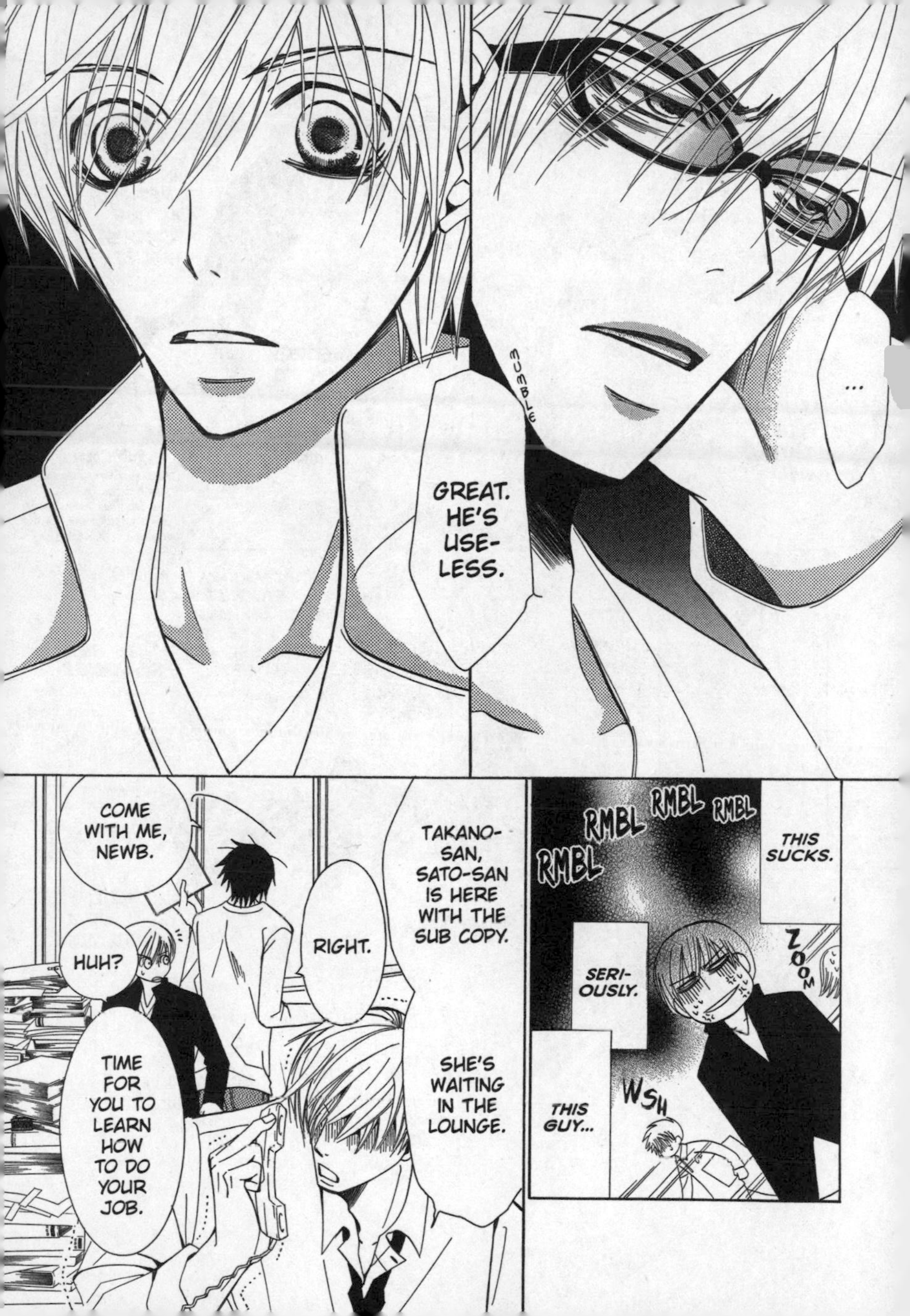
...
MUMBLE
GREAT. HE'S USELESS.
THIS SUCKS.
RMBL RMBL RMBL RMBL
ZOOM
SERIOUSLY.
WSH
THIS GUY...
TAKANO-SAN, SATO-SAN IS HERE WITH THE SUB COPY.
SHE'S WAITING IN THE LOUNGE.
RIGHT.
COME WITH ME, NEWB.
HUH?
TIME FOR YOU TO LEARN HOW TO DO YOUR JOB.

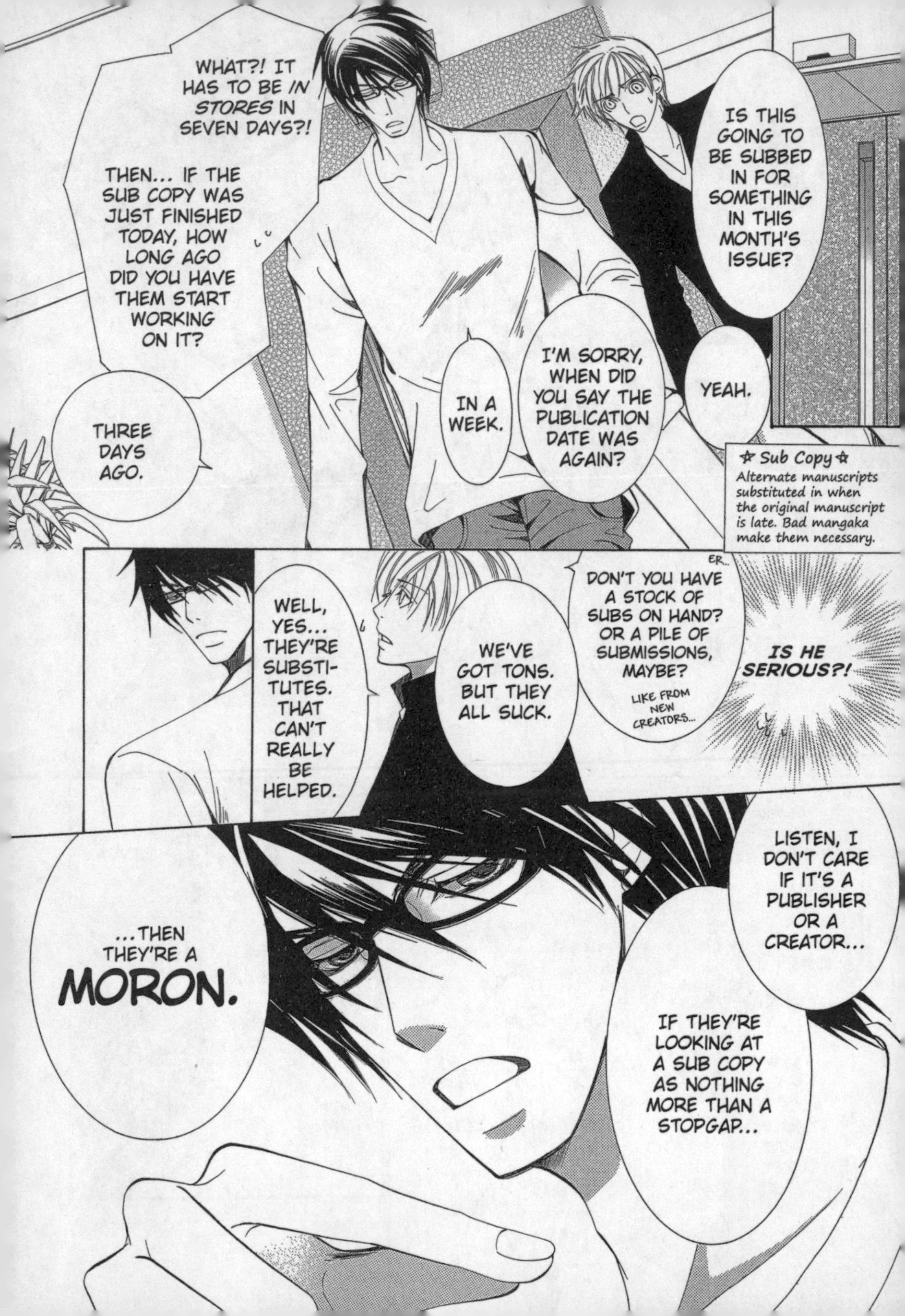
IS THIS GOING TO BE SUBBED IN FOR SOMETHING IN THIS MONTH'S ISSUE?
YEAH.
I'M SORRY, WHEN DID YOU SAY THE PUBLICATION DATE WAS AGAIN?
IN A WEEK.
WHAT?! IT HAS TO BE *IN STORES* IN SEVEN DAYS?!
THEN... IF THE SUB COPY WAS JUST FINISHED TODAY, HOW LONG AGO DID YOU HAVE THEM START WORKING ON IT?
THREE DAYS AGO.
☆ Sub Copy ☆ Alternate manuscripts substituted in when the original manuscript is late. Bad mangaka make them necessary.
IS HE SERIOUS?!
ER..
DON'T YOU HAVE A STOCK OF SUBS ON HAND? OR A PILE OF SUBMISSIONS, MAYBE?
LIKE FROM NEW CREATORS...
WE'VE GOT TONS. BUT THEY ALL SUCK.
WELL, YES... THEY'RE SUBSTI-TUTES. THAT CAN'T REALLY BE HELPED.
LISTEN, I DON'T CARE IF IT'S A PUBLISHER OR A CREATOR...
IF THEY'RE LOOKING AT A SUB COPY AS NOTHING MORE THAN A STOPGAP...
...THEN THEY'RE A **MORON.**

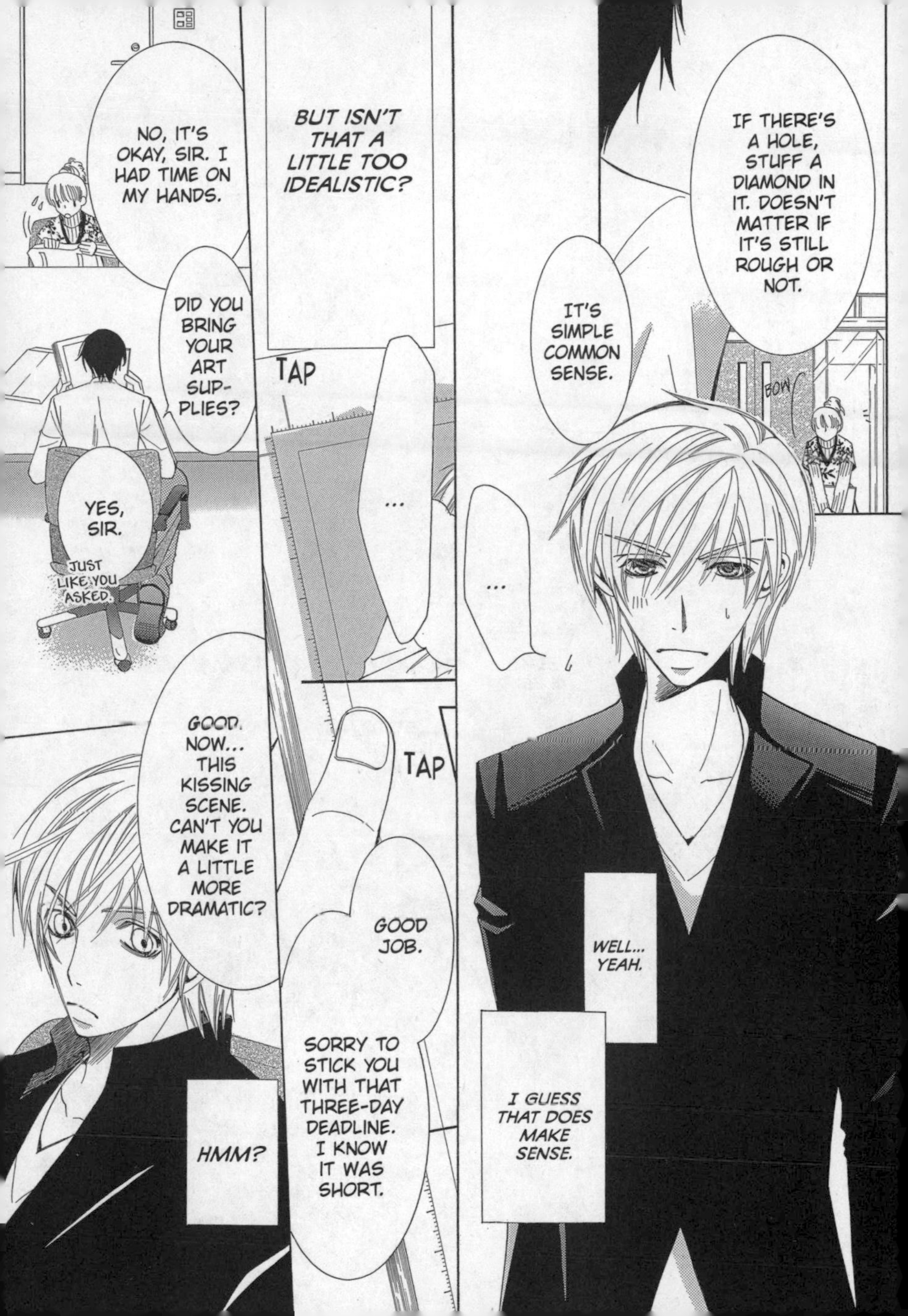
IF THERE'S A HOLE, STUFF A DIAMOND IN IT. DOESN'T MATTER IF IT'S STILL ROUGH OR NOT.
IT'S SIMPLE COMMON SENSE.
BOW
BUT ISN'T THAT A LITTLE TOO IDEALISTIC?
TAP
...
...
WELL... YEAH.
I GUESS THAT DOES MAKE SENSE.
TAP
GOOD JOB.
SORRY TO STICK YOU WITH THAT THREE-DAY DEADLINE. I KNOW IT WAS SHORT.
HMM?
NO, IT'S OKAY, SIR. I HAD TIME ON MY HANDS.
DID YOU BRING YOUR ART SUP-PLIES?
YES, SIR.
JUST LIKE YOU ASKED.
GOOD. NOW... THIS KISSING SCENE. CAN'T YOU MAKE IT A LITTLE MORE DRAMATIC?

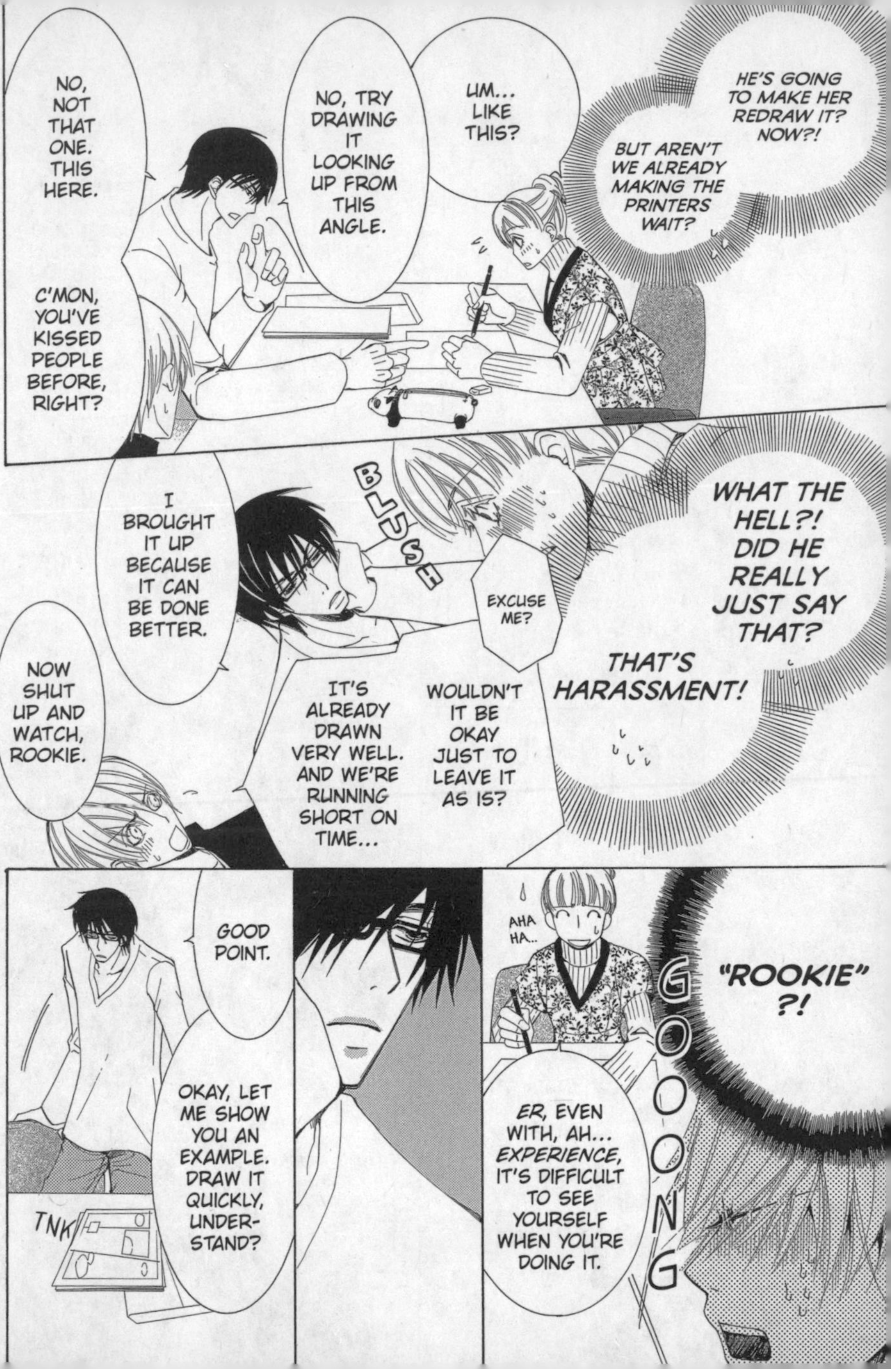
HE'S GOING TO MAKE HER REDRAW IT? NOW?!
BUT AREN'T WE ALREADY MAKING THE PRINTERS WAIT?
UM... LIKE THIS?
NO, TRY DRAWING IT LOOKING UP FROM THIS ANGLE.
NO, NOT THAT ONE. THIS HERE.
C'MON, YOU'VE KISSED PEOPLE BEFORE, RIGHT?
WHAT THE HELL?! DID HE REALLY JUST SAY THAT?
THAT'S HARASSMENT!
BLUSH
EXCUSE ME?
I BROUGHT IT UP BECAUSE IT CAN BE DONE BETTER.
WOULDN'T IT BE OKAY JUST TO LEAVE IT AS IS?
IT'S ALREADY DRAWN VERY WELL. AND WE'RE RUNNING SHORT ON TIME...
NOW SHUT UP AND WATCH, ROOKIE.
"ROOKIE" ?!
GOOONG
AHA HA...
ER, EVEN WITH, AH... *EXPERIENCE*, IT'S DIFFICULT TO SEE YOURSELF WHEN YOU'RE DOING IT.
GOOD POINT.
OKAY, LET ME SHOW YOU AN EXAMPLE. DRAW IT QUICKLY, UNDERSTAND?
TNK

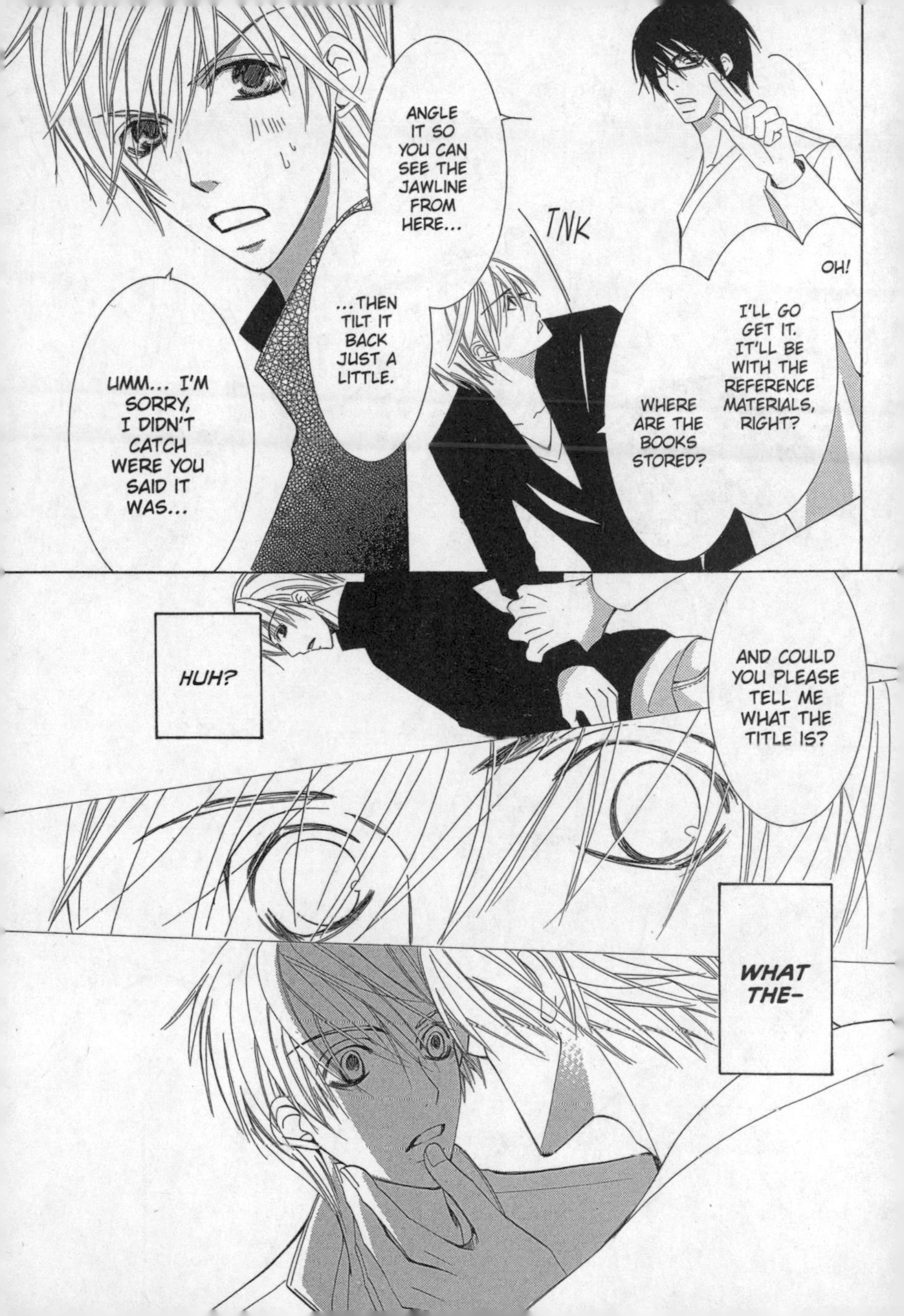
OH!
I'LL GO GET IT. IT'LL BE WITH THE REFERENCE MATERIALS, RIGHT?
WHERE ARE THE BOOKS STORED?
TNK
ANGLE IT SO YOU CAN SEE THE JAWLINE FROM HERE...
...THEN TILT IT BACK JUST A LITTLE.
UMM... I'M SORRY, I DIDN'T CATCH WERE YOU SAID IT WAS...
AND COULD YOU PLEASE TELL ME WHAT THE TITLE IS?
HUH?
WHAT THE-

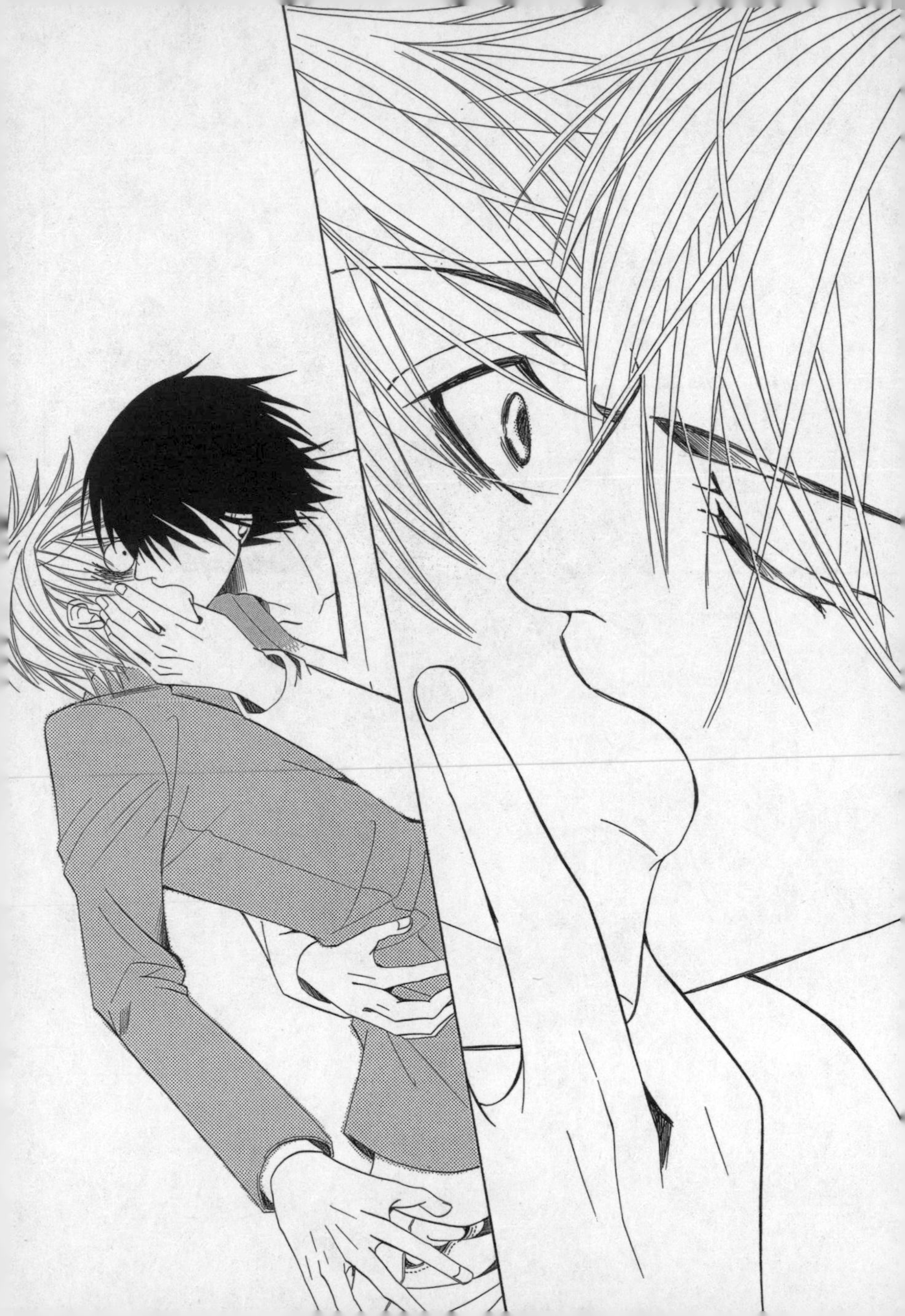

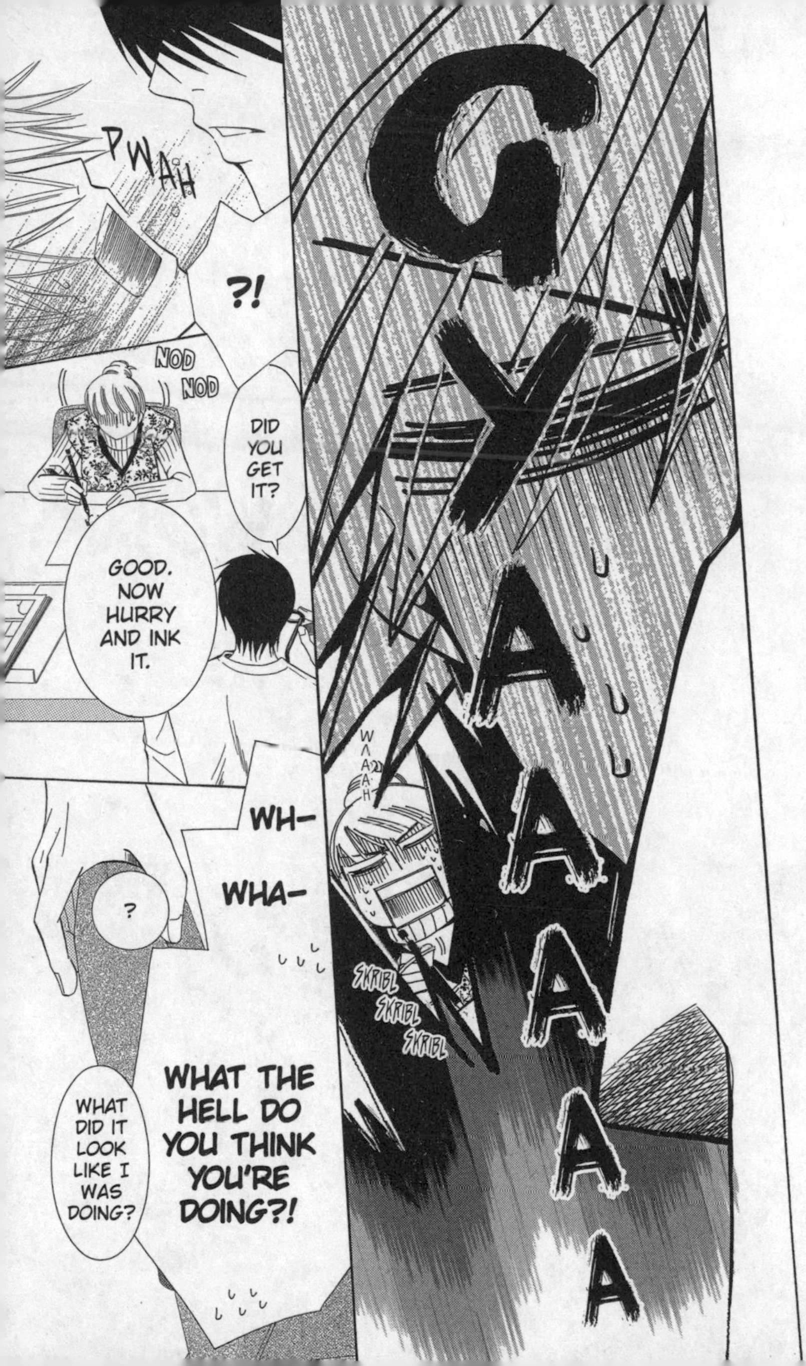
GYAAAAAA
WAAAH
SKRIBL SKRIBL SKRIBL
PWAH
?!
NOD NOD
DID YOU GET IT?
GOOD. NOW HURRY AND INK IT.
WH-
WHA-
?
WHAT THE HELL DO YOU THINK YOU'RE DOING?!
WHAT DID IT LOOK LIKE I WAS DOING?

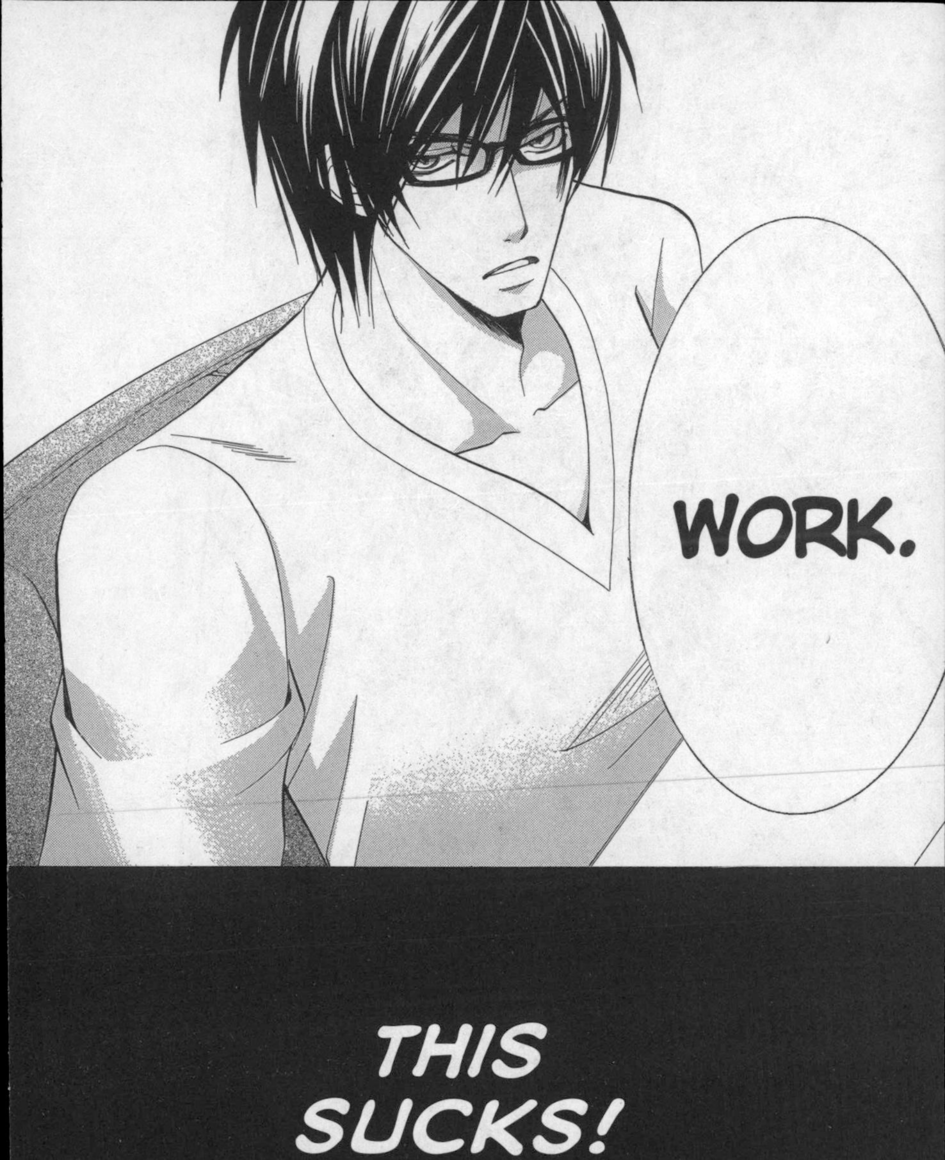
WORK.
THIS SUCKS!

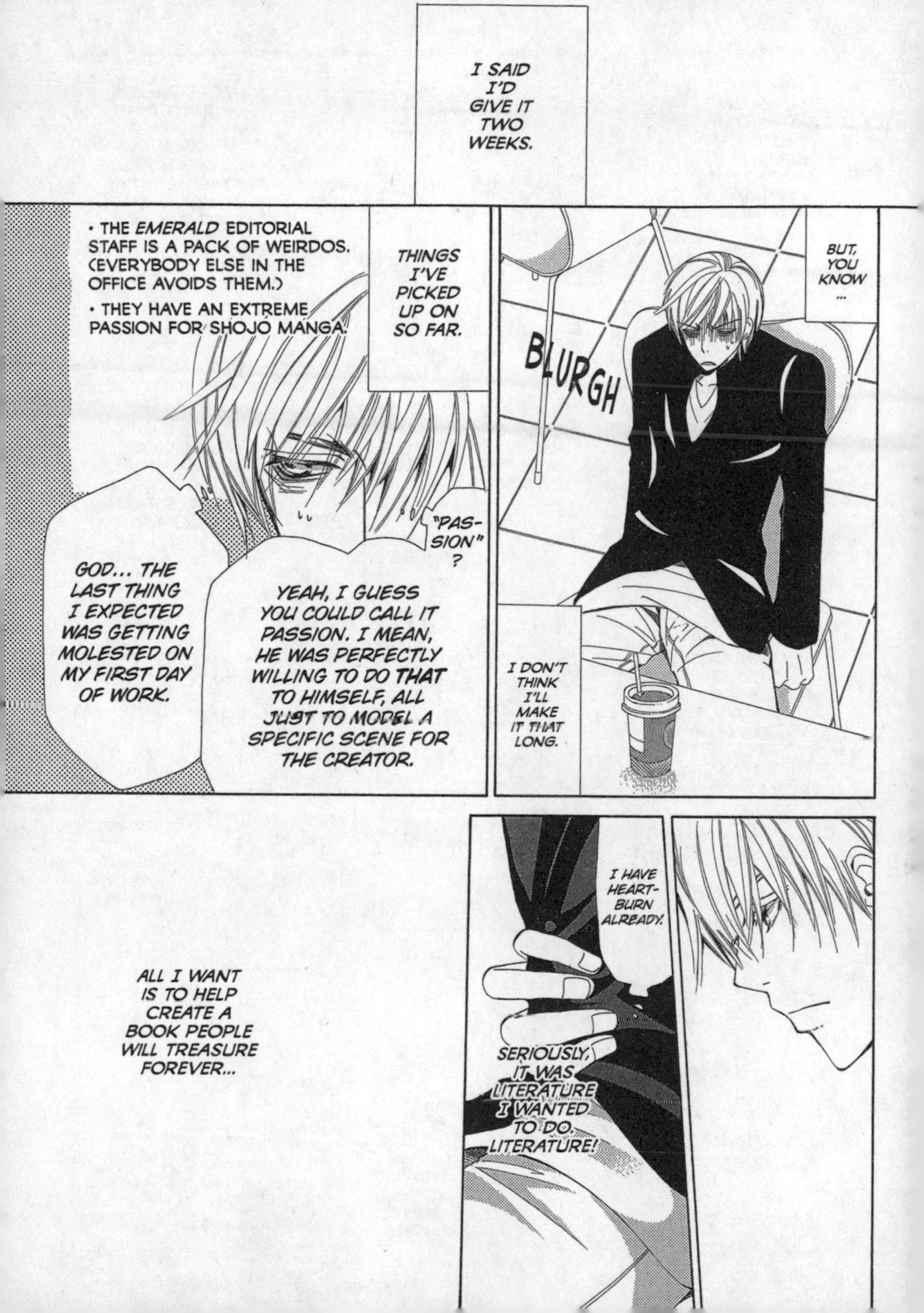
I SAID I'D GIVE IT TWO WEEKS.
BUT, YOU KNOW ...
BLURGH
I DON'T THINK I'LL MAKE IT THAT LONG.
THINGS I'VE PICKED UP ON SO FAR.
• THE *EMERALD* EDITORIAL STAFF IS A PACK OF WEIRDOS. (EVERYBODY ELSE IN THE OFFICE AVOIDS THEM.)
• THEY HAVE AN EXTREME PASSION FOR SHOJO MANGA.
"PASSION"?
YEAH, I GUESS YOU COULD CALL IT PASSION. I MEAN, HE WAS PERFECTLY WILLING TO DO THAT TO HIMSELF, ALL JUST TO MODEL A SPECIFIC SCENE FOR THE CREATOR.
GOD... THE LAST THING I EXPECTED WAS GETTING MOLESTED ON MY FIRST DAY OF WORK.
I HAVE HEART-BURN ALREADY.
SERIOUSLY, IT WAS LITERATURE I WANTED TO DO. LITERATURE!
ALL I WANT IS TO HELP CREATE A BOOK PEOPLE WILL TREASURE FOREVER...

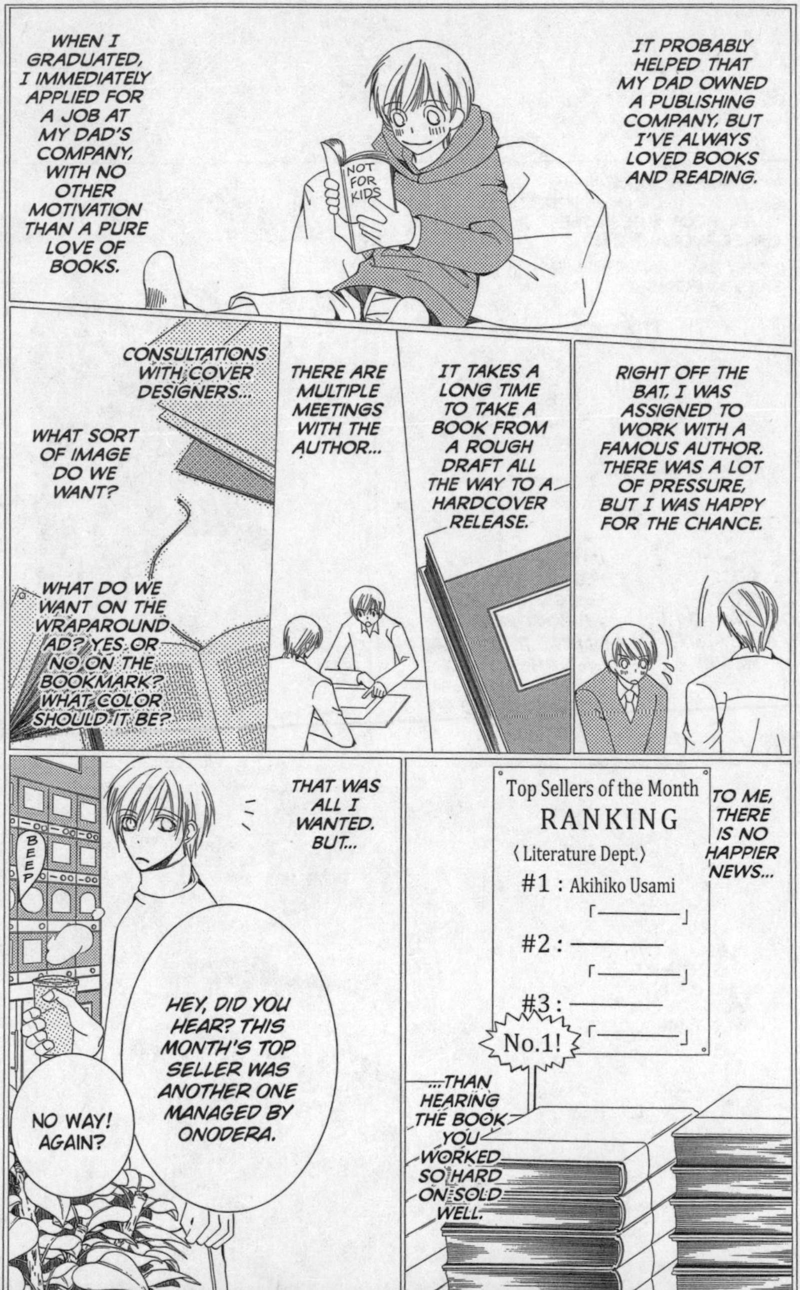
IT PROBABLY HELPED THAT MY DAD OWNED A PUBLISHING COMPANY, BUT I'VE ALWAYS LOVED BOOKS AND READING.
WHEN I GRADUATED, I IMMEDIATELY APPLIED FOR A JOB AT MY DAD'S COMPANY, WITH NO OTHER MOTIVATION THAN A PURE LOVE OF BOOKS.
NOT FOR KIDS
RIGHT OFF THE BAT, I WAS ASSIGNED TO WORK WITH A FAMOUS AUTHOR. THERE WAS A LOT OF PRESSURE, BUT I WAS HAPPY FOR THE CHANCE.
IT TAKES A LONG TIME TO TAKE A BOOK FROM A ROUGH DRAFT ALL THE WAY TO A HARDCOVER RELEASE.
THERE ARE MULTIPLE MEETINGS WITH THE AUTHOR...
CONSULTATIONS WITH COVER DESIGNERS...
WHAT SORT OF IMAGE DO WE WANT?
WHAT DO WE WANT ON THE WRAPAROUND AD? YES OR NO ON THE BOOKMARK? WHAT COLOR SHOULD IT BE?
TO ME, THERE IS NO HAPPIER NEWS...
Top Sellers of the Month
RANKING
〈Literature Dept.〉
#1 : Akihiko Usami
#2 :
#3 :
No.1!
...THAN HEARING THE BOOK YOU WORKED SO HARD ON SOLD WELL.
THAT WAS ALL I WANTED. BUT...
BEEP
HEY, DID YOU HEAR? THIS MONTH'S TOP SELLER WAS ANOTHER ONE MANAGED BY ONODERA.
NO WAY! AGAIN?

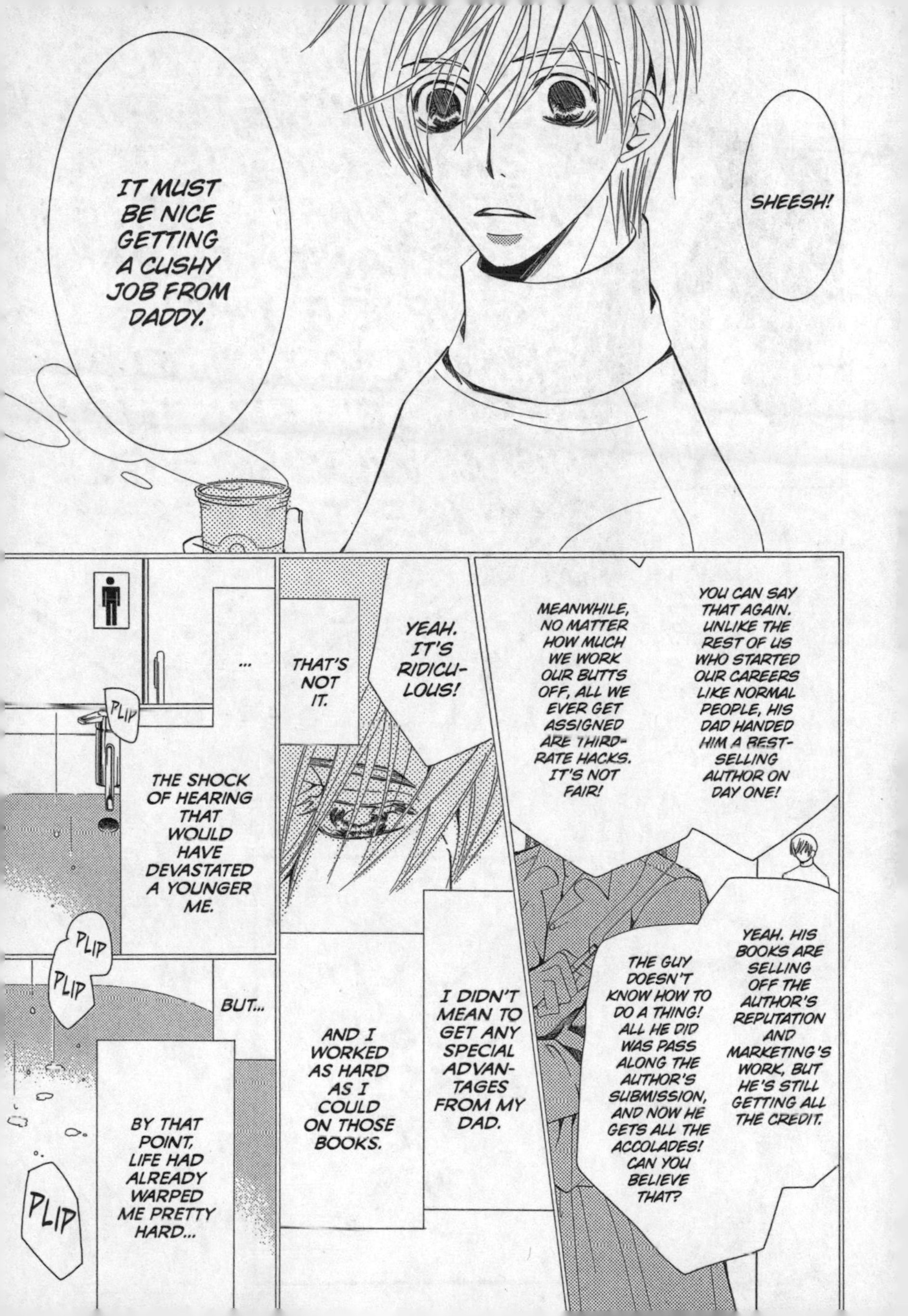
SHEESH!
IT MUST BE NICE GETTING A CUSHY JOB FROM DADDY.
MEANWHILE, NO MATTER HOW MUCH WE WORK OUR BUTTS OFF, ALL WE EVER GET ASSIGNED ARE THIRD-RATE HACKS. IT'S NOT FAIR!
YOU CAN SAY THAT AGAIN. UNLIKE THE REST OF US WHO STARTED OUR CAREERS LIKE NORMAL PEOPLE, HIS DAD HANDED HIM A BEST-SELLING AUTHOR ON DAY ONE!
THE GUY DOESN'T KNOW HOW TO DO A THING! ALL HE DID WAS PASS ALONG THE AUTHOR'S SUBMISSION, AND NOW HE GETS ALL THE ACCOLADES! CAN YOU BELIEVE THAT?
YEAH. HIS BOOKS ARE SELLING OFF THE AUTHOR'S REPUTATION AND MARKETING'S WORK, BUT HE'S STILL GETTING ALL THE CREDIT.
YEAH. IT'S RIDICULOUS!
THAT'S NOT IT.
I DIDN'T MEAN TO GET ANY SPECIAL ADVANTAGES FROM MY DAD.
AND I WORKED AS HARD AS I COULD ON THOSE BOOKS.
...
PLIP
THE SHOCK OF HEARING THAT WOULD HAVE DEVASTATED A YOUNGER ME.
PLIP
PLIP
BUT...
BY THAT POINT, LIFE HAD ALREADY WARPED ME PRETTY HARD...
PLIP

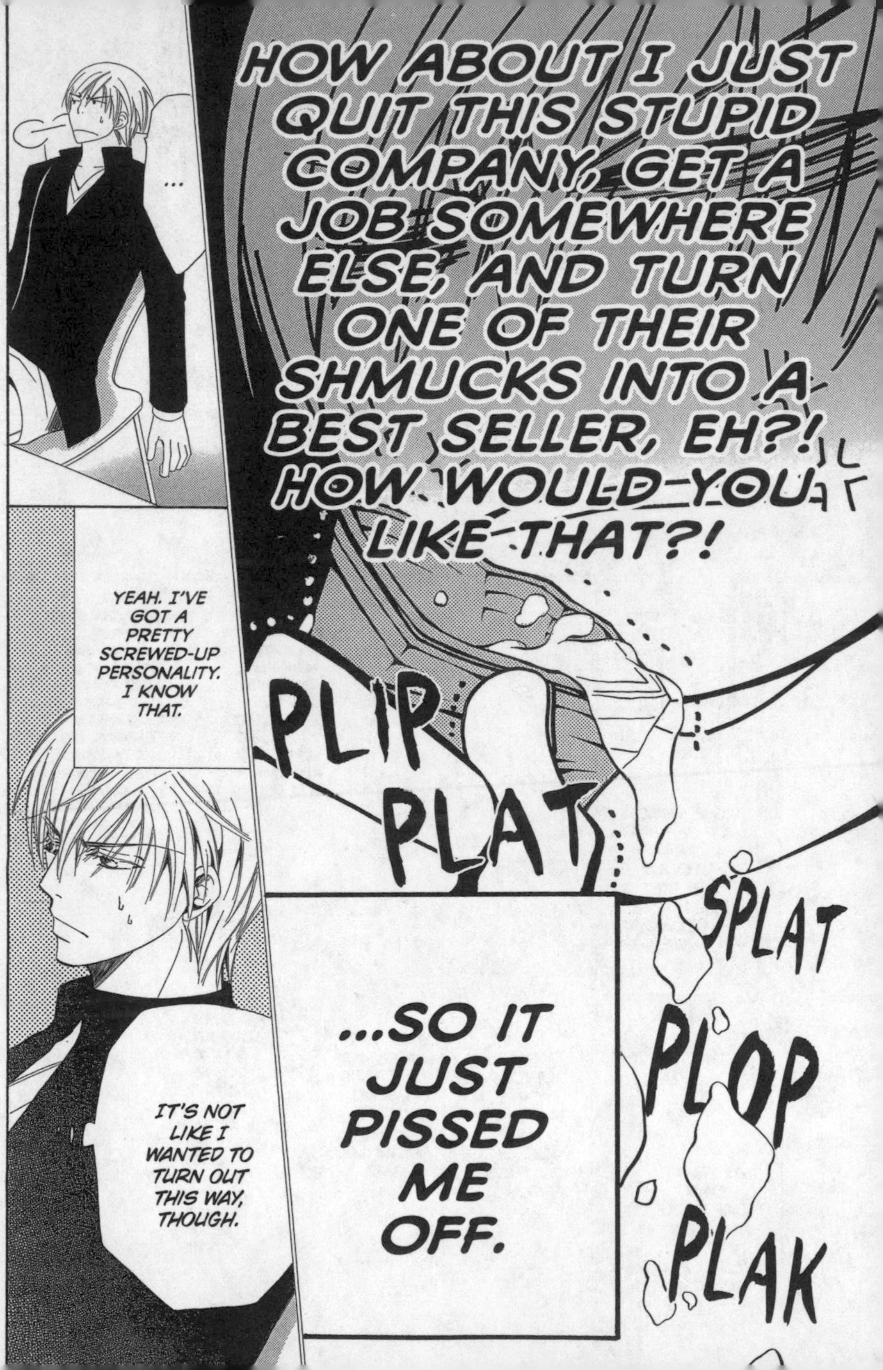
HOW ABOUT I JUST QUIT THIS STUPID COMPANY, GET A JOB SOMEWHERE ELSE, AND TURN ONE OF THEIR SHMUCKS INTO A BEST SELLER, EH?! HOW WOULD YOU LIKE THAT?!
...
PLIP
PLAT
SPLAT
PLOP
PLAK
...SO IT JUST PISSED ME OFF.
YEAH. I'VE GOT A PRETTY SCREWED-UP PERSONALITY. I KNOW THAT.
IT'S NOT LIKE I WANTED TO TURN OUT THIS WAY, THOUGH.

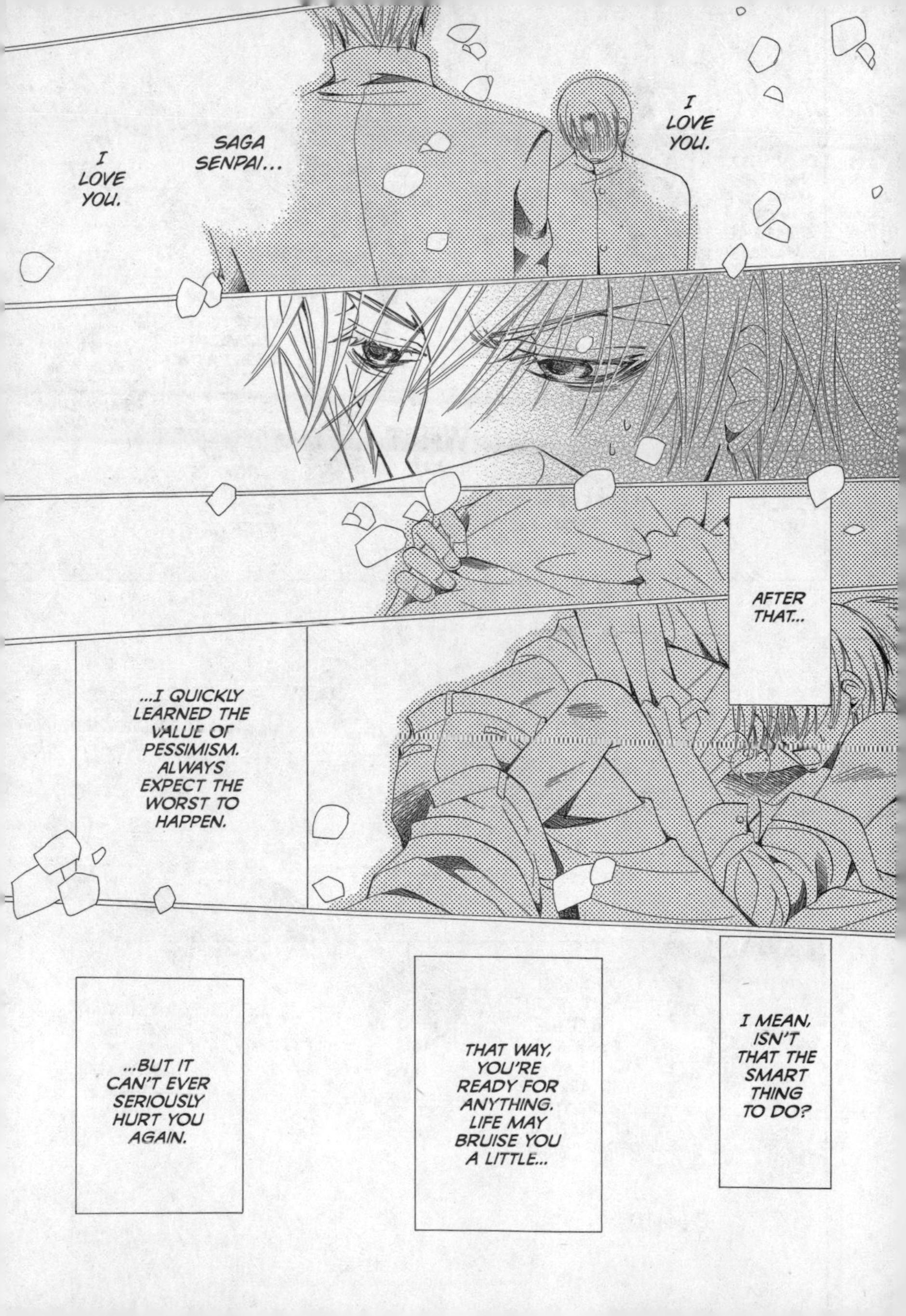
I LOVE YOU.
SAGA SENPAI...
I LOVE YOU.
AFTER THAT...
...I QUICKLY LEARNED THE VALUE OF PESSIMISM. ALWAYS EXPECT THE WORST TO HAPPEN.
I MEAN, ISN'T THAT THE SMART THING TO DO?
THAT WAY, YOU'RE READY FOR ANYTHING. LIFE MAY BRUISE YOU A LITTLE...
...BUT IT CAN'T EVER SERIOUSLY HURT YOU AGAIN.

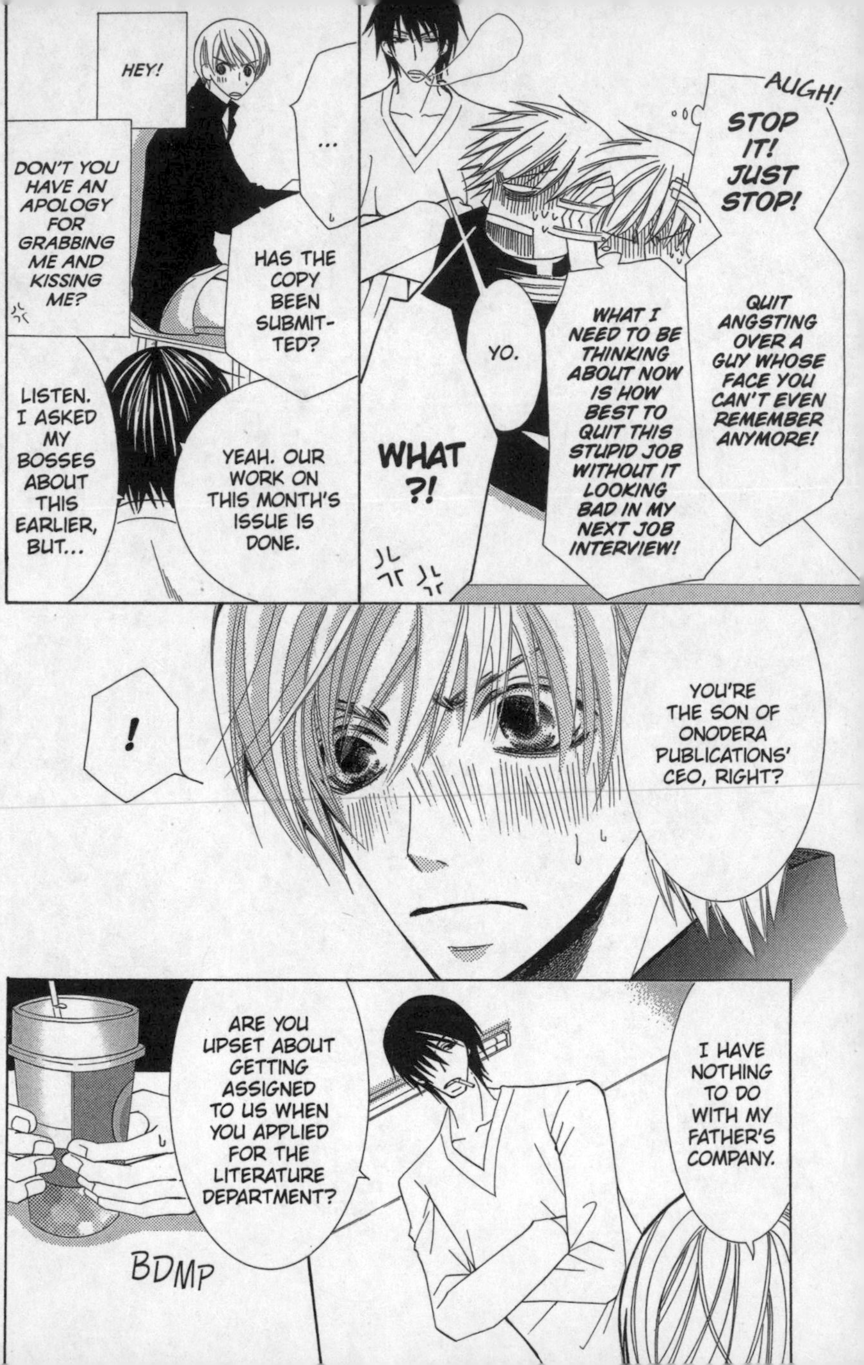
AUGH!
STOP IT! JUST STOP!
QUIT ANGSTING OVER A GUY WHOSE FACE YOU CAN'T EVEN REMEMBER ANYMORE!
WHAT I NEED TO BE THINKING ABOUT NOW IS HOW BEST TO QUIT THIS STUPID JOB WITHOUT IT LOOKING BAD IN MY NEXT JOB INTERVIEW!
YO.
WHAT?!
HEY!
DON'T YOU HAVE AN APOLOGY FOR GRABBING ME AND KISSING ME?
...
HAS THE COPY BEEN SUBMITTED?
YEAH. OUR WORK ON THIS MONTH'S ISSUE IS DONE.
LISTEN. I ASKED MY BOSSES ABOUT THIS EARLIER, BUT...
YOU'RE THE SON OF ONODERA PUBLICATIONS' CEO, RIGHT?
!
I HAVE NOTHING TO DO WITH MY FATHER'S COMPANY.
ARE YOU UPSET ABOUT GETTING ASSIGNED TO US WHEN YOU APPLIED FOR THE LITERATURE DEPARTMENT?
BDMP

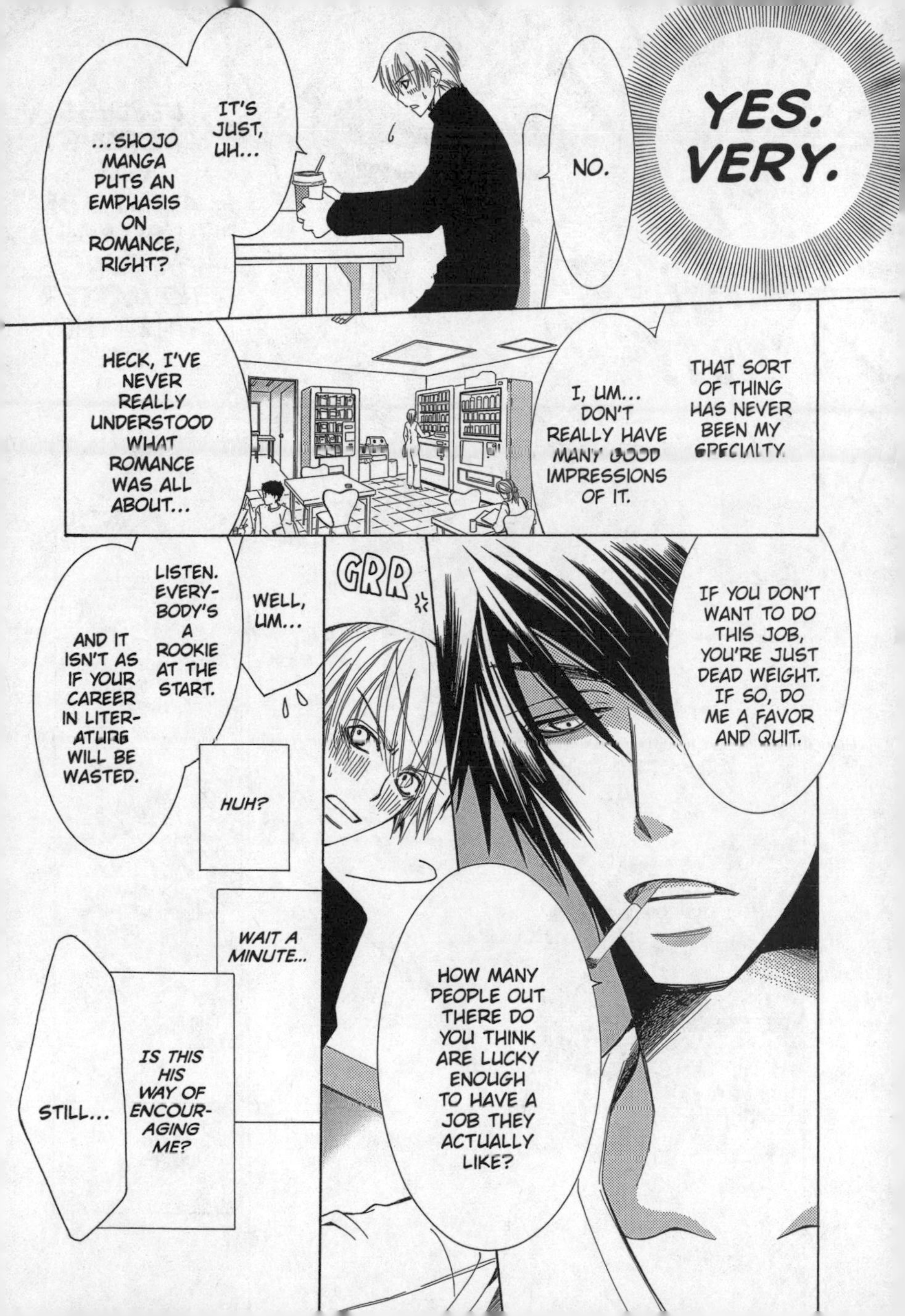
YES. VERY.
NO.
IT'S JUST, UH...
...SHOJO MANGA PUTS AN EMPHASIS ON ROMANCE, RIGHT?
THAT SORT OF THING HAS NEVER BEEN MY SPECIALTY
I, UM... DON'T REALLY HAVE MANY GOOD IMPRESSIONS OF IT.
HECK, I'VE NEVER REALLY UNDERSTOOD WHAT ROMANCE WAS ALL ABOUT...
IF YOU DON'T WANT TO DO THIS JOB, YOU'RE JUST DEAD WEIGHT. IF SO, DO ME A FAVOR AND QUIT.
GRR
HOW MANY PEOPLE OUT THERE DO YOU THINK ARE LUCKY ENOUGH TO HAVE A JOB THEY ACTUALLY LIKE?
WELL, UM...
LISTEN. EVERY-BODY'S A ROOKIE AT THE START.
AND IT ISN'T AS IF YOUR CAREER IN LITER-ATURE WILL BE WASTED.
HUH?
WAIT A MINUTE...
IS THIS HIS WAY OF ENCOUR-AGING ME?
STILL...

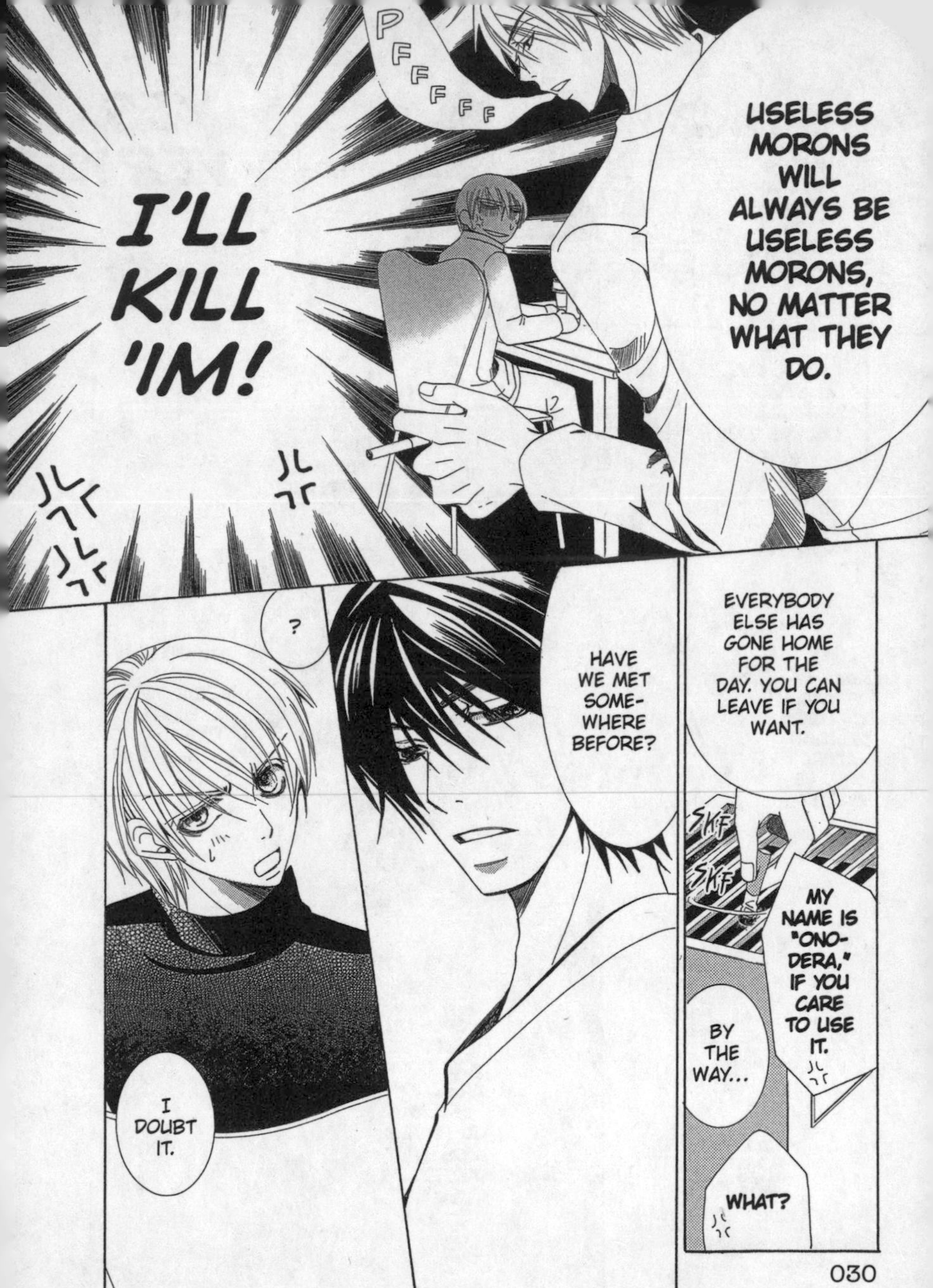

PFFFFF
USELESS MORONS WILL ALWAYS BE USELESS MORONS, NO MATTER WHAT THEY DO.
I'LL KILL 'IM!
EVERYBODY ELSE HAS GONE HOME FOR THE DAY. YOU CAN LEAVE IF YOU WANT.
SKF
SKF
MY NAME IS "ONO-DERA," IF YOU CARE TO USE IT.
BY THE WAY...
WHAT?
HAVE WE MET SOME-WHERE BEFORE?
?
I DOUBT IT.

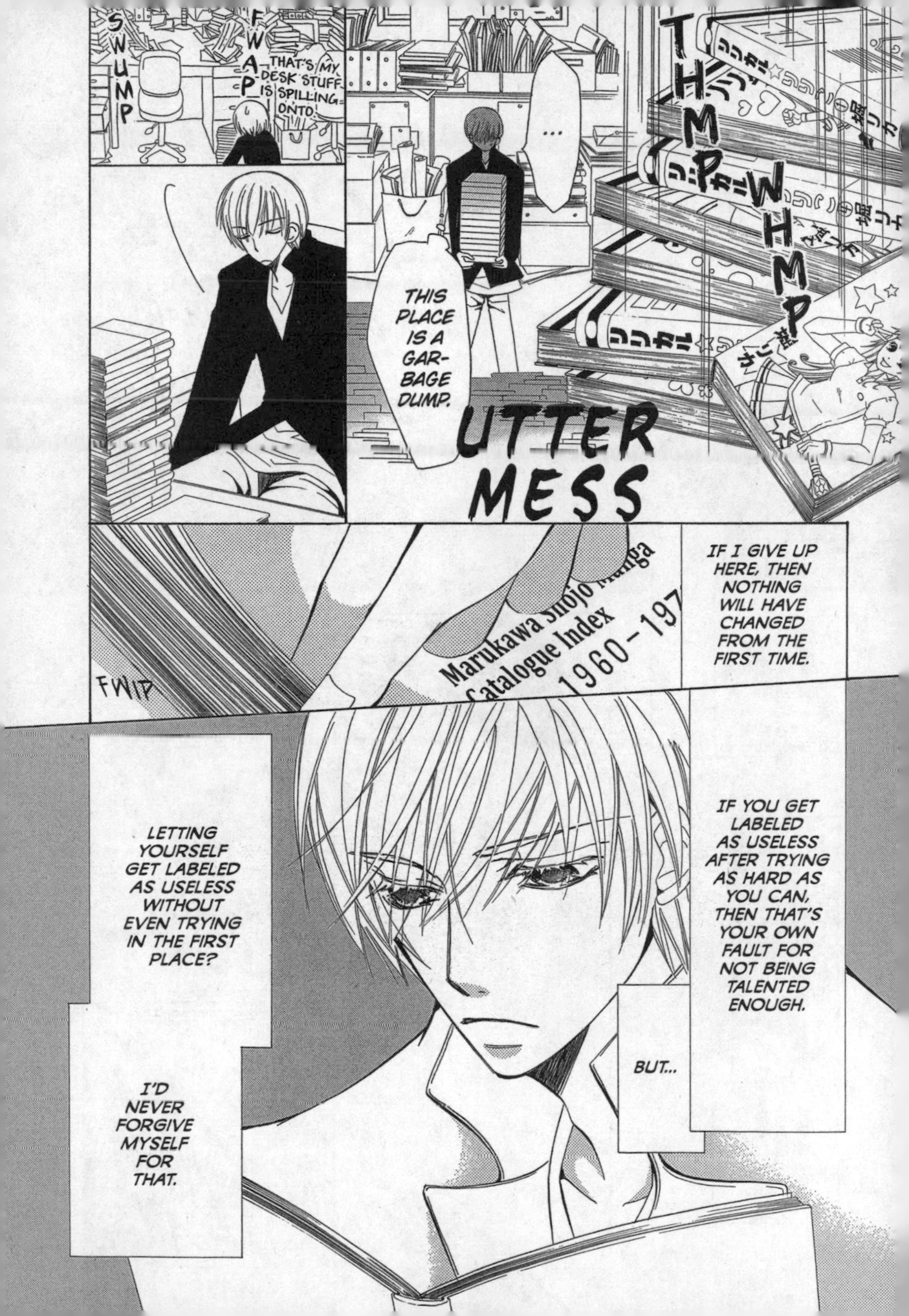
THMP
WHMP
...
THIS PLACE IS A GARBAGE DUMP.
UTTER MESS
SWUMP
FWAP
THAT'S MY DESK STUFF IS SPILLING ONTO.
IF I GIVE UP HERE, THEN NOTHING WILL HAVE CHANGED FROM THE FIRST TIME.
Marukawa Shojo Manga Catalogue Index 1960-197
FWIP
IF YOU GET LABELED AS USELESS AFTER TRYING AS HARD AS YOU CAN, THEN THAT'S YOUR OWN FAULT FOR NOT BEING TALENTED ENOUGH.
BUT...
LETTING YOURSELF GET LABELED AS USELESS WITHOUT EVEN TRYING IN THE FIRST PLACE?
I'D NEVER FORGIVE MYSELF FOR THAT.

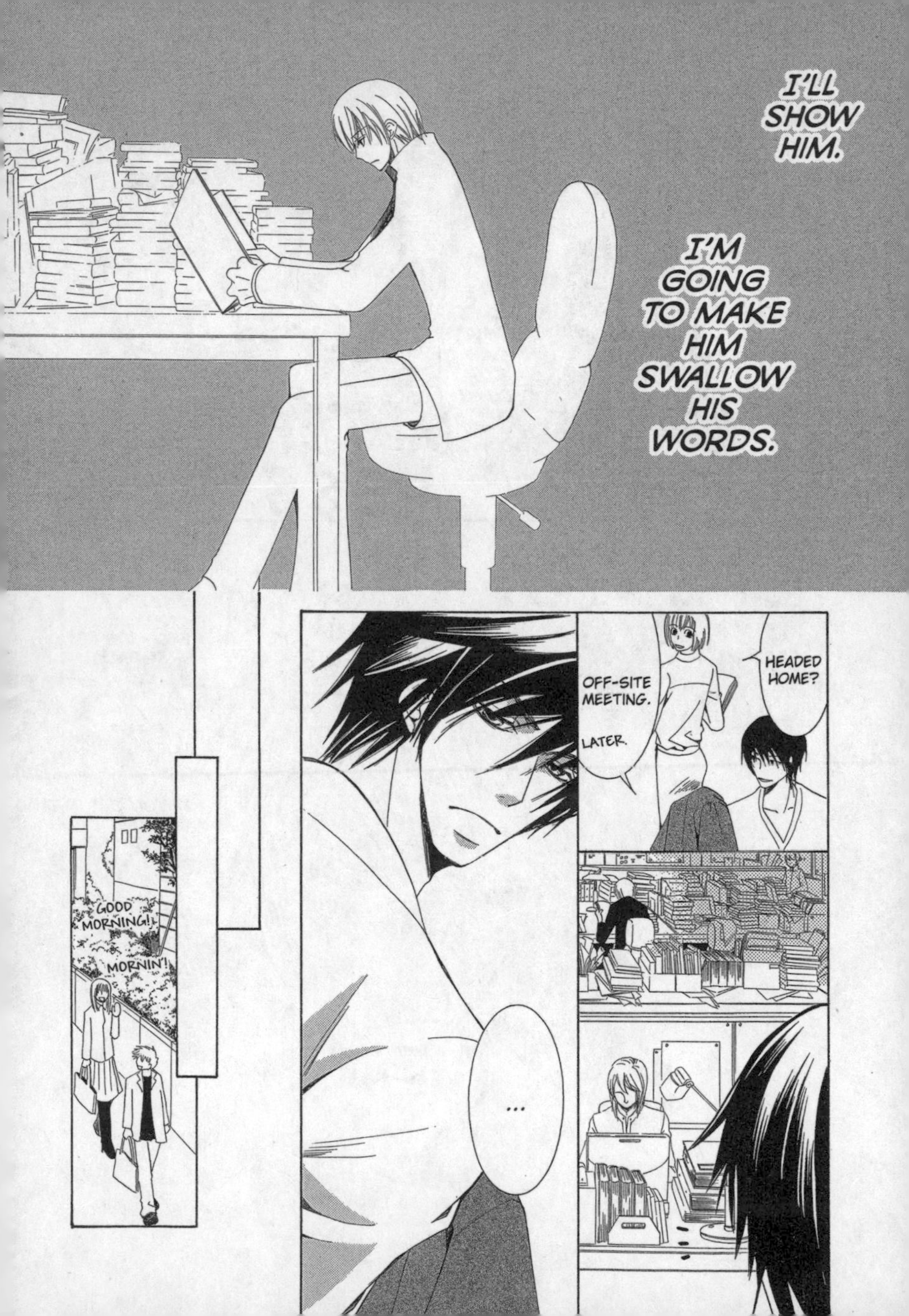
I'LL SHOW HIM.
I'M GOING TO MAKE HIM SWALLOW HIS WORDS.
HEADED HOME?
OFF-SITE MEETING.
LATER.
...
GOOD MORNING!
MORNIN'!

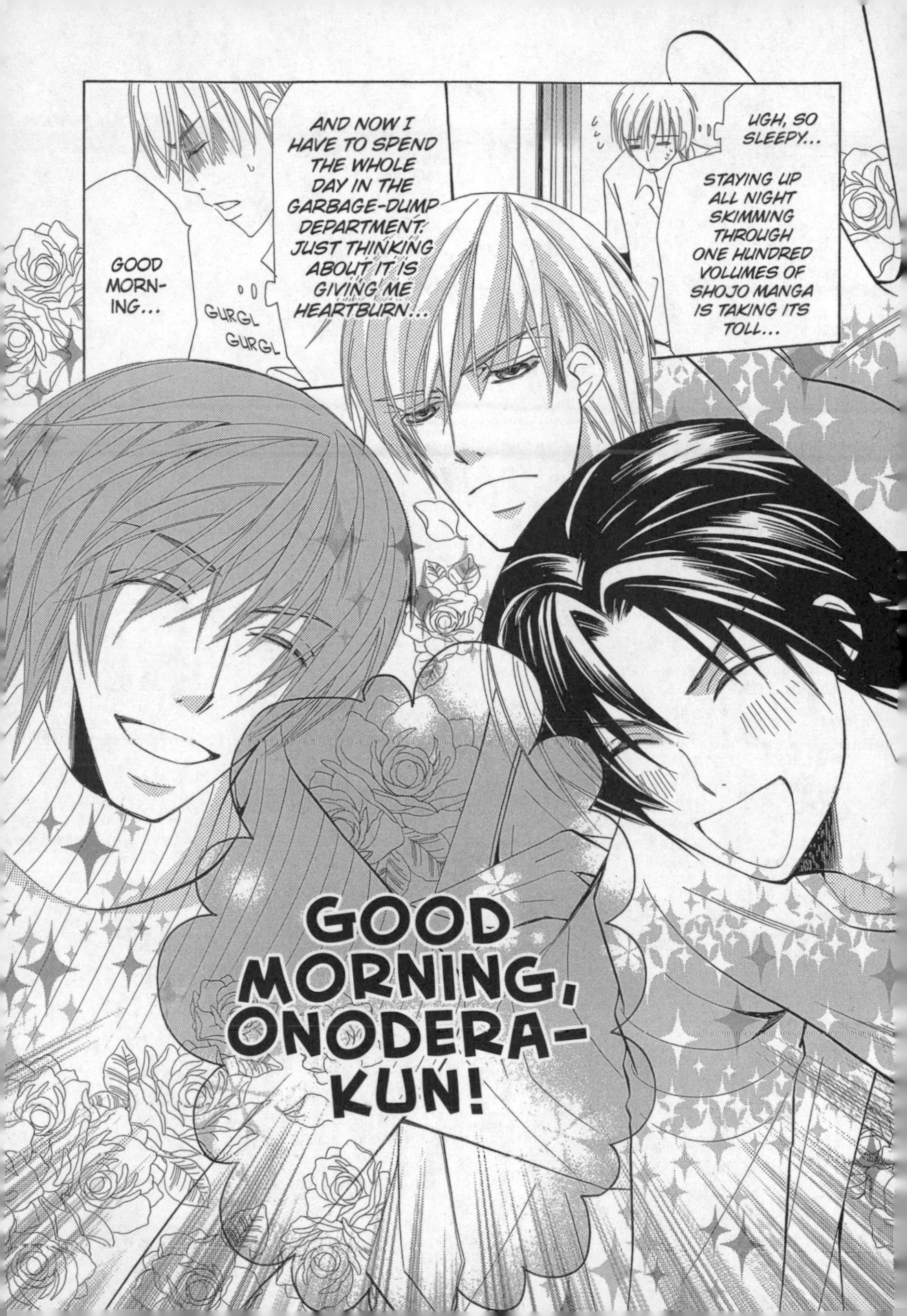
UGH, SO SLEEPY...
STAYING UP ALL NIGHT SKIMMING THROUGH ONE HUNDRED VOLUMES OF SHOJO MANGA IS TAKING ITS TOLL...
AND NOW I HAVE TO SPEND THE WHOLE DAY IN THE GARBAGE-DUMP DEPARTMENT. JUST THINKING ABOUT IT IS GIVING ME HEARTBURN...
GOOD MORN-ING...
GURGL GURGL
GOOD MORNING, ONODERA-KUN!

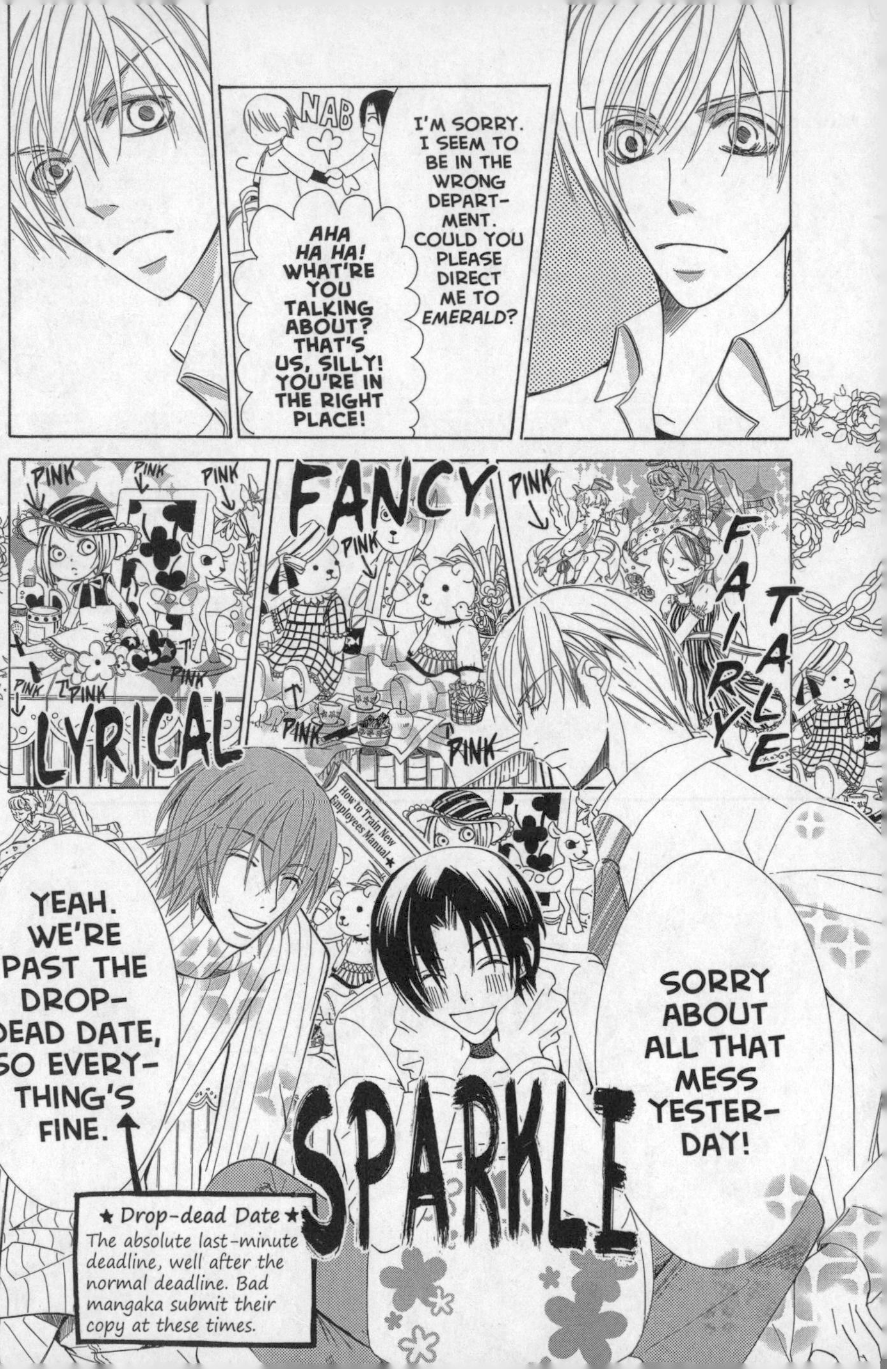

NAB
I'M SORRY. I SEEM TO BE IN THE WRONG DEPARTMENT. COULD YOU PLEASE DIRECT ME TO *EMERALD*?
AHA HA HA! WHAT'RE YOU TALKING ABOUT? THAT'S US, SILLY! YOU'RE IN THE RIGHT PLACE!
PINK
FAIRY TALE
PINK
PINK
FANCY
PINK
PINK
PINK
PINK
PINK
PINK
PINK
LYRICAL
How to Train New Employees Manual
SORRY ABOUT ALL THAT MESS YESTERDAY!
YEAH. WE'RE PAST THE DROP-DEAD DATE, SO EVERYTHING'S FINE.
SPARKLE
★ Drop-dead Date ★
The absolute last-minute deadline, well after the normal deadline. Bad mangaka submit their copy at these times.

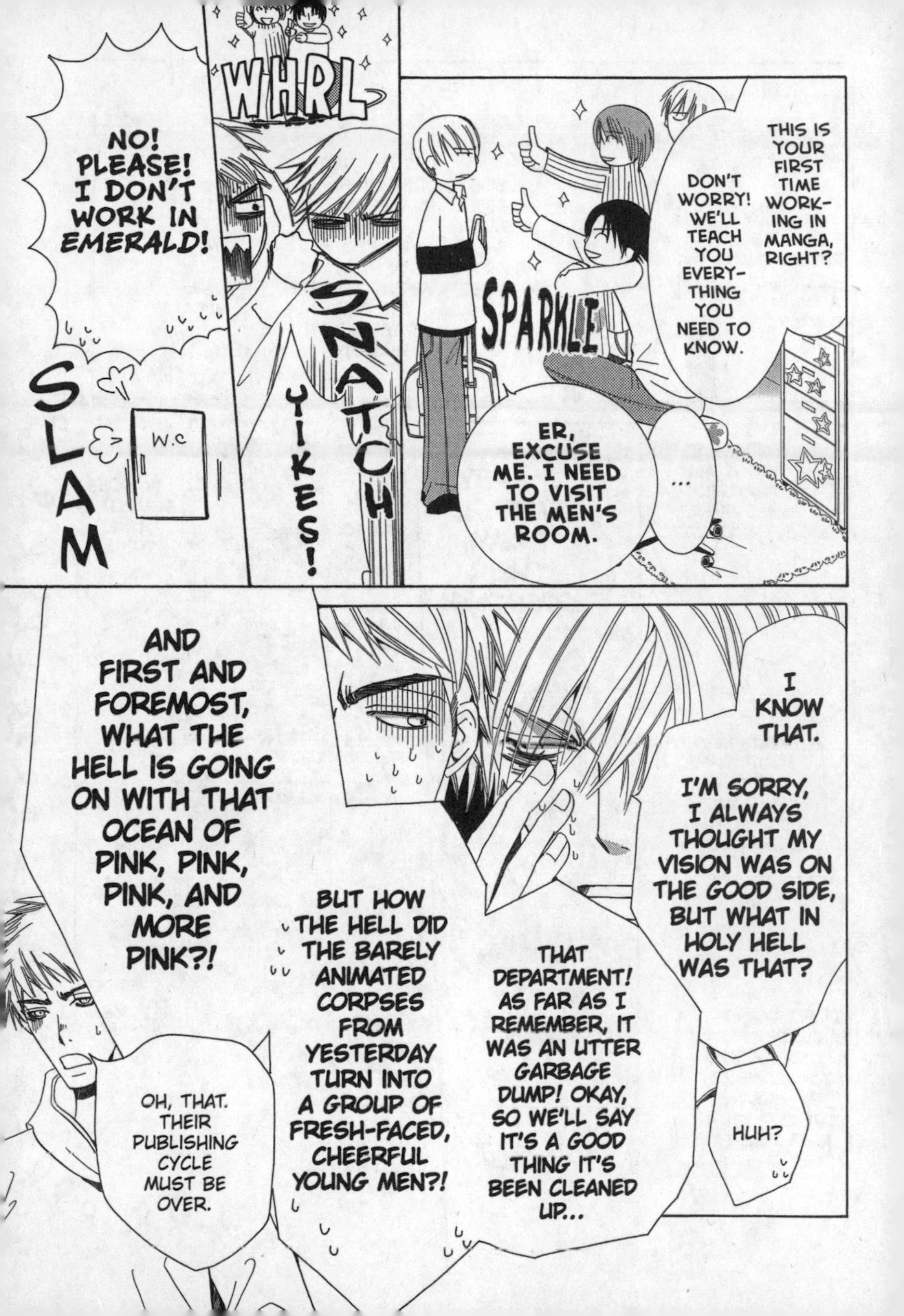
THIS IS YOUR FIRST TIME WORKING IN MANGA, RIGHT?
DON'T WORRY! WE'LL TEACH YOU EVERYTHING YOU NEED TO KNOW.
SPARKLE
...
ER, EXCUSE ME. I NEED TO VISIT THE MEN'S ROOM.
WHRL
SNATCH
YIKES!
NO! PLEASE! I DON'T WORK IN EMERALD!
SLAM
W.C
I KNOW THAT.
I'M SORRY, I ALWAYS THOUGHT MY VISION WAS ON THE GOOD SIDE, BUT WHAT IN HOLY HELL WAS THAT?
HUH?
THAT DEPARTMENT! AS FAR AS I REMEMBER, IT WAS AN UTTER GARBAGE DUMP! OKAY, SO WE'LL SAY IT'S A GOOD THING IT'S BEEN CLEANED UP...
BUT HOW THE HELL DID THE BARELY ANIMATED CORPSES FROM YESTERDAY TURN INTO A GROUP OF FRESH-FACED, CHEERFUL YOUNG MEN?!
AND FIRST AND FOREMOST, WHAT THE HELL IS GOING ON WITH THAT OCEAN OF PINK, PINK, PINK, AND MORE PINK?!
OH, THAT. THEIR PUBLISHING CYCLE MUST BE OVER.

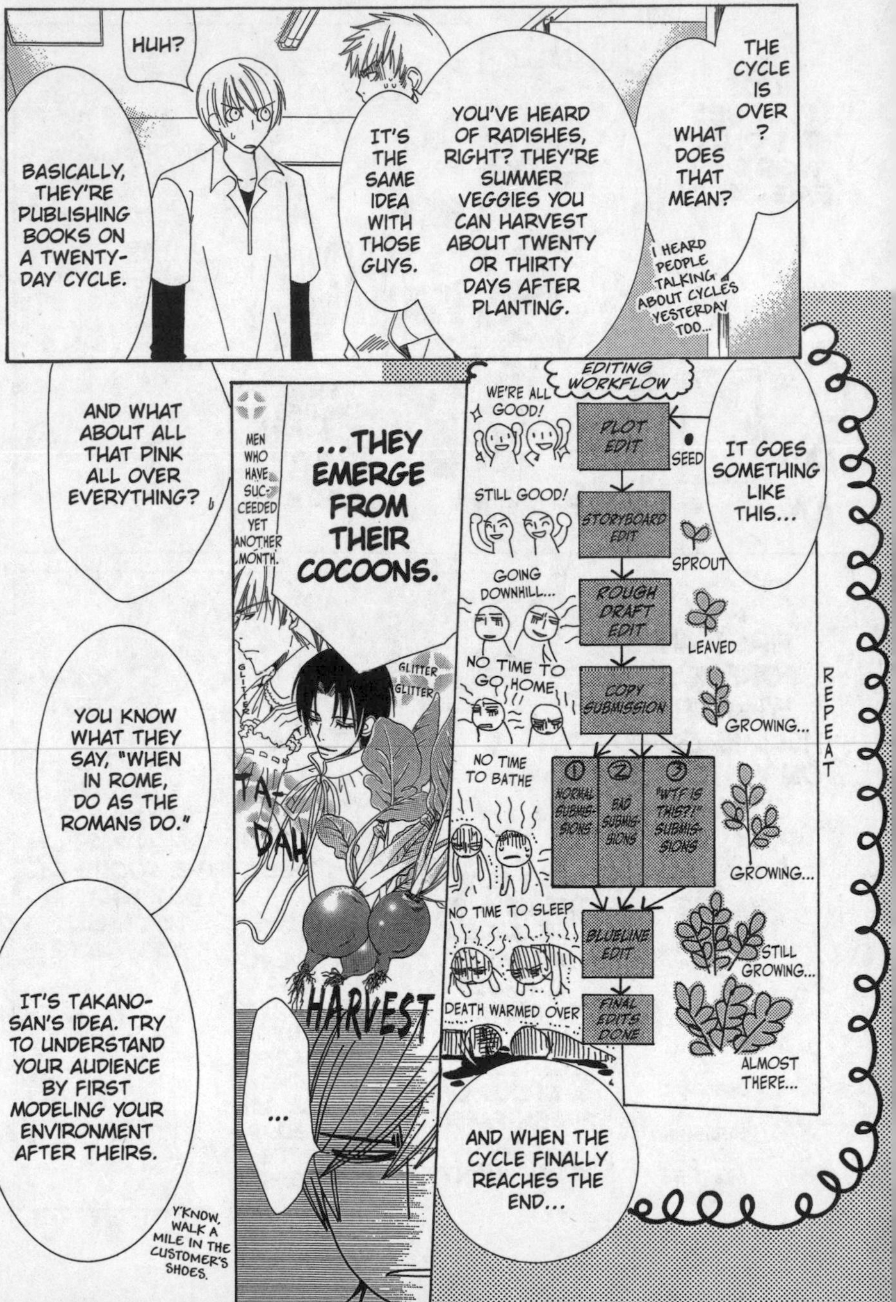
THE CYCLE IS OVER?
WHAT DOES THAT MEAN?
I HEARD PEOPLE TALKING ABOUT CYCLES YESTERDAY TOO...
YOU'VE HEARD OF RADISHES, RIGHT? THEY'RE SUMMER VEGGIES YOU CAN HARVEST ABOUT TWENTY OR THIRTY DAYS AFTER PLANTING.
IT'S THE SAME IDEA WITH THOSE GUYS.
HUH?
BASICALLY, THEY'RE PUBLISHING BOOKS ON A TWENTY-DAY CYCLE.
IT GOES SOMETHING LIKE THIS...
EDITING WORKFLOW
WE'RE ALL GOOD!
PLOT EDIT
SEED
STILL GOOD!
STORYBOARD EDIT
SPROUT
GOING DOWNHILL...
ROUGH DRAFT EDIT
LEAVED
NO TIME TO GO HOME
COPY SUBMISSION
GROWING...
REPEAT
NO TIME TO BATHE
1 NORMAL SUBMISSIONS
2 BAD SUBMISSIONS
3 "WTF IS THIS?!" SUBMISSIONS
GROWING...
NO TIME TO SLEEP
BLUELINE EDIT
STILL GROWING...
DEATH WARMED OVER
FINAL EDITS DONE
ALMOST THERE...
AND WHEN THE CYCLE FINALLY REACHES THE END...
...THEY EMERGE FROM THEIR COCOONS.
MEN WHO HAVE SUCCEEDED YET ANOTHER MONTH.
GLITTER GLITTER
GLITTER
TA-DAH
HARVEST
...
AND WHAT ABOUT ALL THAT PINK ALL OVER EVERYTHING?
YOU KNOW WHAT THEY SAY, "WHEN IN ROME, DO AS THE ROMANS DO."
IT'S TAKANO-SAN'S IDEA. TRY TO UNDERSTAND YOUR AUDIENCE BY FIRST MODELING YOUR ENVIRONMENT AFTER THEIRS.
Y'KNOW, WALK A MILE IN THE CUSTOMER'S SHOES.

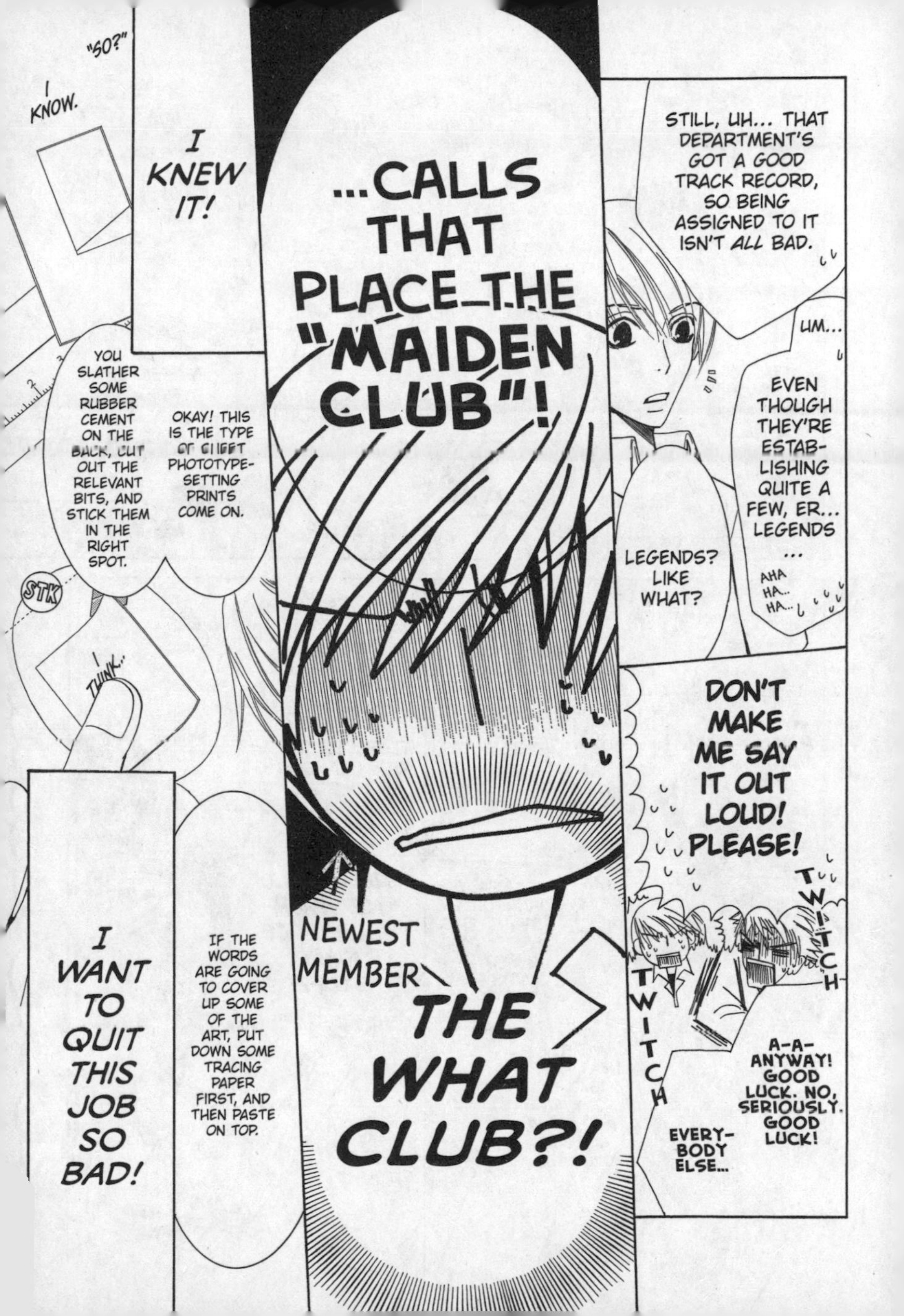
STILL, UH... THAT DEPARTMENT'S GOT A GOOD TRACK RECORD, SO BEING ASSIGNED TO IT ISN'T *ALL* BAD.
UM...
EVEN THOUGH THEY'RE ESTABLISHING QUITE A FEW, ER... LEGENDS ...
AHA HA... HA...
LEGENDS? LIKE WHAT?
DON'T MAKE ME SAY IT OUT LOUD! PLEASE!
TWITCH
TWITCH
A-A-ANYWAY! GOOD LUCK. NO, SERIOUSLY. GOOD LUCK!
EVERYBODY ELSE...
...CALLS THAT PLACE THE "MAIDEN CLUB"!
NEWEST MEMBER
THE WHAT CLUB?!
"SO?"
I KNOW.
I KNEW IT!
YOU SLATHER SOME RUBBER CEMENT ON THE BACK, CUT OUT THE RELEVANT BITS, AND STICK THEM IN THE RIGHT SPOT.
OKAY! THIS IS THE TYPE OF SHEET PHOTOTYPE-SETTING PRINTS COME ON.
STK
I THINK...
I WANT TO QUIT THIS JOB SO BAD!
IF THE WORDS ARE GOING TO COVER UP SOME OF THE ART, PUT DOWN SOME TRACING PAPER FIRST, AND THEN PASTE ON TOP.

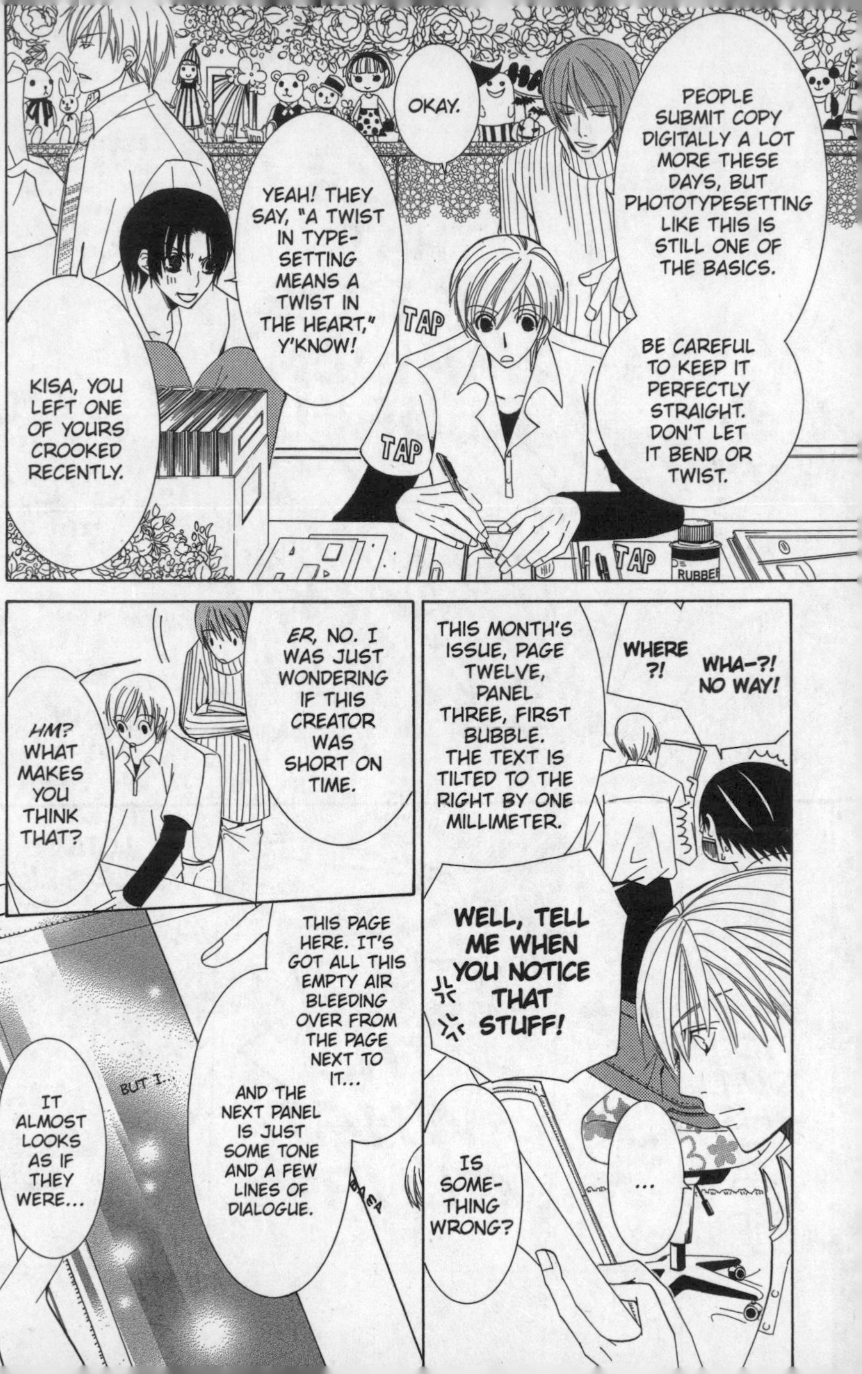
PEOPLE SUBMIT COPY DIGITALLY A LOT MORE THESE DAYS, BUT PHOTOTYPESETTING LIKE THIS IS STILL ONE OF THE BASICS.
BE CAREFUL TO KEEP IT PERFECTLY STRAIGHT. DON'T LET IT BEND OR TWIST.
TAP
TAP
TAP
OKAY.
YEAH! THEY SAY, "A TWIST IN TYPE-SETTING MEANS A TWIST IN THE HEART," Y'KNOW!
KISA, YOU LEFT ONE OF YOURS CROOKED RECENTLY.
WHERE ?!
WHA-?! NO WAY!
THIS MONTH'S ISSUE, PAGE TWELVE, PANEL THREE, FIRST BUBBLE. THE TEXT IS TILTED TO THE RIGHT BY ONE MILLIMETER.
WELL, TELL ME WHEN YOU NOTICE THAT STUFF!
...
IS SOME-THING WRONG?
HM? WHAT MAKES YOU THINK THAT?
ER, NO. I WAS JUST WONDERING IF THIS CREATOR WAS SHORT ON TIME.
THIS PAGE HERE. IT'S GOT ALL THIS EMPTY AIR BLEEDING OVER FROM THE PAGE NEXT TO IT...
AND THE NEXT PANEL IS JUST SOME TONE AND A FEW LINES OF DIALOGUE.
IT ALMOST LOOKS AS IF THEY WERE...
BUT I...

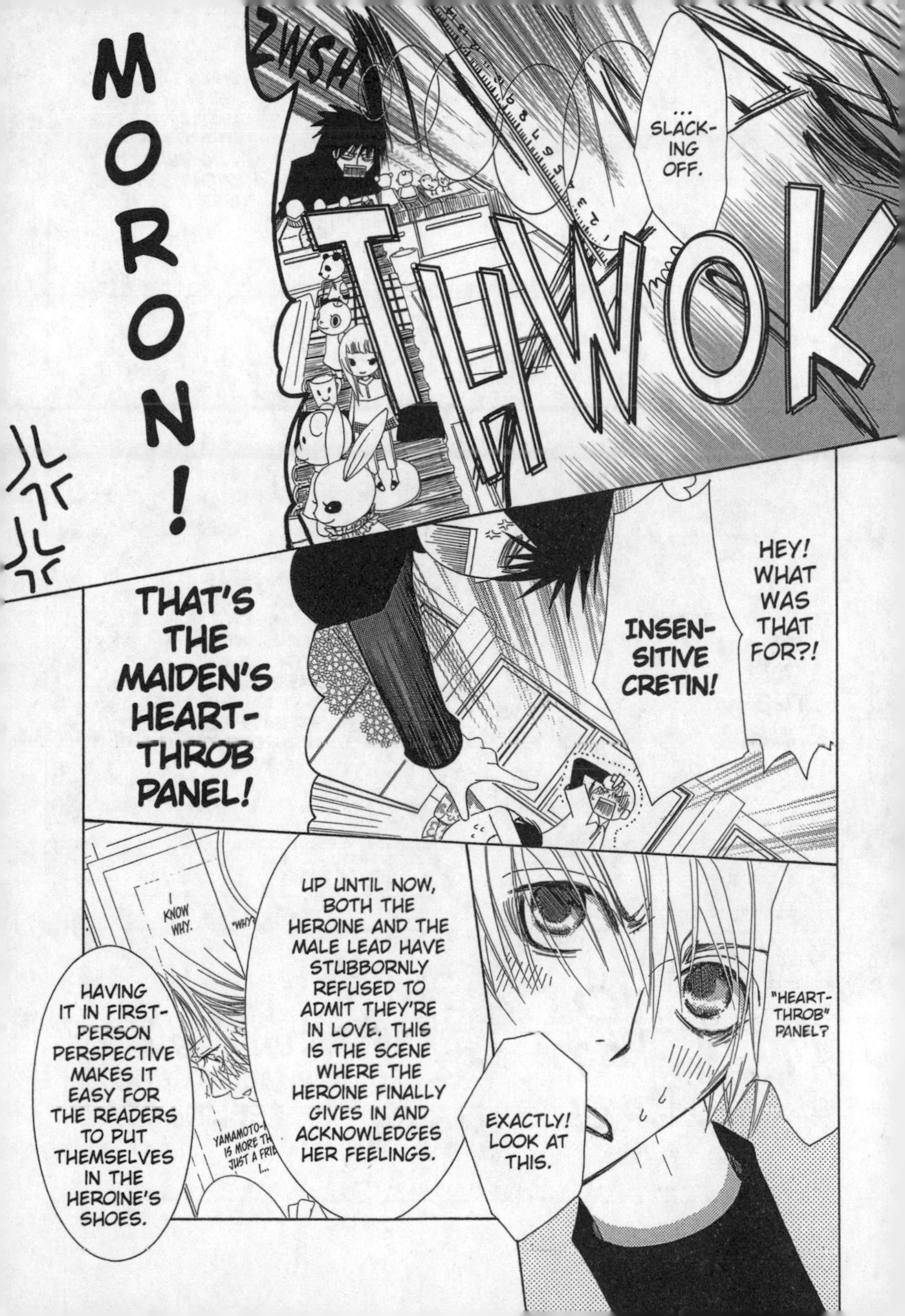
...SLACKING OFF.
ZWSH
THWOK
MORON!
HEY! WHAT WAS THAT FOR?!
INSEN-SITIVE CRETIN!
THAT'S THE MAIDEN'S HEART-THROB PANEL!
"HEART-THROB" PANEL?
EXACTLY! LOOK AT THIS.
UP UNTIL NOW, BOTH THE HEROINE AND THE MALE LEAD HAVE STUBBORNLY REFUSED TO ADMIT THEY'RE IN LOVE. THIS IS THE SCENE WHERE THE HEROINE FINALLY GIVES IN AND ACKNOWLEDGES HER FEELINGS.
I KNOW WHY.
HAVING IT IN FIRST-PERSON PERSPECTIVE MAKES IT EASY FOR THE READERS TO PUT THEMSELVES IN THE HEROINE'S SHOES.

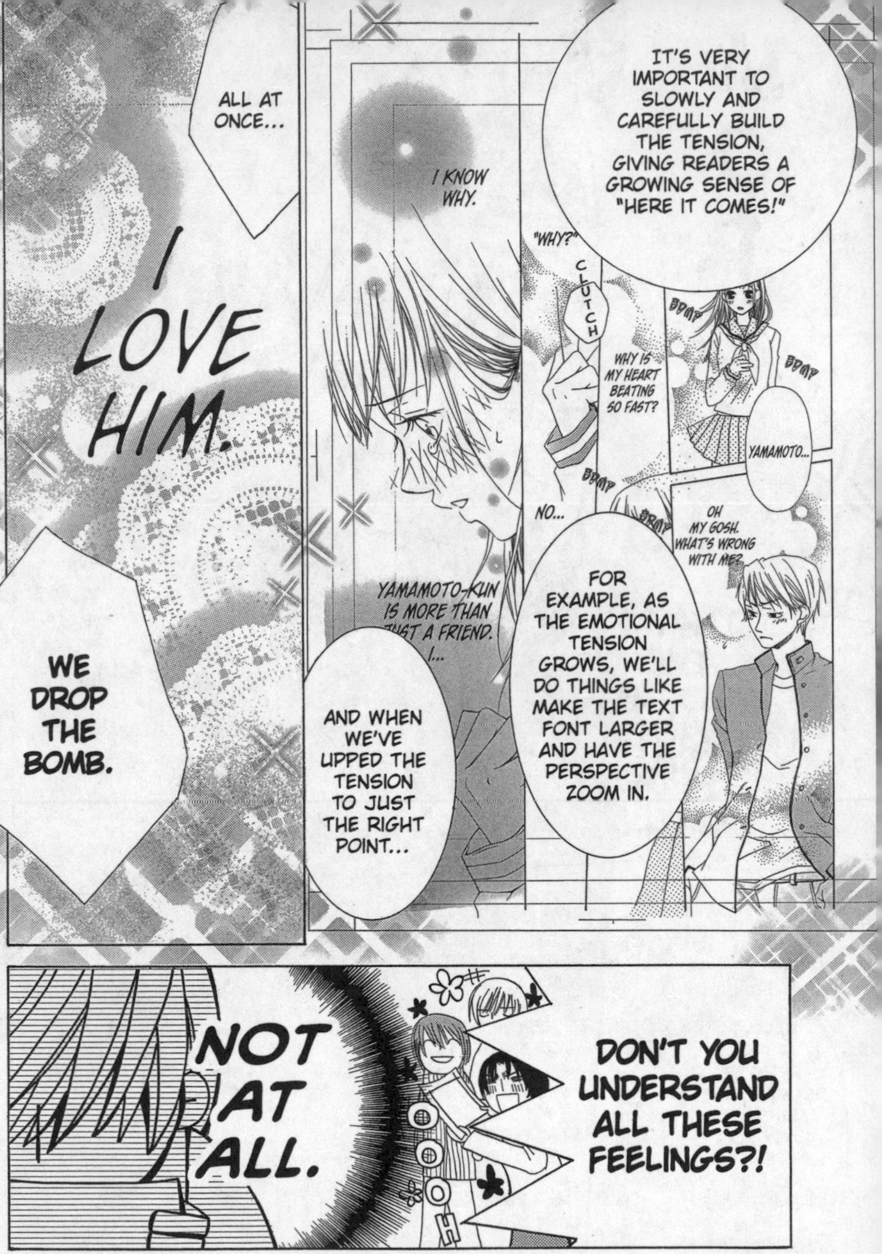

IT'S VERY IMPORTANT TO SLOWLY AND CAREFULLY BUILD THE TENSION, GIVING READERS A GROWING SENSE OF "HERE IT COMES!"
"WHY?"
CLUTCH
BDMP
WHY IS MY HEART BEATING SO FAST?
BDMP
YAMAMOTO...
BDMP
NO...
BDMP
OH MY GOSH. WHAT'S WRONG WITH ME?
FOR EXAMPLE, AS THE EMOTIONAL TENSION GROWS, WE'LL DO THINGS LIKE MAKE THE TEXT FONT LARGER AND HAVE THE PERSPECTIVE ZOOM IN.
I KNOW WHY.
YAMAMOTO-KUN IS MORE THAN JUST A FRIEND. I...
AND WHEN WE'VE UPPED THE TENSION TO JUST THE RIGHT POINT...
ALL AT ONCE...
I LOVE HIM.
WE DROP THE BOMB.
DON'T YOU UNDERSTAND ALL THESE FEELINGS?!
NOT AT ALL.

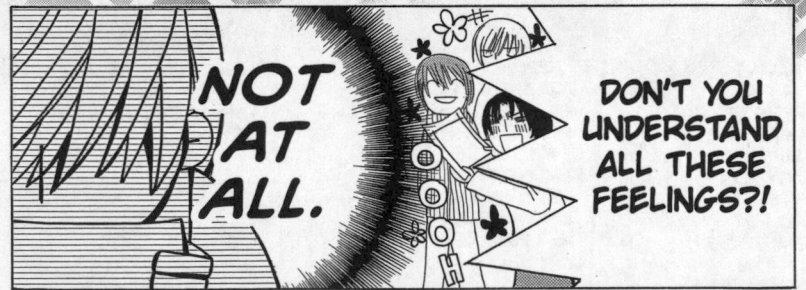

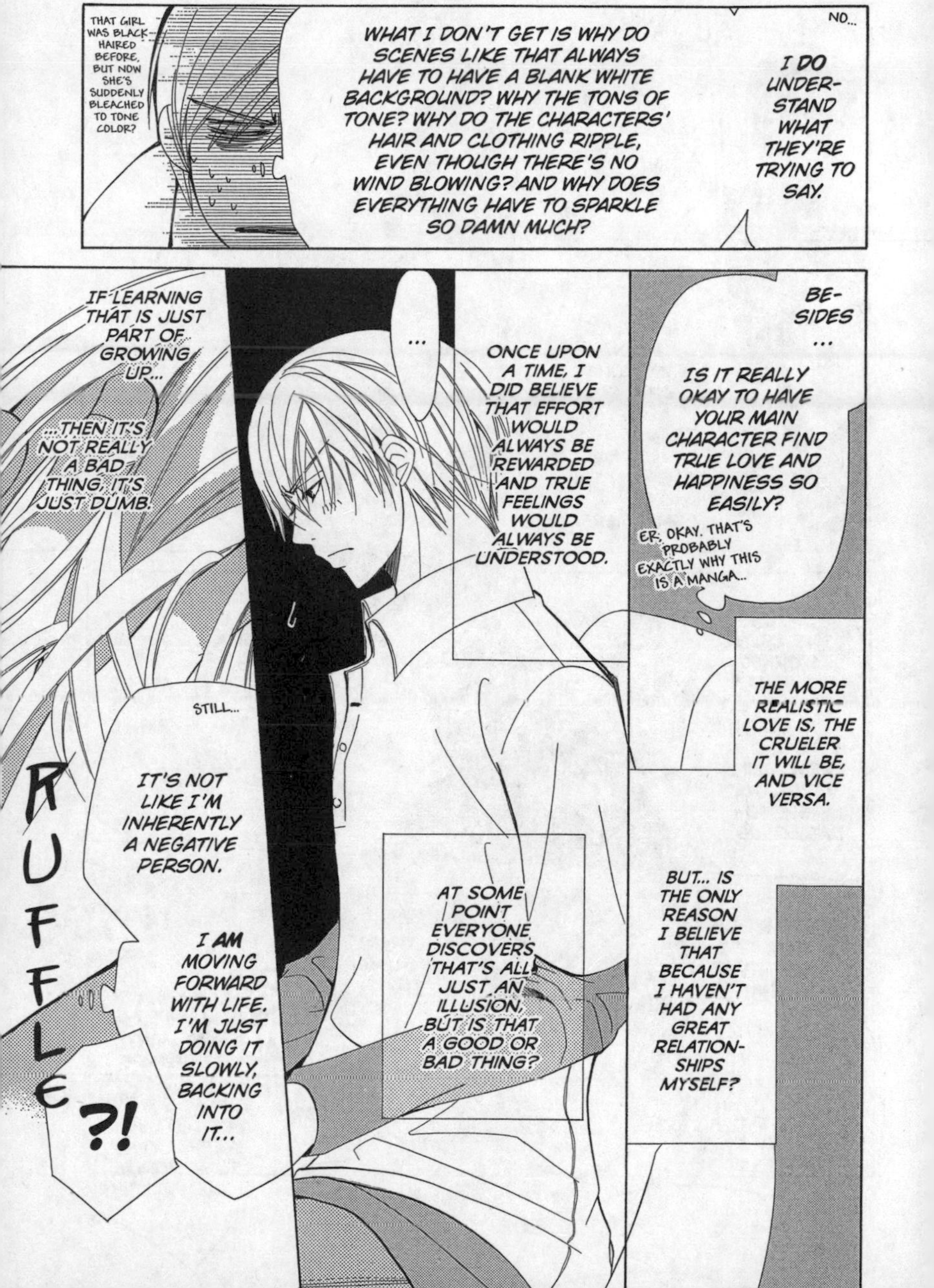
NO...
I DO UNDERSTAND WHAT THEY'RE TRYING TO SAY.
WHAT I DON'T GET IS WHY DO SCENES LIKE THAT ALWAYS HAVE TO HAVE A BLANK WHITE BACKGROUND? WHY THE TONS OF TONE? WHY DO THE CHARACTERS' HAIR AND CLOTHING RIPPLE, EVEN THOUGH THERE'S NO WIND BLOWING? AND WHY DOES EVERYTHING HAVE TO SPARKLE SO DAMN MUCH?
THAT GIRL WAS BLACK-HAIRED BEFORE, BUT NOW SHE'S SUDDENLY BLEACHED TO TONE COLOR?
BESIDES...
IS IT REALLY OKAY TO HAVE YOUR MAIN CHARACTER FIND TRUE LOVE AND HAPPINESS SO EASILY?
ER, OKAY. THAT'S PROBABLY EXACTLY WHY THIS IS A MANGA...
THE MORE REALISTIC LOVE IS, THE CRUELER IT WILL BE, AND VICE VERSA.
BUT... IS THE ONLY REASON I BELIEVE THAT BECAUSE I HAVEN'T HAD ANY GREAT RELATIONSHIPS MYSELF?
...
ONCE UPON A TIME, I DID BELIEVE THAT EFFORT WOULD ALWAYS BE REWARDED AND TRUE FEELINGS WOULD ALWAYS BE UNDERSTOOD.
AT SOME POINT EVERYONE DISCOVERS THAT'S ALL JUST AN ILLUSION, BUT IS THAT A GOOD OR BAD THING?
IF LEARNING THAT IS JUST PART OF GROWING UP...
...THEN IT'S NOT REALLY A BAD THING, IT'S JUST DUMB.
STILL...
IT'S NOT LIKE I'M INHERENTLY A NEGATIVE PERSON.
I AM MOVING FORWARD WITH LIFE. I'M JUST DOING IT SLOWLY, BACKING INTO IT...
RUFFLE
?!

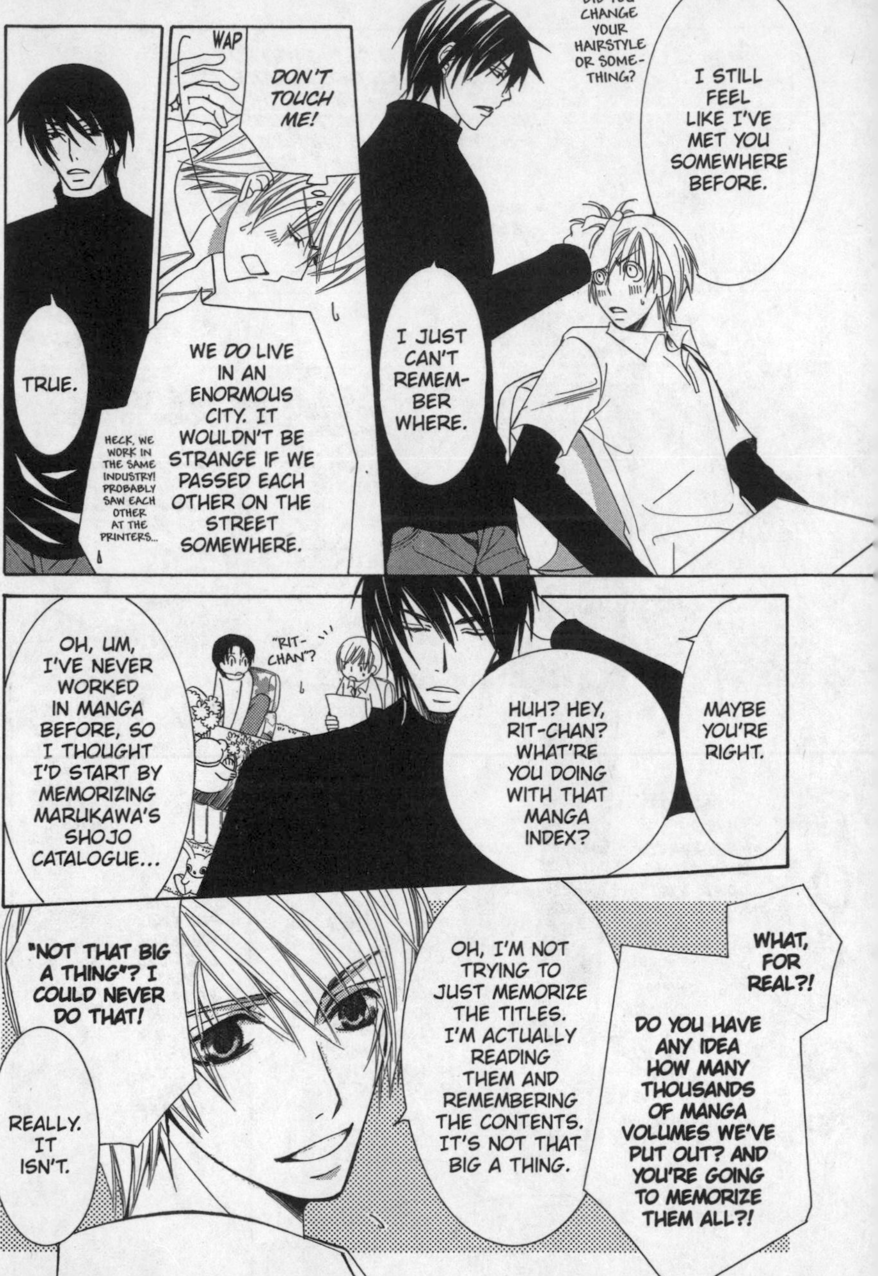
DID YOU CHANGE YOUR HAIRSTYLE OR SOMETHING?
I STILL FEEL LIKE I'VE MET YOU SOMEWHERE BEFORE.
I JUST CAN'T REMEMBER WHERE.
WAP
DON'T TOUCH ME!
WE DO LIVE IN AN ENORMOUS CITY. IT WOULDN'T BE STRANGE IF WE PASSED EACH OTHER ON THE STREET SOMEWHERE.
TRUE.
HECK, WE WORK IN THE SAME INDUSTRY! PROBABLY SAW EACH OTHER AT THE PRINTERS...
MAYBE YOU'RE RIGHT.
HUH? HEY, RIT-CHAN? WHAT'RE YOU DOING WITH THAT MANGA INDEX?
"RIT-CHAN"?
OH, UM, I'VE NEVER WORKED IN MANGA BEFORE, SO I THOUGHT I'D START BY MEMORIZING MARUKAWA'S SHOJO CATALOGUE...
WHAT, FOR REAL?!
DO YOU HAVE ANY IDEA HOW MANY THOUSANDS OF MANGA VOLUMES WE'VE PUT OUT? AND YOU'RE GOING TO MEMORIZE THEM ALL?!
OH, I'M NOT TRYING TO JUST MEMORIZE THE TITLES. I'M ACTUALLY READING THEM AND REMEMBERING THE CONTENTS. IT'S NOT THAT BIG A THING.
"NOT THAT BIG A THING"? I COULD NEVER DO THAT!
REALLY. IT ISN'T.

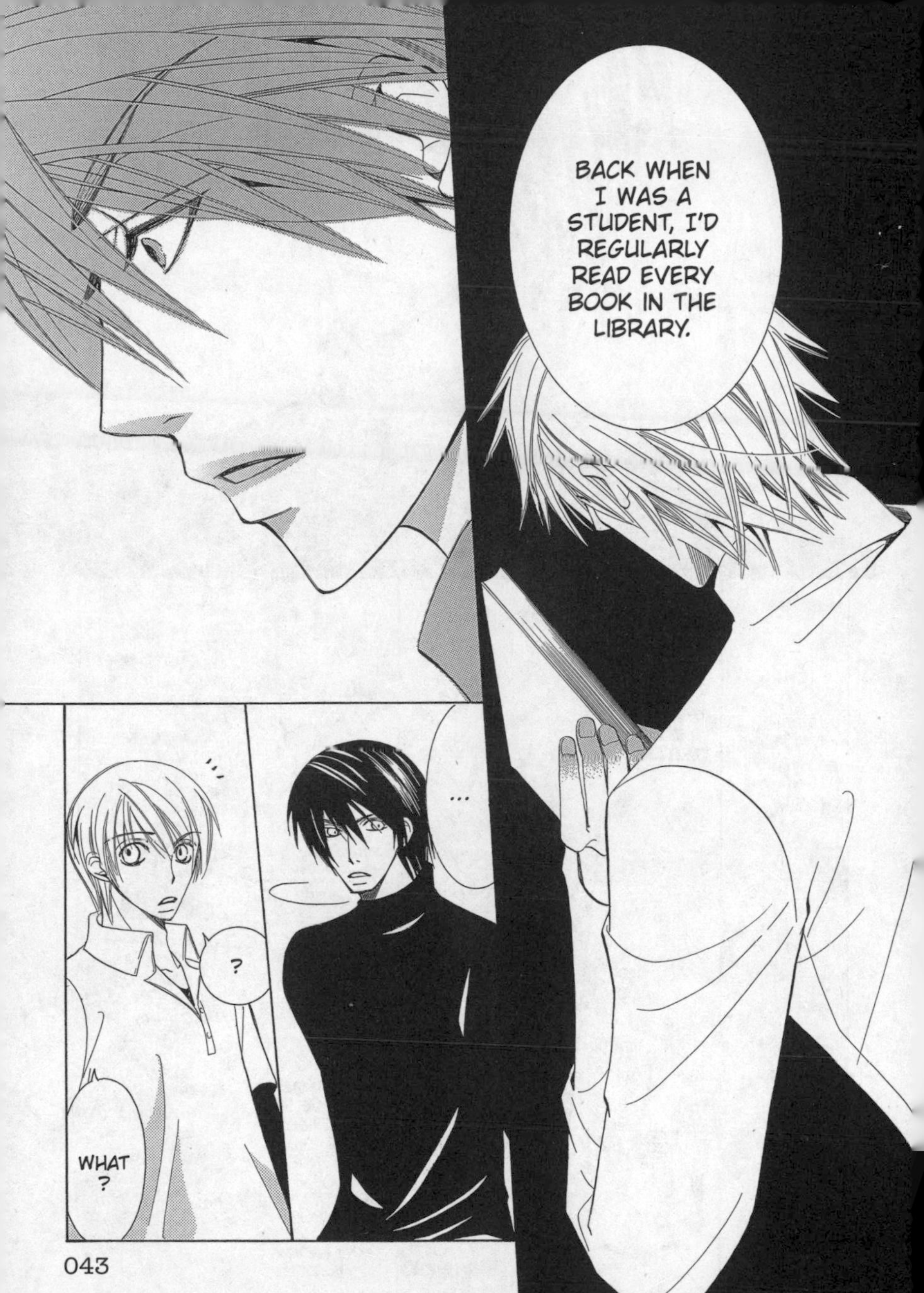
BACK WHEN I WAS A STUDENT, I'D REGULARLY READ EVERY BOOK IN THE LIBRARY.
...
?
WHAT?

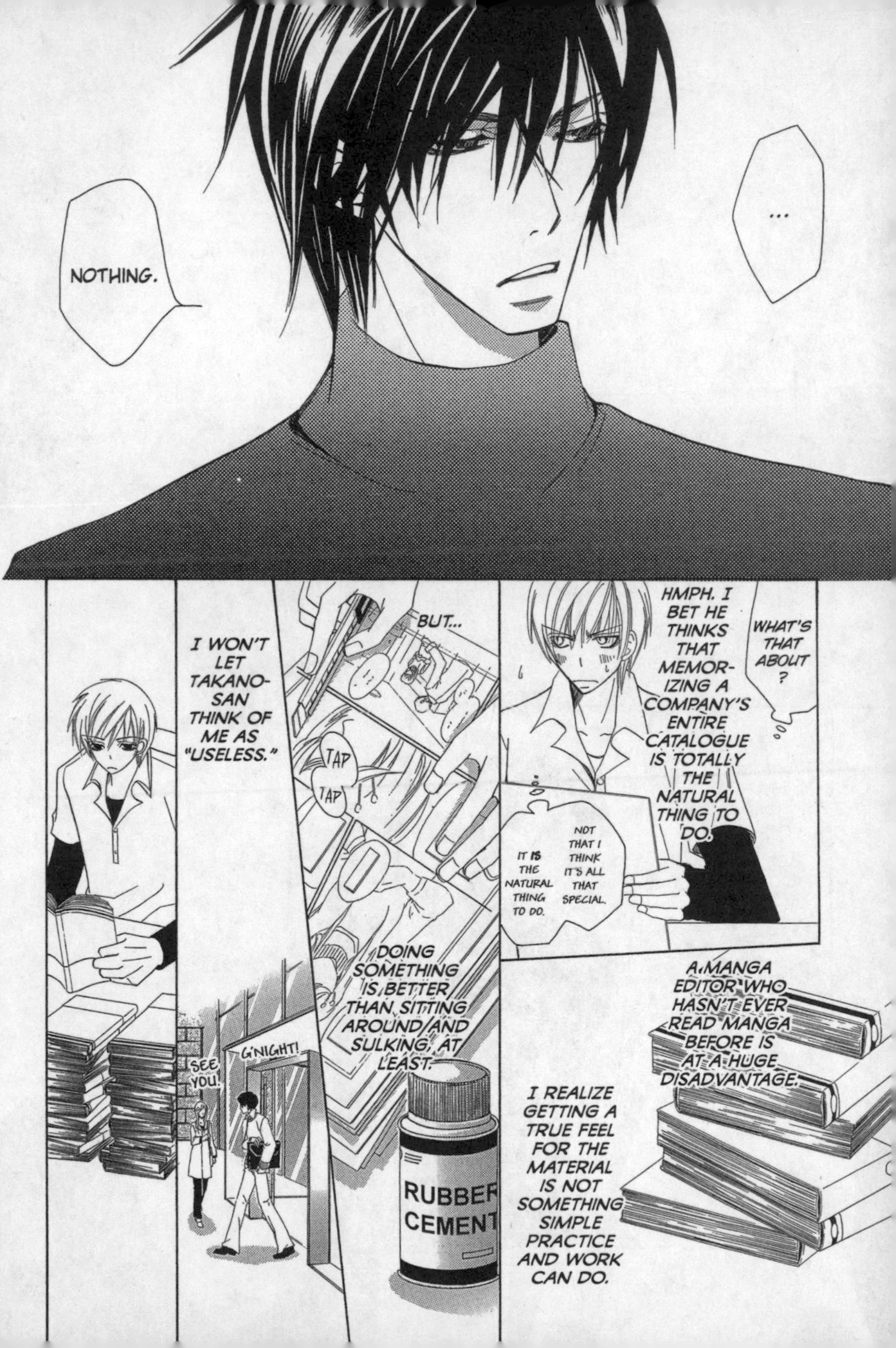
...
NOTHING.
WHAT'S THAT ABOUT?
HMPH. I BET HE THINKS THAT MEMORIZING A COMPANY'S ENTIRE CATALOGUE IS TOTALLY THE NATURAL THING TO DO.
NOT THAT I THINK IT'S ALL THAT SPECIAL.
IT IS THE NATURAL THING TO DO.
A MANGA EDITOR WHO HASN'T EVER READ MANGA BEFORE IS AT A HUGE DISADVANTAGE.
I REALIZE GETTING A TRUE FEEL FOR THE MATERIAL IS NOT SOMETHING SIMPLE PRACTICE AND WORK CAN DO.
BUT...
TAP
TAP
DOING SOMETHING IS BETTER THAN SITTING AROUND AND SULKING, AT LEAST.
RUBBER CEMENT
I WON'T LET TAKANO-SAN THINK OF ME AS "USELESS."
G'NIGHT!
SEE YOU!

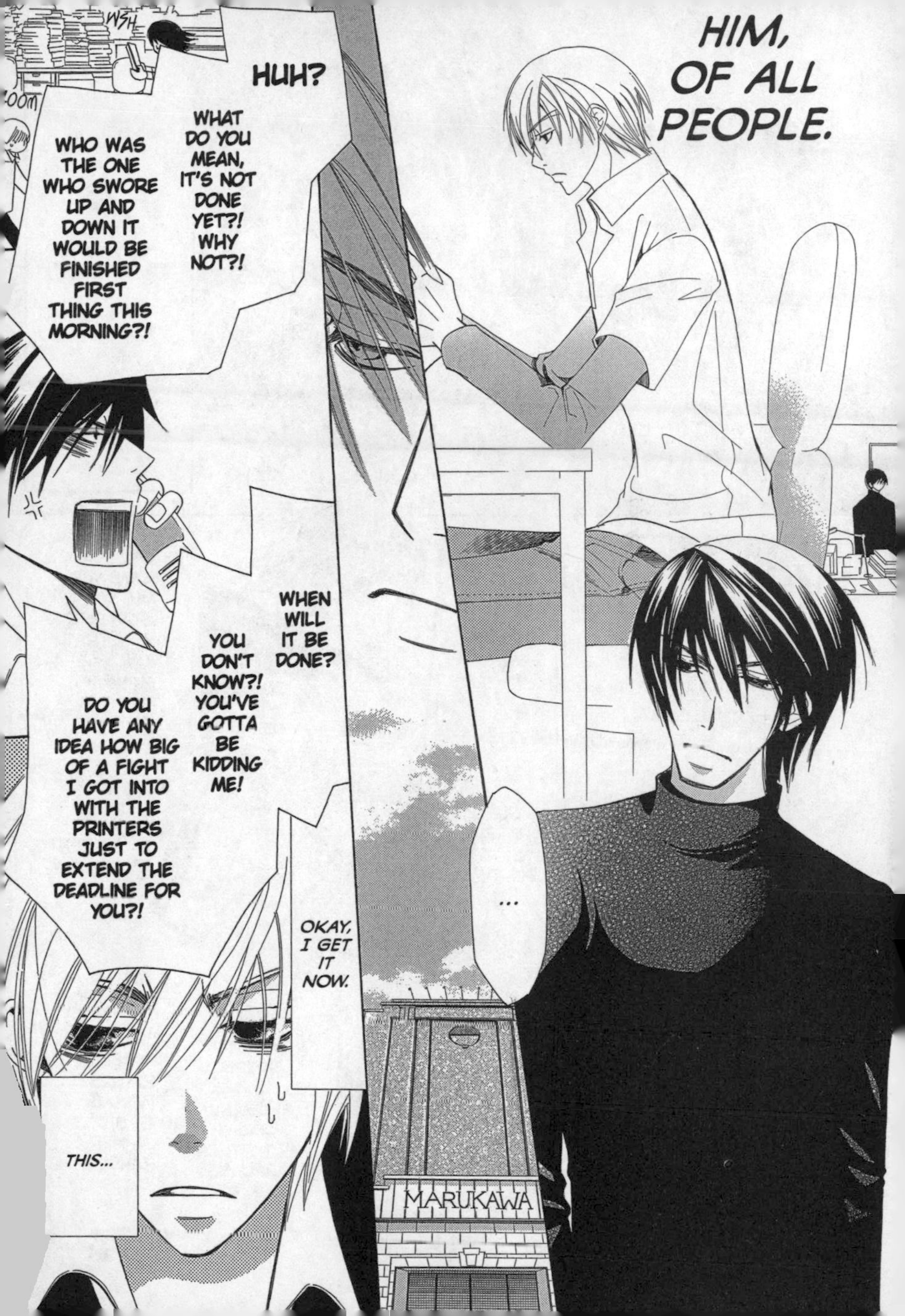
HIM, OF ALL PEOPLE.
HUH?
WHAT DO YOU MEAN, IT'S NOT DONE YET?! WHY NOT?!
WHO WAS THE ONE WHO SWORE UP AND DOWN IT WOULD BE FINISHED FIRST THING THIS MORNING?!
WSH
WHEN WILL IT BE DONE?
YOU DON'T KNOW?! YOU'VE GOTTA BE KIDDING ME!
DO YOU HAVE ANY IDEA HOW BIG OF A FIGHT I GOT INTO WITH THE PRINTERS JUST TO EXTEND THE DEADLINE FOR YOU?!
...
OKAY, I GET IT NOW.
THIS...
MARUKAWA

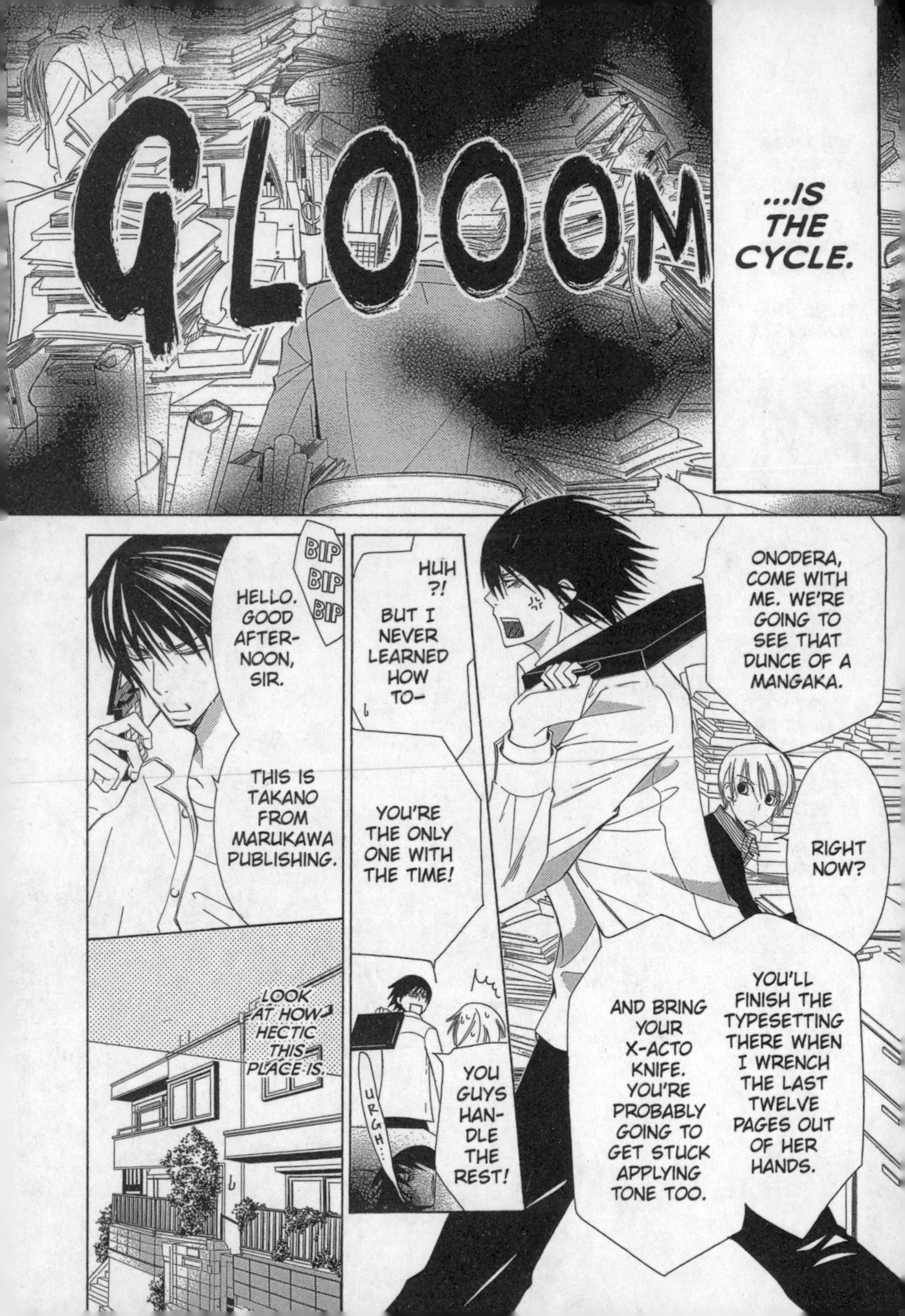
...IS THE CYCLE.
GLOOOM
ONODERA, COME WITH ME. WE'RE GOING TO SEE THAT DUNCE OF A MANGAKA.
RIGHT NOW?
YOU'LL FINISH THE TYPESETTING THERE WHEN I WRENCH THE LAST TWELVE PAGES OUT OF HER HANDS.
AND BRING YOUR X-ACTO KNIFE. YOU'RE PROBABLY GOING TO GET STUCK APPLYING TONE TOO.
HUH?!
BUT I NEVER LEARNED HOW TO—
YOU'RE THE ONLY ONE WITH THE TIME!
YOU GUYS HANDLE THE REST!
URGH...
BIP BIP BIP
HELLO. GOOD AFTERNOON, SIR.
THIS IS TAKANO FROM MARUKAWA PUBLISHING.
LOOK AT HOW HECTIC THIS PLACE IS.

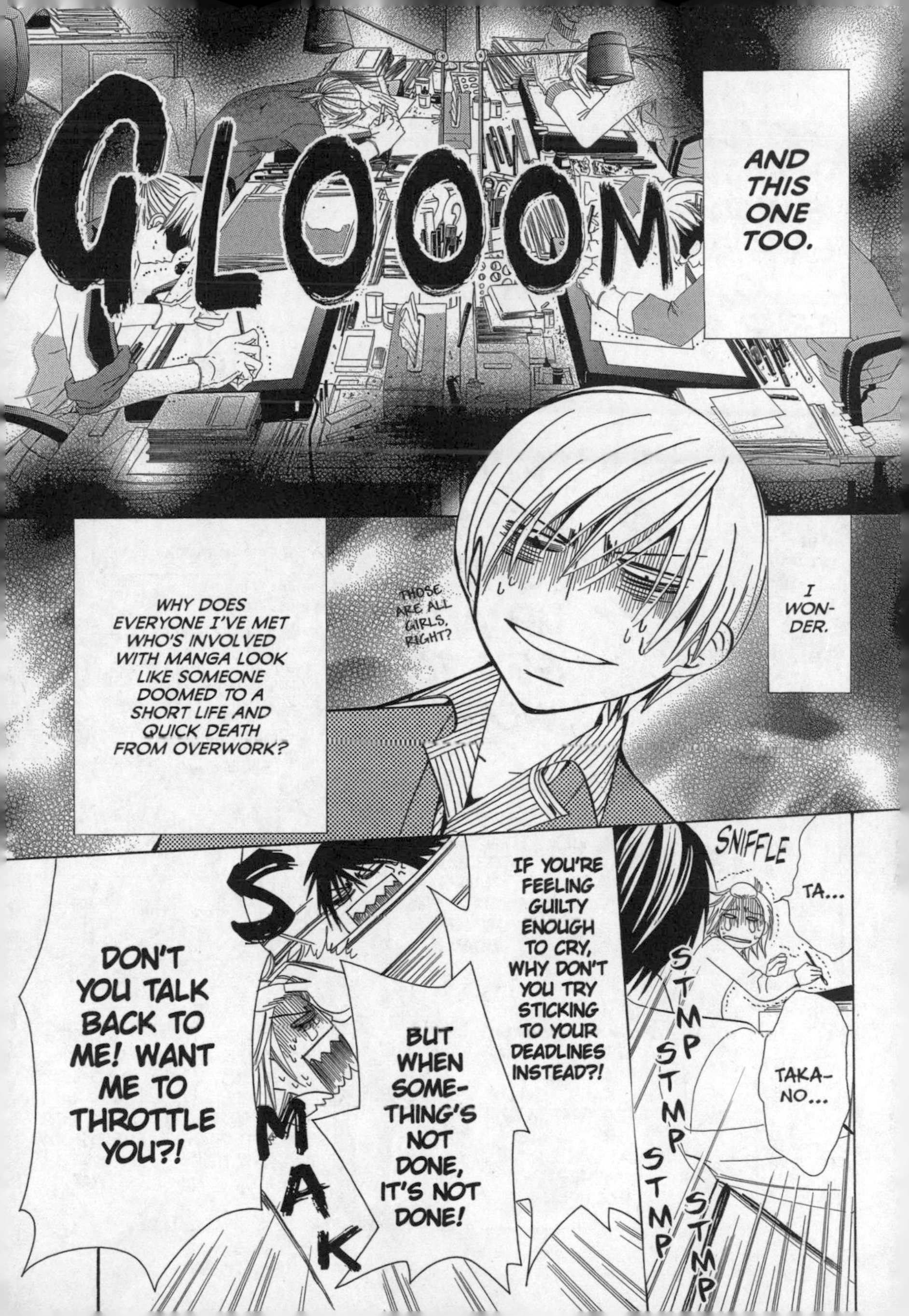
AND THIS ONE TOO.
GLOOOM
I WON-DER.
THOSE ARE ALL GIRLS, RIGHT?
WHY DOES EVERYONE I'VE MET WHO'S INVOLVED WITH MANGA LOOK LIKE SOMEONE DOOMED TO A SHORT LIFE AND QUICK DEATH FROM OVERWORK?
SNIFFLE
TA...
TAKA-NO...
STMP STMP STMP STMP STMP STMP
IF YOU'RE FEELING GUILTY ENOUGH TO CRY, WHY DON'T YOU TRY STICKING TO YOUR DEADLINES INSTEAD?!
BUT WHEN SOME-THING'S NOT DONE, IT'S NOT DONE!
DON'T YOU TALK BACK TO ME! WANT ME TO THROTTLE YOU?!
SMAK

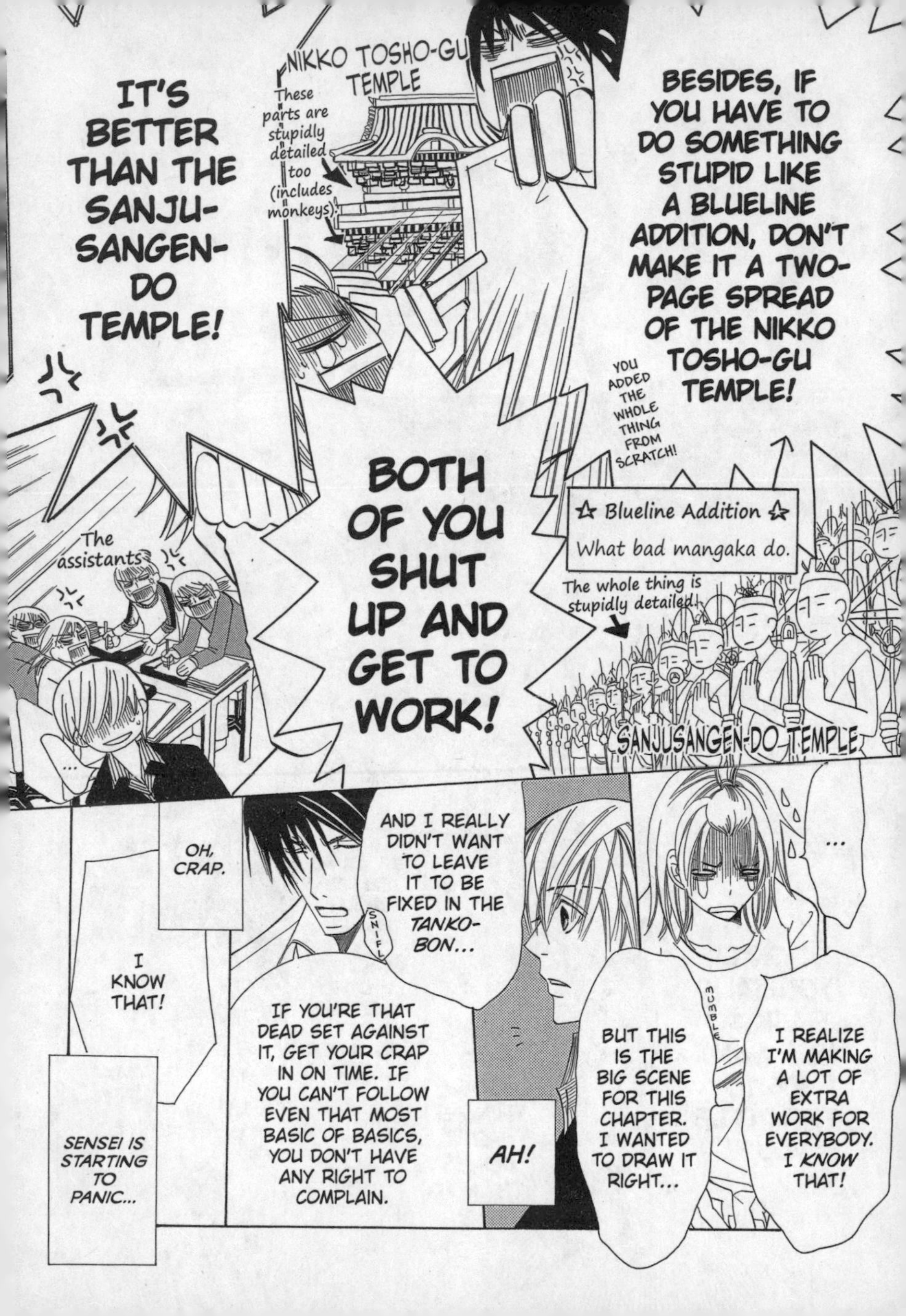
BESIDES, IF YOU HAVE TO DO SOMETHING STUPID LIKE A BLUELINE ADDITION, DON'T MAKE IT A TWO-PAGE SPREAD OF THE NIKKO TOSHO-GU TEMPLE!
YOU ADDED THE WHOLE THING FROM SCRATCH!
NIKKO TOSHO-GU TEMPLE
These parts are stupidly detailed too (includes monkeys).
IT'S BETTER THAN THE SANJU-SANGEN-DO TEMPLE!
☆ Blueline Addition ☆
What bad mangaka do.
The whole thing is stupidly detailed!
SANJUSANGEN-DO TEMPLE
BOTH OF YOU SHUT UP AND GET TO WORK!
The assistants
...
...
I REALIZE I'M MAKING A LOT OF EXTRA WORK FOR EVERYBODY. I KNOW THAT!
BUT THIS IS THE BIG SCENE FOR THIS CHAPTER. I WANTED TO DRAW IT RIGHT...
AND I REALLY DIDN'T WANT TO LEAVE IT TO BE FIXED IN THE *TANKOBON*...
SNIFL
IF YOU'RE THAT DEAD SET AGAINST IT, GET YOUR CRAP IN ON TIME. IF YOU CAN'T FOLLOW EVEN THAT MOST BASIC OF BASICS, YOU DON'T HAVE ANY RIGHT TO COMPLAIN.
AH!
OH, CRAP.
I KNOW THAT!
SENSEI IS STARTING TO PANIC...

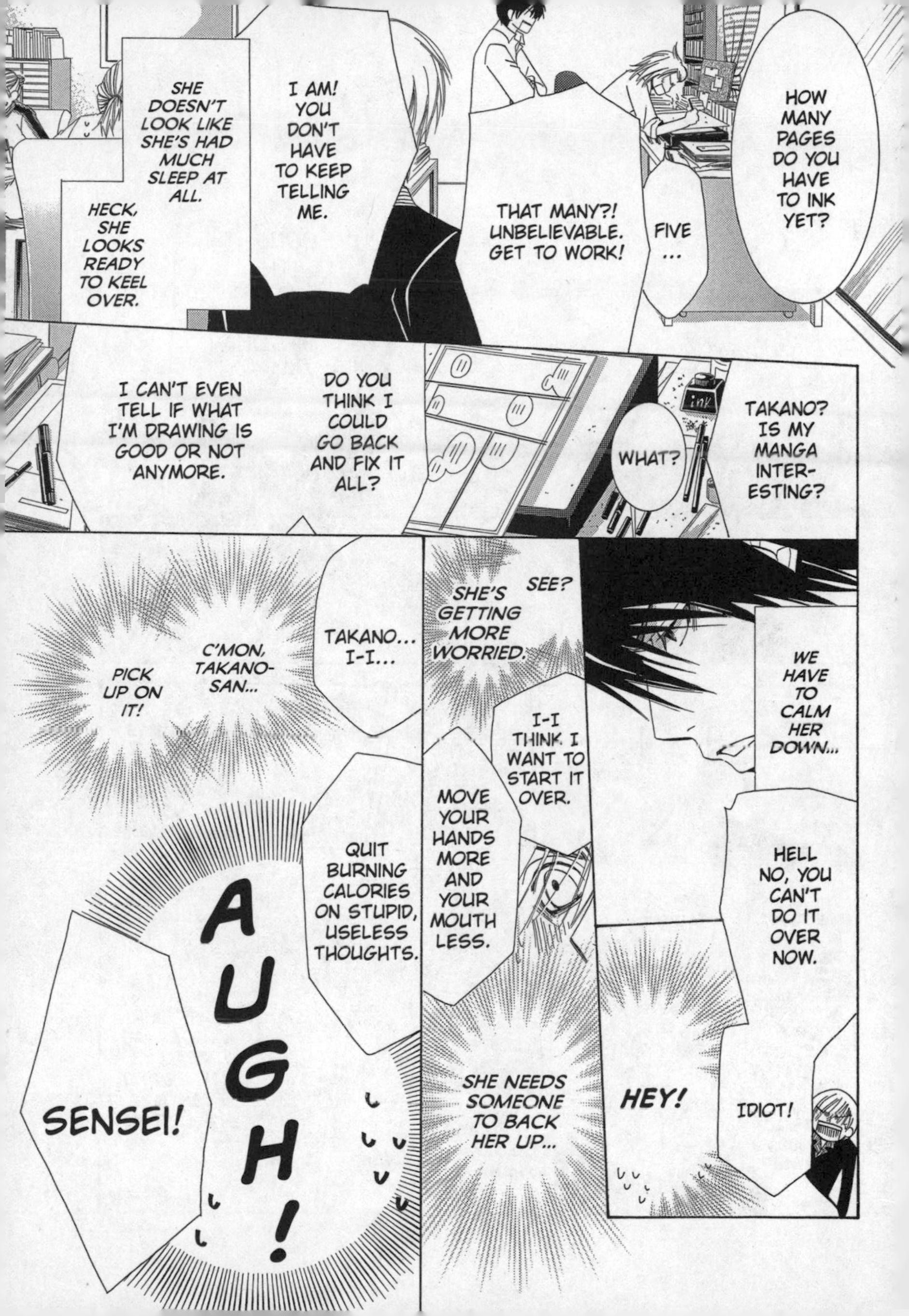
HOW MANY PAGES DO YOU HAVE TO INK YET?
FIVE...
THAT MANY?! UNBELIEVABLE. GET TO WORK!
I AM! YOU DON'T HAVE TO KEEP TELLING ME.
SHE DOESN'T LOOK LIKE SHE'S HAD MUCH SLEEP AT ALL.
HECK, SHE LOOKS READY TO KEEL OVER.
TAKANO? IS MY MANGA INTER-ESTING?
WHAT?
DO YOU THINK I COULD GO BACK AND FIX IT ALL?
I CAN'T EVEN TELL IF WHAT I'M DRAWING IS GOOD OR NOT ANYMORE.
SEE?
SHE'S GETTING MORE WORRIED.
WE HAVE TO CALM HER DOWN...
I-I THINK I WANT TO START IT OVER.
HELL NO, YOU CAN'T DO IT OVER NOW.
MOVE YOUR HANDS MORE AND YOUR MOUTH LESS.
IDIOT!
HEY!
SHE NEEDS SOMEONE TO BACK HER UP...
TAKANO... I-I...
C'MON, TAKANO-SAN...
PICK UP ON IT!
QUIT BURNING CALORIES ON STUPID, USELESS THOUGHTS.
AUGH!
SENSEI!

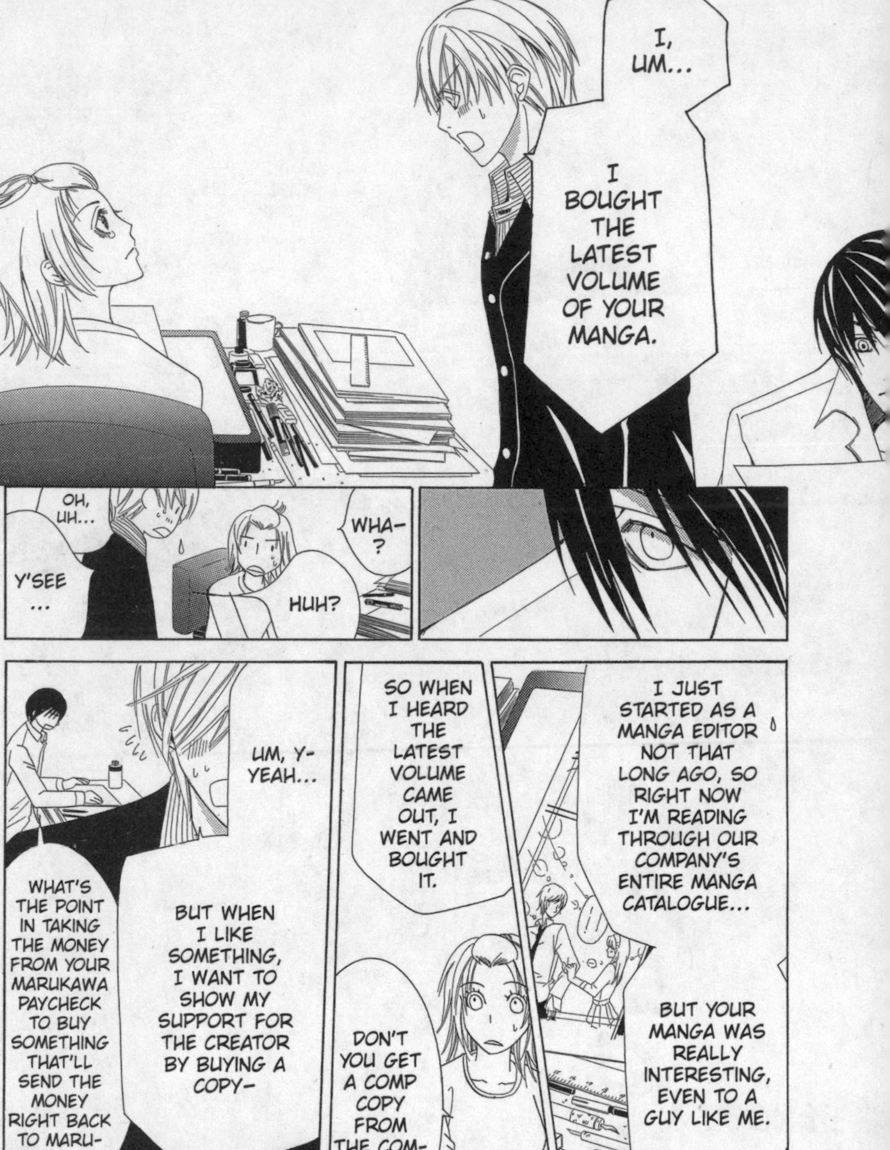
I, UM...
I BOUGHT THE LATEST VOLUME OF YOUR MANGA.
WHA- ?
HUH?
OH, UH...
Y'SEE ...
I JUST STARTED AS A MANGA EDITOR NOT THAT LONG AGO, SO RIGHT NOW I'M READING THROUGH OUR COMPANY'S ENTIRE MANGA CATALOGUE...
BUT YOUR MANGA WAS REALLY INTERESTING, EVEN TO A GUY LIKE ME.
SO WHEN I HEARD THE LATEST VOLUME CAME OUT, I WENT AND BOUGHT IT.
DON'T YOU GET A COMP COPY FROM THE COM-PANY?
UM, Y-YEAH...
BUT WHEN I LIKE SOMETHING, I WANT TO SHOW MY SUPPORT FOR THE CREATOR BY BUYING A COPY-
WHAT'S THE POINT IN TAKING THE MONEY FROM YOUR MARUKAWA PAYCHECK TO BUY SOMETHING THAT'LL SEND THE MONEY RIGHT BACK TO MARU-KAWA?

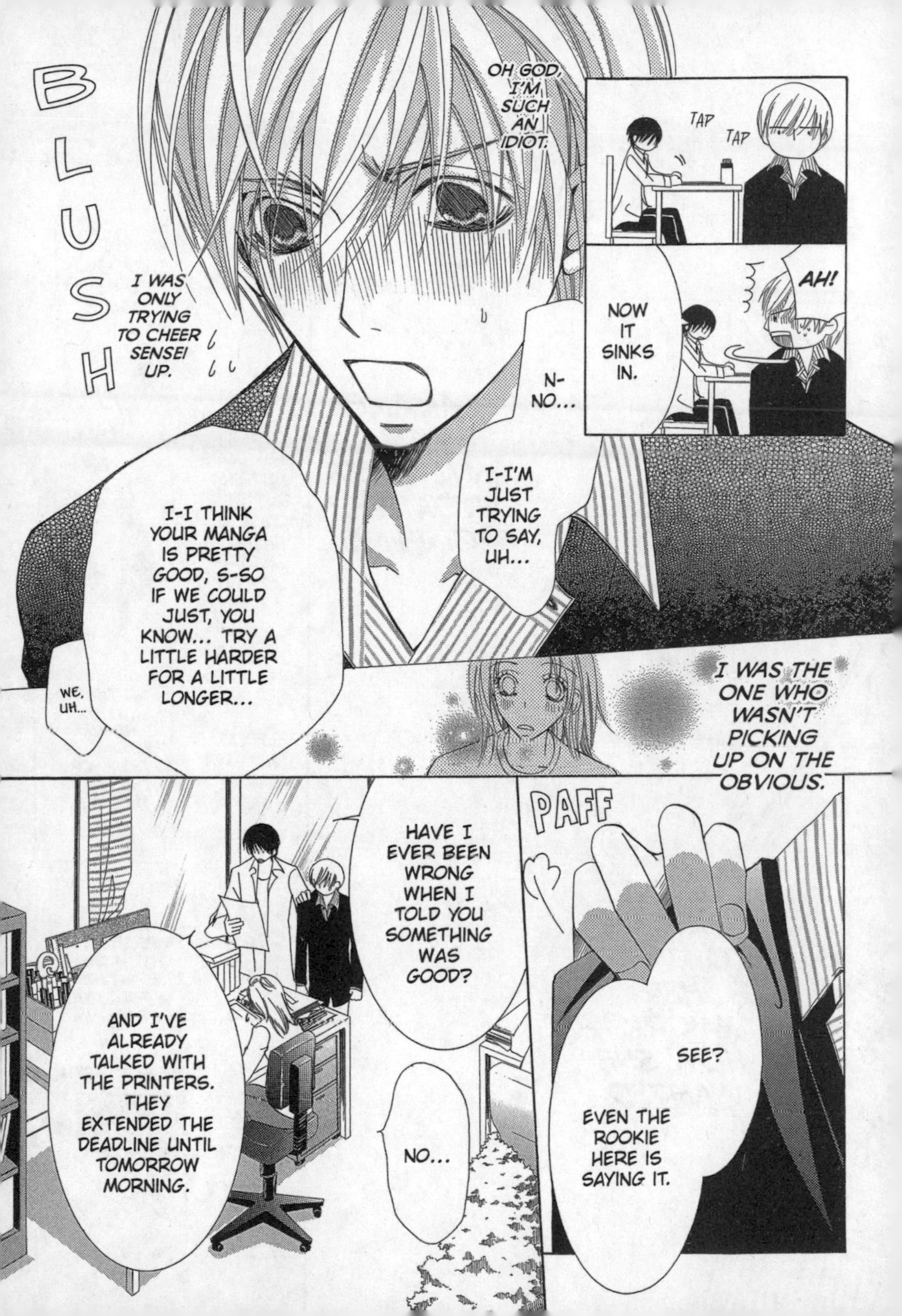
TAP
TAP
AH!
NOW IT SINKS IN.
OH GOD, I'M SUCH AN IDIOT.
BLUSH
N-NO...
I WAS ONLY TRYING TO CHEER SENSEI UP.
I-I'M JUST TRYING TO SAY, UH...
I-I THINK YOUR MANGA IS PRETTY GOOD, S-SO IF WE COULD JUST, YOU KNOW... TRY A LITTLE HARDER FOR A LITTLE LONGER...
WE, UH...
I WAS THE ONE WHO WASN'T PICKING UP ON THE OBVIOUS.
PAFF
SEE?
EVEN THE ROOKIE HERE IS SAYING IT.
HAVE I EVER BEEN WRONG WHEN I TOLD YOU SOMETHING WAS GOOD?
NO...
AND I'VE ALREADY TALKED WITH THE PRINTERS. THEY EXTENDED THE DEADLINE UNTIL TOMORROW MORNING.

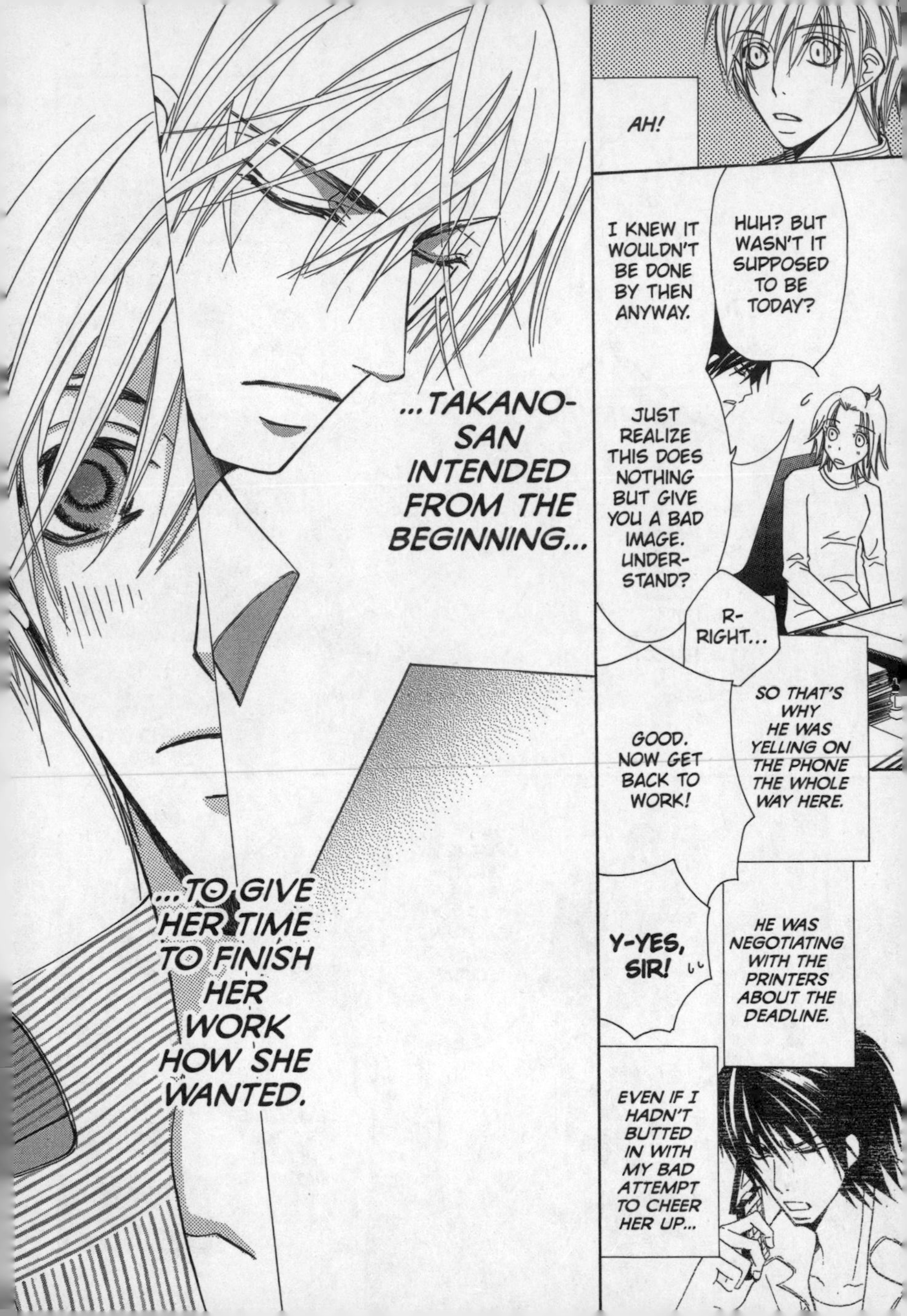
AH!
HUH? BUT WASN'T IT SUPPOSED TO BE TODAY?
I KNEW IT WOULDN'T BE DONE BY THEN ANYWAY.
JUST REALIZE THIS DOES NOTHING BUT GIVE YOU A BAD IMAGE. UNDER-STAND?
R-RIGHT...
SO THAT'S WHY HE WAS YELLING ON THE PHONE THE WHOLE WAY HERE.
GOOD. NOW GET BACK TO WORK!
HE WAS NEGOTIATING WITH THE PRINTERS ABOUT THE DEADLINE.
Y-YES, SIR!
EVEN IF I HADN'T BUTTED IN WITH MY BAD ATTEMPT TO CHEER HER UP...
...TAKANO-SAN INTENDED FROM THE BEGINNING...
...TO GIVE HER TIME TO FINISH HER WORK HOW SHE WANTED.

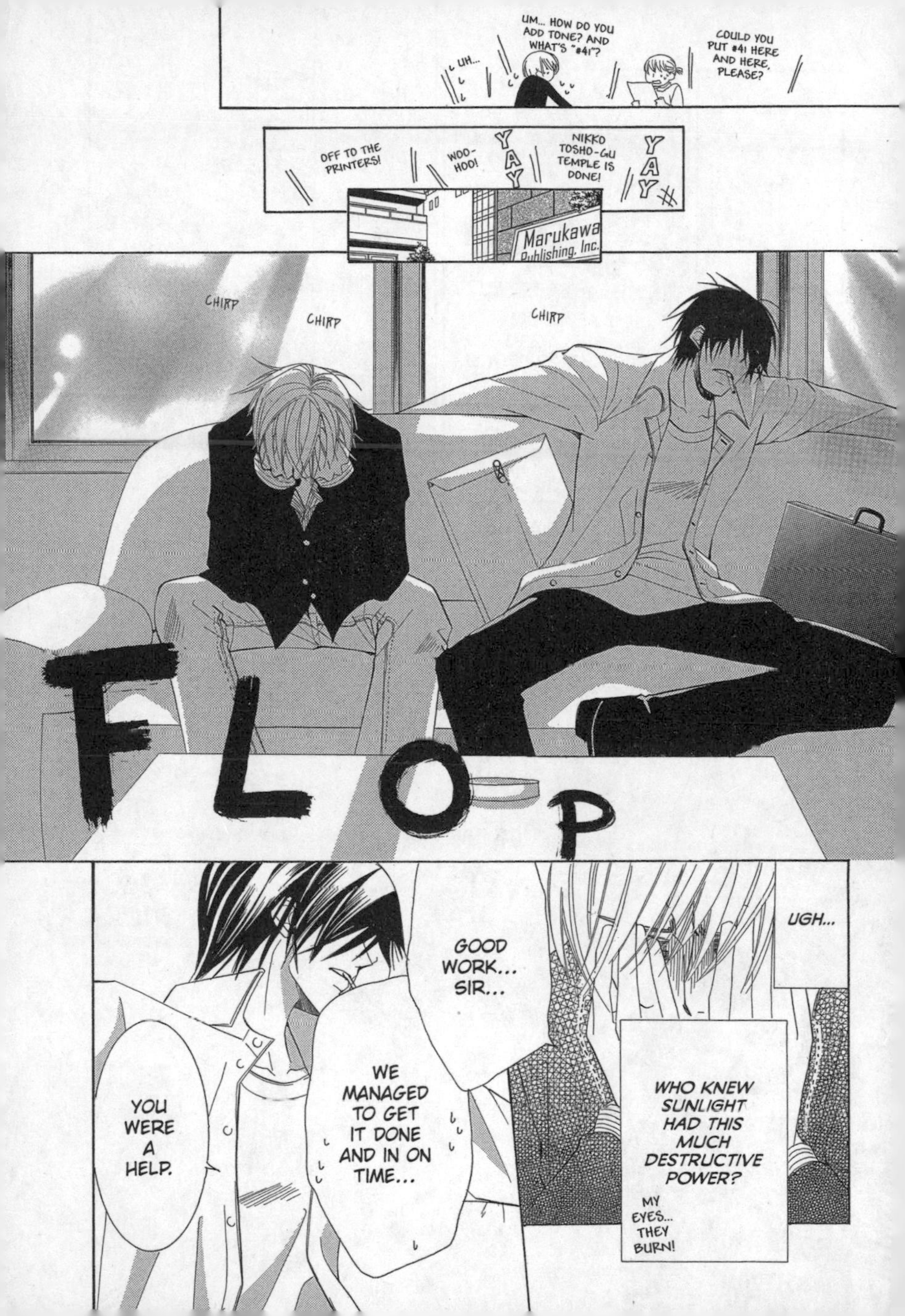
COULD YOU PUT #41 HERE AND HERE, PLEASE?
UM... HOW DO YOU ADD TONE? AND WHAT'S "#41"?
UH...
YAY
NIKKO TOSHO-GU TEMPLE IS DONE!
YAY
WOO-HOO!
OFF TO THE PRINTERS!
Marukawa Publishing, Inc.
CHIRP
CHIRP
CHIRP
FLOP
UGH...
WHO KNEW SUNLIGHT HAD THIS MUCH DESTRUCTIVE POWER?
MY EYES... THEY BURN!
GOOD WORK... SIR...
WE MANAGED TO GET IT DONE AND IN ON TIME...
YOU WERE A HELP.

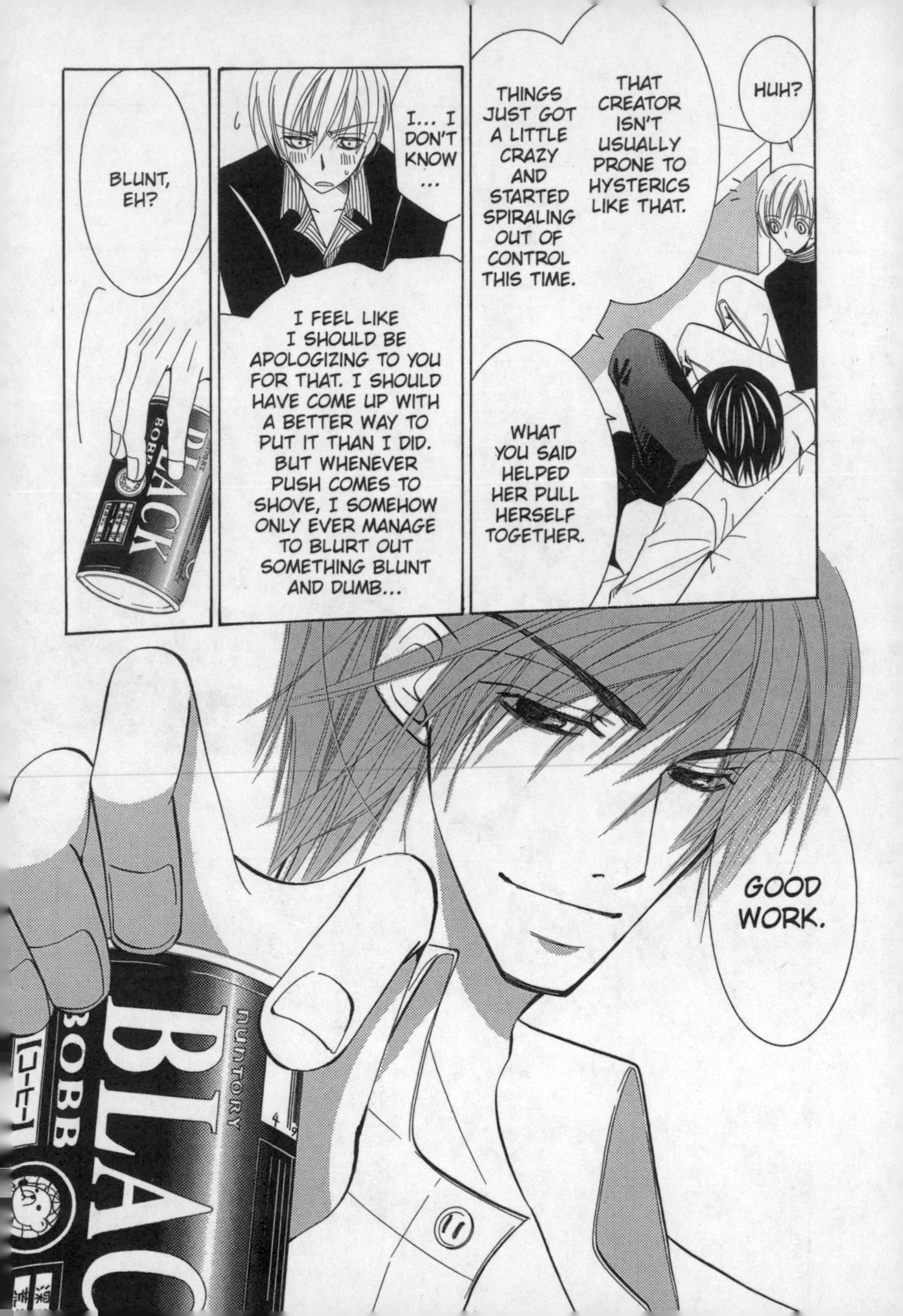
HUH?
THAT CREATOR ISN'T USUALLY PRONE TO HYSTERICS LIKE THAT.
THINGS JUST GOT A LITTLE CRAZY AND STARTED SPIRALING OUT OF CONTROL THIS TIME.
WHAT YOU SAID HELPED HER PULL HERSELF TOGETHER.
I... I DON'T KNOW ...
I FEEL LIKE I SHOULD BE APOLOGIZING TO YOU FOR THAT. I SHOULD HAVE COME UP WITH A BETTER WAY TO PUT IT THAN I DID. BUT WHENEVER PUSH COMES TO SHOVE, I SOMEHOW ONLY EVER MANAGE TO BLURT OUT SOMETHING BLUNT AND DUMB...
BLUNT, EH?
GOOD WORK.

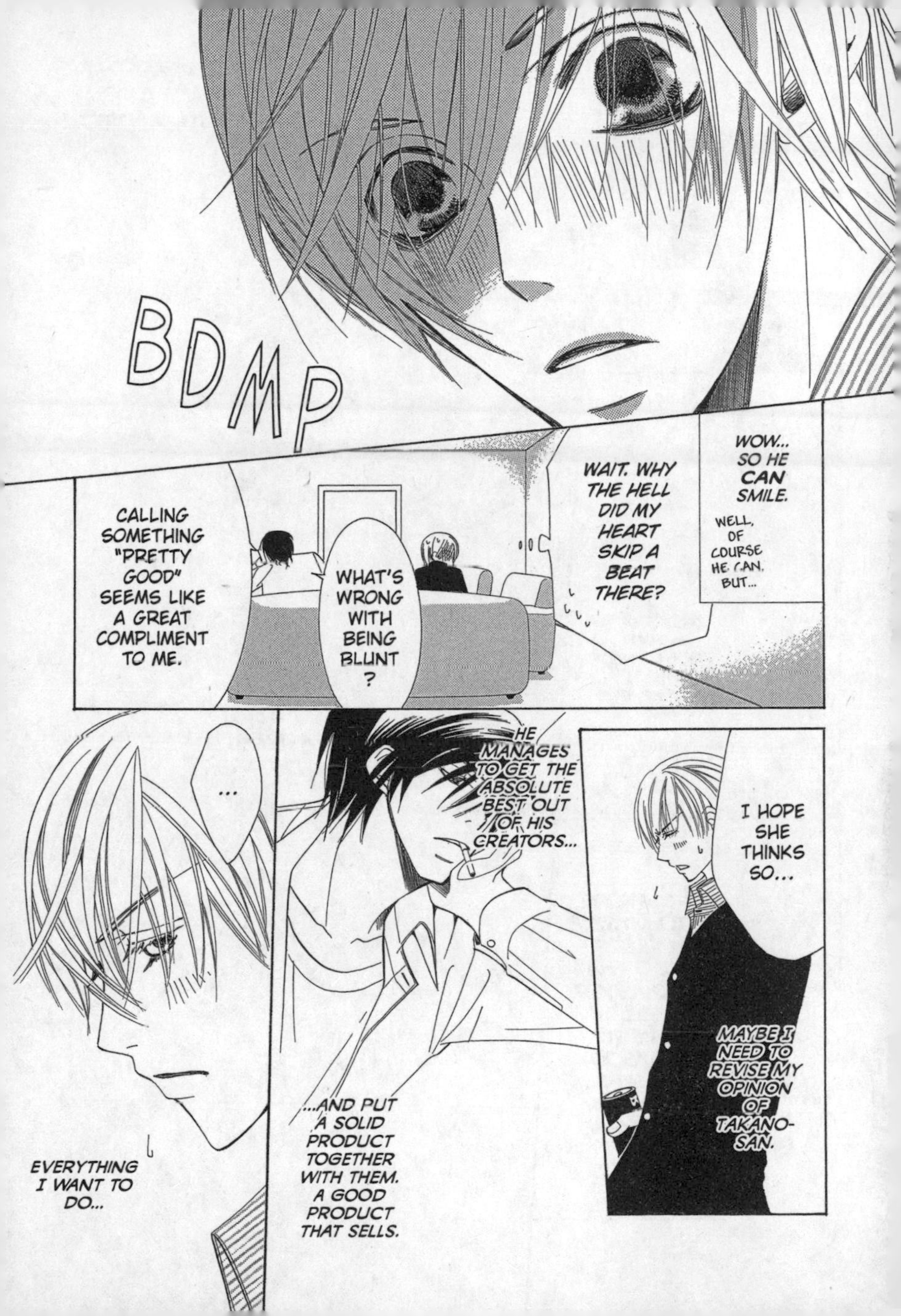
BDMP
WOW... SO HE CAN SMILE.
WELL, OF COURSE HE CAN, BUT...
WAIT. WHY THE HELL DID MY HEART SKIP A BEAT THERE?
WHAT'S WRONG WITH BEING BLUNT ?
CALLING SOMETHING "PRETTY GOOD" SEEMS LIKE A GREAT COMPLIMENT TO ME.
I HOPE SHE THINKS SO...
MAYBE I NEED TO REVISE MY OPINION OF TAKANO-SAN.
HE MANAGES TO GET THE ABSOLUTE BEST OUT OF HIS CREATORS...
...AND PUT A SOLID PRODUCT TOGETHER WITH THEM. A GOOD PRODUCT THAT SELLS.
...
EVERYTHING I WANT TO DO...

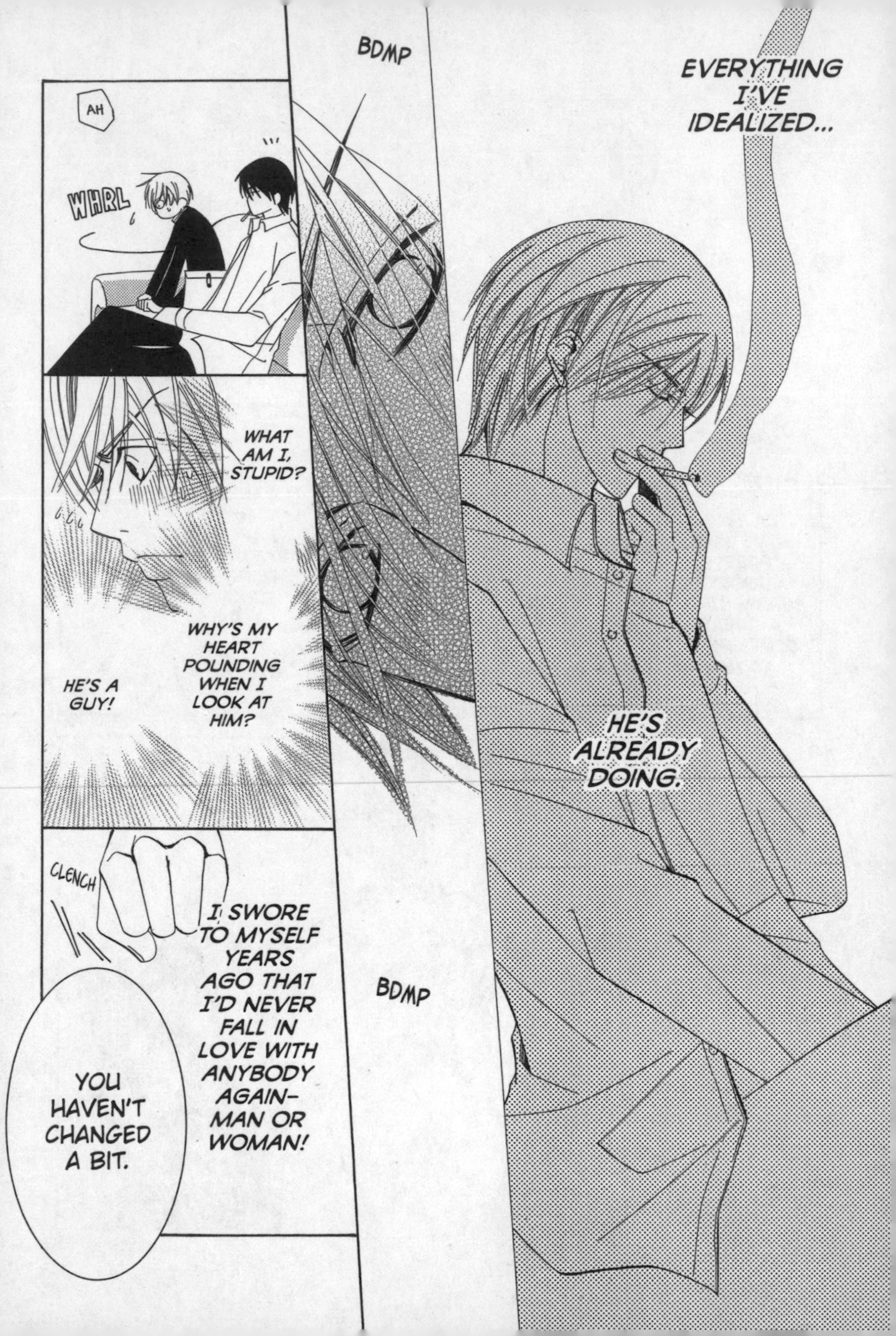
EVERYTHING I'VE IDEALIZED...
HE'S ALREADY DOING.
BDMP
BDMP
AH
WHRL
WHAT AM I, STUPID?
WHY'S MY HEART POUNDING WHEN I LOOK AT HIM?
HE'S A GUY!
CLENCH
I SWORE TO MYSELF YEARS AGO THAT I'D NEVER FALL IN LOVE WITH ANYBODY AGAIN—MAN OR WOMAN!
YOU HAVEN'T CHANGED A BIT.

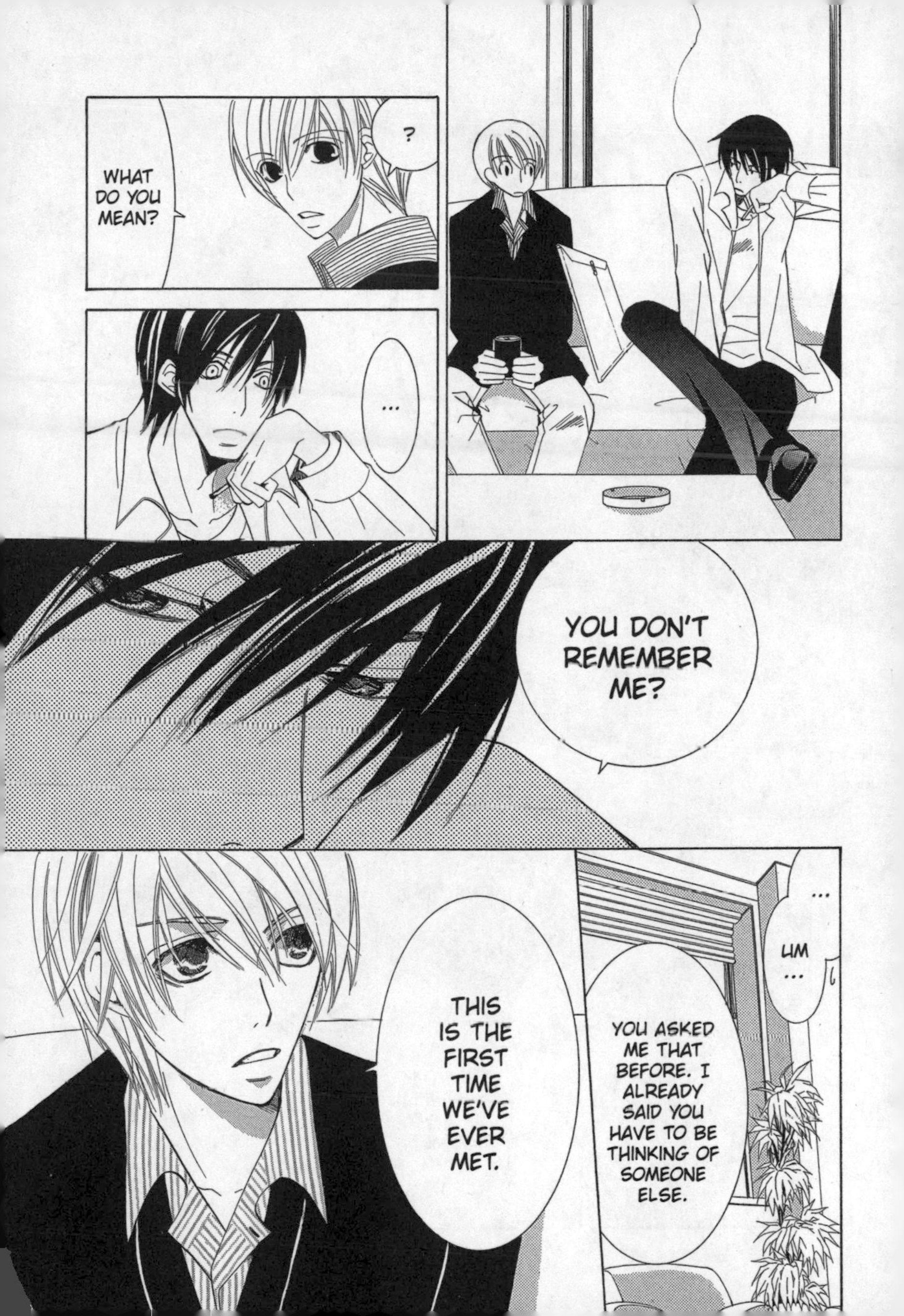
?
WHAT DO YOU MEAN?
...
YOU DON'T REMEMBER ME?
... UM ...
YOU ASKED ME THAT BEFORE. I ALREADY SAID YOU HAVE TO BE THINKING OF SOMEONE ELSE.
THIS IS THE FIRST TIME WE'VE EVER MET.

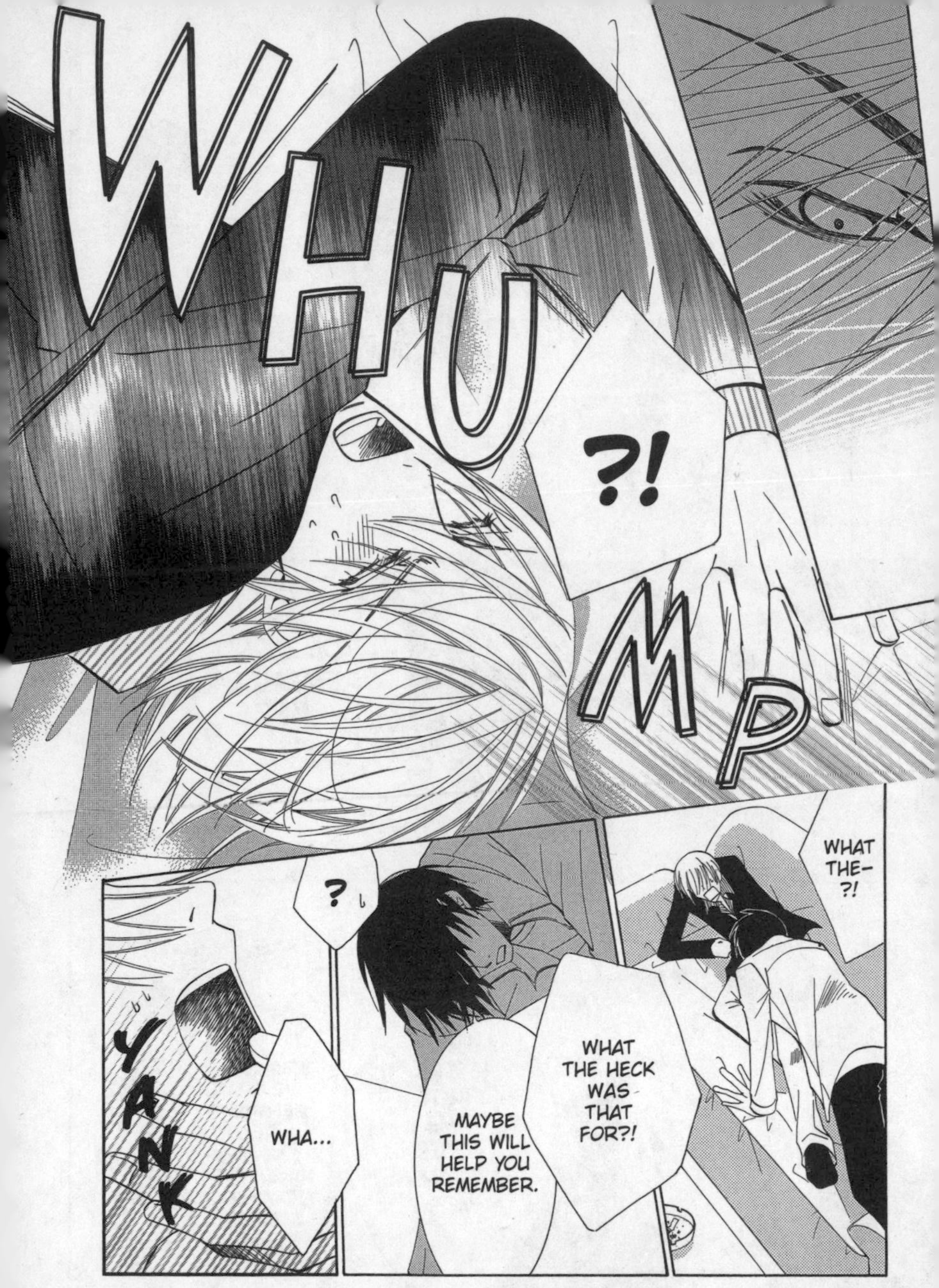
WHUMP
?!
WHAT THE-?!
WHAT THE HECK WAS THAT FOR?!
?
MAYBE THIS WILL HELP YOU REMEMBER.
WHA...
YANK

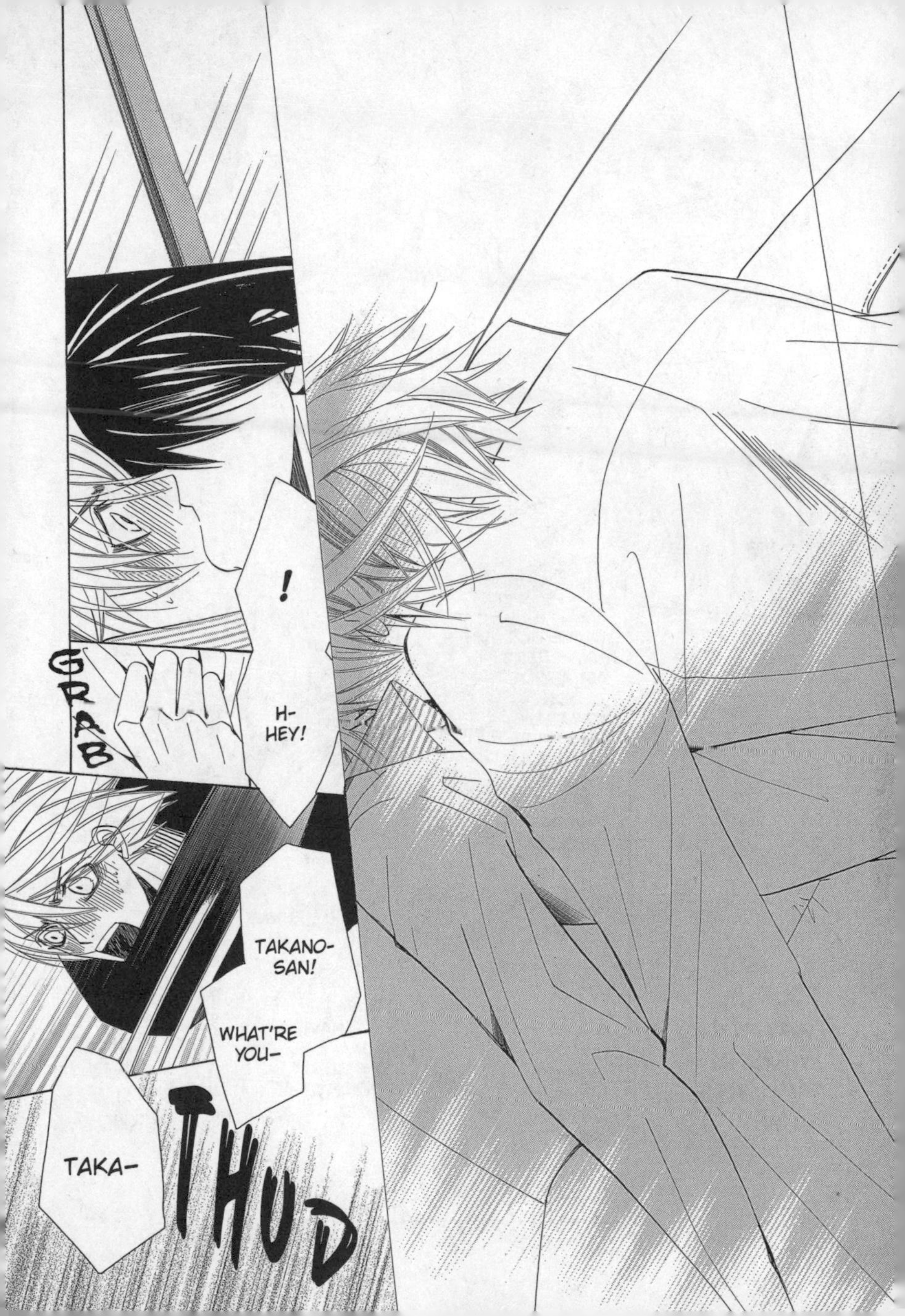
!
GRAB
H-
HEY!
TAKANO-
SAN!
WHAT'RE
YOU-
TAKA-
THUD

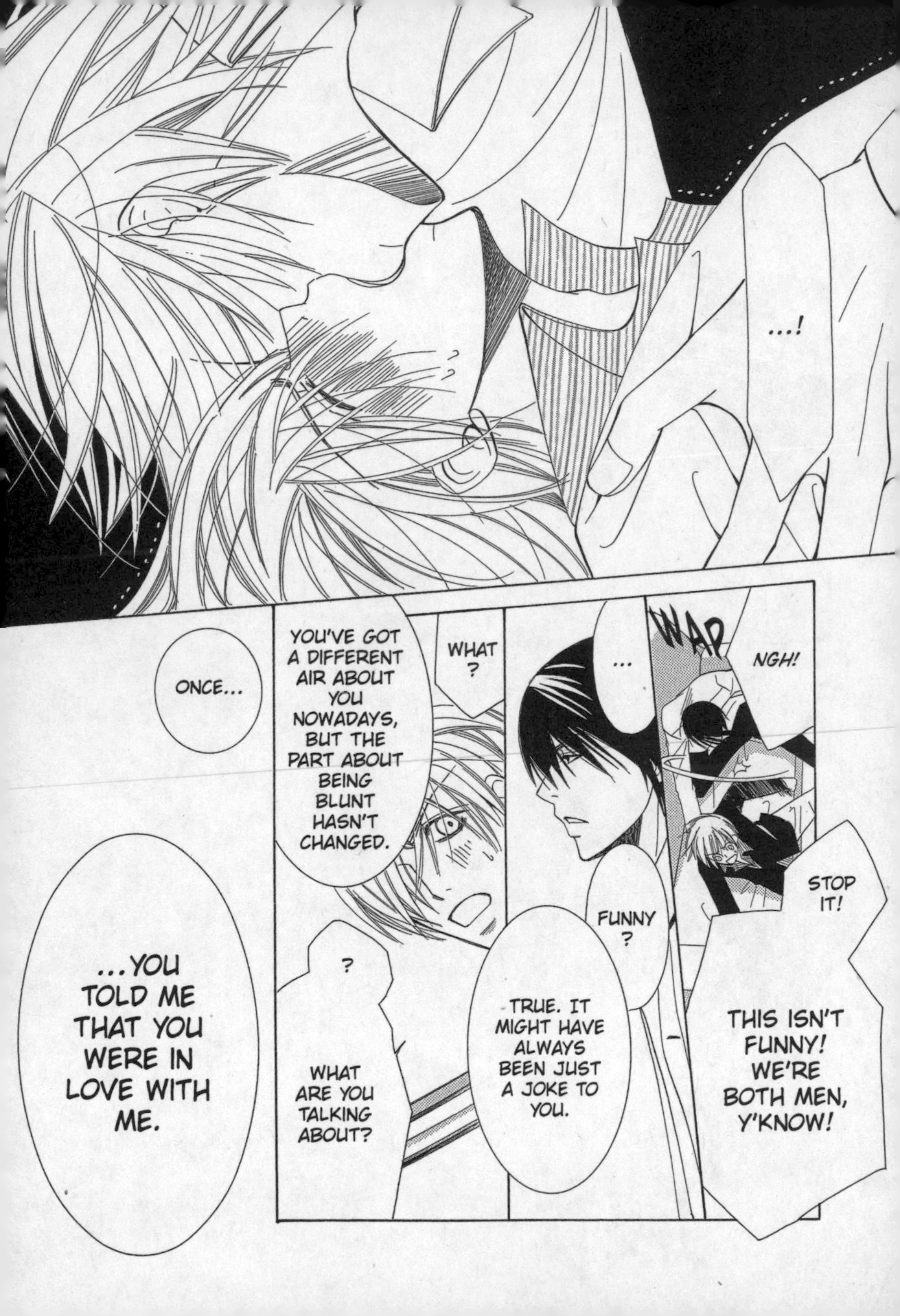
...!
WAP
NGH!
STOP IT!
THIS ISN'T FUNNY! WE'RE BOTH MEN, Y'KNOW!
...
FUNNY?
TRUE. IT MIGHT HAVE ALWAYS BEEN JUST A JOKE TO YOU.
WHAT?
YOU'VE GOT A DIFFERENT AIR ABOUT YOU NOWADAYS, BUT THE PART ABOUT BEING BLUNT HASN'T CHANGED.
?
WHAT ARE YOU TALKING ABOUT?
ONCE...
...YOU TOLD ME THAT YOU WERE IN LOVE WITH ME.

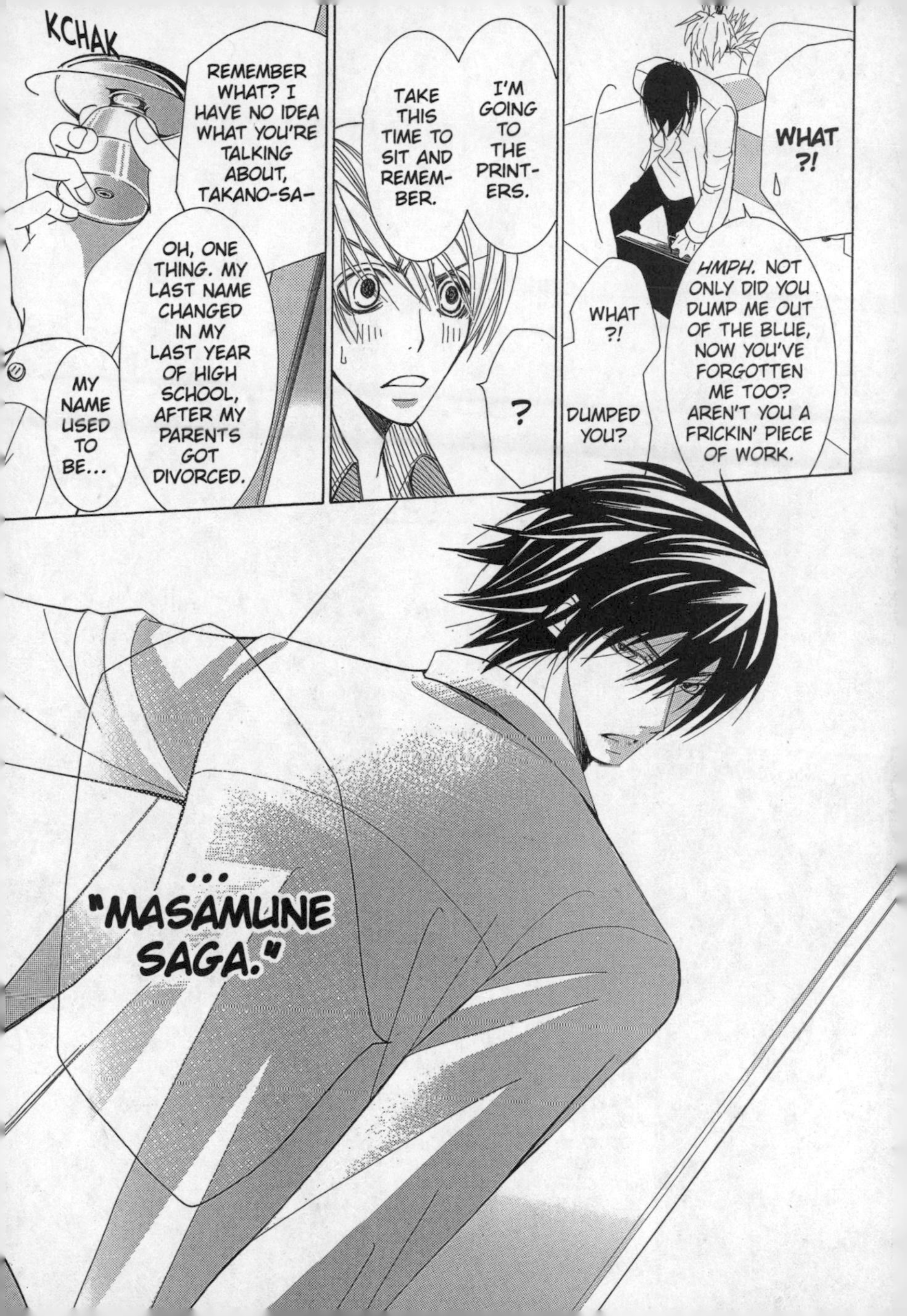
WHAT ?!
HMPH. NOT ONLY DID YOU DUMP ME OUT OF THE BLUE, NOW YOU'VE FORGOTTEN ME TOO? AREN'T YOU A FRICKIN' PIECE OF WORK.
WHAT ?!
DUMPED YOU?
I'M GOING TO THE PRINTERS.
TAKE THIS TIME TO SIT AND REMEMBER.
?
REMEMBER WHAT? I HAVE NO IDEA WHAT YOU'RE TALKING ABOUT, TAKANO-SA–
KCHAK
OH, ONE THING. MY LAST NAME CHANGED IN MY LAST YEAR OF HIGH SCHOOL, AFTER MY PARENTS GOT DIVORCED.
MY NAME USED TO BE...
... "MASAMUNE SAGA."

"*SAGA SENPAI...*"

MASA-
MUNE
SAGA.

SAGA
...

SENPAI
...

SAGA!

WE'RE
DATING
NOW,
RIGHT?
DOES THIS
MAKE
US, UM...
LOVERS?

I MEAN,
YOU'VE
NEVER
REALLY
SAID ANY-
THING
OUT LOUD,
SENPAI.

HM?

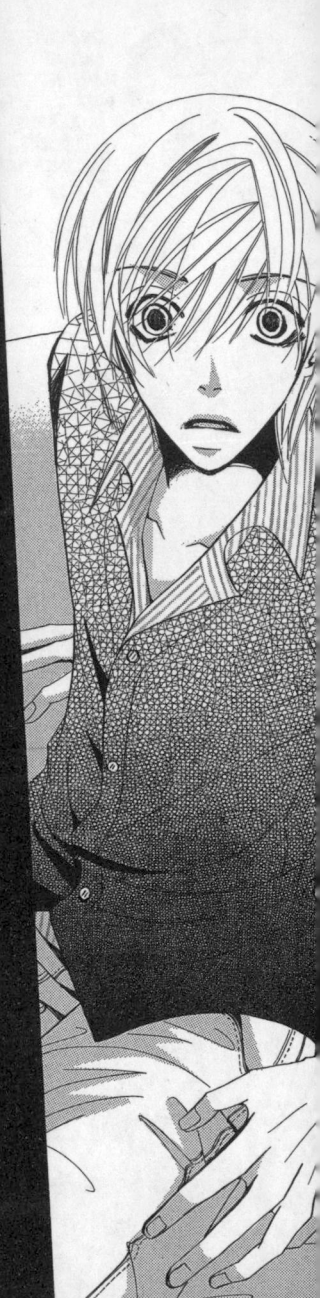

MASAMUNE... SAGA?

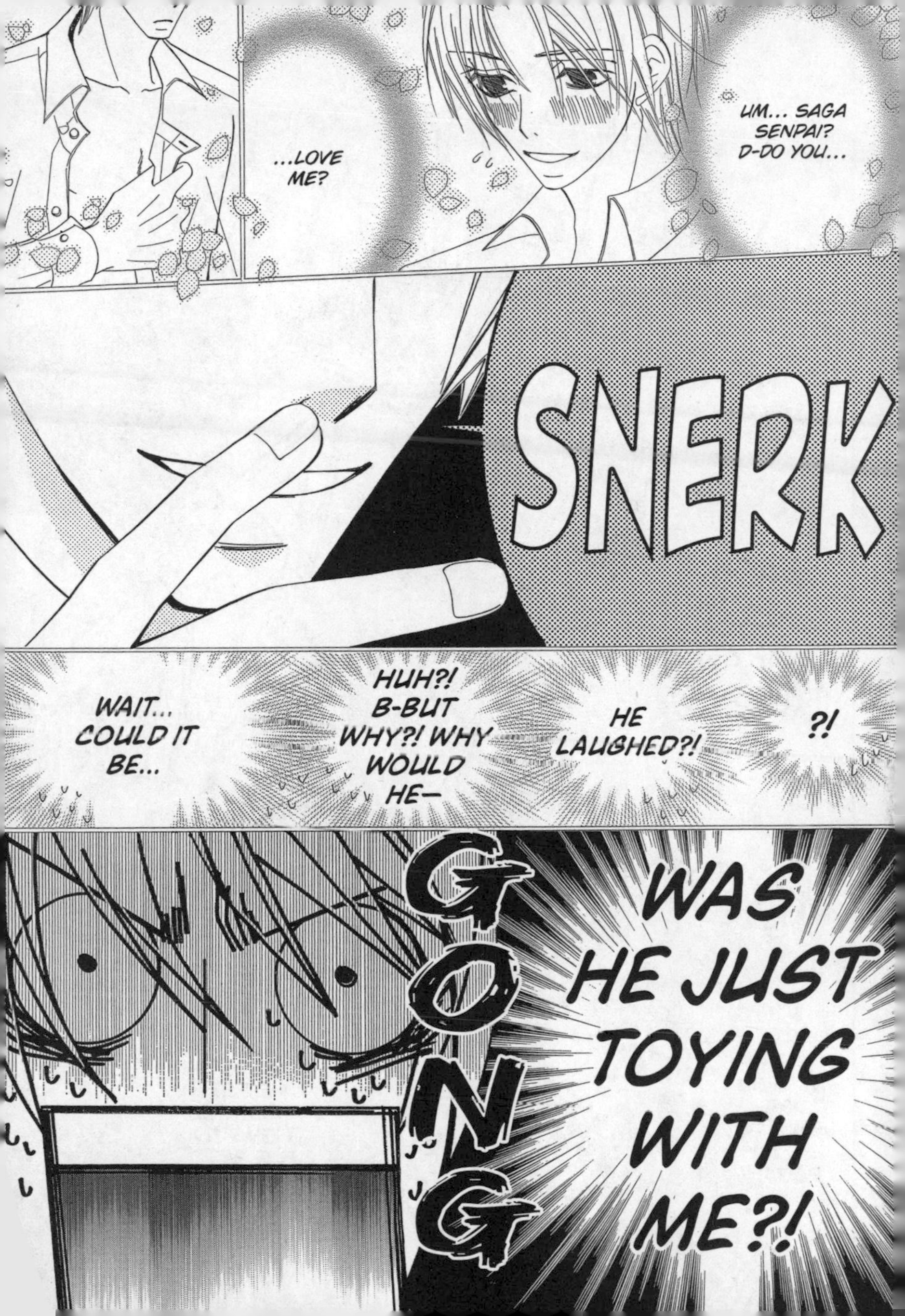
UM... SAGA SENPAI? D-DO YOU...
...LOVE ME?
SNERK
?!
HE LAUGHED?!
HUH?! B-BUT WHY?! WHY WOULD HE—
WAIT... COULD IT BE...
WAS HE JUST TOYING WITH ME?!
GONG

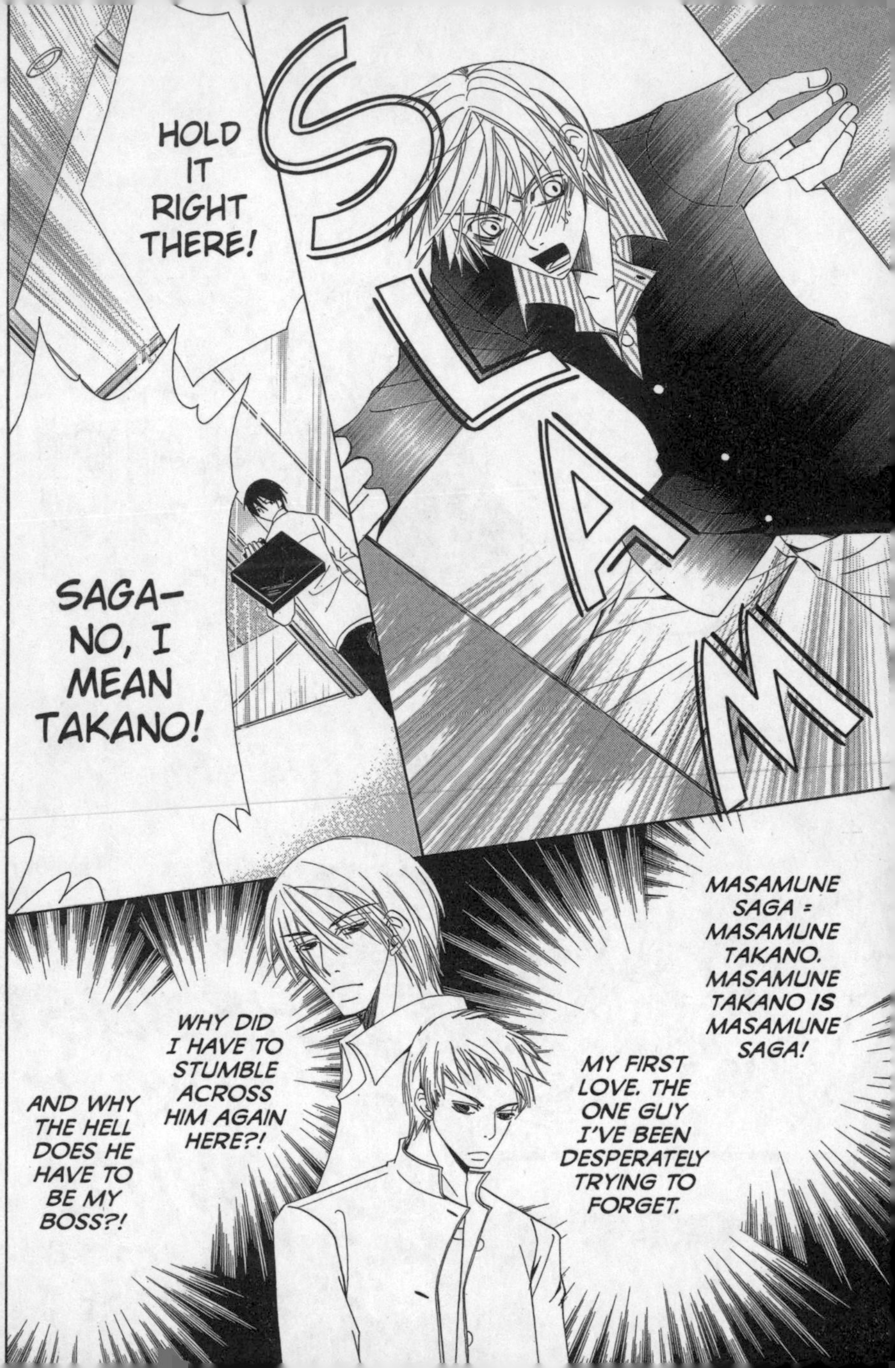
SLAM
HOLD IT RIGHT THERE!
SAGA- NO, I MEAN TAKANO!
MASAMUNE SAGA = MASAMUNE TAKANO. MASAMUNE TAKANO IS MASAMUNE SAGA!
MY FIRST LOVE. THE ONE GUY I'VE BEEN DESPERATELY TRYING TO FORGET.
WHY DID I HAVE TO STUMBLE ACROSS HIM AGAIN HERE?!
AND WHY THE HELL DOES HE HAVE TO BE MY BOSS?!

I'M SURPRISED YOU EVEN DARED TO TELL ME WHO YOU WERE, LIKE IT WAS NOTHING!

COME BACK HERE!

DON'T JUST SAY WHATEVER YOU WANT AND THEN RUN AWAY!

HOW ABOUT AN APOLOGY OR TWO?! I DESERVE ONE, AFTER THE HORRIBLE, TRAUMATIC THINGS YOU DID TO ME!

HUH?

YOU WERE THE ONE WHO DID HORRIBLE THINGS TO ME.

WHO ELSE?! THANKS TO WHAT YOU DID, I'VE—

THAT I DID TO YOU?

"HORRIBLE THINGS"?

YEAH!

TELL ME AGAIN JUST WHO IT WAS THAT ROUNDHOUSE KICKED ME OUT OF NOWHERE AND THEN VANISHED OFF THE FACE OF THE EARTH?!

HUH?

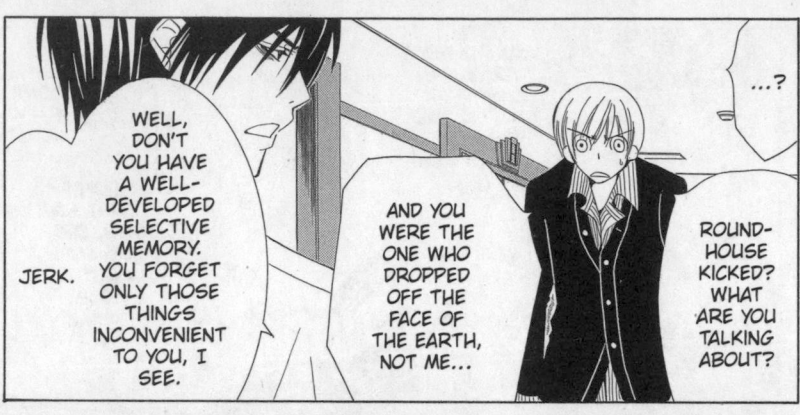

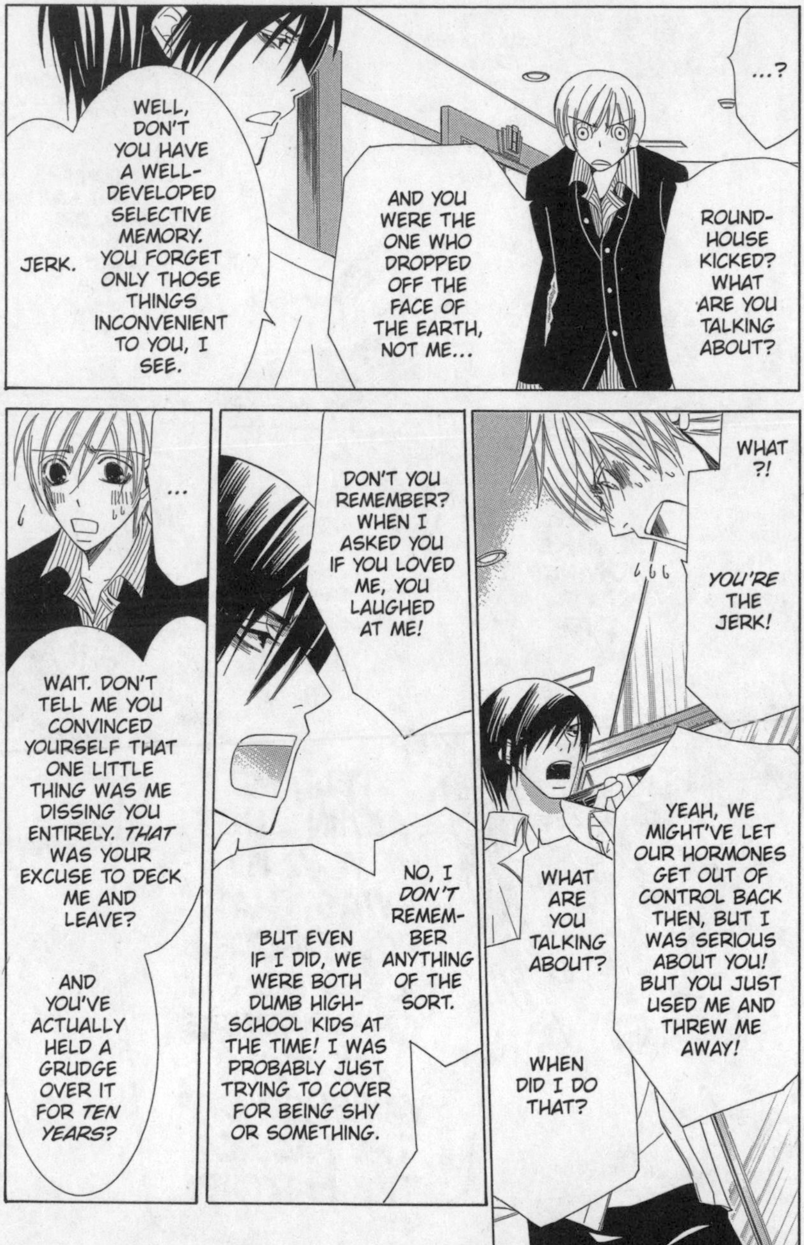
...?
ROUND-HOUSE KICKED? WHAT ARE YOU TALKING ABOUT?
AND YOU WERE THE ONE WHO DROPPED OFF THE FACE OF THE EARTH, NOT ME...
WELL, DON'T YOU HAVE A WELL-DEVELOPED SELECTIVE MEMORY. YOU FORGET ONLY THOSE THINGS INCONVENIENT TO YOU, I SEE.
JERK.
WHAT ?!
YOU'RE THE JERK!
YEAH, WE MIGHT'VE LET OUR HORMONES GET OUT OF CONTROL BACK THEN, BUT I WAS SERIOUS ABOUT YOU! BUT YOU JUST USED ME AND THREW ME AWAY!
WHAT ARE YOU TALKING ABOUT?
WHEN DID I DO THAT?
DON'T YOU REMEMBER? WHEN I ASKED YOU IF YOU LOVED ME, YOU LAUGHED AT ME!
NO, I *DON'T* REMEMBER ANYTHING OF THE SORT.
BUT EVEN IF I DID, WE WERE BOTH DUMB HIGH-SCHOOL KIDS AT THE TIME! I WAS PROBABLY JUST TRYING TO COVER FOR BEING SHY OR SOMETHING.
...
WAIT. DON'T TELL ME YOU CONVINCED YOURSELF THAT ONE LITTLE THING WAS ME DISSING YOU ENTIRELY. *THAT* WAS YOUR EXCUSE TO DECK ME AND LEAVE?
AND YOU'VE ACTUALLY HELD A GRUDGE OVER IT FOR *TEN YEARS?*

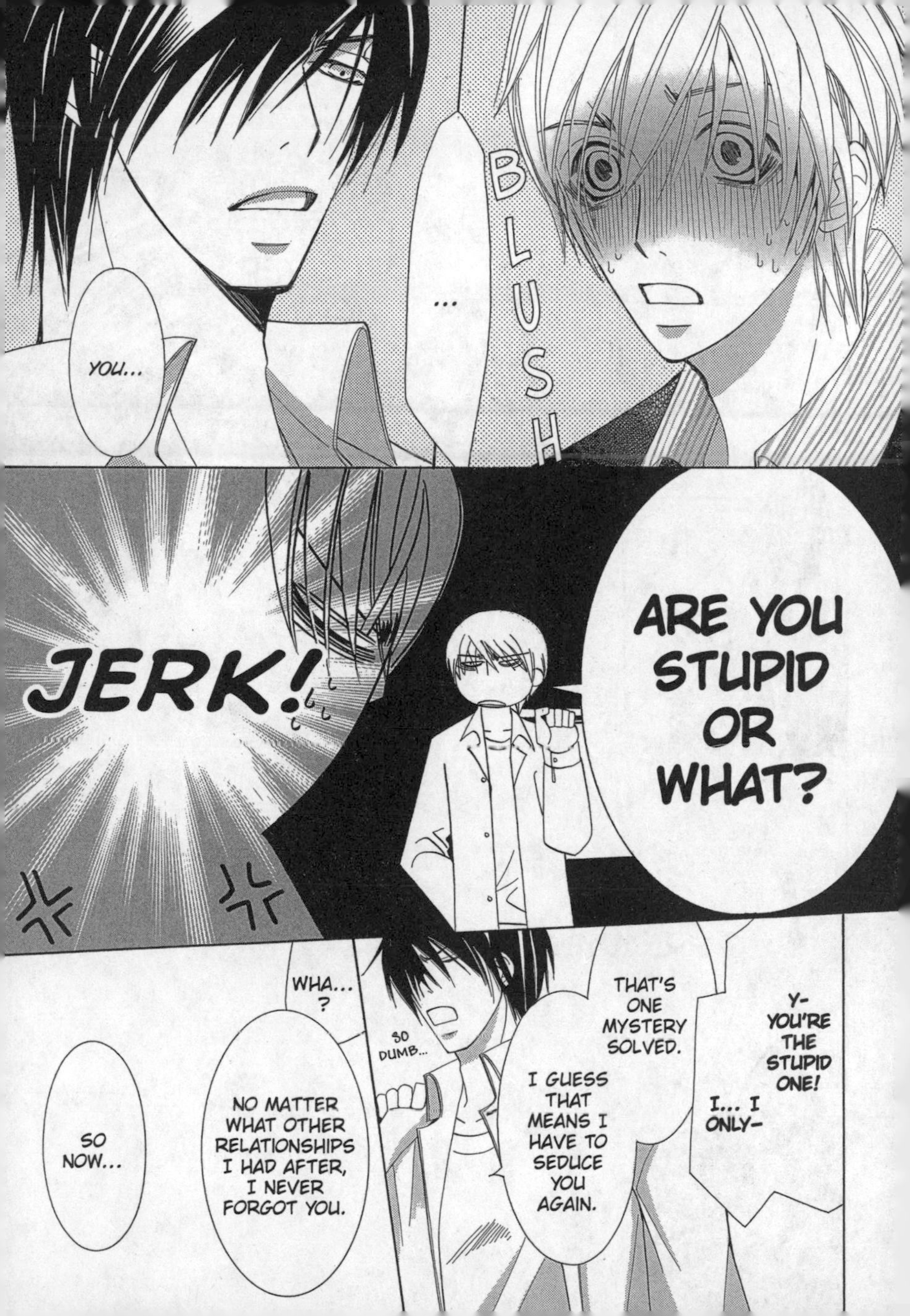
BLUSH
...
YOU...
ARE YOU STUPID OR WHAT?
JERK!
Y- YOU'RE THE STUPID ONE!
I... I ONLY-
THAT'S ONE MYSTERY SOLVED.
I GUESS THAT MEANS I HAVE TO SEDUCE YOU AGAIN.
WHA... ?
SO DUMB...
NO MATTER WHAT OTHER RELATIONSHIPS I HAD AFTER, I NEVER FORGOT YOU.
SO NOW...

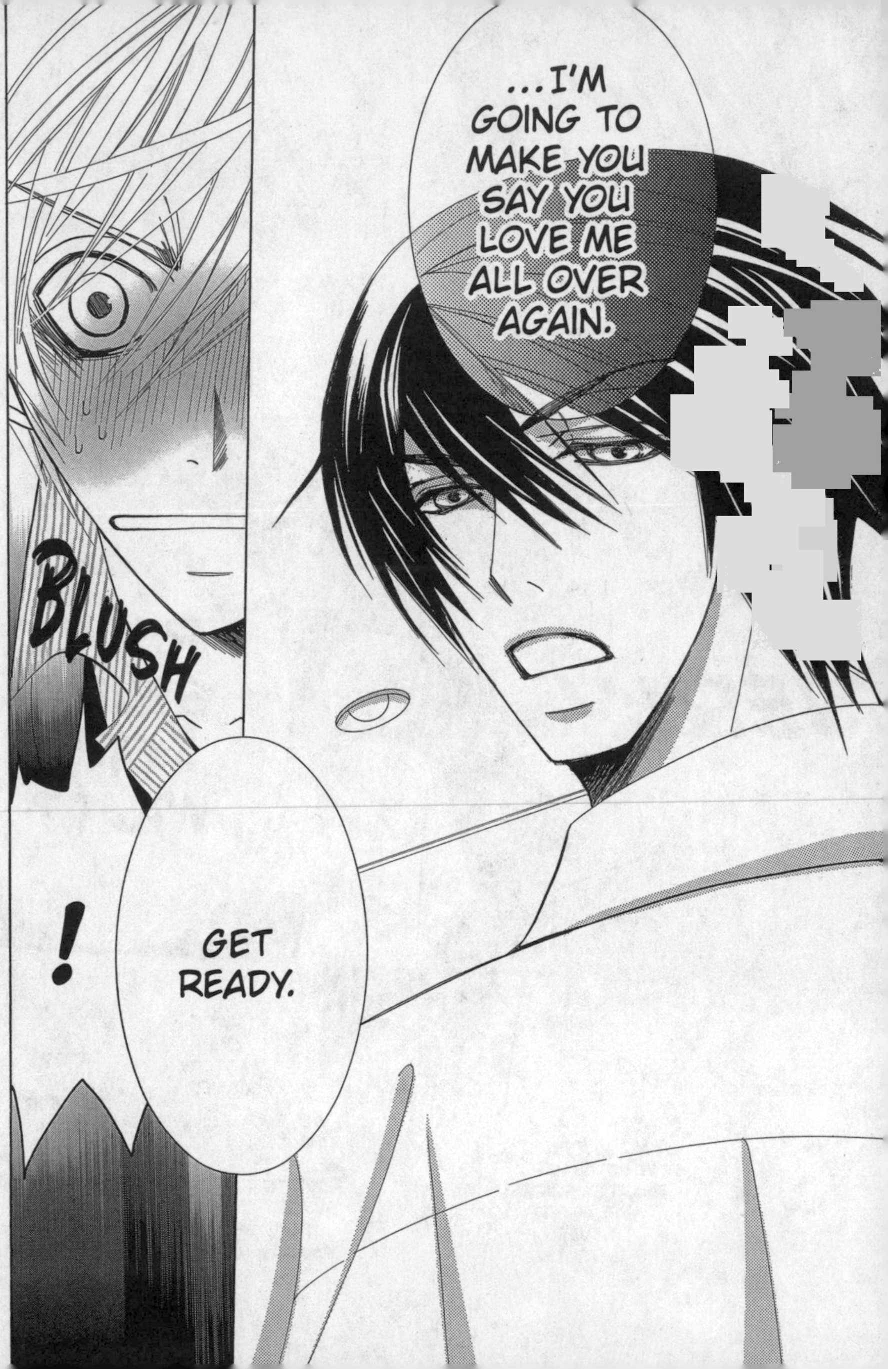
...I'M GOING TO MAKE YOU SAY YOU LOVE ME ALL OVER AGAIN.
BLUSH
GET READY.
!

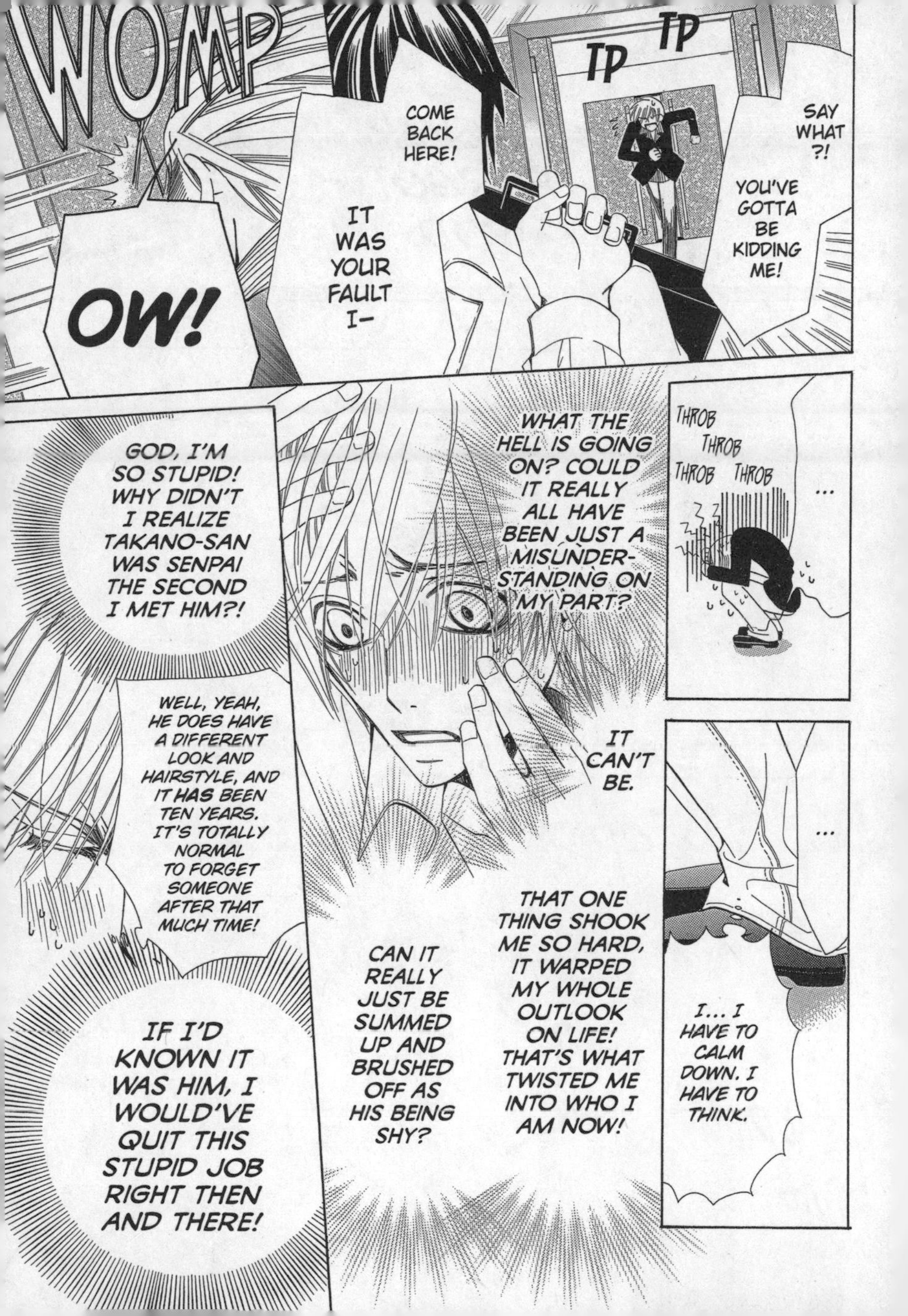
SAY WHAT?!
YOU'VE GOTTA BE KIDDING ME!
TP TP
COME BACK HERE!
IT WAS YOUR FAULT I—
WOMP
OW!
THROB THROB THROB THROB
...
...
I... I HAVE TO CALM DOWN. I HAVE TO THINK.
WHAT THE HELL IS GOING ON? COULD IT REALLY ALL HAVE BEEN JUST A MISUNDER-STANDING ON MY PART?
GOD, I'M SO STUPID! WHY DIDN'T I REALIZE TAKANO-SAN WAS SENPAI THE SECOND I MET HIM?!
IT CAN'T BE.
WELL, YEAH, HE DOES HAVE A DIFFERENT LOOK AND HAIRSTYLE, AND IT HAS BEEN TEN YEARS. IT'S TOTALLY NORMAL TO FORGET SOMEONE AFTER THAT MUCH TIME!
THAT ONE THING SHOOK ME SO HARD, IT WARPED MY WHOLE OUTLOOK ON LIFE! THAT'S WHAT TWISTED ME INTO WHO I AM NOW!
CAN IT REALLY JUST BE SUMMED UP AND BRUSHED OFF AS HIS BEING SHY?
IF I'D KNOWN IT WAS HIM, I WOULD'VE QUIT THIS STUPID JOB RIGHT THEN AND THERE!

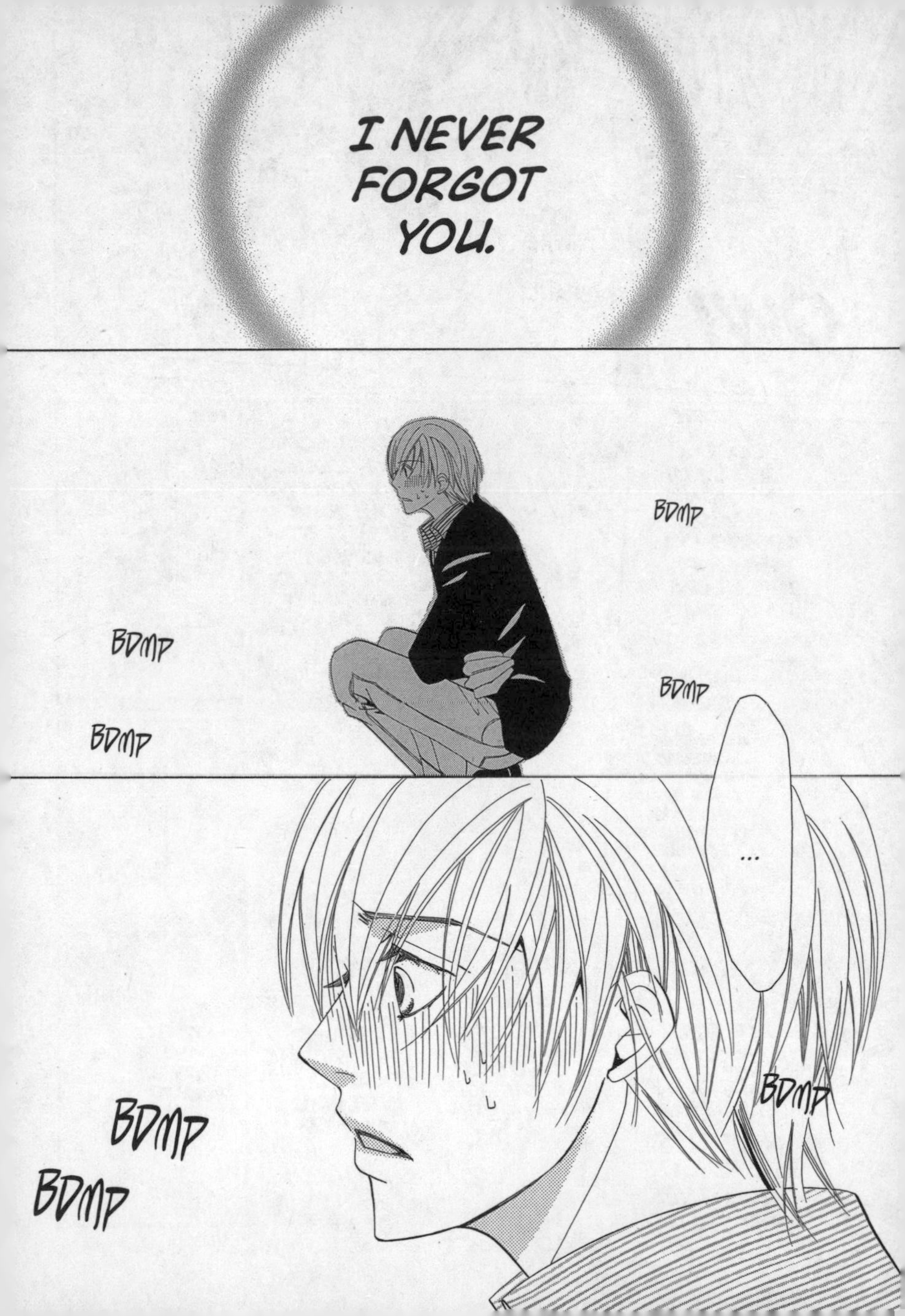
I NEVER FORGOT YOU.
BDMP
BDMP
BDMP
BDMP
...
BDMP
BDMP
BDMP

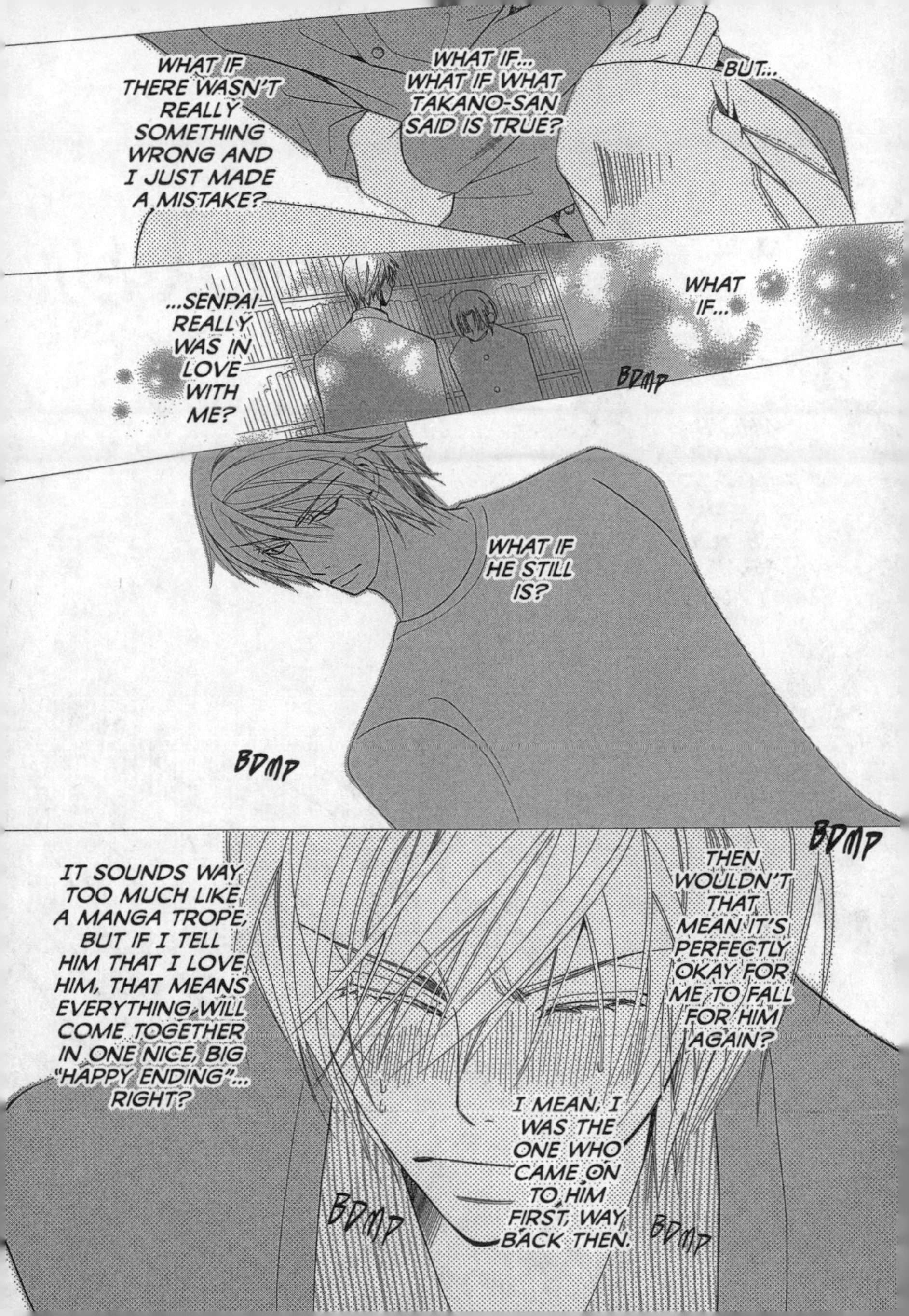
BUT...
WHAT IF... WHAT IF WHAT TAKANO-SAN SAID IS TRUE?
WHAT IF THERE WASN'T REALLY SOMETHING WRONG AND I JUST MADE A MISTAKE?
WHAT IF...
BDMP
...SENPAI REALLY WAS IN LOVE WITH ME?
WHAT IF HE STILL IS?
BDMP
BDMP
THEN WOULDN'T THAT MEAN IT'S PERFECTLY OKAY FOR ME TO FALL FOR HIM AGAIN?
IT SOUNDS WAY TOO MUCH LIKE A MANGA TROPE, BUT IF I TELL HIM THAT I LOVE HIM, THAT MEANS EVERYTHING WILL COME TOGETHER IN ONE NICE, BIG "HAPPY ENDING"... RIGHT?
BDMP
I MEAN, I WAS THE ONE WHO CAME ON TO HIM FIRST WAY BACK THEN.
BDMP

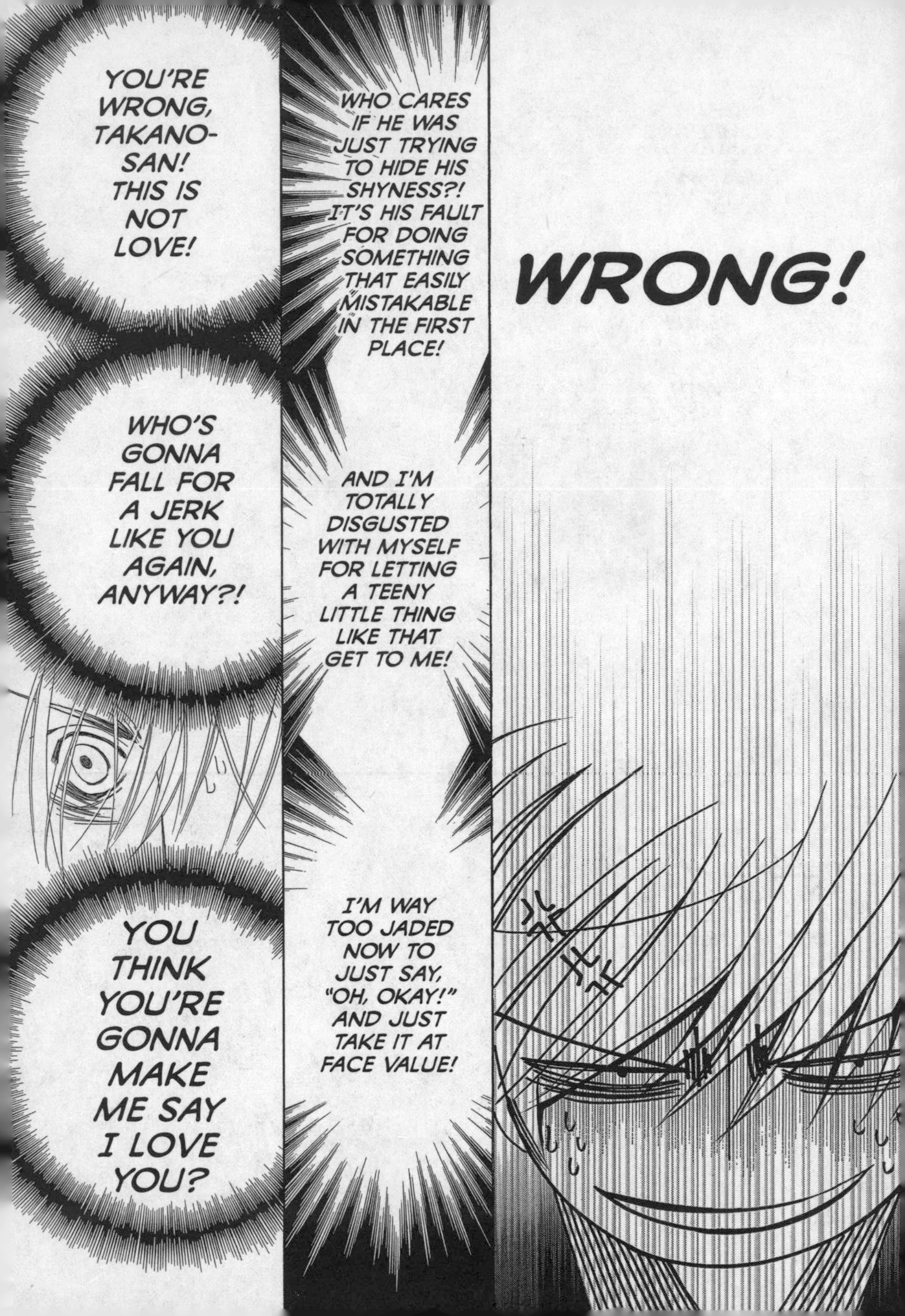
WRONG!
WHO CARES IF HE WAS JUST TRYING TO HIDE HIS SHYNESS?! IT'S HIS FAULT FOR DOING SOMETHING THAT EASILY MISTAKABLE IN THE FIRST PLACE!
AND I'M TOTALLY DISGUSTED WITH MYSELF FOR LETTING A TEENY LITTLE THING LIKE THAT GET TO ME!
I'M WAY TOO JADED NOW TO JUST SAY, "OH, OKAY!" AND JUST TAKE IT AT FACE VALUE!
YOU'RE WRONG, TAKANO-SAN! THIS IS NOT LOVE!
WHO'S GONNA FALL FOR A JERK LIKE YOU AGAIN, ANYWAY?!
YOU THINK YOU'RE GONNA MAKE ME SAY I LOVE YOU?

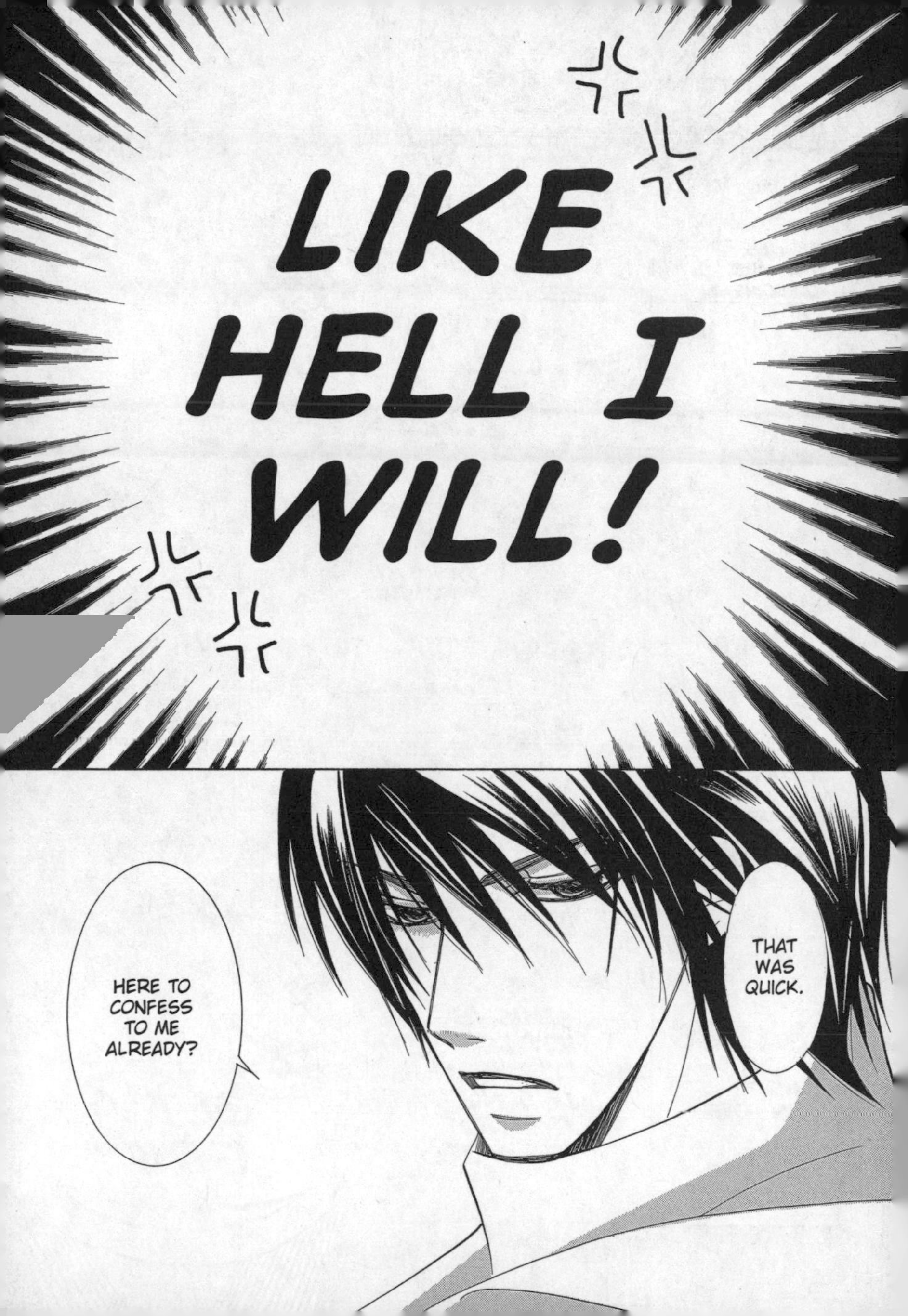
LIKE HELL I WILL!
THAT WAS QUICK.
HERE TO CONFESS TO ME ALREADY?

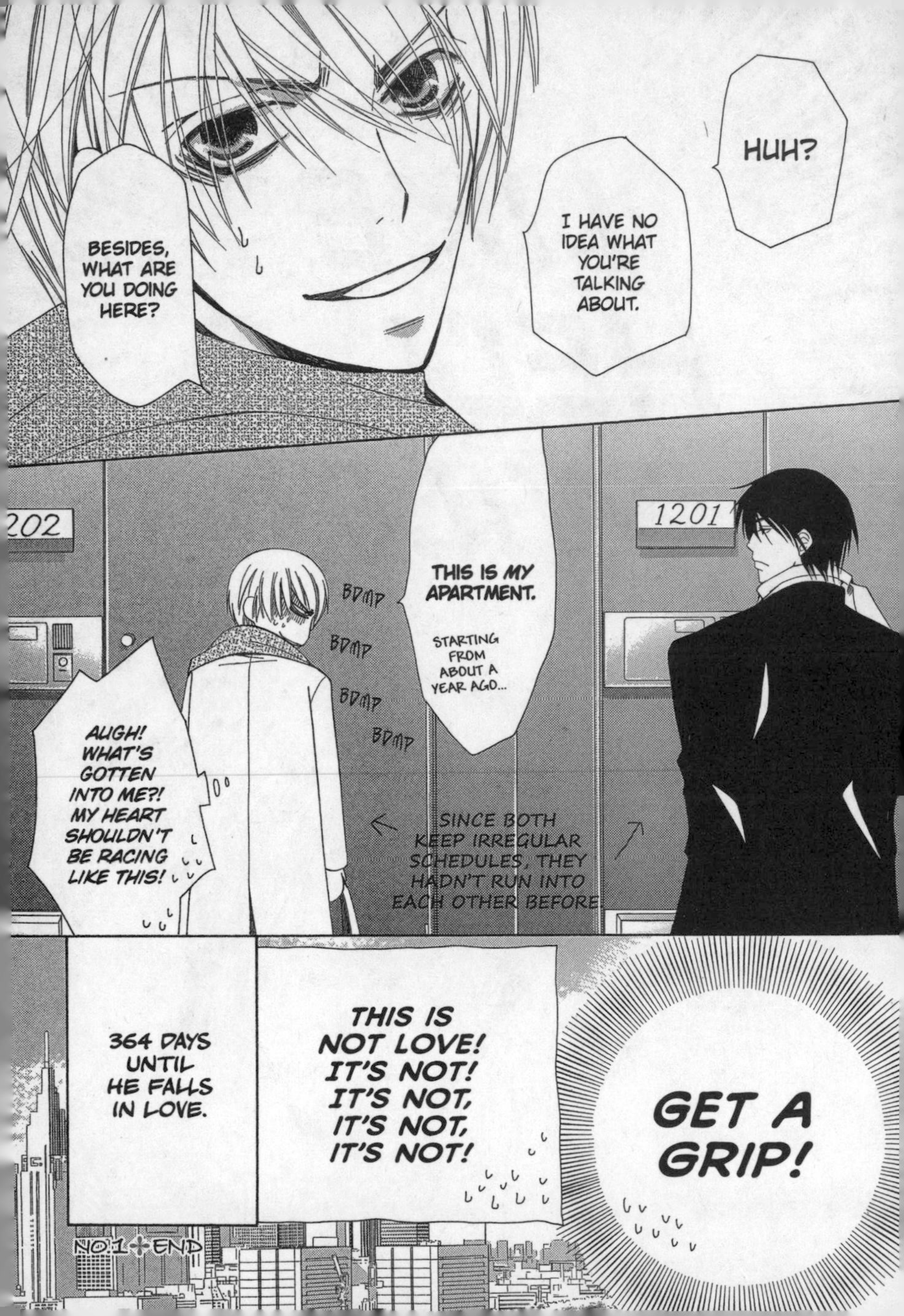
HUH?
I HAVE NO IDEA WHAT YOU'RE TALKING ABOUT.
BESIDES, WHAT ARE YOU DOING HERE?
1201
THIS IS MY APARTMENT.
STARTING FROM ABOUT A YEAR AGO...
202
BDMP
BDMP
BDMP
BDMP
SINCE BOTH KEEP IRREGULAR SCHEDULES, THEY HADN'T RUN INTO EACH OTHER BEFORE.
AUGH! WHAT'S GOTTEN INTO ME?! MY HEART SHOULDN'T BE RACING LIKE THIS!
GET A GRIP!
THIS IS NOT LOVE! IT'S NOT! IT'S NOT, IT'S NOT, IT'S NOT!
364 DAYS UNTIL HE FALLS IN LOVE.
NO.1 END

MARUKAWA PUBLISHING TERMINOLOGY & JARGON (PART 1)

*NOTE: ALL OF THE TERMINOLOGY LISTED HEREIN IS SPECIFIC TO MARUKAWA PUBLISHING AND MAY NOT BE APPLICABLE TO THE GENERAL PUBLISHING INDUSTRY.

[MARUKAWA PUBLISHING]

A PUBLISHING COMPANY THAT PRODUCES BOOKS AND MANGA. ITS CATALOGUE IS DIVERSE AND CONTAINS LITERARY NOVELS, SHOJO MANGA, SHONEN (SEINEN) MANGA, AND BOYS' LOVE. BEST-SELLING AUTHOR AKIHIKO USAMI DEBUTED WITH MARUKAWA PUBLISHING. THEY ARE ALSO FAMOUS FOR RELEASING THE WIDELY POPULAR MANGA *THE ☆ KAN* (BY HIBIKI IJUUIN) AND BEING THE HOME OF THE MUCH-TALKED-ABOUT BOYS' LOVE NOVELIST YAYOI AKIGAWA.

[*EMERALD* EDITING DEPARTMENT]

AN EDITORIAL DEPARTMENT IN MARUKAWA PUBLISHING. THEY PUBLISH THE MONTHLY SHOJO MANGA ANTHOLOGY *EMERALD*. THEY HAVE BEEN STEADILY INCREASING THEIR SALES OUTPUT ACROSS THE LAST SEVERAL YEARS. THOUGH AN EDITORIAL DEPARTMENT FOR SHOJO (GIRLS) MANGA, IT IS STAFFED ENTIRELY BY MEN. THE REST OF THE COMPANY REFERS TO IT AS THE "MAIDEN CLUB."

[BLUELINE]

BLUELINES ARE PRINTING PROOFS OF A MANUSCRIPT RUN OFF OF THE PRINTER'S MASTER FILM IN ORDER TO ALLOW FOR A FINAL EDITING PASS OF THE PRINTER'S PLATE SETTINGS. THEY GENERALLY APPEAR ENTIRELY IN SHADES OF BLUE. THIS IS THE LAST STAGE IN WHICH ANY EDITS CAN BE MADE TO A MANUSCRIPT.

The World's Greatest First Love
The Case of Ritsu Onodera

TO MOVE,
OR NOT
TO MOVE.
THAT
IS THE
QUESTION...

JUST
RENEWED
HIS LEASE.

HOUSING
INFORMATION

FOR RENT
APARTMENTS/CONDOS
HOUSING INFORMATION

HOUSES APARTMENTS

MARUKAWA PUBLISHING TERMINOLOGY & JARGON (PART 2)

*NOTE: ALL OF THE TERMINOLOGY LISTED HEREIN IS SPECIFIC TO MARUKAWA PUBLISHING AND MAY NOT BE APPLICABLE TO THE GENERAL PUBLISHING INDUSTRY.

[EDITOR IN CHIEF]

THE HEAD OF AN EDITORIAL DEPARTMENT, THE EDITOR IN CHIEF IS RESPONSIBLE FOR THE ORGANIZATION, DIRECTION, AND POLICIES OF A PUBLICATION. AT MARUKAWA, MASAMUNE TAKANO IS THE EDITOR IN CHIEF OF THE *EMERALD* EDITORIAL DEPARTMENT. OTHER POSITIONS IN THE DEPARTMENT INCLUDE THE SECOND-IN-COMMAND, THE MANAGING EDITOR, AND REGULAR DESK WORKERS.

[RADISHES]

KNOWN AS *HATSUKA DAIKON* (TWENTY-DAY RADISH) IN JAPANESE, RADISHES ARE A ROOT VEGETABLE THAT ORIGINATED IN EUROPE. HARDY AND CULTIVATABLE ANY TIME OF THE YEAR, RADISHES ARE EXCELLENT PLANTS FOR BEGINNER GARDENERS TO GROW. SINCE RADISHES GENERALLY GROW TO MATURITY IN TWENTY TO THIRTY DAYS, THE *EMERALD* EDITORIAL DEPARTMENT'S TWENTY-DAY PUBLICATION CYCLE IS SOMETIMES REFERRED TO AS A "RADISH CYCLE."

[SUB COPY]

EDITORIAL SHORTHAND FOR A "SUBSTITUTE MANUSCRIPT," SUB COPIES ARE MANUSCRIPTS ADDED TO A PUBLICATION IN PLACE OF THE ORIGINALLY SCHEDULED MANUSCRIPT WHEN THAT MANUSCRIPT IS NOT AVAILABLE FOR WHATEVER REASON.

The World's Greatest First Love
The Case of Ritsu Onodera

ONODERA

DIVVYING UP THE WORKLOAD

MINO   KISA   TORI

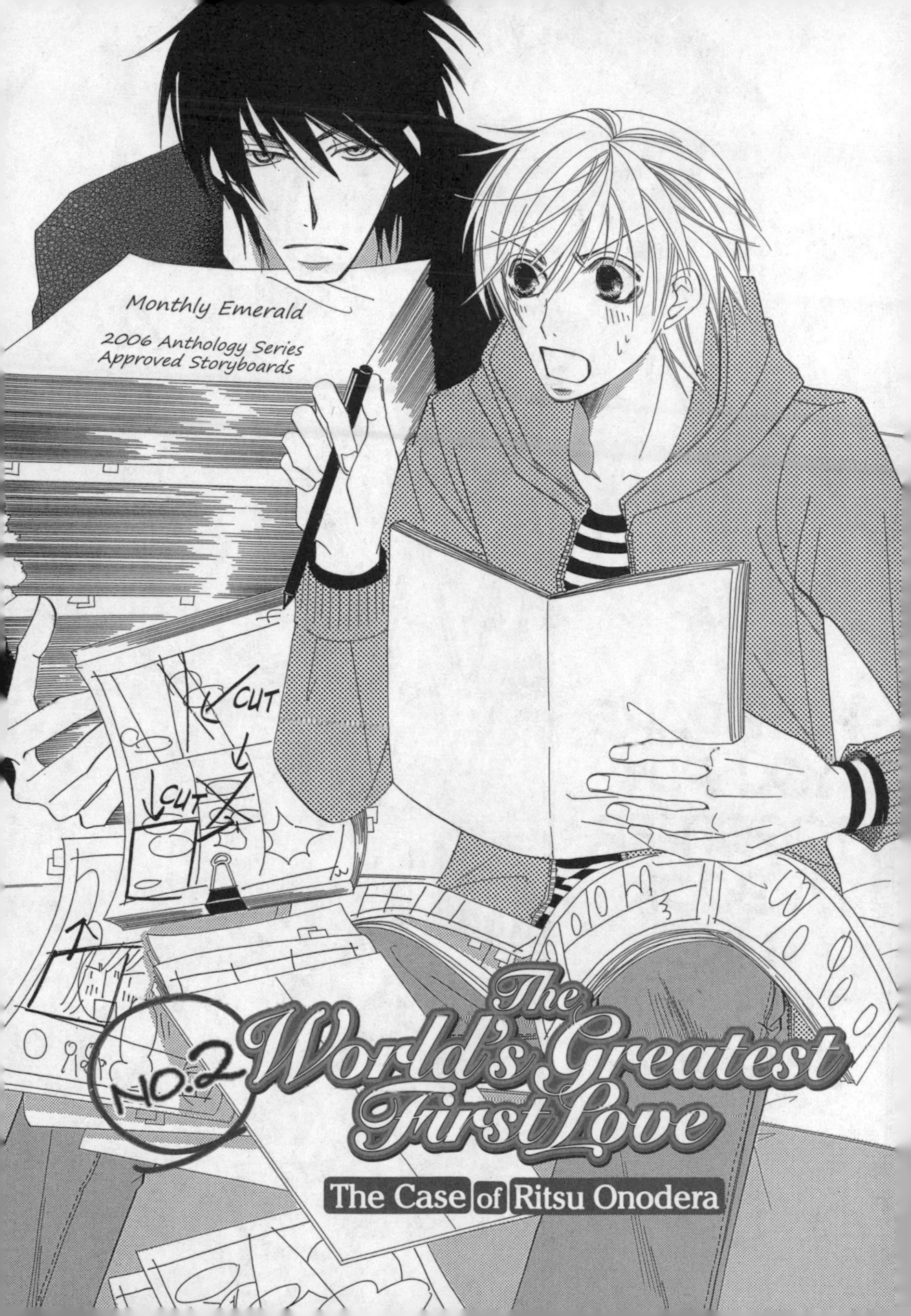
Monthly Emerald
2006 Anthology Series
Approved Storyboards
CUT
CUT
No.2
The World's Greatest First Love
The Case of Ritsu Onodera

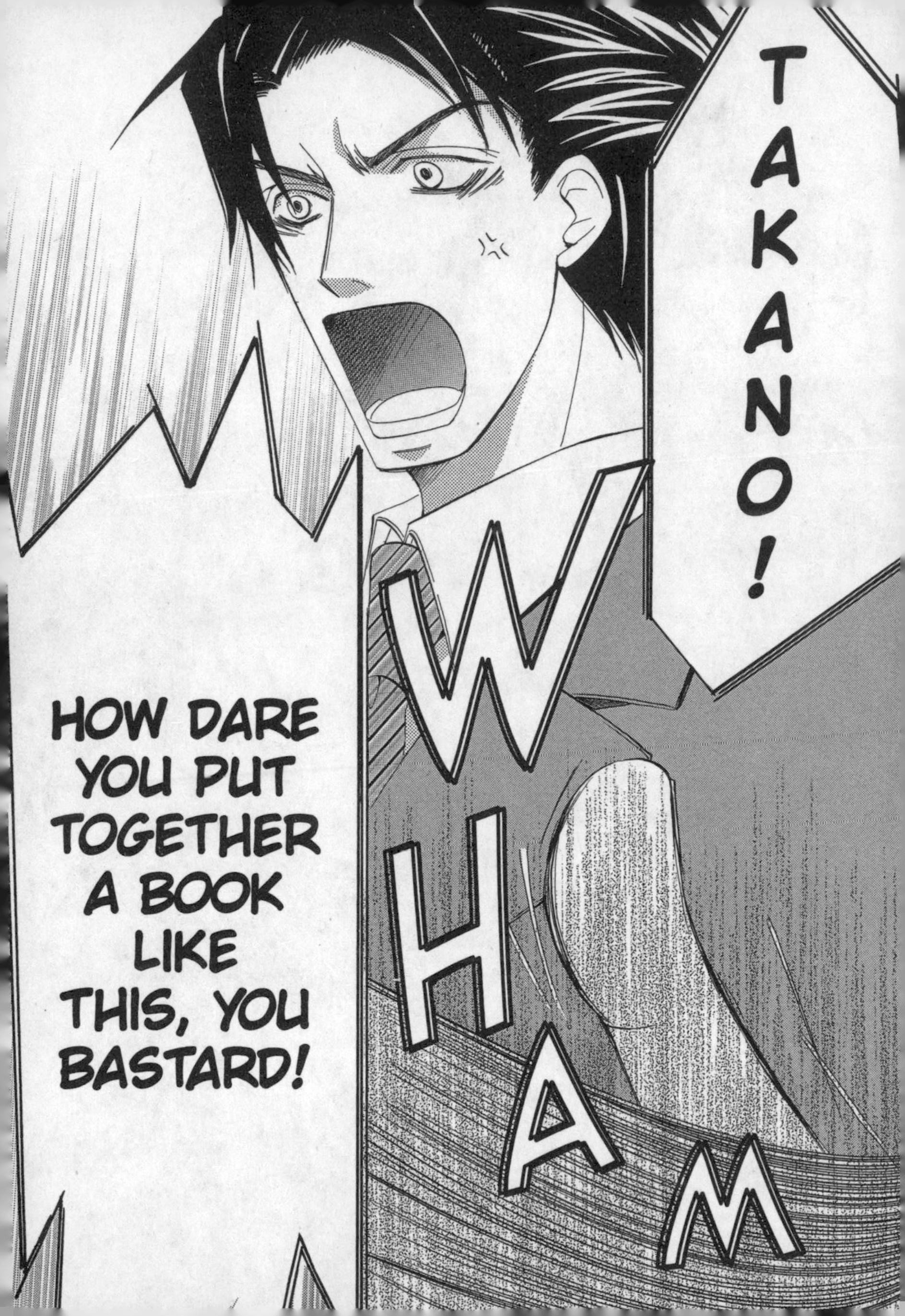
TAKANO!
WHAM
HOW DARE YOU PUT TOGETHER A BOOK LIKE THIS, YOU BASTARD!

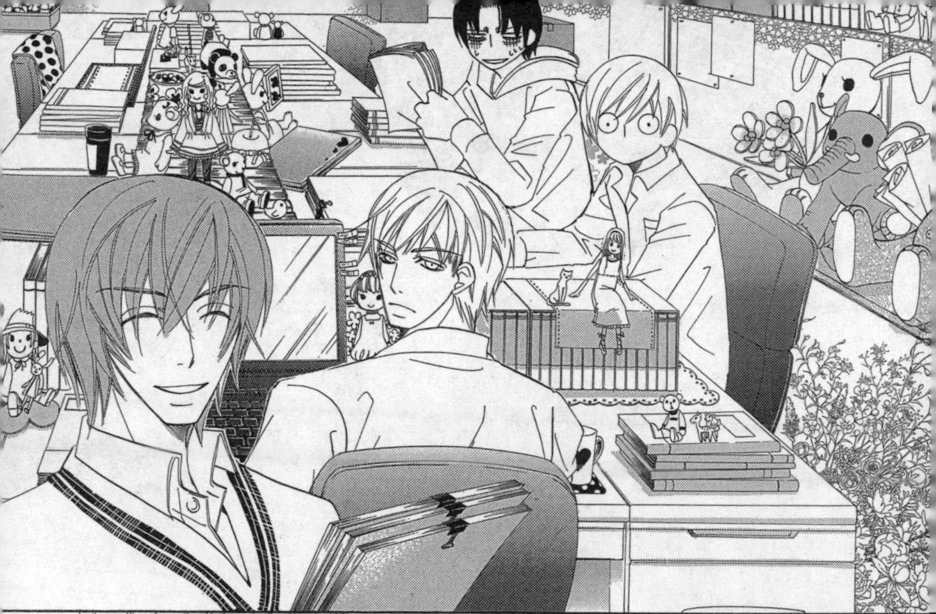

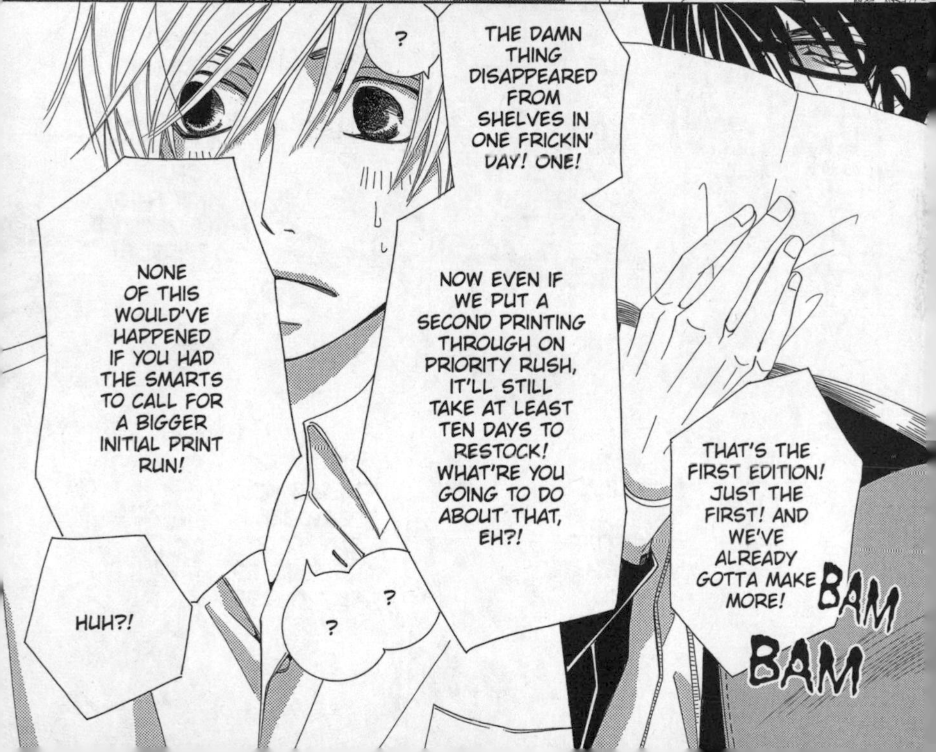
?
THE DAMN THING DISAPPEARED FROM SHELVES IN ONE FRICKIN' DAY! ONE!
THAT'S THE FIRST EDITION! JUST THE FIRST! AND WE'VE ALREADY GOTTA MAKE MORE!
BAM BAM
NOW EVEN IF WE PUT A SECOND PRINTING THROUGH ON PRIORITY RUSH, IT'LL STILL TAKE AT LEAST TEN DAYS TO RESTOCK! WHAT'RE YOU GOING TO DO ABOUT THAT, EH?!
NONE OF THIS WOULD'VE HAPPENED IF YOU HAD THE SMARTS TO CALL FOR A BIGGER INITIAL PRINT RUN!
? ?
HUH?!

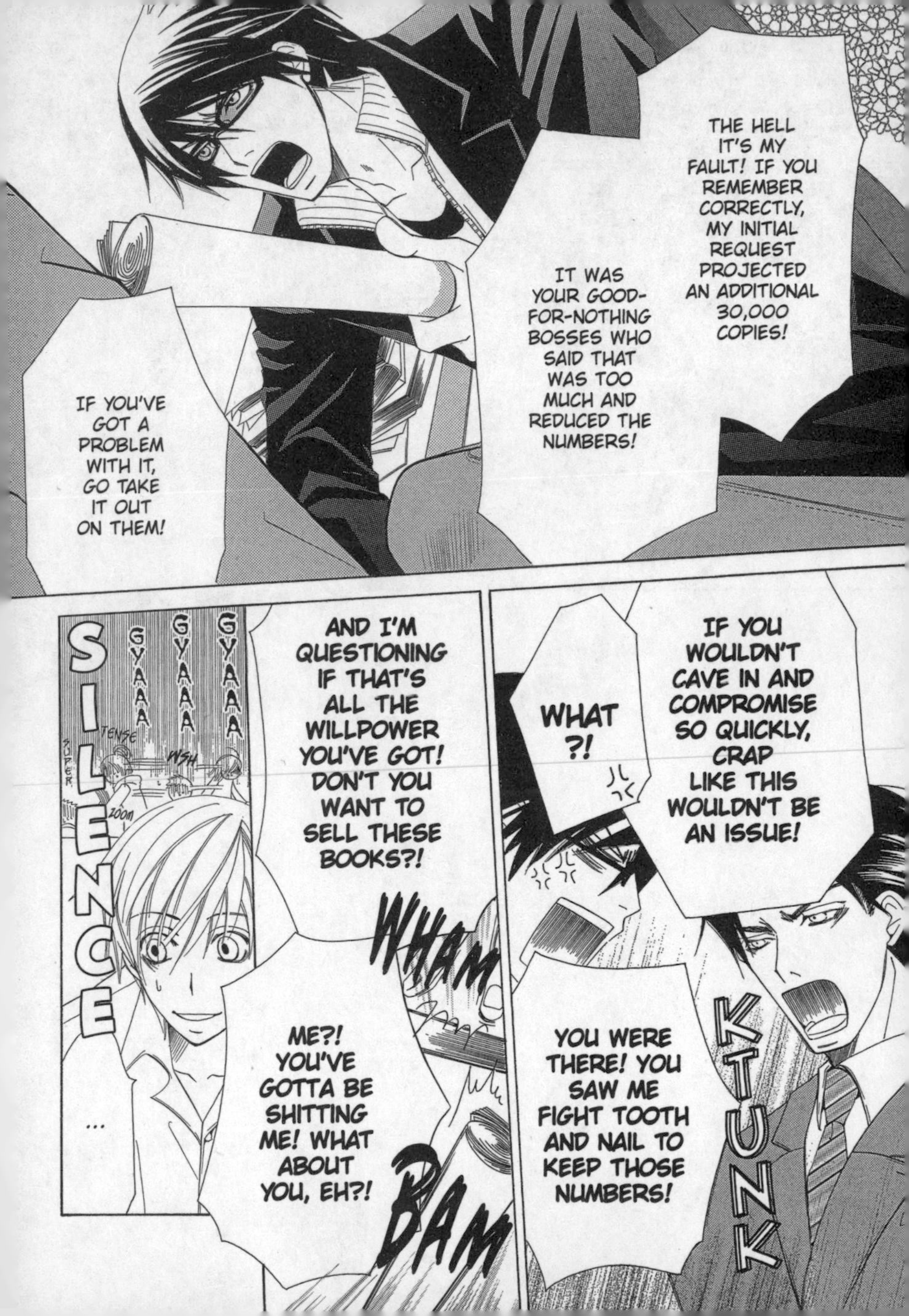
THE HELL IT'S MY FAULT! IF YOU REMEMBER CORRECTLY, MY INITIAL REQUEST PROJECTED AN ADDITIONAL 30,000 COPIES!
IT WAS YOUR GOOD-FOR-NOTHING BOSSES WHO SAID THAT WAS TOO MUCH AND REDUCED THE NUMBERS!
IF YOU'VE GOT A PROBLEM WITH IT, GO TAKE IT OUT ON THEM!
IF YOU WOULDN'T CAVE IN AND COMPROMISE SO QUICKLY, CRAP LIKE THIS WOULDN'T BE AN ISSUE!
WHAT?!
KTUNK
YOU WERE THERE! YOU SAW ME FIGHT TOOTH AND NAIL TO KEEP THOSE NUMBERS!
AND I'M QUESTIONING IF THAT'S ALL THE WILLPOWER YOU'VE GOT! DON'T YOU WANT TO SELL THESE BOOKS?!
WHAM
ME?! YOU'VE GOTTA BE SHITTING ME! WHAT ABOUT YOU, EH?!
BAM
GYAAA
GYAAA
GYAAA
TENSE
WSH
SUPER
ZOOM
SILENCE
...

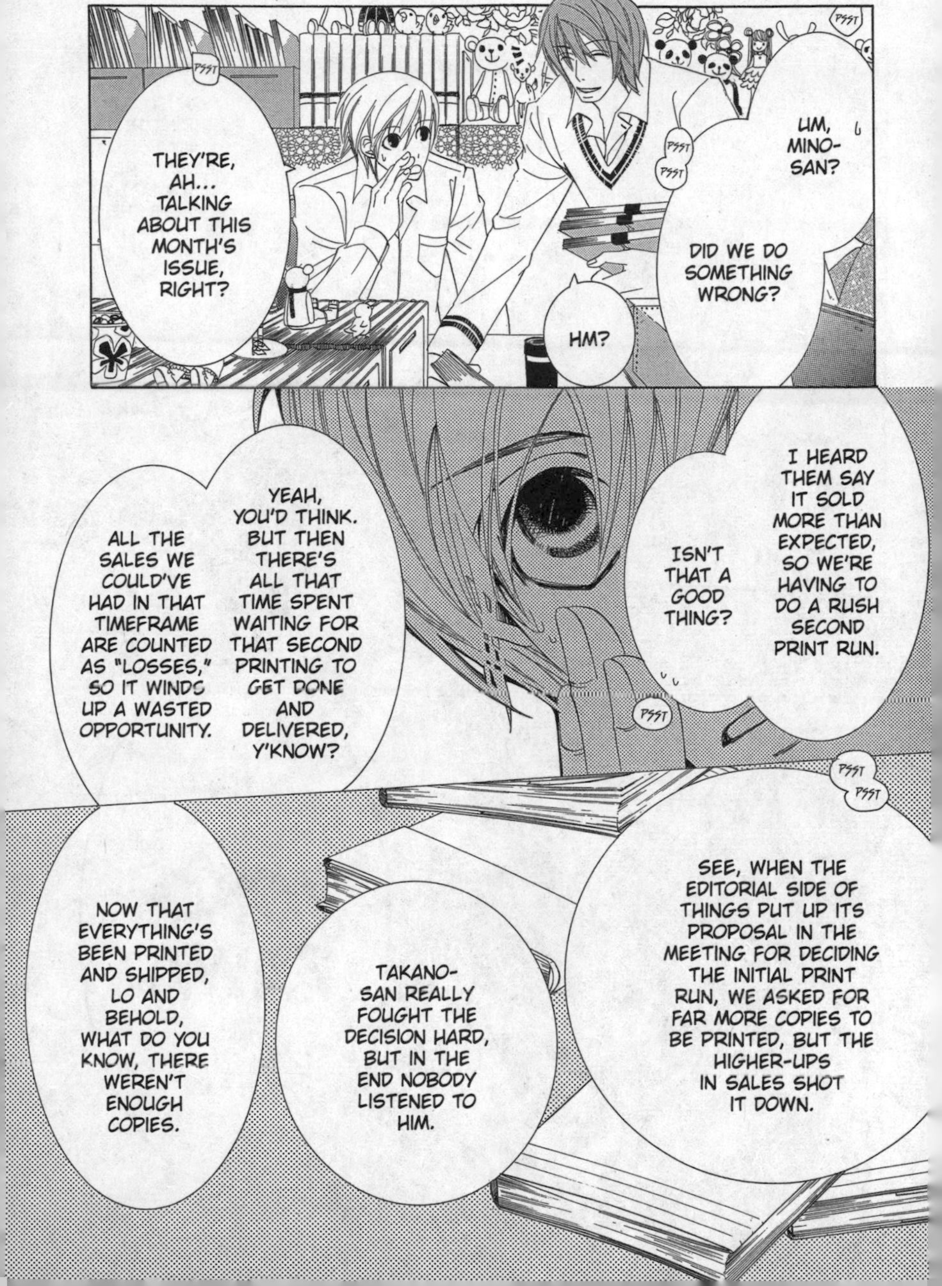
PSST
PSST
PSST
PSST
UM, MINO-SAN?
DID WE DO SOMETHING WRONG?
HM?
THEY'RE, AH... TALKING ABOUT THIS MONTH'S ISSUE, RIGHT?
I HEARD THEM SAY IT SOLD MORE THAN EXPECTED, SO WE'RE HAVING TO DO A RUSH SECOND PRINT RUN.
ISN'T THAT A GOOD THING?
PSST
YEAH, YOU'D THINK. BUT THEN THERE'S ALL THAT TIME SPENT WAITING FOR THAT SECOND PRINTING TO GET DONE AND DELIVERED, Y'KNOW?
ALL THE SALES WE COULD'VE HAD IN THAT TIMEFRAME ARE COUNTED AS "LOSSES," SO IT WINDS UP A WASTED OPPORTUNITY.
PSST
PSST
SEE, WHEN THE EDITORIAL SIDE OF THINGS PUT UP ITS PROPOSAL IN THE MEETING FOR DECIDING THE INITIAL PRINT RUN, WE ASKED FOR FAR MORE COPIES TO BE PRINTED, BUT THE HIGHER-UPS IN SALES SHOT IT DOWN.
TAKANO-SAN REALLY FOUGHT THE DECISION HARD, BUT IN THE END NOBODY LISTENED TO HIM.
NOW THAT EVERYTHING'S BEEN PRINTED AND SHIPPED, LO AND BEHOLD, WHAT DO YOU KNOW, THERE WEREN'T ENOUGH COPIES.

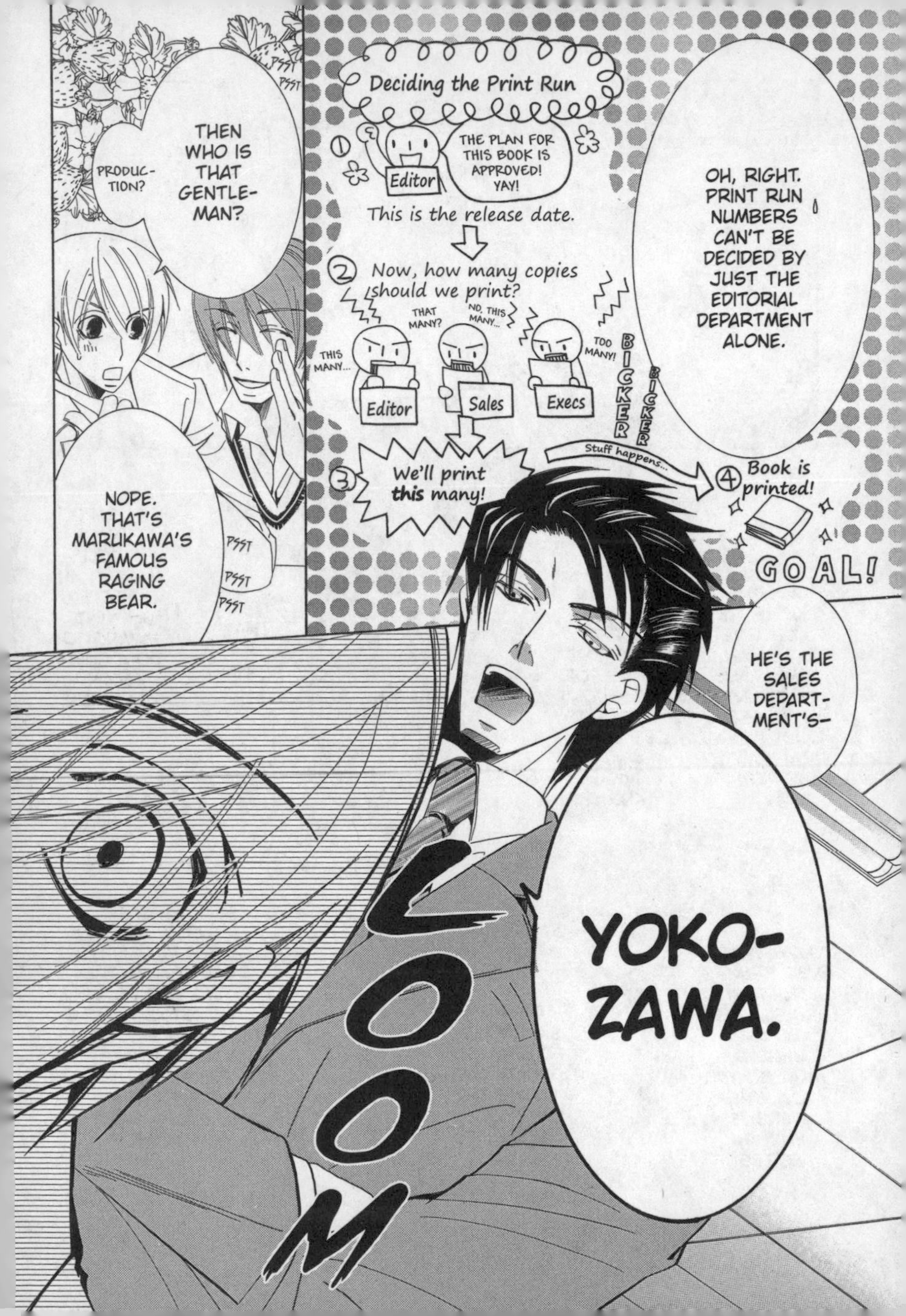
OH, RIGHT. PRINT RUN NUMBERS CAN'T BE DECIDED BY JUST THE EDITORIAL DEPARTMENT ALONE.
Deciding the Print Run
①
Editor
THE PLAN FOR THIS BOOK IS APPROVED! YAY!
This is the release date.
② Now, how many copies should we print?
THIS MANY...
THAT MANY?
NO, THIS MANY...
TOO MANY!
Editor
Sales
Execs
BICKER
BICKER
③ We'll print this many!
Stuff happens...
④ Book is printed!
GOAL!
THEN WHO IS THAT GENTLE-MAN?
PRODUC-TION?
PSST
PSST
NOPE. THAT'S MARUKAWA'S FAMOUS RAGING BEAR.
PSST
PSST
PSST
HE'S THE SALES DEPART-MENT'S-
YOKO-ZAWA.
VOOOM

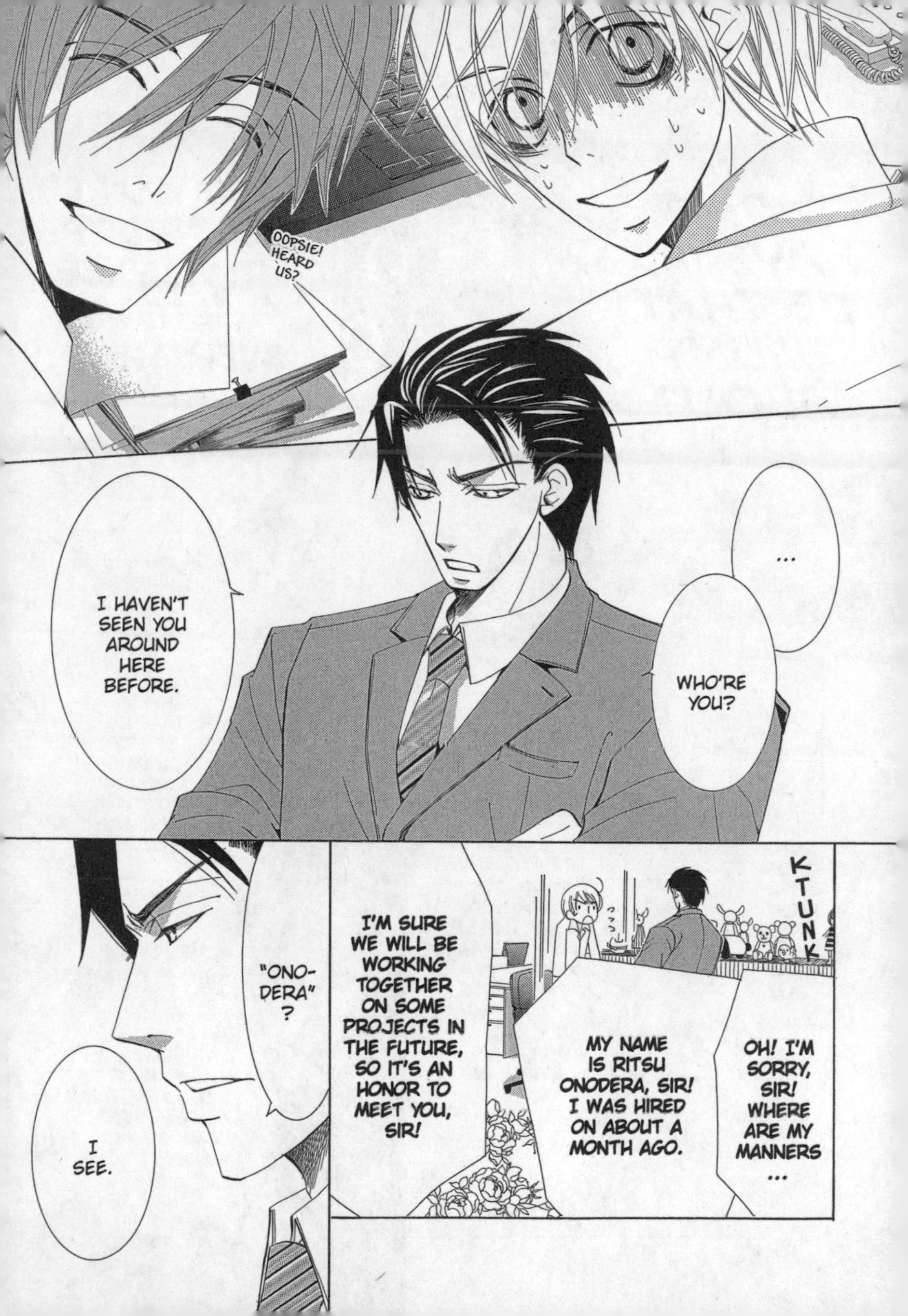
OOPSIE! HEARD US?
...
WHO'RE YOU?
I HAVEN'T SEEN YOU AROUND HERE BEFORE.
KTUNK
OH! I'M SORRY, SIR! WHERE ARE MY MANNERS...
MY NAME IS RITSU ONODERA, SIR! I WAS HIRED ON ABOUT A MONTH AGO.
I'M SURE WE WILL BE WORKING TOGETHER ON SOME PROJECTS IN THE FUTURE, SO IT'S AN HONOR TO MEET YOU, SIR!
"ONODERA"?
I SEE.

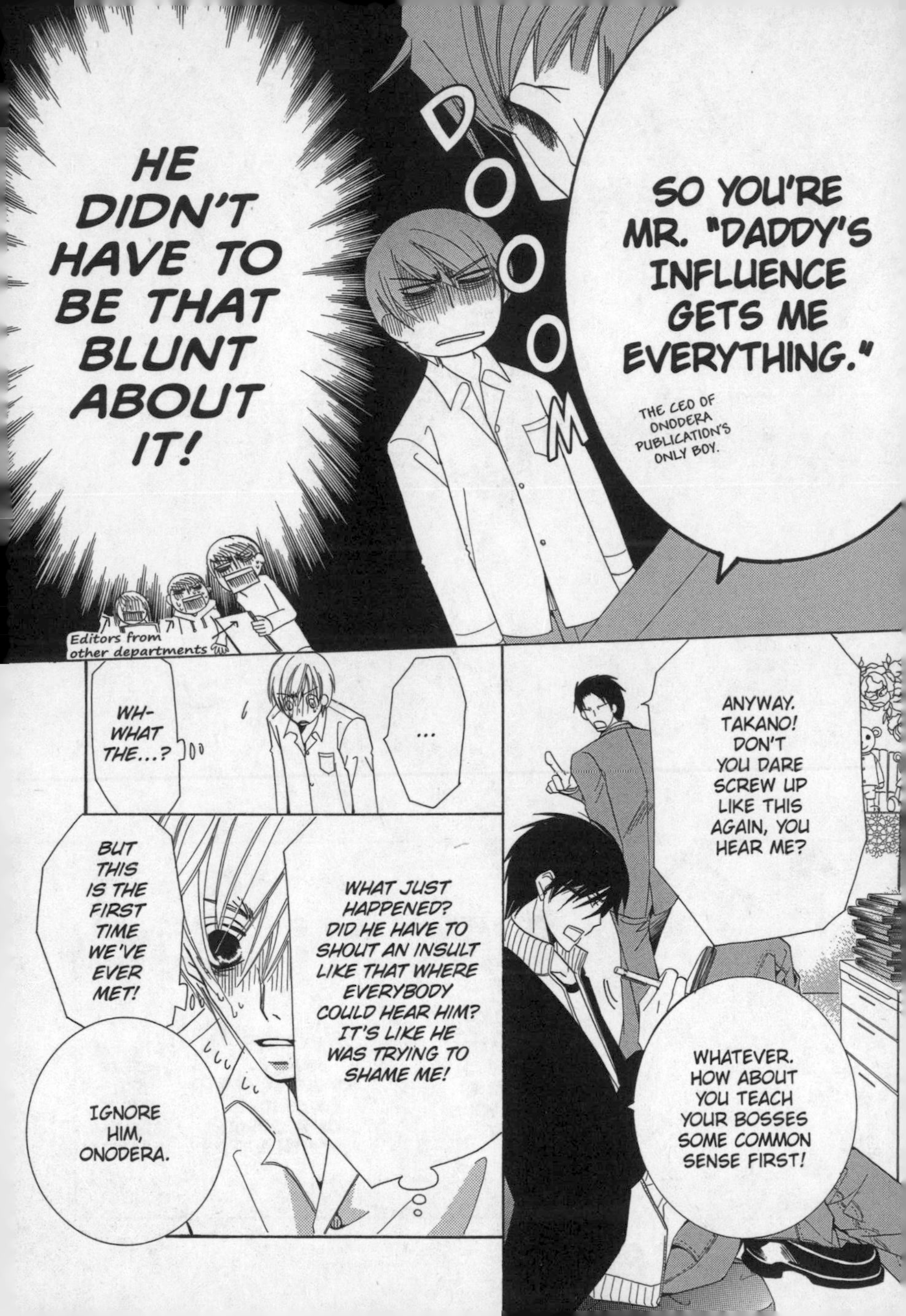
SO YOU'RE MR. "DADDY'S INFLUENCE GETS ME EVERYTHING."
THE CEO OF ONODERA PUBLICATION'S ONLY BOY.
DOOOOM
HE DIDN'T HAVE TO BE THAT BLUNT ABOUT IT!
Editors from other departments
ANYWAY. TAKANO! DON'T YOU DARE SCREW UP LIKE THIS AGAIN, YOU HEAR ME?
WHATEVER. HOW ABOUT YOU TEACH YOUR BOSSES SOME COMMON SENSE FIRST!
...
WH- WHAT THE...?
WHAT JUST HAPPENED? DID HE HAVE TO SHOUT AN INSULT LIKE THAT WHERE EVERYBODY COULD HEAR HIM? IT'S LIKE HE WAS TRYING TO SHAME ME!
BUT THIS IS THE FIRST TIME WE'VE EVER MET!
IGNORE HIM, ONODERA.

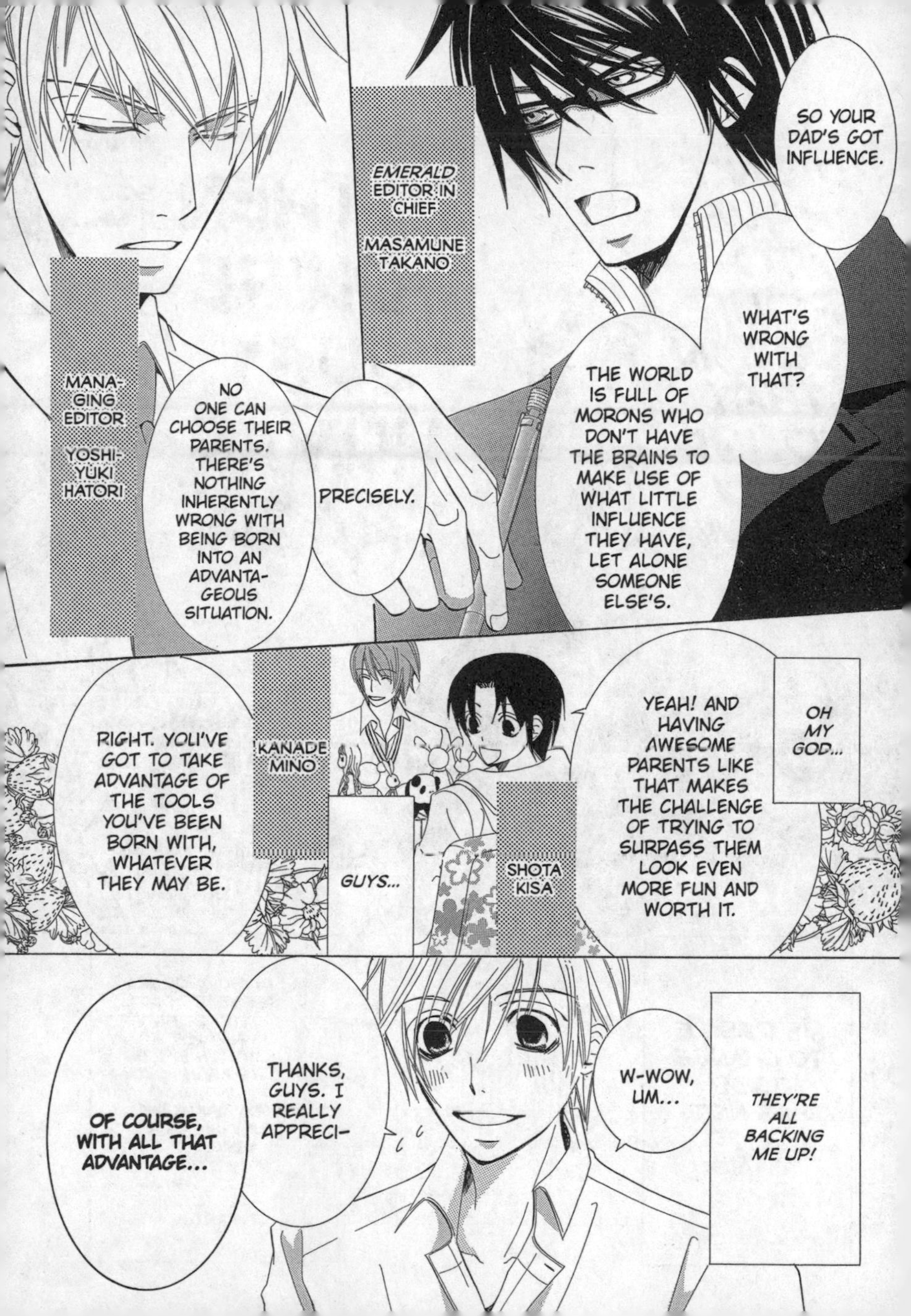
SO YOUR DAD'S GOT INFLUENCE.
EMERALD EDITOR IN CHIEF
MASAMUNE TAKANO
WHAT'S WRONG WITH THAT?
THE WORLD IS FULL OF MORONS WHO DON'T HAVE THE BRAINS TO MAKE USE OF WHAT LITTLE INFLUENCE THEY HAVE, LET ALONE SOMEONE ELSE'S.
PRECISELY.
NO ONE CAN CHOOSE THEIR PARENTS. THERE'S NOTHING INHERENTLY WRONG WITH BEING BORN INTO AN ADVANTAGEOUS SITUATION.
MANAGING EDITOR
YOSHIYUKI HATORI
OH MY GOD...
YEAH! AND HAVING AWESOME PARENTS LIKE THAT MAKES THE CHALLENGE OF TRYING TO SURPASS THEM LOOK EVEN MORE FUN AND WORTH IT.
SHOTA KISA
GUYS...
KANADE MINO
RIGHT. YOU'VE GOT TO TAKE ADVANTAGE OF THE TOOLS YOU'VE BEEN BORN WITH, WHATEVER THEY MAY BE.
THEY'RE ALL BACKING ME UP!
W-WOW, UM...
THANKS, GUYS. I REALLY APPRECI-
OF COURSE, WITH ALL THAT ADVANTAGE...

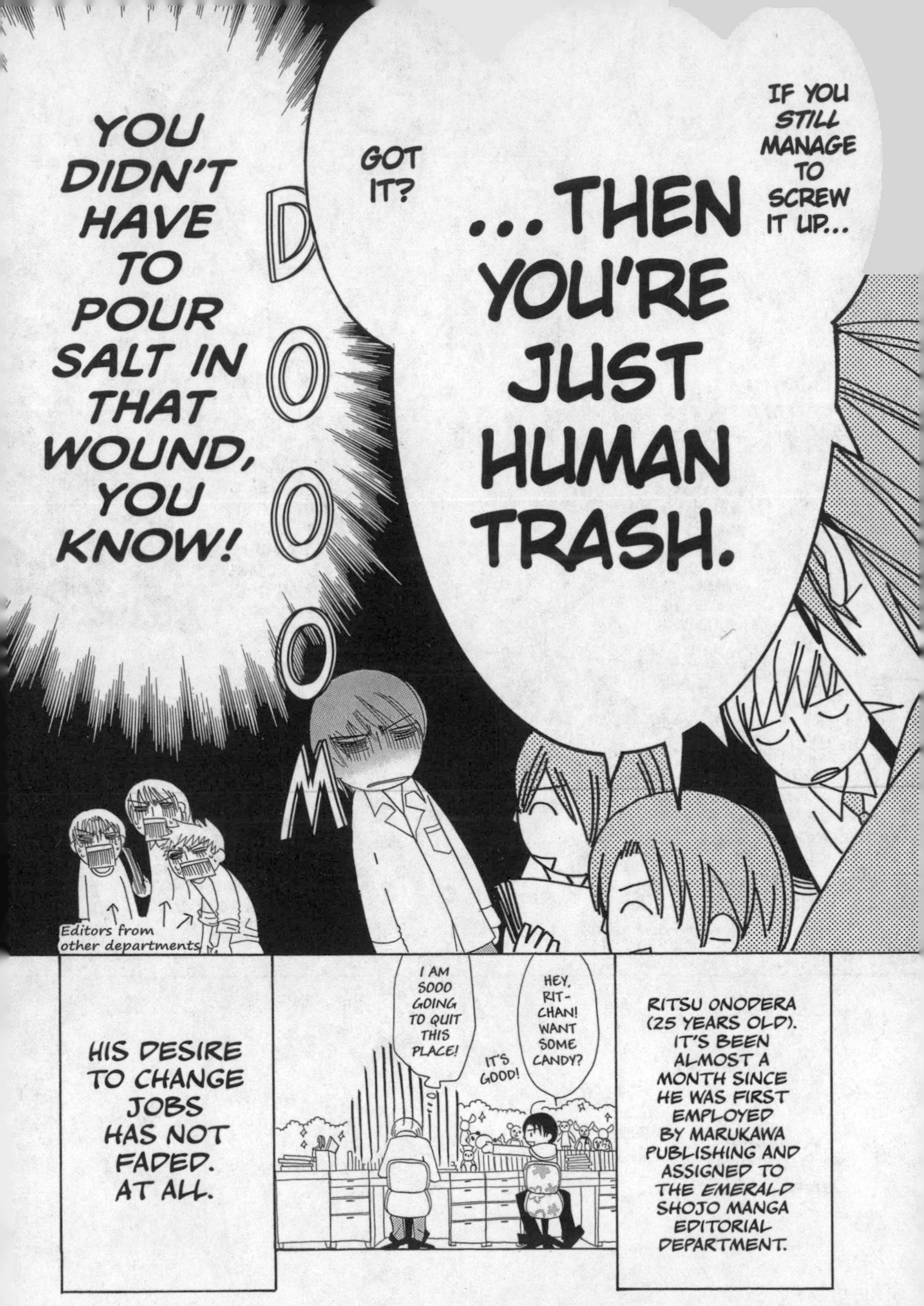
IF YOU STILL MANAGE TO SCREW IT UP...
...THEN YOU'RE JUST HUMAN TRASH.
GOT IT?
DOOOOM
YOU DIDN'T HAVE TO POUR SALT IN THAT WOUND, YOU KNOW!
Editors from other departments
RITSU ONODERA (25 YEARS OLD). IT'S BEEN ALMOST A MONTH SINCE HE WAS FIRST EMPLOYED BY MARUKAWA PUBLISHING AND ASSIGNED TO THE EMERALD SHOJO MANGA EDITORIAL DEPARTMENT.
HEY, RIT-CHAN! WANT SOME CANDY?
IT'S GOOD!
I AM SOOO GOING TO QUIT THIS PLACE!
HIS DESIRE TO CHANGE JOBS HAS NOT FADED. AT ALL.

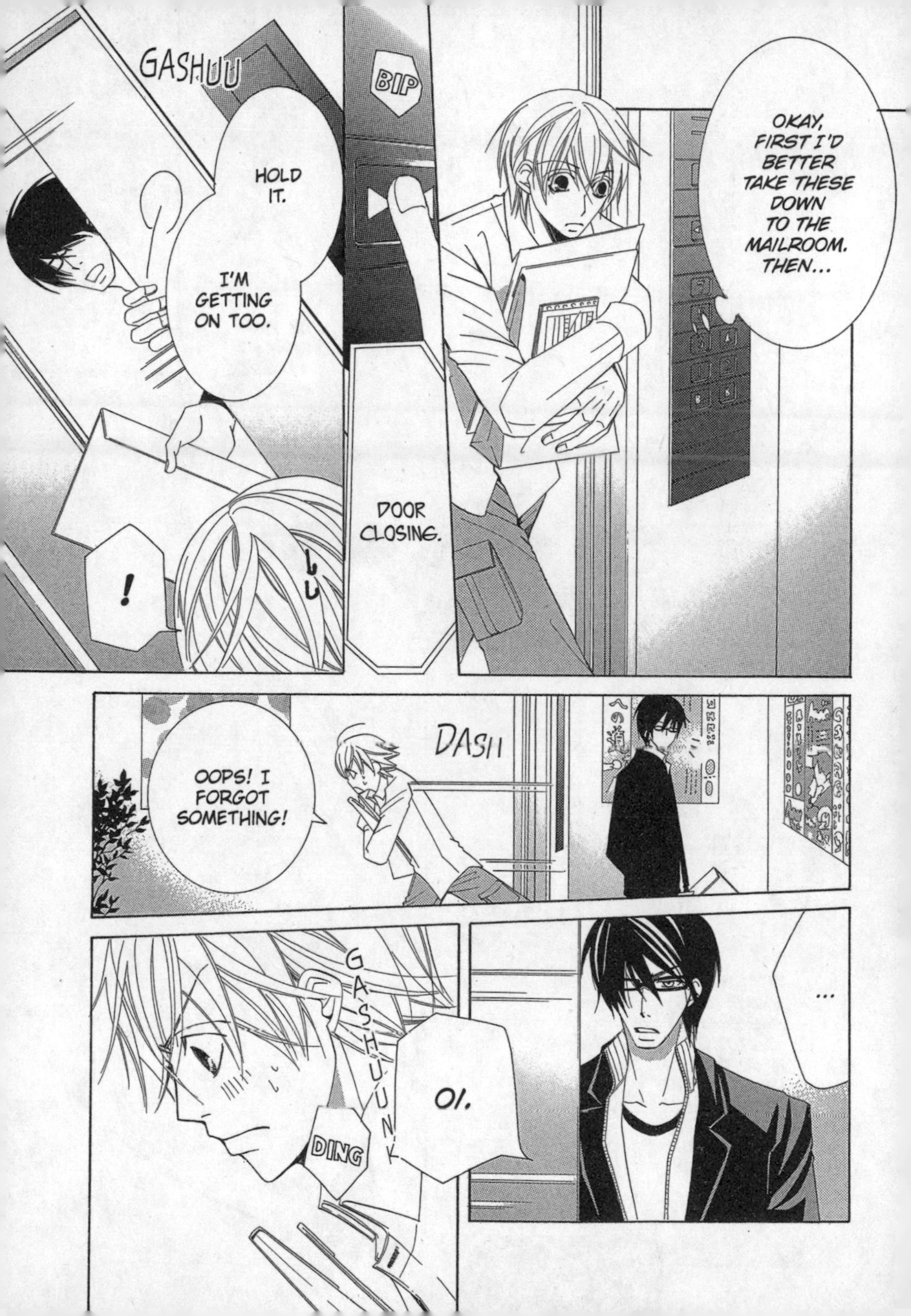
OKAY, FIRST I'D BETTER TAKE THESE DOWN TO THE MAILROOM. THEN...
BIP
DOOR CLOSING.
GASHUU
HOLD IT.
I'M GETTING ON TOO.
!
DASH
OOPS! I FORGOT SOMETHING!
...
GASHUUNK
OI.
DING

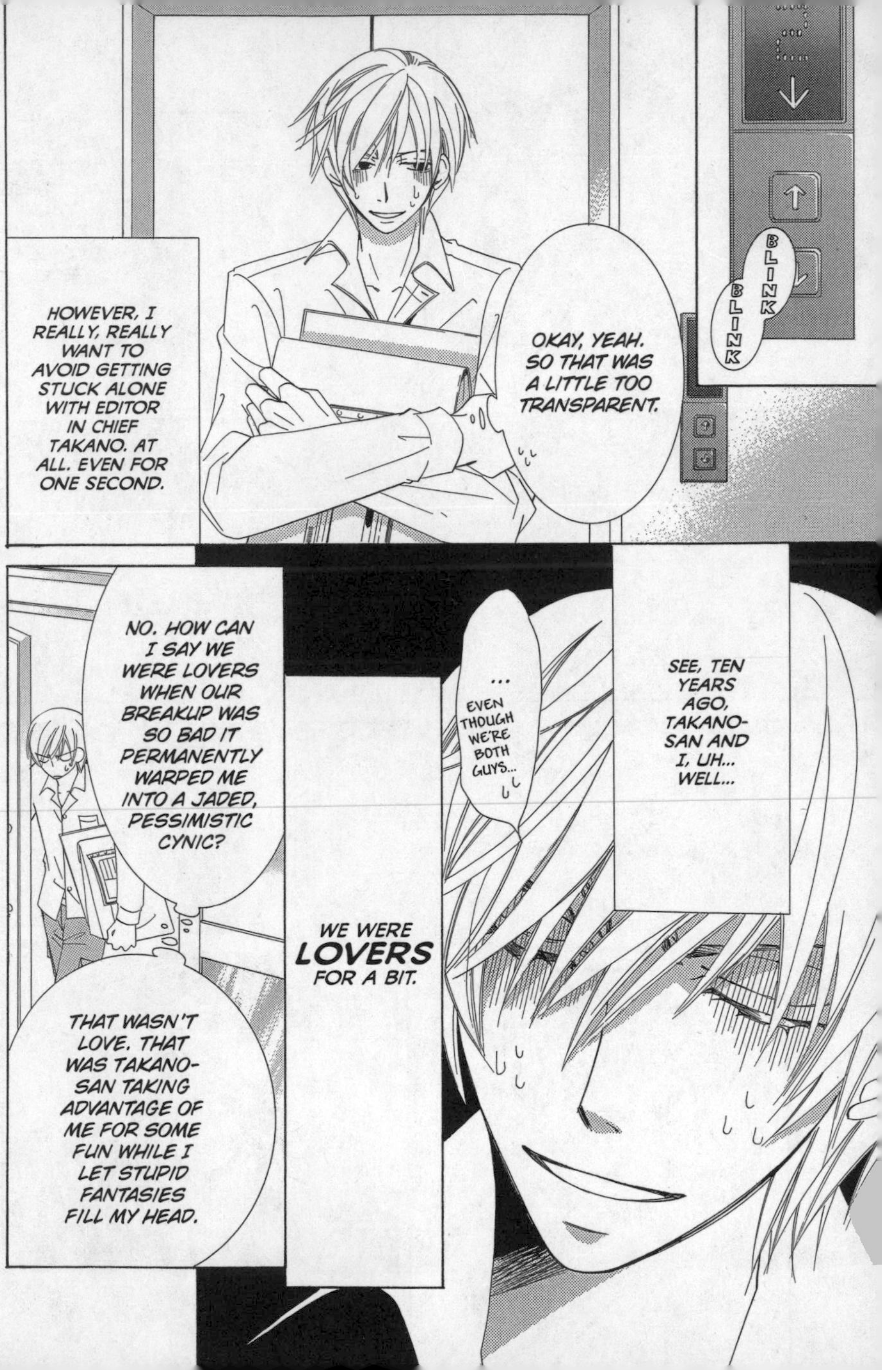
BLINK
BLINK
OKAY, YEAH. SO THAT WAS A LITTLE TOO TRANSPARENT.
HOWEVER, I REALLY, REALLY WANT TO AVOID GETTING STUCK ALONE WITH EDITOR IN CHIEF TAKANO. AT ALL. EVEN FOR ONE SECOND.
SEE, TEN YEARS AGO, TAKANO-SAN AND I, UH... WELL...
... EVEN THOUGH WE'RE BOTH GUYS...
WE WERE LOVERS FOR A BIT.
NO. HOW CAN I SAY WE WERE LOVERS WHEN OUR BREAKUP WAS SO BAD IT PERMANENTLY WARPED ME INTO A JADED, PESSIMISTIC CYNIC?
THAT WASN'T LOVE. THAT WAS TAKANO-SAN TAKING ADVANTAGE OF ME FOR SOME FUN WHILE I LET STUPID FANTASIES FILL MY HEAD.

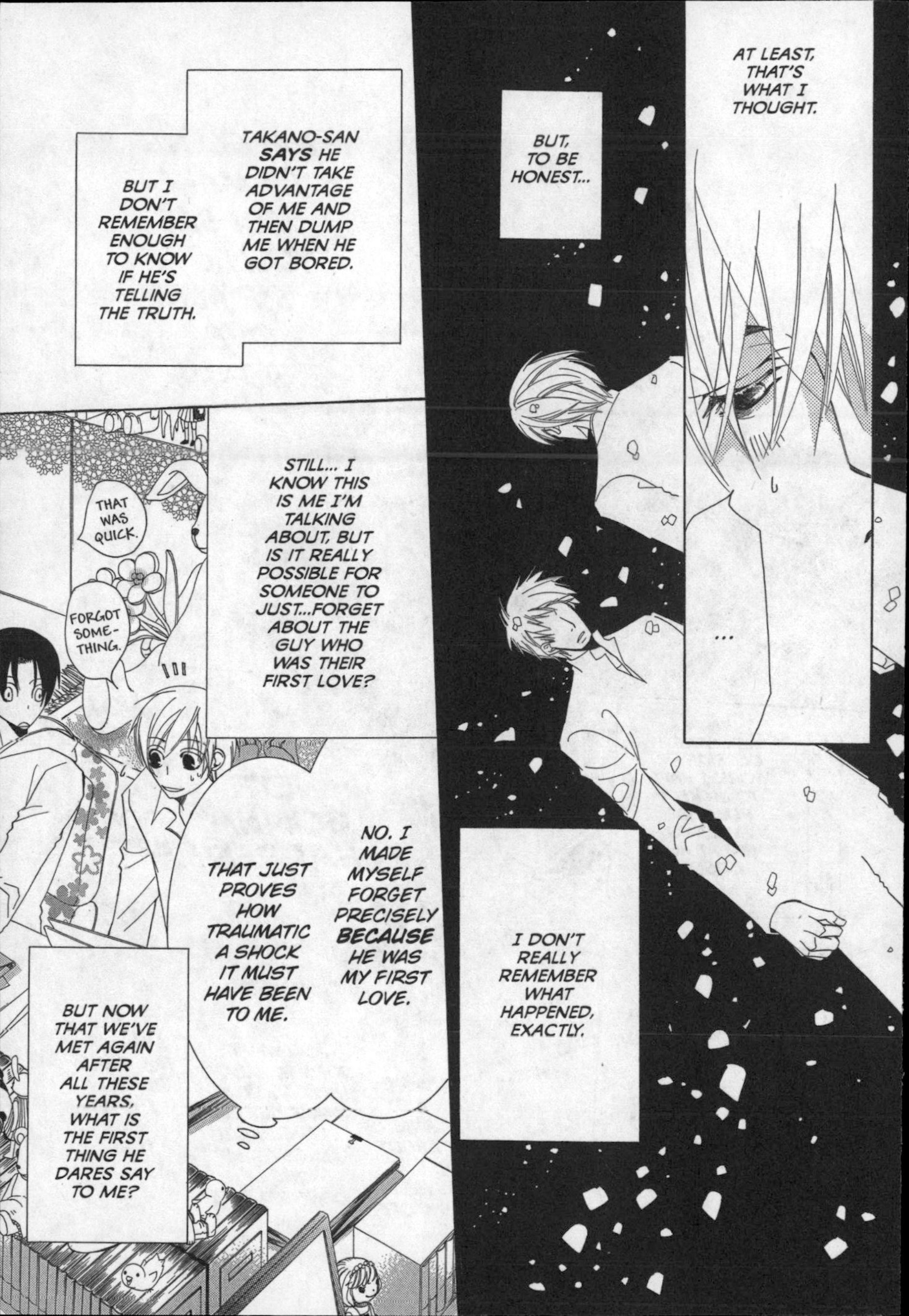
AT LEAST, THAT'S WHAT I THOUGHT.
BUT, TO BE HONEST...
...
I DON'T REALLY REMEMBER WHAT HAPPENED, EXACTLY.
TAKANO-SAN **SAYS** HE DIDN'T TAKE ADVANTAGE OF ME AND THEN DUMP ME WHEN HE GOT BORED.
BUT I DON'T REMEMBER ENOUGH TO KNOW IF HE'S TELLING THE TRUTH.
STILL... I KNOW THIS IS ME I'M TALKING ABOUT, BUT IS IT REALLY POSSIBLE FOR SOMEONE TO JUST...FORGET ABOUT THE GUY WHO WAS THEIR FIRST LOVE?
THAT WAS QUICK.
FORGOT SOME-THING.
NO. I MADE MYSELF FORGET PRECISELY **BECAUSE** HE WAS MY FIRST LOVE.
THAT JUST PROVES HOW TRAUMATIC A SHOCK IT MUST HAVE BEEN TO ME.
BUT NOW THAT WE'VE MET AGAIN AFTER ALL THESE YEARS, WHAT IS THE FIRST THING HE DARES SAY TO ME?

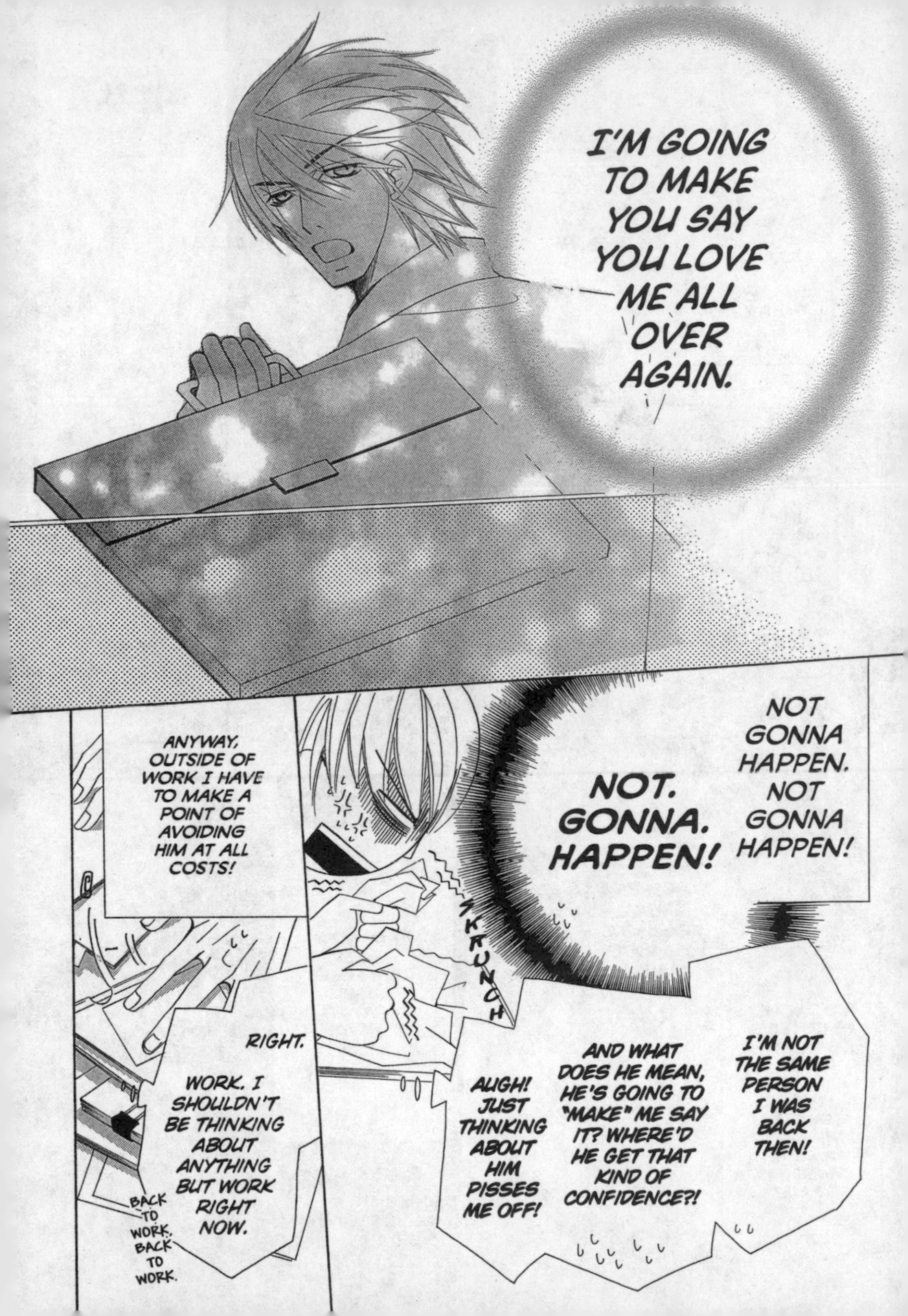
I'M GOING TO MAKE YOU SAY YOU LOVE ME ALL OVER AGAIN.
NOT GONNA HAPPEN. NOT GONNA HAPPEN. NOT GONNA HAPPEN!
NOT. GONNA. HAPPEN!
SKRUNCH
I'M NOT THE SAME PERSON I WAS BACK THEN!
AND WHAT DOES HE MEAN, HE'S GOING TO "MAKE" ME SAY IT? WHERE'D HE GET THAT KIND OF CONFIDENCE?!
AUGH! JUST THINKING ABOUT HIM PISSES ME OFF!
ANYWAY, OUTSIDE OF WORK I HAVE TO MAKE A POINT OF AVOIDING HIM AT ALL COSTS!
RIGHT.
WORK. I SHOULDN'T BE THINKING ABOUT ANYTHING BUT WORK RIGHT NOW.
BACK TO WORK, BACK TO WORK.

IS MUTO SENSEI STILL NOT FINISHED WITH THE STORY-BOARDS?

SHE'S ALREADY FIVE DAYS LATE FROM THE FIRST DEADLINE WE SET.

IF WE LET THINGS SLIDE ANY FURTHER, IT MIGHT HAVE AN IMPACT ON THE TIME SHE HAS TO DRAW UP THE DRAFTS.

SUN	MON	TUE
	1	2
7	3:00 Meeting (8)	9
14	Muto-san Storyboard Due (15)	16
21		

OH, UM...

SHE'S ON THE LATE SIDE WITH HER STORYBOARD, AND SINCE YOU WERE HER PREVIOUS EDITOR, I WAS JUST WONDERING IF YOU MIGHT KNOW ANYTHING.

HATORI-SAN?

HOW FAST DOES MUTO SENSEI USUALLY FINISH HER DRAFTS? DOES SHE GET THEM DONE QUICKLY?

HUH?

IT'S A GOOD IDEA TO CHECK ON HER PROGRESS ON A REGULAR BASIS.

THANKS. I'LL DO THAT.

SHE'S NOT THE WORST OF DEADLINE BREAKERS, NO.

BUT WHEN SHE DOES GET WRITER'S BLOCK, SHE'S THE TYPE TO BECOME VERY DEPRESSED. IT TAKES SOME TIME FOR HER TO RECOVER.

K CHIK

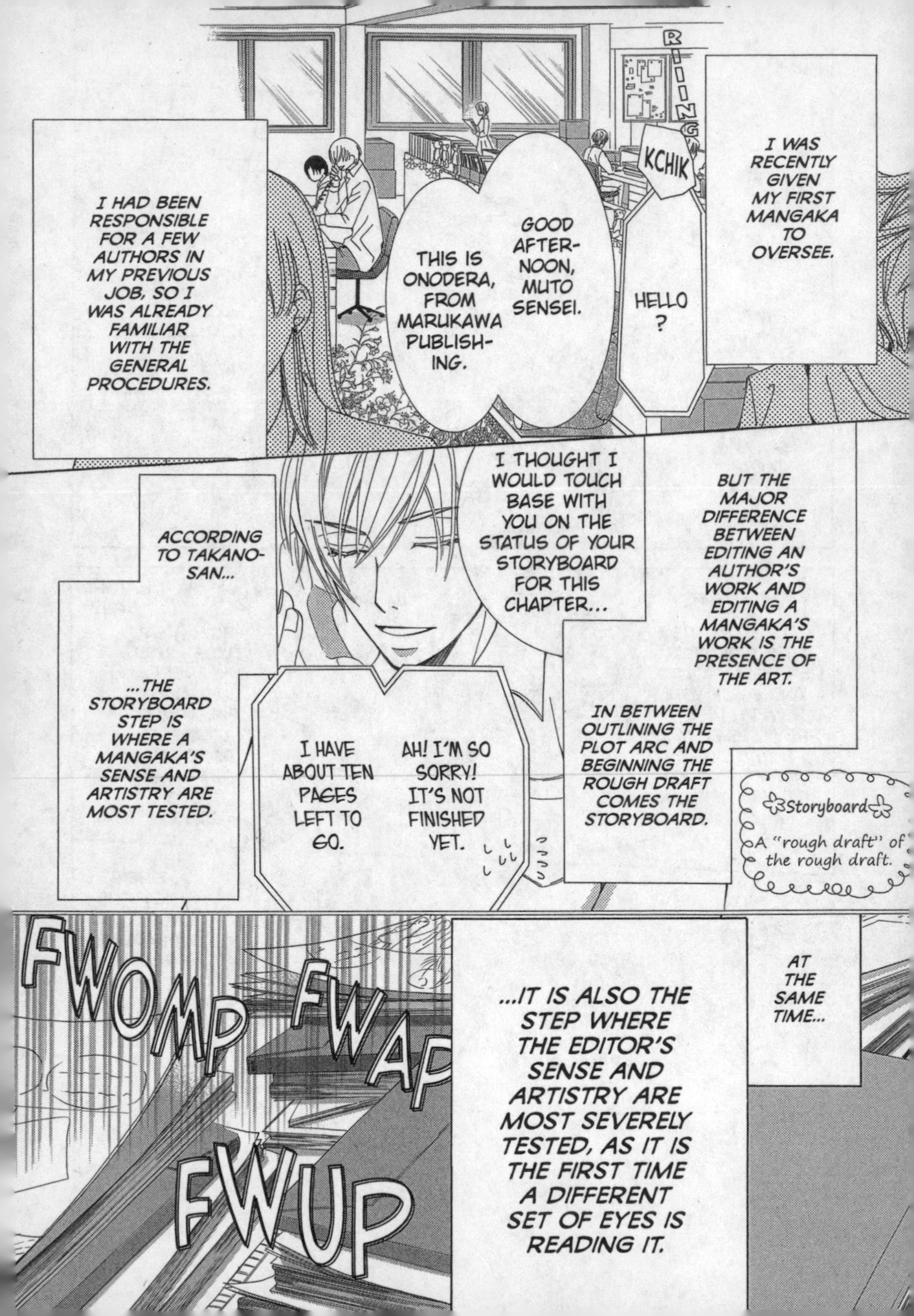
I WAS RECENTLY GIVEN MY FIRST MANGAKA TO OVERSEE.
RIIIING
KCHIK
HELLO?
GOOD AFTERNOON, MUTO SENSEI.
THIS IS ONODERA, FROM MARUKAWA PUBLISHING.
I HAD BEEN RESPONSIBLE FOR A FEW AUTHORS IN MY PREVIOUS JOB, SO I WAS ALREADY FAMILIAR WITH THE GENERAL PROCEDURES.
BUT THE MAJOR DIFFERENCE BETWEEN EDITING AN AUTHOR'S WORK AND EDITING A MANGAKA'S WORK IS THE PRESENCE OF THE ART.
Storyboard
A "rough draft" of the rough draft.
I THOUGHT I WOULD TOUCH BASE WITH YOU ON THE STATUS OF YOUR STORYBOARD FOR THIS CHAPTER...
IN BETWEEN OUTLINING THE PLOT ARC AND BEGINNING THE ROUGH DRAFT COMES THE STORYBOARD.
AH! I'M SO SORRY! IT'S NOT FINISHED YET.
I HAVE ABOUT TEN PAGES LEFT TO GO.
ACCORDING TO TAKANO-SAN...
...THE STORYBOARD STEP IS WHERE A MANGAKA'S SENSE AND ARTISTRY ARE MOST TESTED.
AT THE SAME TIME...
...IT IS ALSO THE STEP WHERE THE EDITOR'S SENSE AND ARTISTRY ARE MOST SEVERELY TESTED, AS IT IS THE FIRST TIME A DIFFERENT SET OF EYES IS READING IT.
FWOMP
FWAP
FWUP

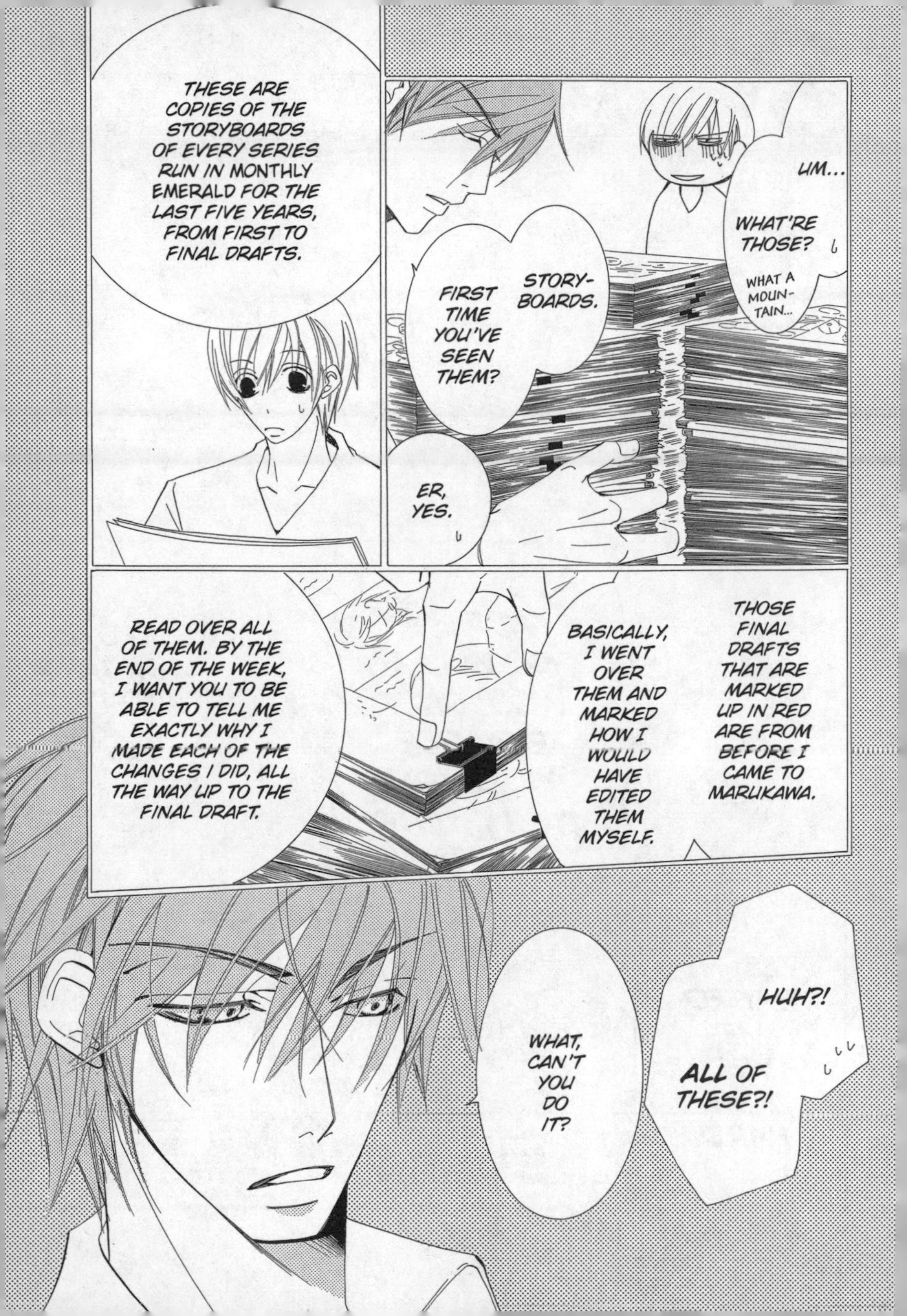
UM...
WHAT'RE THOSE?
WHAT A MOUNTAIN...
STORYBOARDS.
FIRST TIME YOU'VE SEEN THEM?
ER, YES.
THESE ARE COPIES OF THE STORYBOARDS OF EVERY SERIES RUN IN MONTHLY EMERALD FOR THE LAST FIVE YEARS, FROM FIRST TO FINAL DRAFTS.
THOSE FINAL DRAFTS THAT ARE MARKED UP IN RED ARE FROM BEFORE I CAME TO MARUKAWA.
BASICALLY, I WENT OVER THEM AND MARKED HOW I WOULD HAVE EDITED THEM MYSELF.
READ OVER ALL OF THEM. BY THE END OF THE WEEK, I WANT YOU TO BE ABLE TO TELL ME EXACTLY WHY I MADE EACH OF THE CHANGES I DID, ALL THE WAY UP TO THE FINAL DRAFT.
HUH?!
ALL OF THESE?!
WHAT, CAN'T YOU DO IT?

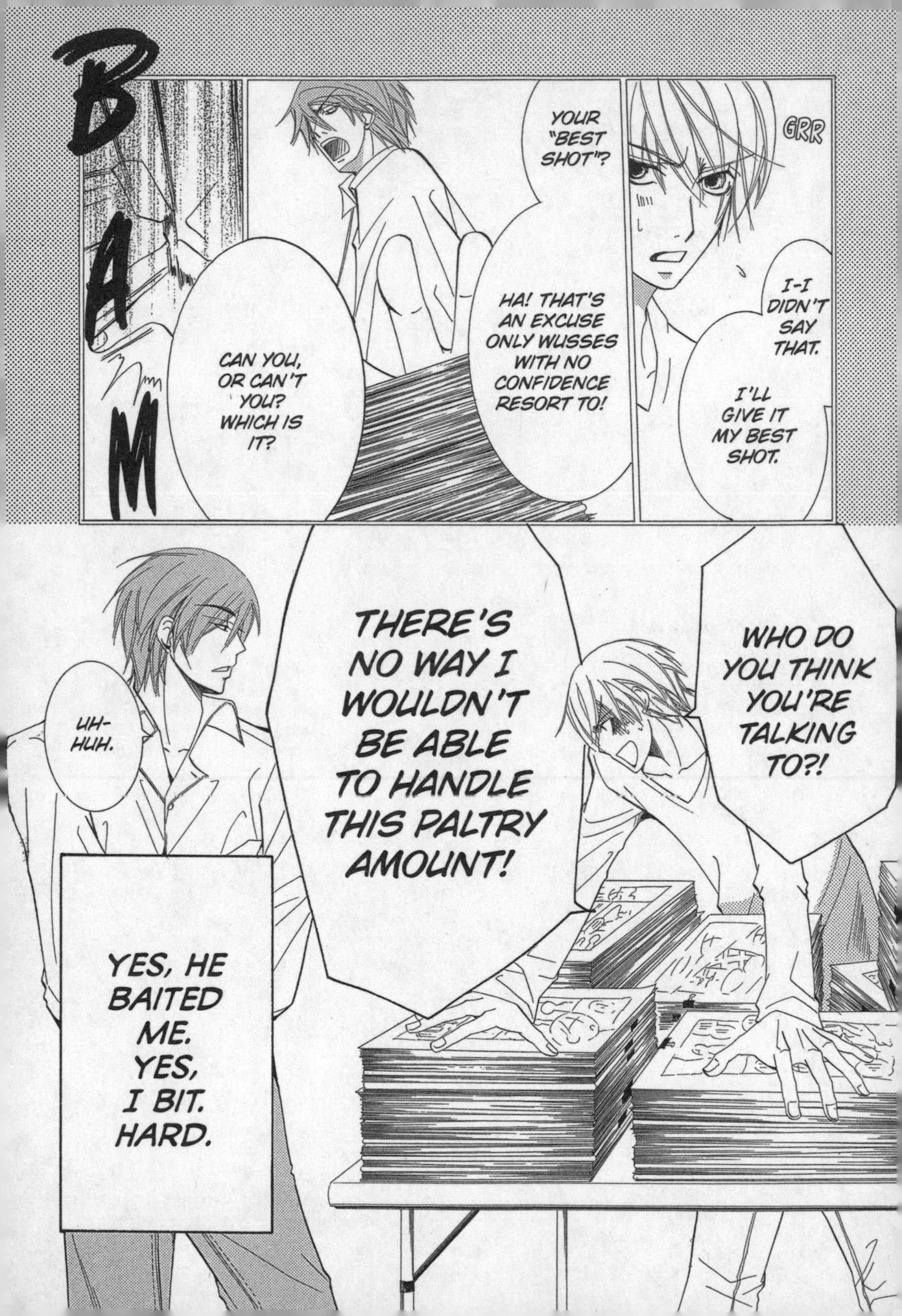
GRR
I-I DIDN'T SAY THAT.
I'LL GIVE IT MY BEST SHOT.
YOUR "BEST SHOT"?
HA! THAT'S AN EXCUSE ONLY WUSSES WITH NO CONFIDENCE RESORT TO!
CAN YOU, OR CAN'T YOU? WHICH IS IT?
BAM
WHO DO YOU THINK YOU'RE TALKING TO?!
THERE'S NO WAY I WOULDN'T BE ABLE TO HANDLE THIS PALTRY AMOUNT!
UH-HUH.
YES, HE BAITED ME. YES, I BIT. HARD.

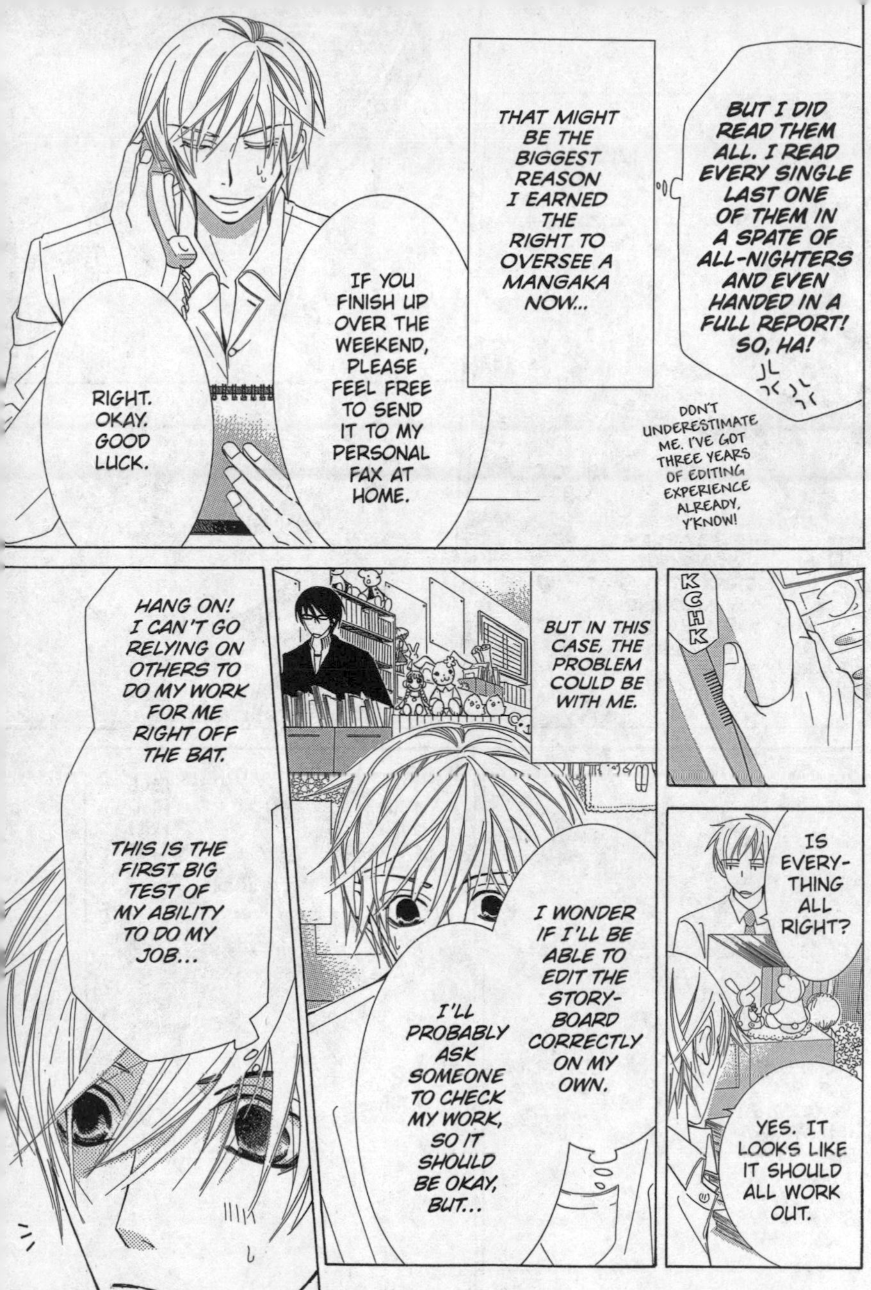
BUT I DID READ THEM ALL. I READ EVERY SINGLE LAST ONE OF THEM IN A SPATE OF ALL-NIGHTERS AND EVEN HANDED IN A FULL REPORT! SO, HA!
DON'T UNDERESTIMATE ME. I'VE GOT THREE YEARS OF EDITING EXPERIENCE ALREADY, Y'KNOW!
THAT MIGHT BE THE BIGGEST REASON I EARNED THE RIGHT TO OVERSEE A MANGAKA NOW...
IF YOU FINISH UP OVER THE WEEKEND, PLEASE FEEL FREE TO SEND IT TO MY PERSONAL FAX AT HOME.
RIGHT. OKAY. GOOD LUCK.
KCHK
IS EVERY-THING ALL RIGHT?
YES. IT LOOKS LIKE IT SHOULD ALL WORK OUT.
BUT IN THIS CASE, THE PROBLEM COULD BE WITH ME.
I WONDER IF I'LL BE ABLE TO EDIT THE STORY-BOARD CORRECTLY ON MY OWN.
I'LL PROBABLY ASK SOMEONE TO CHECK MY WORK, SO IT SHOULD BE OKAY, BUT...
HANG ON! I CAN'T GO RELYING ON OTHERS TO DO MY WORK FOR ME RIGHT OFF THE BAT.
THIS IS THE FIRST BIG TEST OF MY ABILITY TO DO MY JOB...

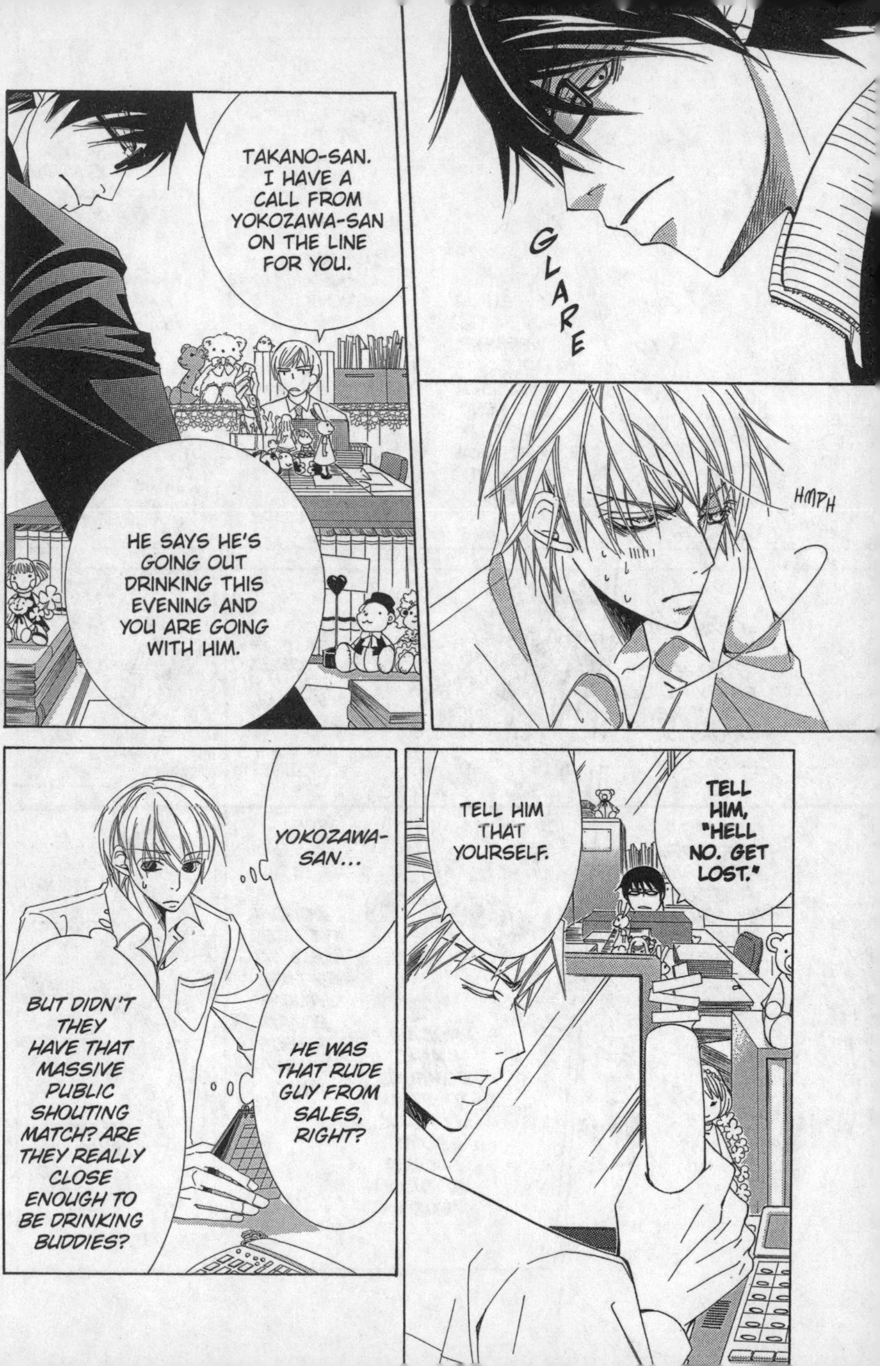
GLARE
HMPH
TAKANO-SAN. I HAVE A CALL FROM YOKOZAWA-SAN ON THE LINE FOR YOU.
HE SAYS HE'S GOING OUT DRINKING THIS EVENING AND YOU ARE GOING WITH HIM.
TELL HIM, "HELL NO. GET LOST."
TELL HIM THAT YOURSELF.
YOKOZAWA-SAN...
HE WAS THAT RUDE GUY FROM SALES, RIGHT?
BUT DIDN'T THEY HAVE THAT MASSIVE PUBLIC SHOUTING MATCH? ARE THEY REALLY CLOSE ENOUGH TO BE DRINKING BUDDIES?

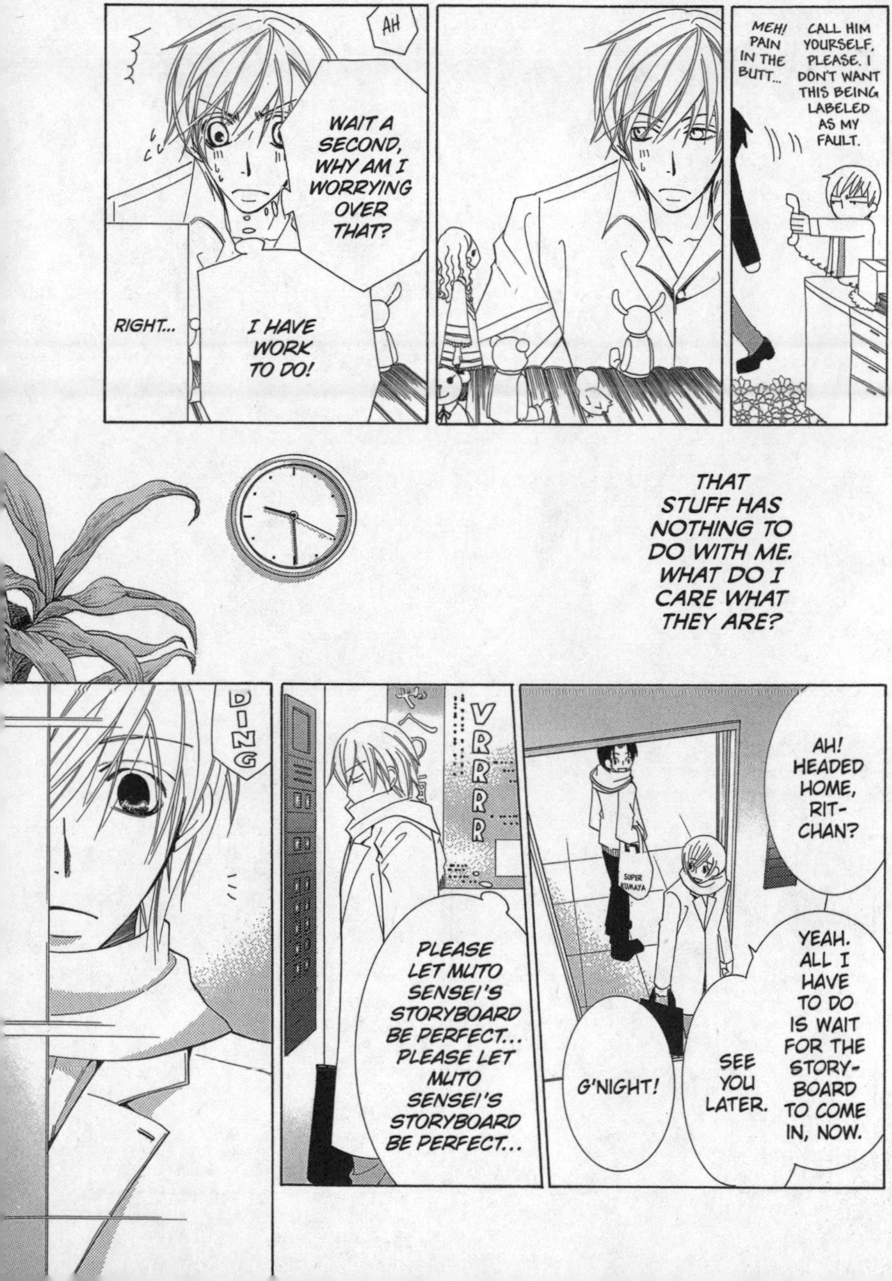
CALL HIM YOURSELF, PLEASE. I DON'T WANT THIS BEING LABELED AS MY FAULT.
MEH! PAIN IN THE BUTT...
AH
WAIT A SECOND, WHY AM I WORRYING OVER THAT?
I HAVE WORK TO DO!
RIGHT...
THAT STUFF HAS NOTHING TO DO WITH ME. WHAT DO I CARE WHAT THEY ARE?
AH! HEADED HOME, RIT-CHAN?
YEAH. ALL I HAVE TO DO IS WAIT FOR THE STORY-BOARD TO COME IN, NOW.
SEE YOU LATER.
SUPER KUMAYA
G'NIGHT!
VRRRR
PLEASE LET MUTO SENSEI'S STORYBOARD BE PERFECT... PLEASE LET MUTO SENSEI'S STORYBOARD BE PERFECT...
DING

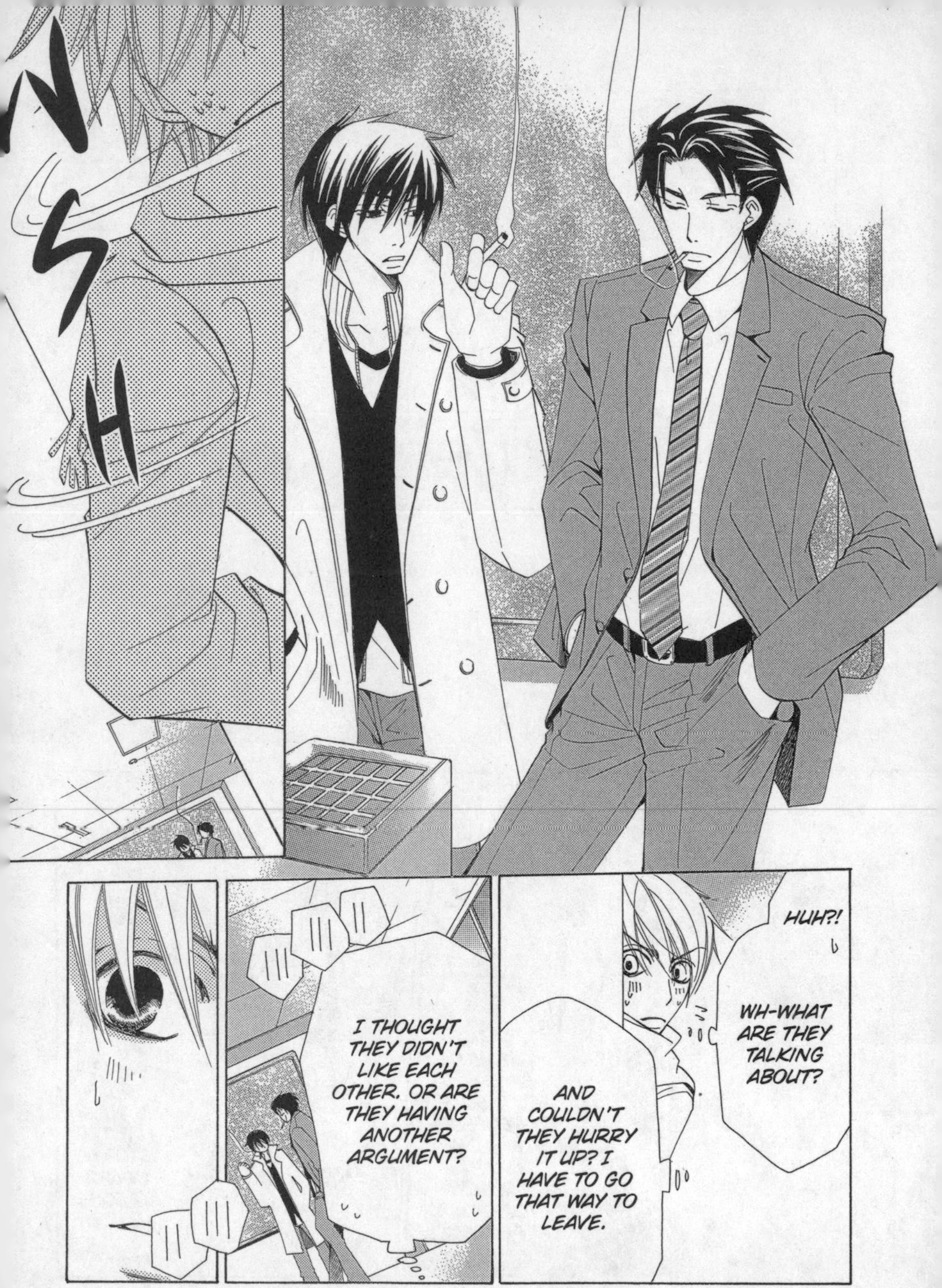
HUH?!
WH-WHAT ARE THEY TALKING ABOUT?
AND COULDN'T THEY HURRY IT UP? I HAVE TO GO THAT WAY TO LEAVE.
I THOUGHT THEY DIDN'T LIKE EACH OTHER. OR ARE THEY HAVING ANOTHER ARGUMENT?

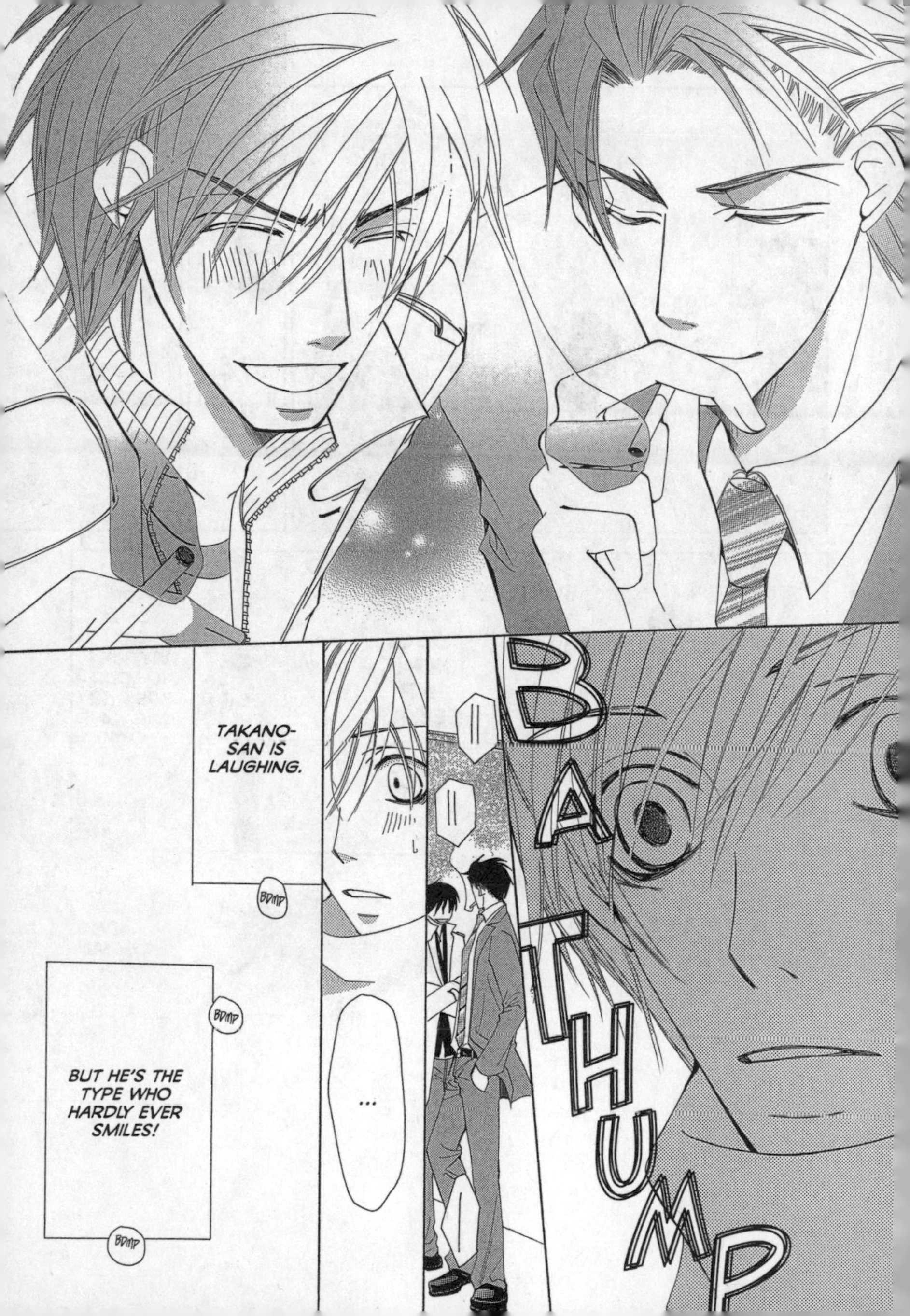
BA-THUMP
!!
...
TAKANO-SAN IS LAUGHING.
BDMP
BDMP
BUT HE'S THE TYPE WHO HARDLY EVER SMILES!
BDMP

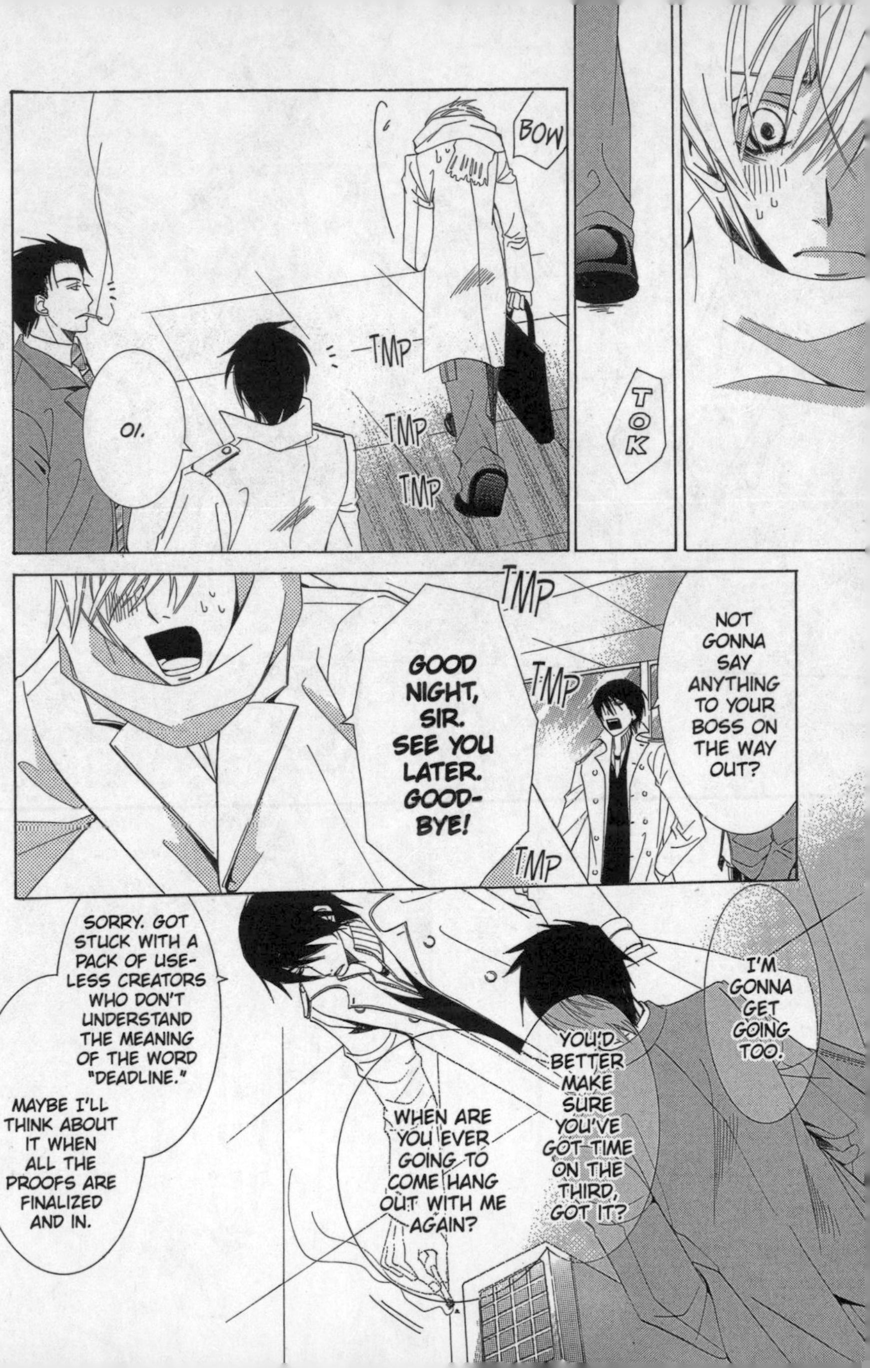
TOK
BOW
TMP
TMP
TMP
OI.
NOT GONNA SAY ANYTHING TO YOUR BOSS ON THE WAY OUT?
TMP
TMP
GOOD NIGHT, SIR. SEE YOU LATER. GOOD-BYE!
TMP
I'M GONNA GET GOING TOO.
YOU'D BETTER MAKE SURE YOU'VE GOT TIME ON THE THIRD, GOT IT?
WHEN ARE YOU EVER GOING TO COME HANG OUT WITH ME AGAIN?
SORRY. GOT STUCK WITH A PACK OF USELESS CREATORS WHO DON'T UNDERSTAND THE MEANING OF THE WORD "DEADLINE."
MAYBE I'LL THINK ABOUT IT WHEN ALL THE PROOFS ARE FINALIZED AND IN.

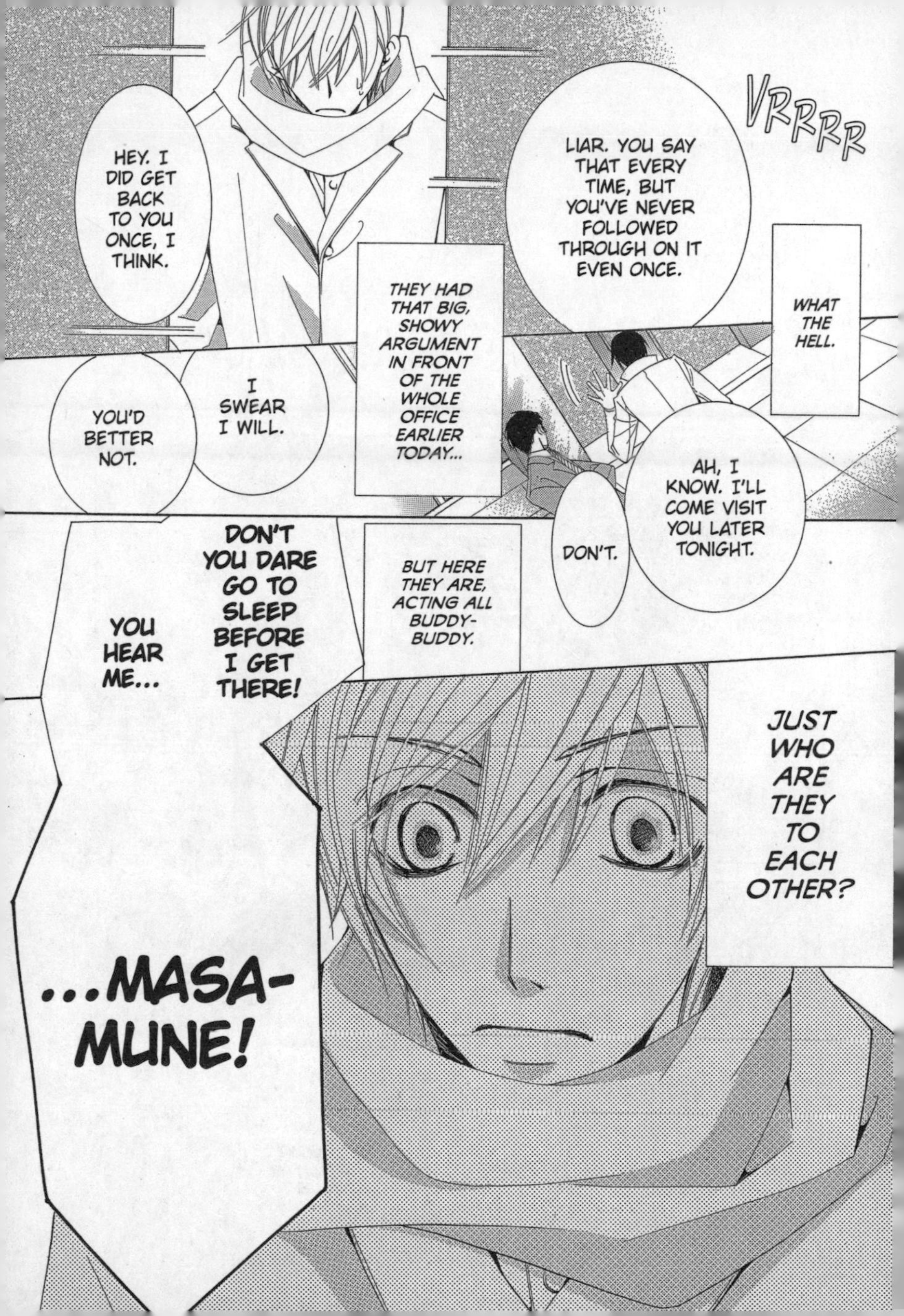
VRRRR
LIAR. YOU SAY THAT EVERY TIME, BUT YOU'VE NEVER FOLLOWED THROUGH ON IT EVEN ONCE.
HEY. I DID GET BACK TO YOU ONCE, I THINK.
WHAT THE HELL.
THEY HAD THAT BIG, SHOWY ARGUMENT IN FRONT OF THE WHOLE OFFICE EARLIER TODAY...
I SWEAR I WILL.
YOU'D BETTER NOT.
AH, I KNOW. I'LL COME VISIT YOU LATER TONIGHT.
DON'T.
BUT HERE THEY ARE, ACTING ALL BUDDY-BUDDY.
DON'T YOU DARE GO TO SLEEP BEFORE I GET THERE!
YOU HEAR ME...
...MASA-MUNE!
JUST WHO ARE THEY TO EACH OTHER?

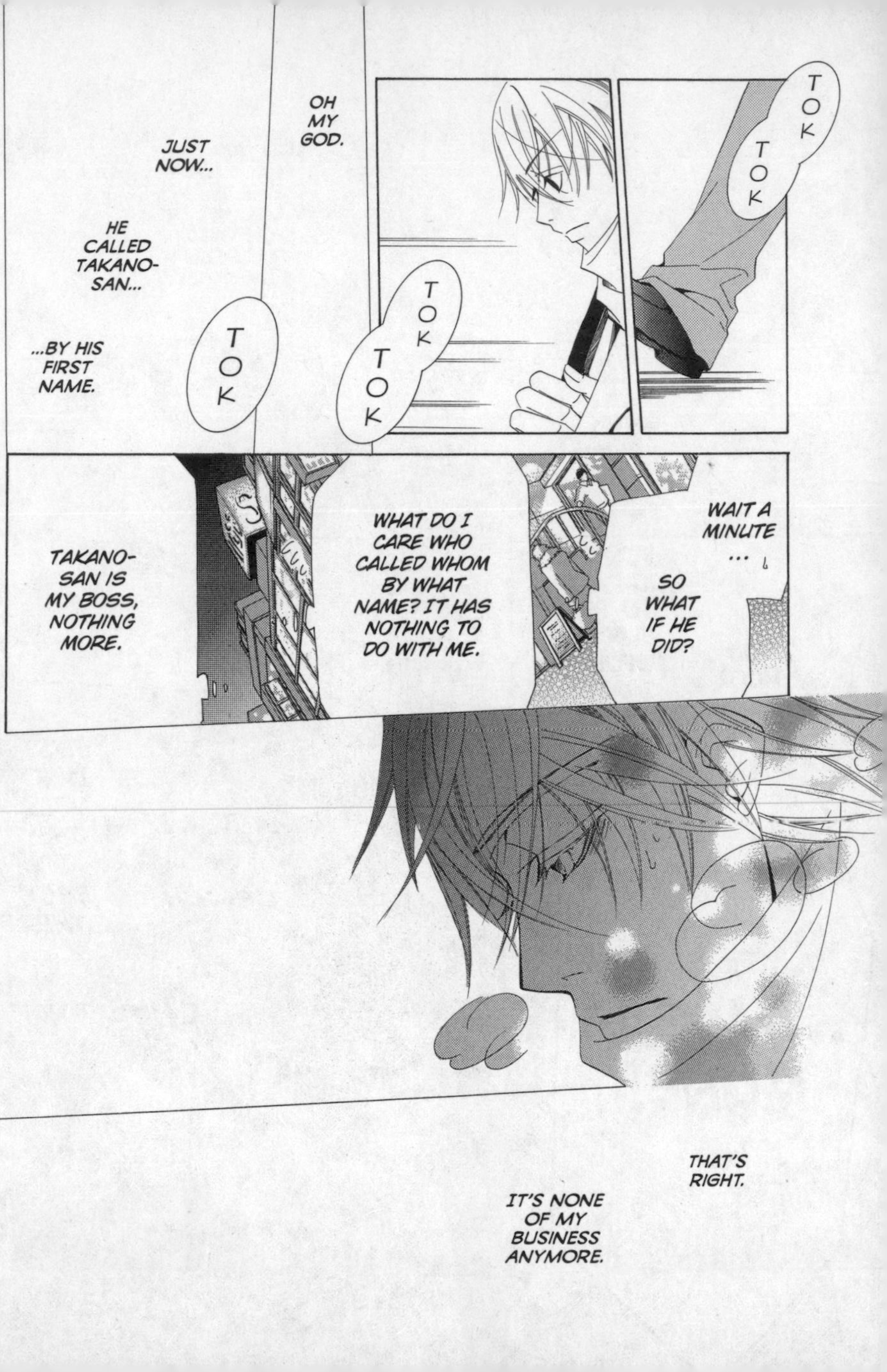
TOK TOK
TOK TOK
OH MY GOD.
TOK
JUST NOW...
HE CALLED TAKANO-SAN...
...BY HIS FIRST NAME.
WAIT A MINUTE...
SO WHAT IF HE DID?
WHAT DO I CARE WHO CALLED WHOM BY WHAT NAME? IT HAS NOTHING TO DO WITH ME.
TAKANO-SAN IS MY BOSS, NOTHING MORE.
THAT'S RIGHT.
IT'S NONE OF MY BUSINESS ANYMORE.

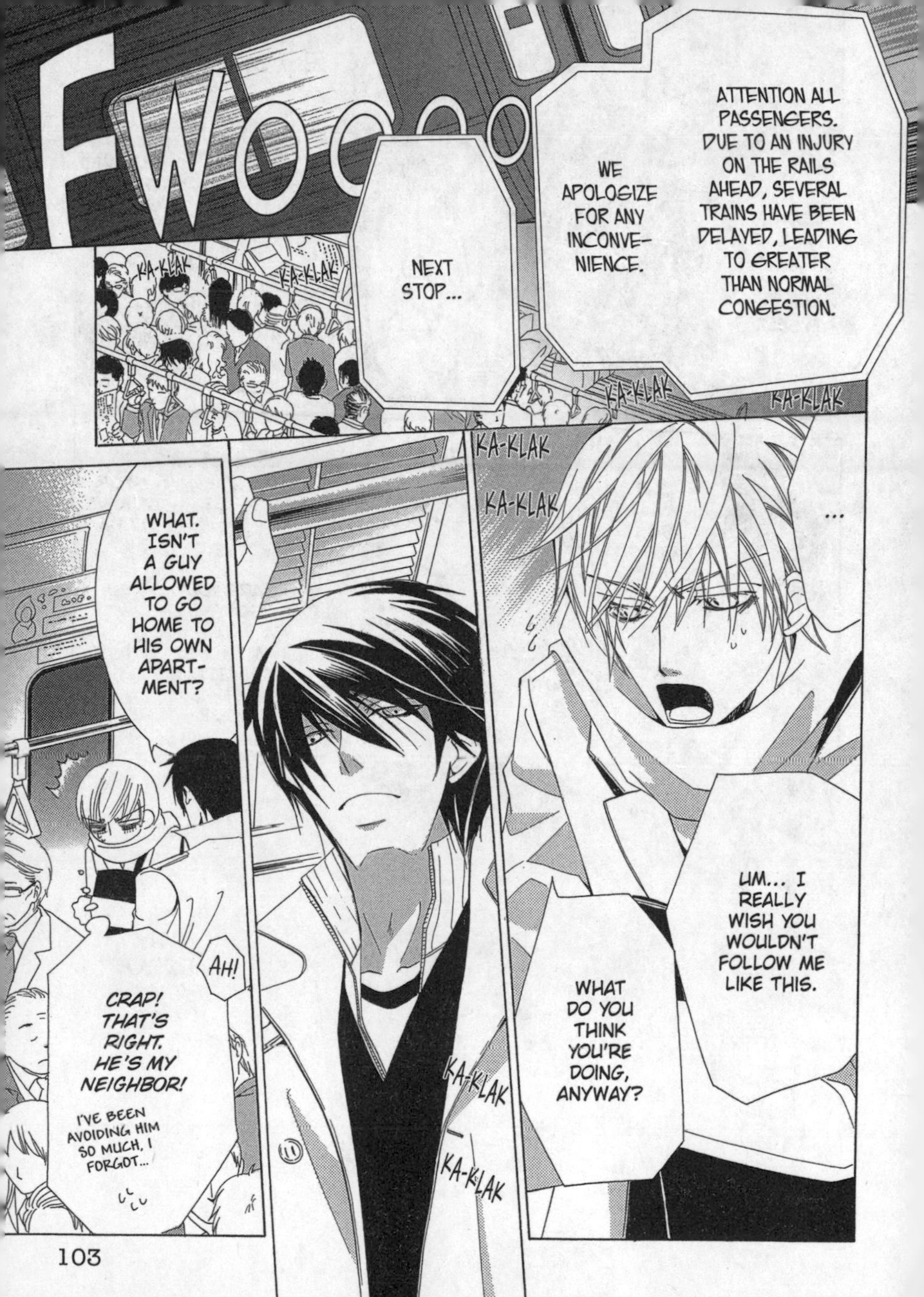
FWOOOO
ATTENTION ALL PASSENGERS. DUE TO AN INJURY ON THE RAILS AHEAD, SEVERAL TRAINS HAVE BEEN DELAYED, LEADING TO GREATER THAN NORMAL CONGESTION.
WE APOLOGIZE FOR ANY INCONVE- NIENCE.
NEXT STOP...
KA-KLAK
KA-KLAK
KA-KLAK
KA-KLAK
KA-KLAK
KA-KLAK
...
UM... I REALLY WISH YOU WOULDN'T FOLLOW ME LIKE THIS.
WHAT DO YOU THINK YOU'RE DOING, ANYWAY?
KA-KLAK
KA-KLAK
WHAT. ISN'T A GUY ALLOWED TO GO HOME TO HIS OWN APART- MENT?
AH!
CRAP! THAT'S RIGHT. HE'S MY NEIGHBOR!
I'VE BEEN AVOIDING HIM SO MUCH, I FORGOT...

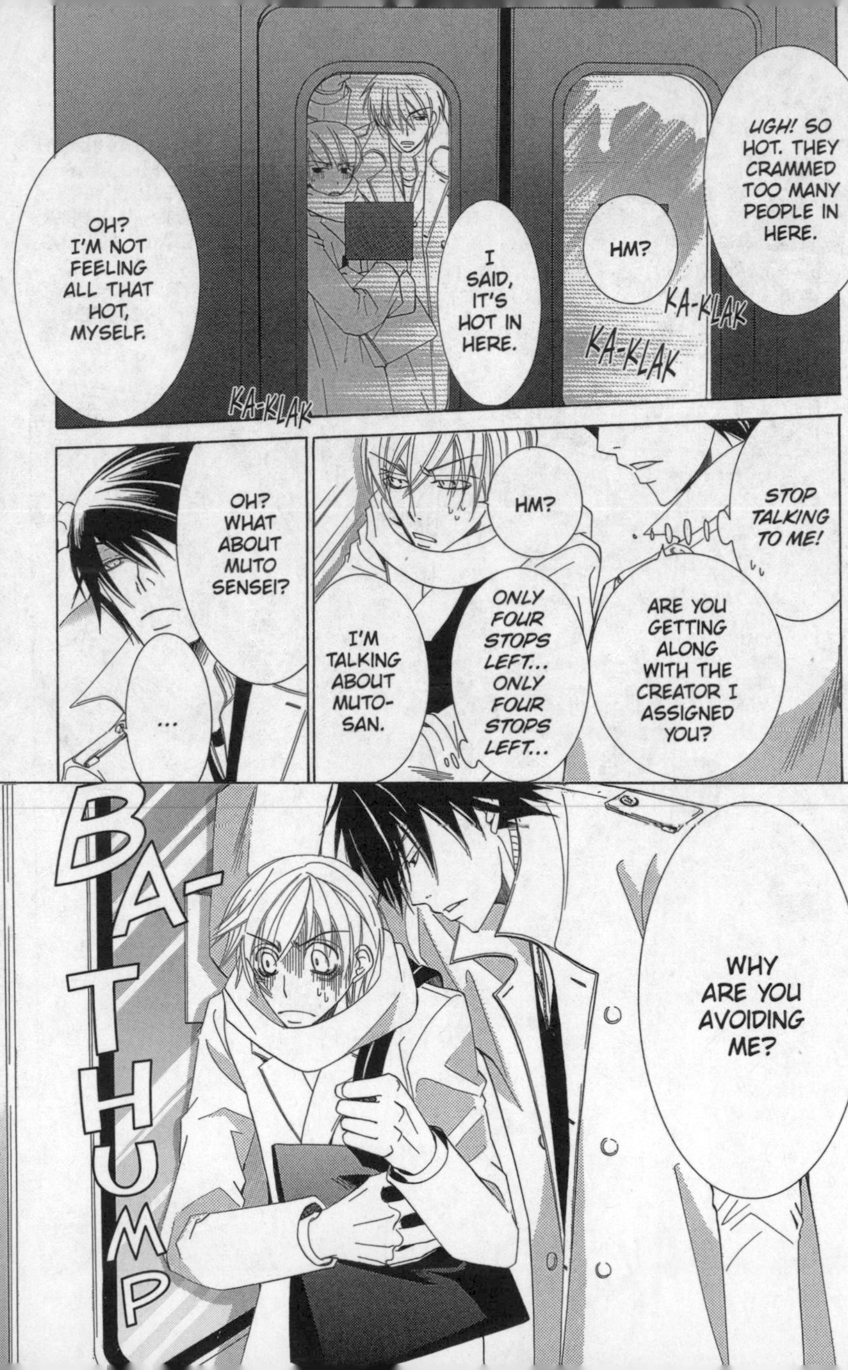
UGH! SO HOT. THEY CRAMMED TOO MANY PEOPLE IN HERE.
HM?
KA-KLAK
KA-KLAK
I SAID, IT'S HOT IN HERE.
OH? I'M NOT FEELING ALL THAT HOT, MYSELF.
KA-KLAK
STOP TALKING TO ME!
HM?
ARE YOU GETTING ALONG WITH THE CREATOR I ASSIGNED YOU?
ONLY FOUR STOPS LEFT... ONLY FOUR STOPS LEFT...
I'M TALKING ABOUT MUTO-SAN.
OH? WHAT ABOUT MUTO SENSEI?
...
WHY ARE YOU AVOIDING ME?
BA-THUMP

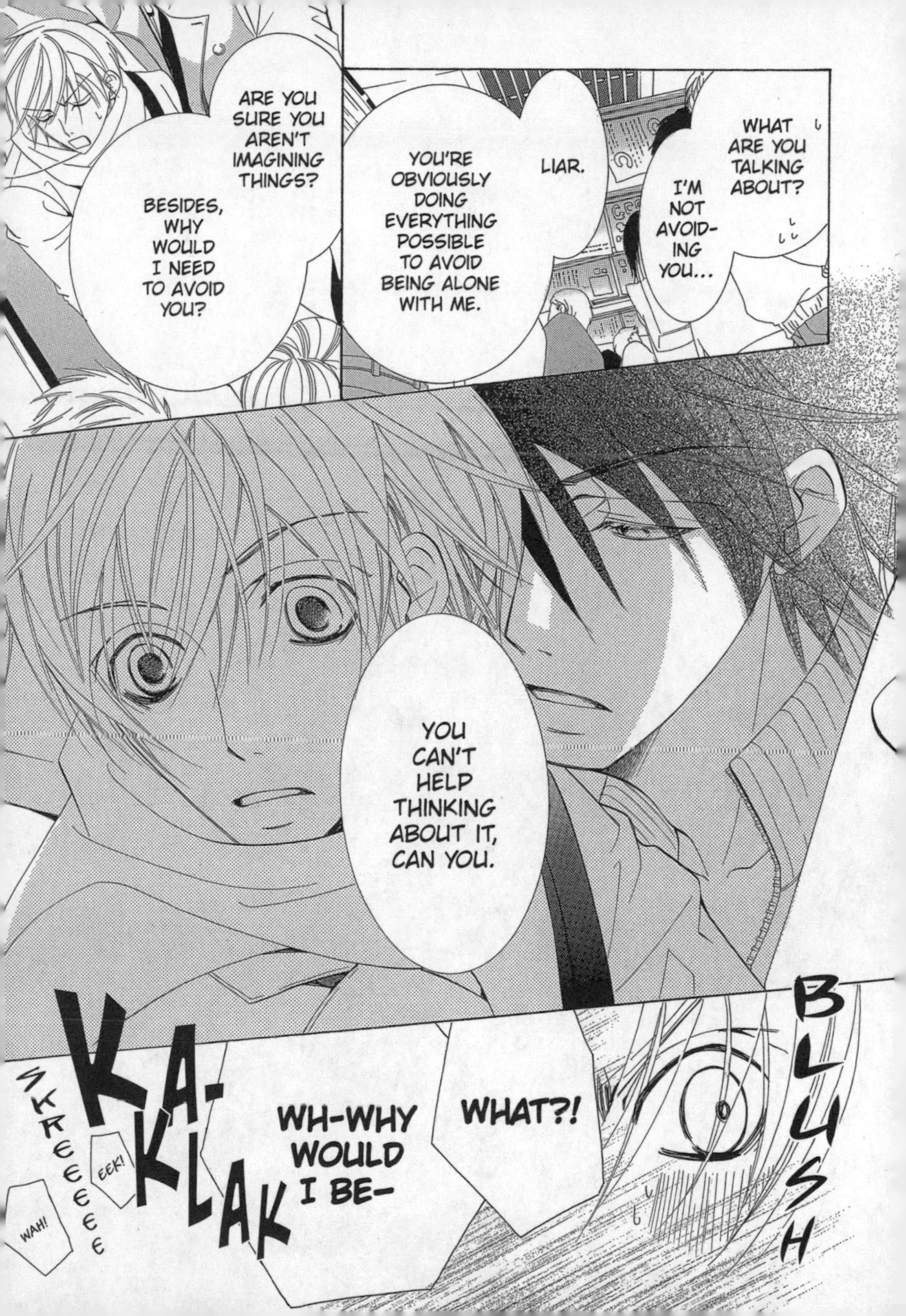
WHAT ARE YOU TALKING ABOUT?
I'M NOT AVOID-ING YOU...
LIAR.
YOU'RE OBVIOUSLY DOING EVERYTHING POSSIBLE TO AVOID BEING ALONE WITH ME.
ARE YOU SURE YOU AREN'T IMAGINING THINGS?
BESIDES, WHY WOULD I NEED TO AVOID YOU?
YOU CAN'T HELP THINKING ABOUT IT, CAN YOU.
BLUSH
WHAT?!
WH-WHY WOULD I BE-
KA-KLAK
SKREEEEEEE
EEK!
WAH!

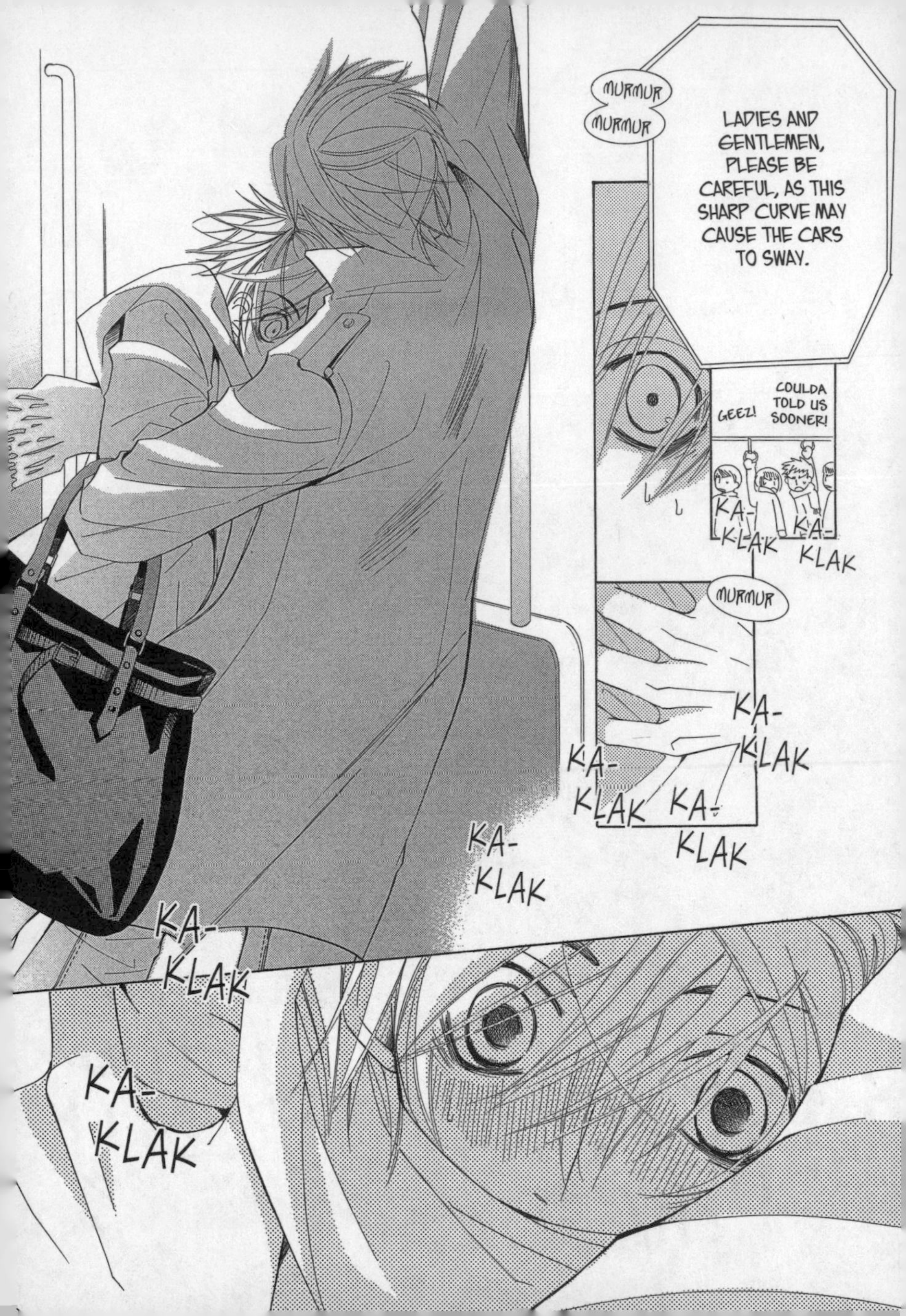
MURMUR
MURMUR
LADIES AND GENTLEMEN, PLEASE BE CAREFUL, AS THIS SHARP CURVE MAY CAUSE THE CARS TO SWAY.
COULDA TOLD US SOONER!
GEEZ!
KA-KLAK
KA-KLAK
MURMUR
KA-KLAK
KA-KLAK
KA-KLAK
KA-KLAK
KA-KLAK
KA-KLAK

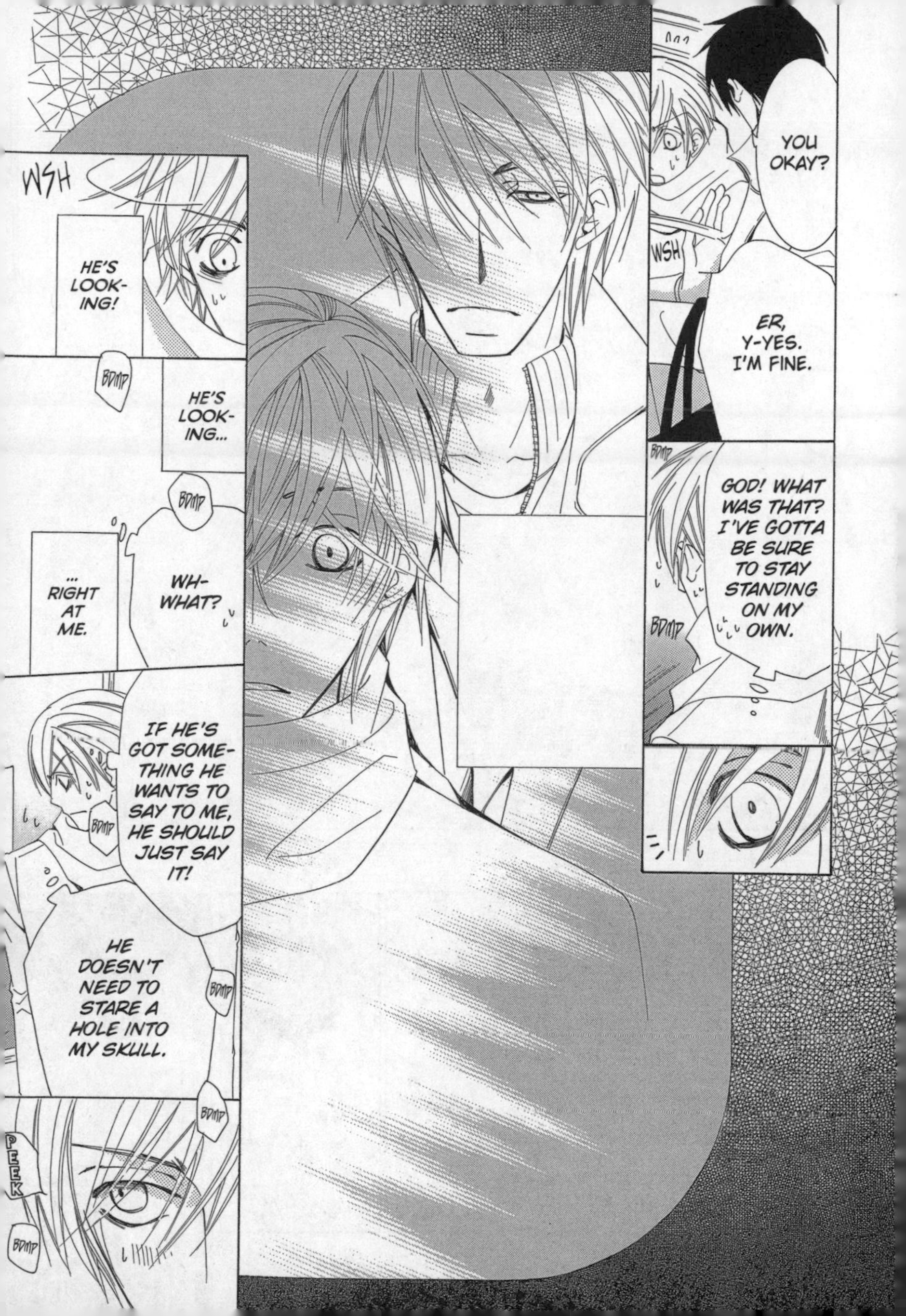
YOU OKAY?
WSH
ER, Y-YES. I'M FINE.
BDMP
GOD! WHAT WAS THAT? I'VE GOTTA BE SURE TO STAY STANDING ON MY OWN.
BDMP
WSH
HE'S LOOKING!
BDMP
HE'S LOOKING...
BDMP
WH-WHAT?
...RIGHT AT ME.
IF HE'S GOT SOMETHING HE WANTS TO SAY TO ME, HE SHOULD JUST SAY IT!
BDMP
HE DOESN'T NEED TO STARE A HOLE INTO MY SKULL.
BDMP
BDMP
PEEK
BDMP

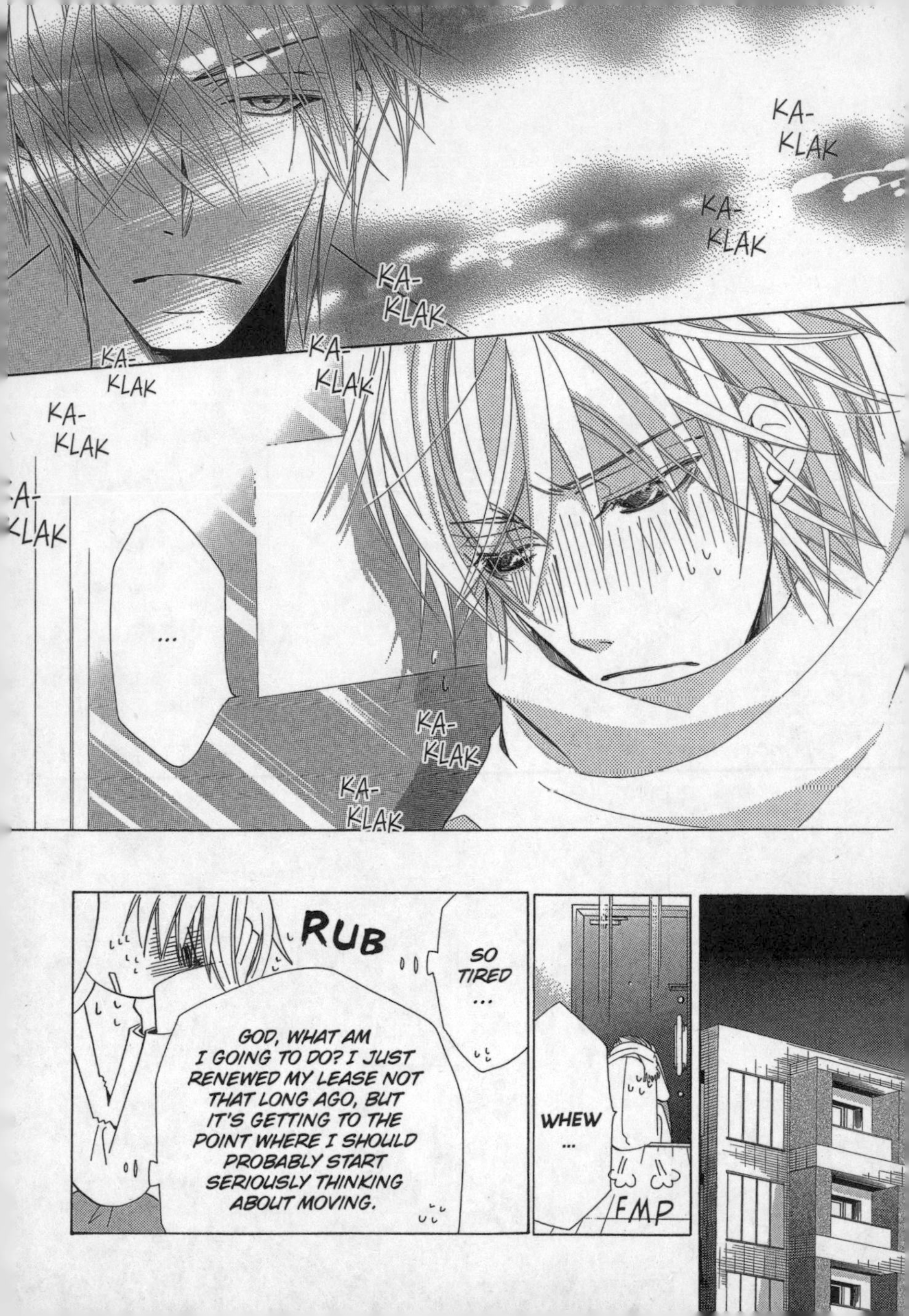
KA-
KLAK
KA-
KLAK
KA-
KLAK
KA-
KLAK
KA-
KLAK
KA-
KLAK
KA-
KLAK
...
KA-
KLAK
KA-
KLAK
WHEW
...
FMP
RUB
SO
TIRED
...
GOD, WHAT AM I GOING TO DO? I JUST RENEWED MY LEASE NOT THAT LONG AGO, BUT IT'S GETTING TO THE POINT WHERE I SHOULD PROBABLY START SERIOUSLY THINKING ABOUT MOVING.

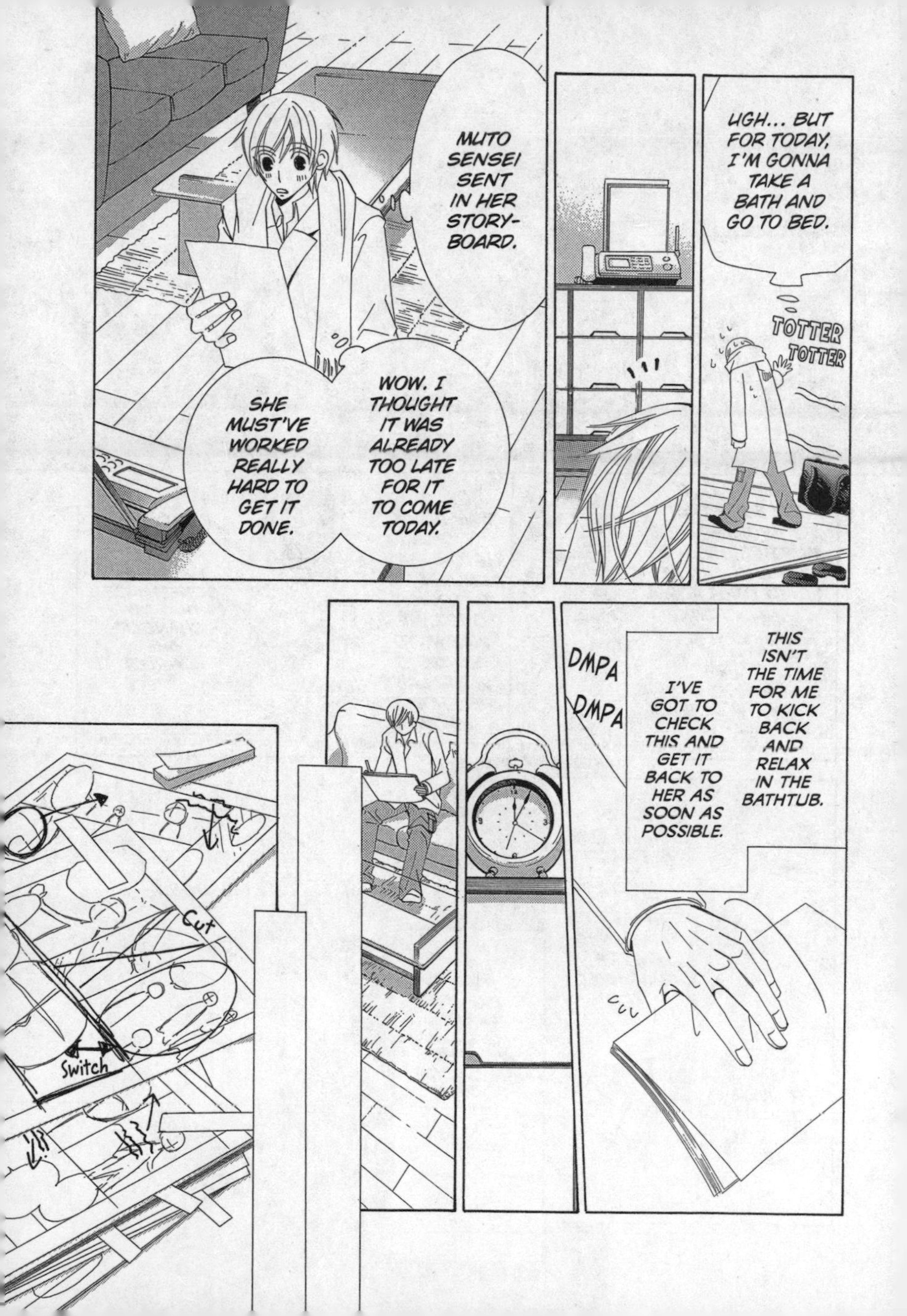
UGH... BUT FOR TODAY, I'M GONNA TAKE A BATH AND GO TO BED.
TOTTER TOTTER
MUTO SENSEI SENT IN HER STORY-BOARD.
WOW. I THOUGHT IT WAS ALREADY TOO LATE FOR IT TO COME TODAY.
SHE MUST'VE WORKED REALLY HARD TO GET IT DONE.
THIS ISN'T THE TIME FOR ME TO KICK BACK AND RELAX IN THE BATHTUB.
I'VE GOT TO CHECK THIS AND GET IT BACK TO HER AS SOON AS POSSIBLE.
DMPA DMPA
Cut
Switch

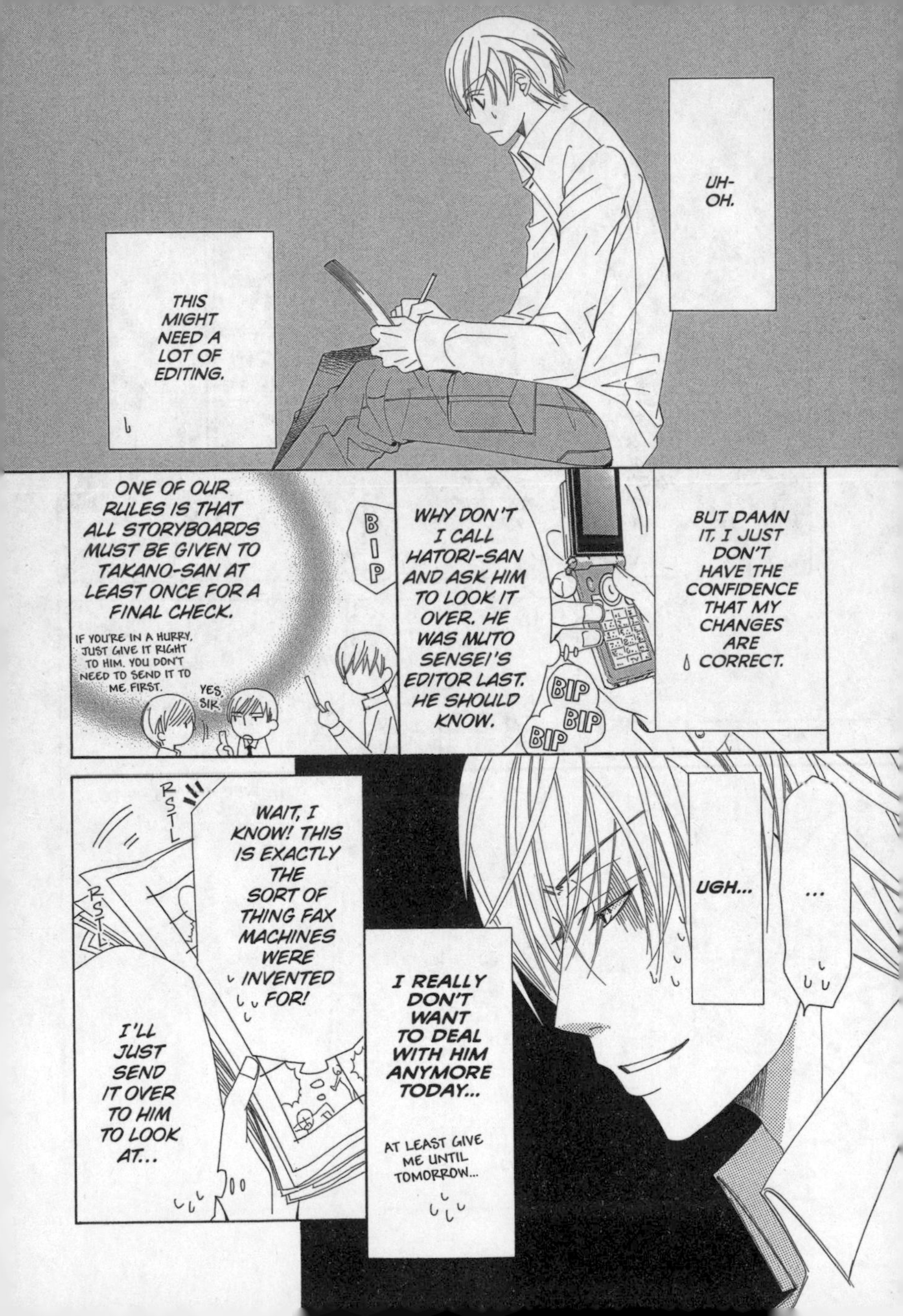
UH-OH.
THIS MIGHT NEED A LOT OF EDITING.
BUT DAMN IT, I JUST DON'T HAVE THE CONFIDENCE THAT MY CHANGES ARE CORRECT.
BIP BIP BIP
WHY DON'T I CALL HATORI-SAN AND ASK HIM TO LOOK IT OVER. HE WAS MUTO SENSEI'S EDITOR LAST. HE SHOULD KNOW.
BIP
ONE OF OUR RULES IS THAT ALL STORYBOARDS MUST BE GIVEN TO TAKANO-SAN AT LEAST ONCE FOR A FINAL CHECK.
IF YOU'RE IN A HURRY, JUST GIVE IT RIGHT TO HIM. YOU DON'T NEED TO SEND IT TO ME FIRST.
YES, SIR.
...
UGH...
I REALLY DON'T WANT TO DEAL WITH HIM ANYMORE TODAY...
AT LEAST GIVE ME UNTIL TOMORROW...
WAIT, I KNOW! THIS IS EXACTLY THE SORT OF THING FAX MACHINES WERE INVENTED FOR!
RSTL
RSTL
I'LL JUST SEND IT OVER TO HIM TO LOOK AT...

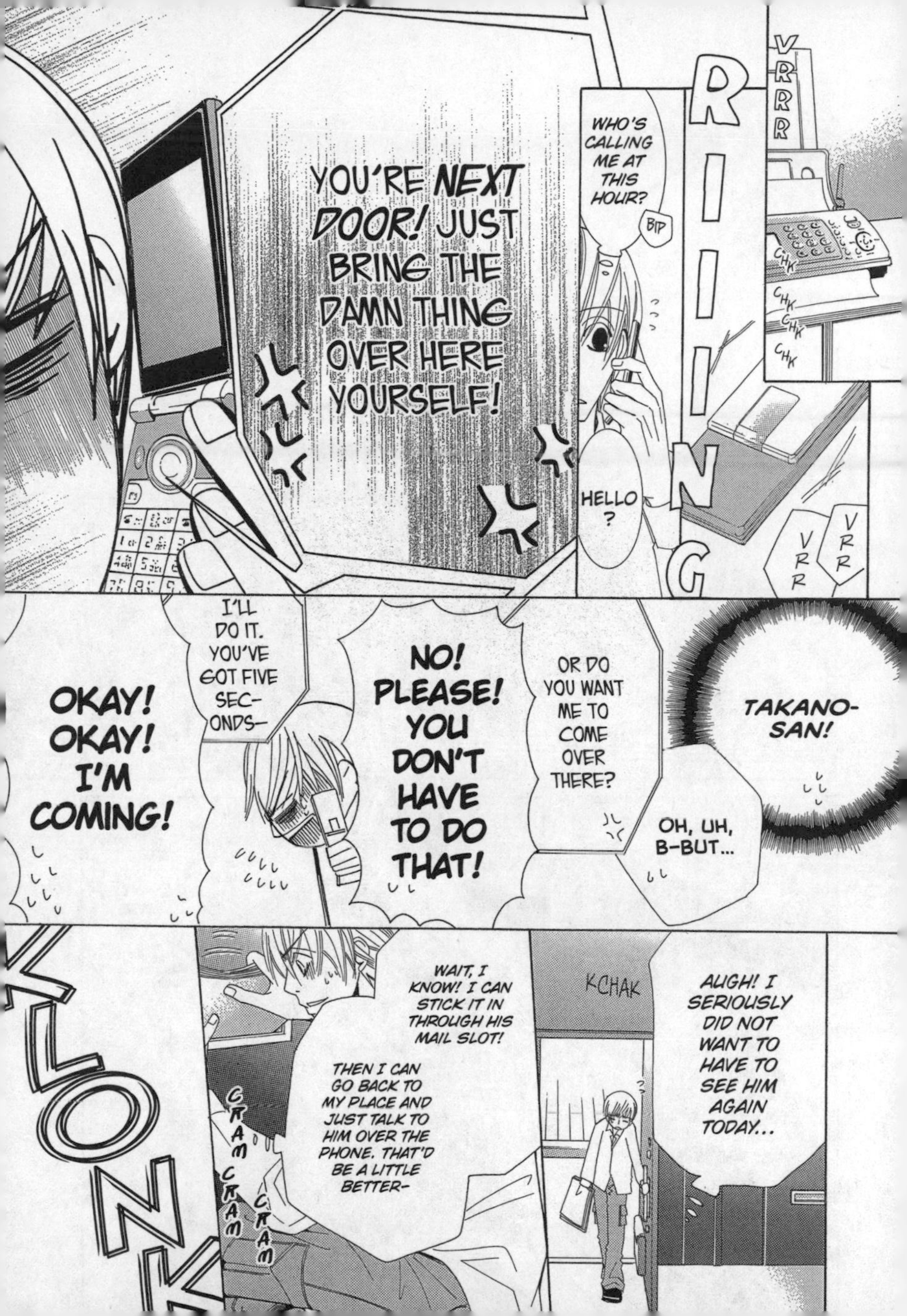
VRRR
CHK
CHK
CHK
CHK
RIIING
WHO'S CALLING ME AT THIS HOUR?
BIP
HELLO?
VRR
VRR
YOU'RE NEXT DOOR! JUST BRING THE DAMN THING OVER HERE YOURSELF!
TAKANO-SAN!
OH, UH, B-BUT...
OR DO YOU WANT ME TO COME OVER THERE?
NO! PLEASE! YOU DON'T HAVE TO DO THAT!
I'LL DO IT. YOU'VE GOT FIVE SEC-ONDS–
OKAY! OKAY! I'M COMING!
KCHAK
AUGH! I SERIOUSLY DID NOT WANT TO HAVE TO SEE HIM AGAIN TODAY...
WAIT, I KNOW! I CAN STICK IT IN THROUGH HIS MAIL SLOT!
THEN I CAN GO BACK TO MY PLACE AND JUST TALK TO HIM OVER THE PHONE. THAT'D BE A LITTLE BETTER–
CRAM
CRAM
CRAM
CRAM
KLONK

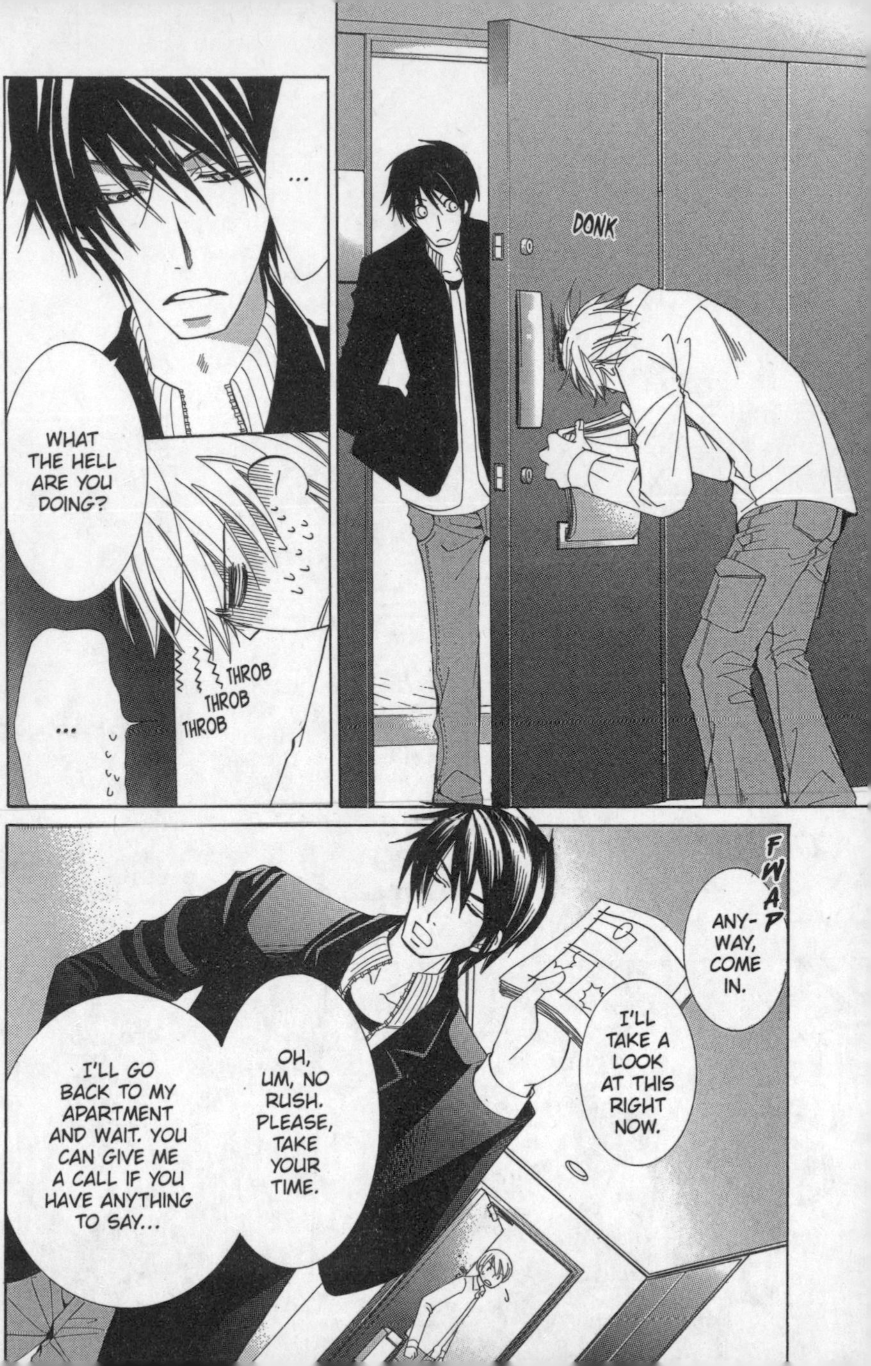
DONK
...
WHAT THE HELL ARE YOU DOING?
THROB
THROB
THROB
...
FWAP
ANY-WAY, COME IN.
I'LL TAKE A LOOK AT THIS RIGHT NOW.
OH, UM, NO RUSH. PLEASE, TAKE YOUR TIME.
I'LL GO BACK TO MY APARTMENT AND WAIT. YOU CAN GIVE ME A CALL IF YOU HAVE ANYTHING TO SAY...

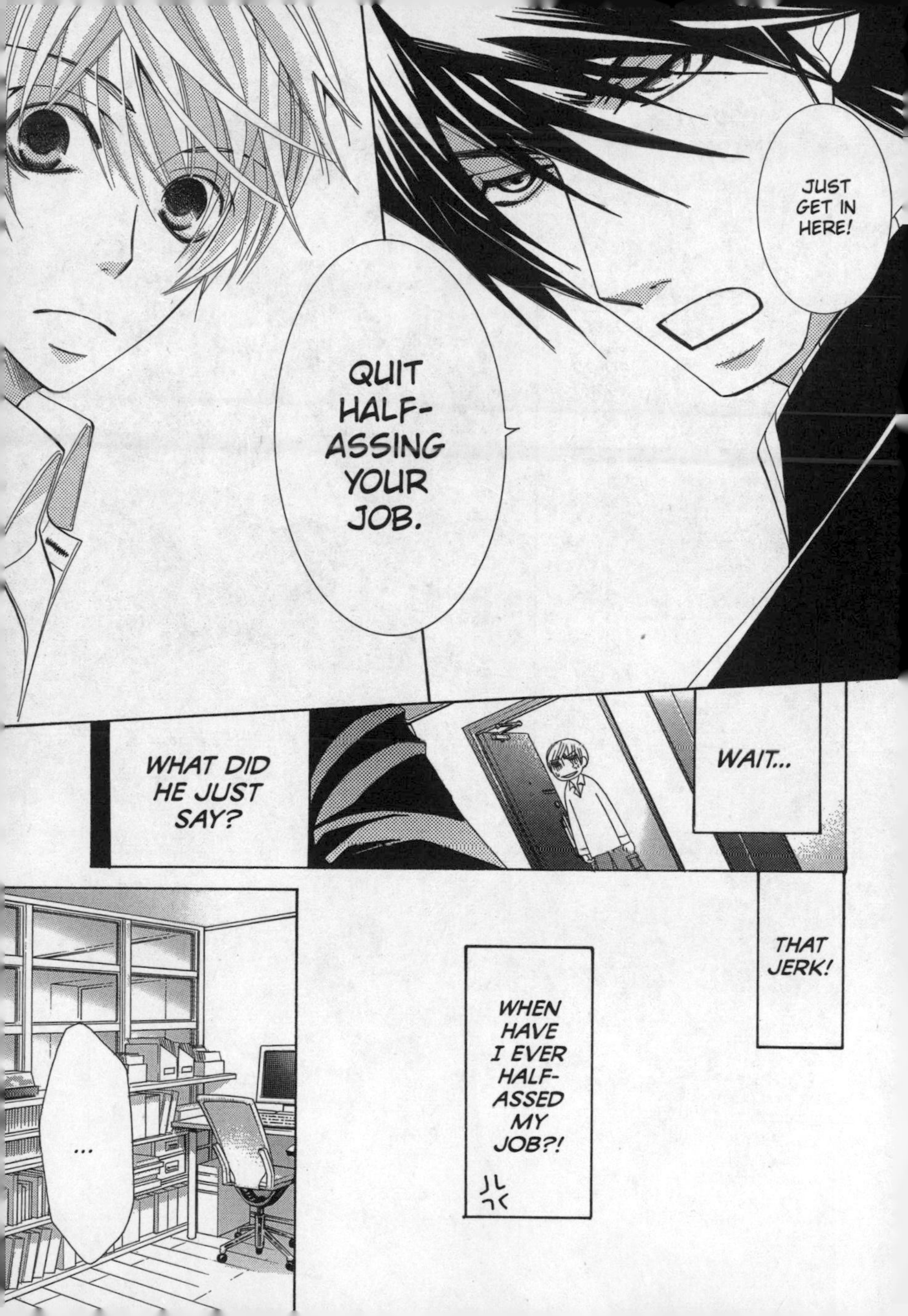
JUST GET IN HERE!
QUIT HALF-ASSING YOUR JOB.
WAIT...
WHAT DID HE JUST SAY?
THAT JERK!
WHEN HAVE I EVER HALF-ASSED MY JOB?!
...

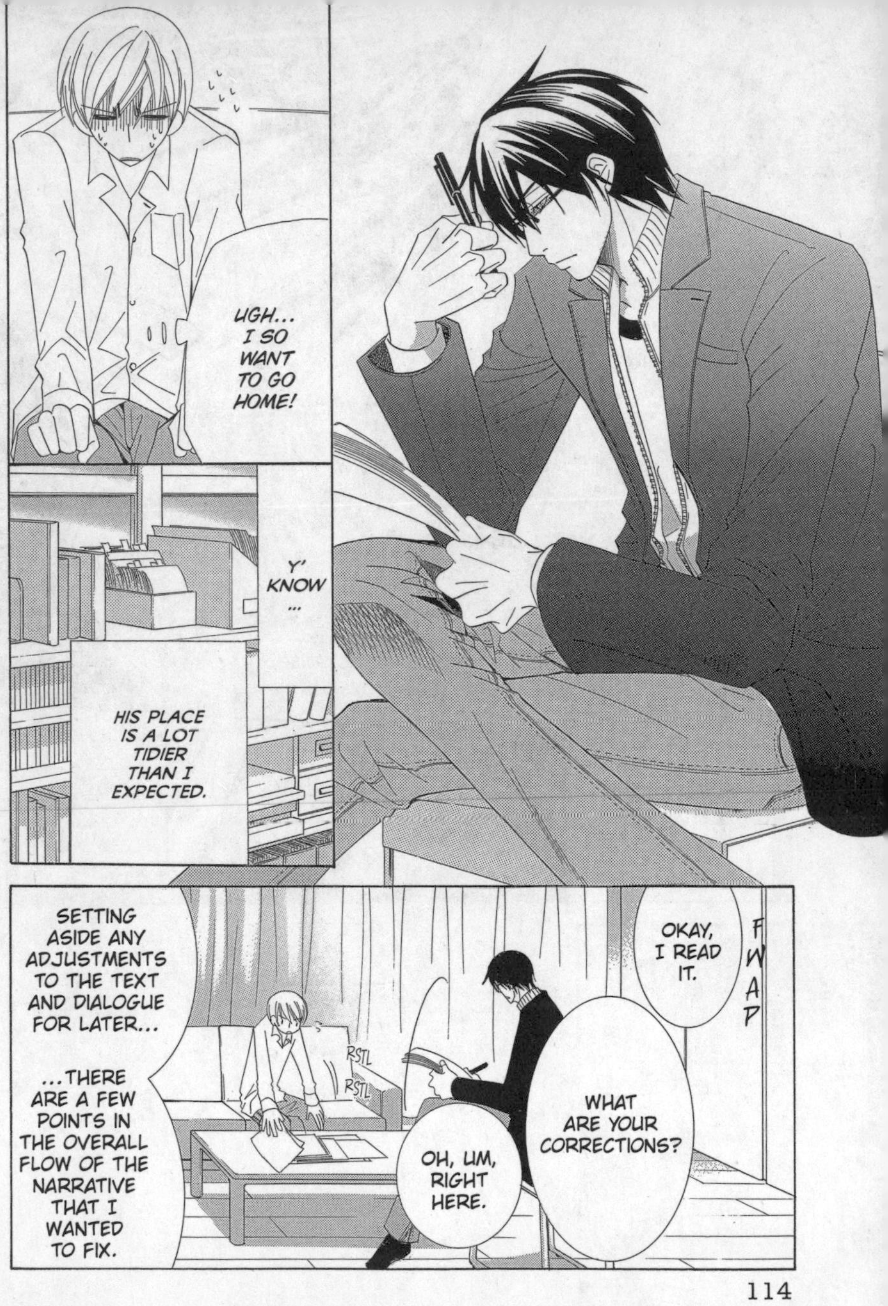
UGH... I SO WANT TO GO HOME!
Y' KNOW ...
HIS PLACE IS A LOT TIDIER THAN I EXPECTED.
OKAY, I READ IT.
FWAP
WHAT ARE YOUR CORRECTIONS?
OH, UM, RIGHT HERE.
RSTL
RSTL
SETTING ASIDE ANY ADJUSTMENTS TO THE TEXT AND DIALOGUE FOR LATER...
...THERE ARE A FEW POINTS IN THE OVERALL FLOW OF THE NARRATIVE THAT I WANTED TO FIX.

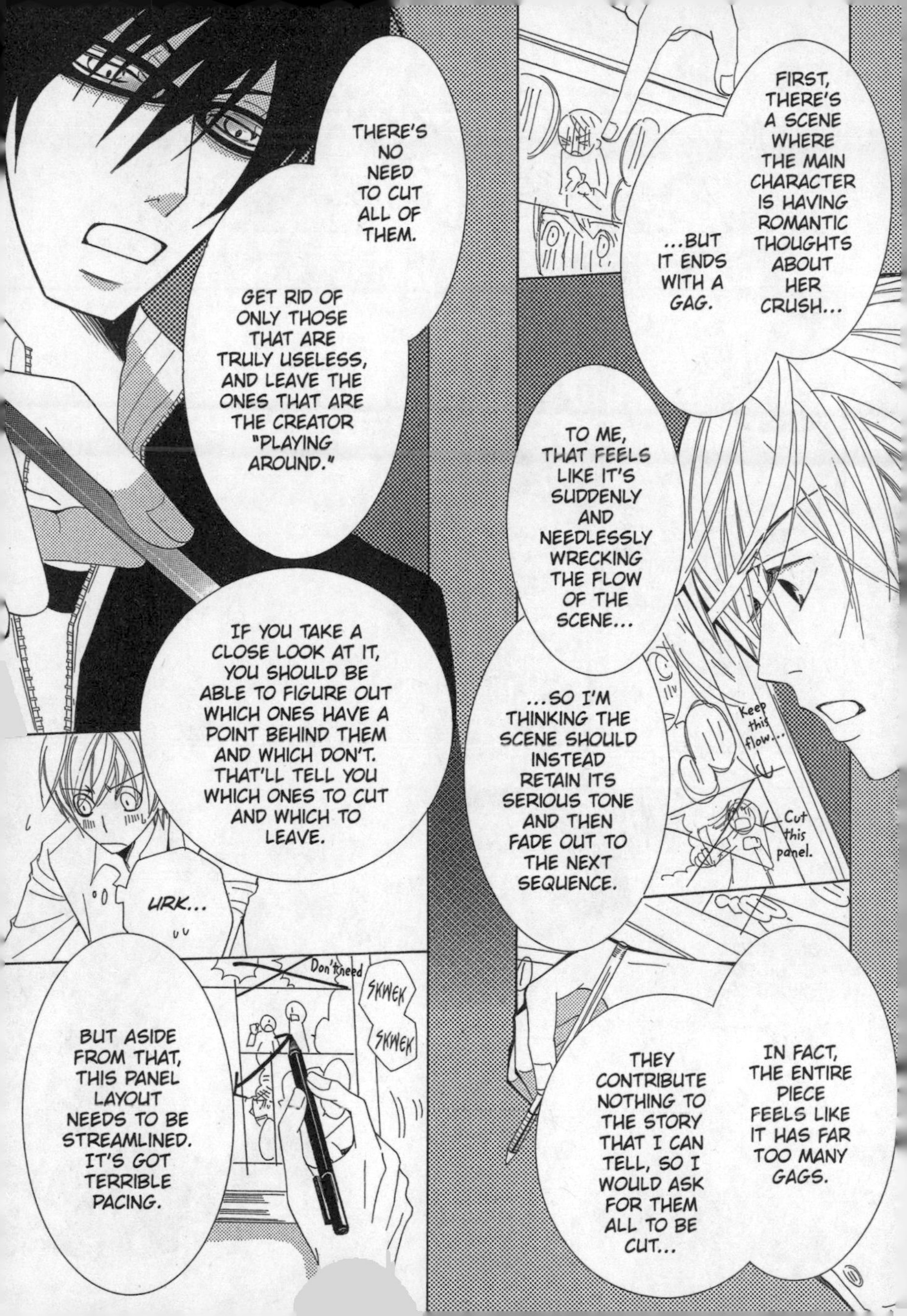
FIRST, THERE'S A SCENE WHERE THE MAIN CHARACTER IS HAVING ROMANTIC THOUGHTS ABOUT HER CRUSH...
...BUT IT ENDS WITH A GAG.
TO ME, THAT FEELS LIKE IT'S SUDDENLY AND NEEDLESSLY WRECKING THE FLOW OF THE SCENE...
Keep this flow...
Cut this panel.
...SO I'M THINKING THE SCENE SHOULD INSTEAD RETAIN ITS SERIOUS TONE AND THEN FADE OUT TO THE NEXT SEQUENCE.
IN FACT, THE ENTIRE PIECE FEELS LIKE IT HAS FAR TOO MANY GAGS.
THEY CONTRIBUTE NOTHING TO THE STORY THAT I CAN TELL, SO I WOULD ASK FOR THEM ALL TO BE CUT...
THERE'S NO NEED TO CUT ALL OF THEM.
GET RID OF ONLY THOSE THAT ARE TRULY USELESS, AND LEAVE THE ONES THAT ARE THE CREATOR "PLAYING AROUND."
IF YOU TAKE A CLOSE LOOK AT IT, YOU SHOULD BE ABLE TO FIGURE OUT WHICH ONES HAVE A POINT BEHIND THEM AND WHICH DON'T. THAT'LL TELL YOU WHICH ONES TO CUT AND WHICH TO LEAVE.
URK...
Don't need
SKWEK
SKWEK
BUT ASIDE FROM THAT, THIS PANEL LAYOUT NEEDS TO BE STREAMLINED. IT'S GOT TERRIBLE PACING.

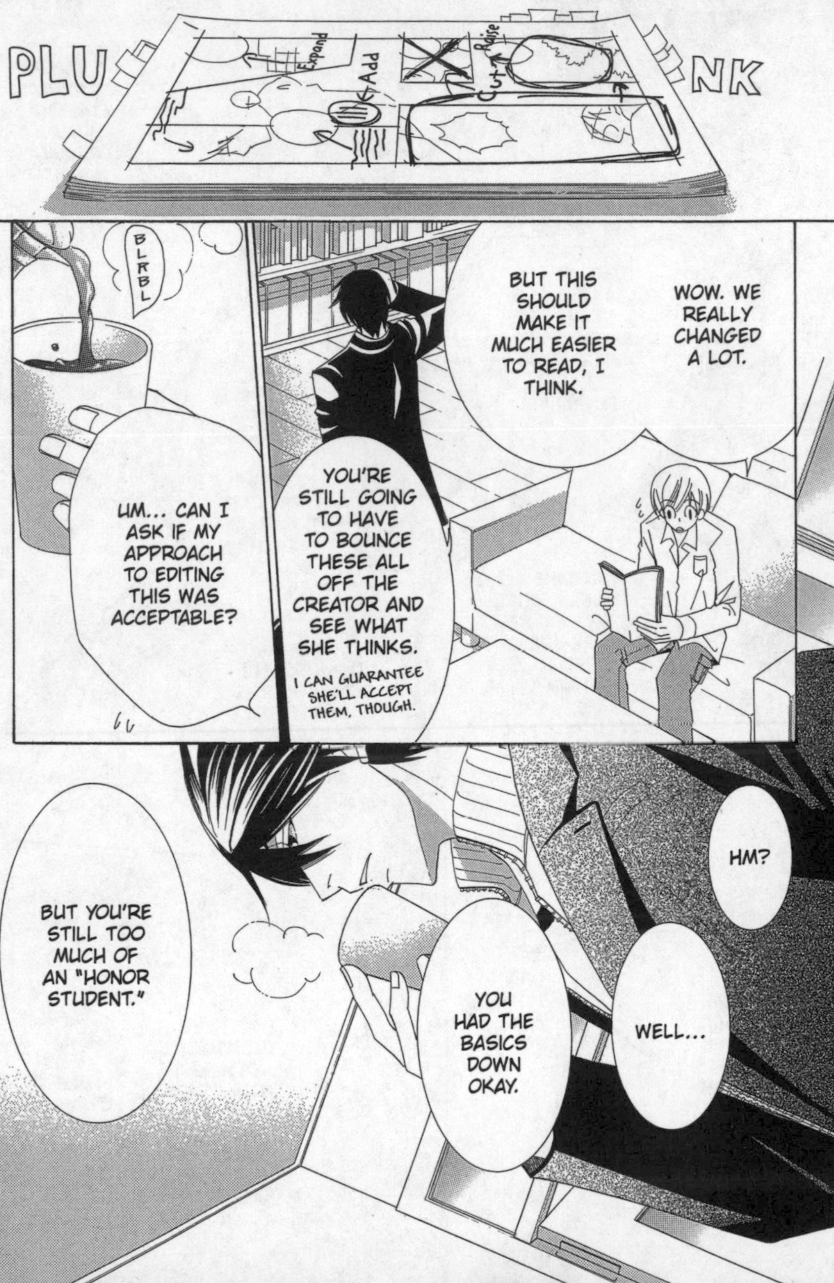
PLUNK
Expand
Add
Cut
Raise
WOW. WE REALLY CHANGED A LOT.
BUT THIS SHOULD MAKE IT MUCH EASIER TO READ, I THINK.
YOU'RE STILL GOING TO HAVE TO BOUNCE THESE ALL OFF THE CREATOR AND SEE WHAT SHE THINKS.
I CAN GUARANTEE SHE'LL ACCEPT THEM, THOUGH.
BLRBL
UM... CAN I ASK IF MY APPROACH TO EDITING THIS WAS ACCEPTABLE?
HM?
WELL...
YOU HAD THE BASICS DOWN OKAY.
BUT YOU'RE STILL TOO MUCH OF AN "HONOR STUDENT."

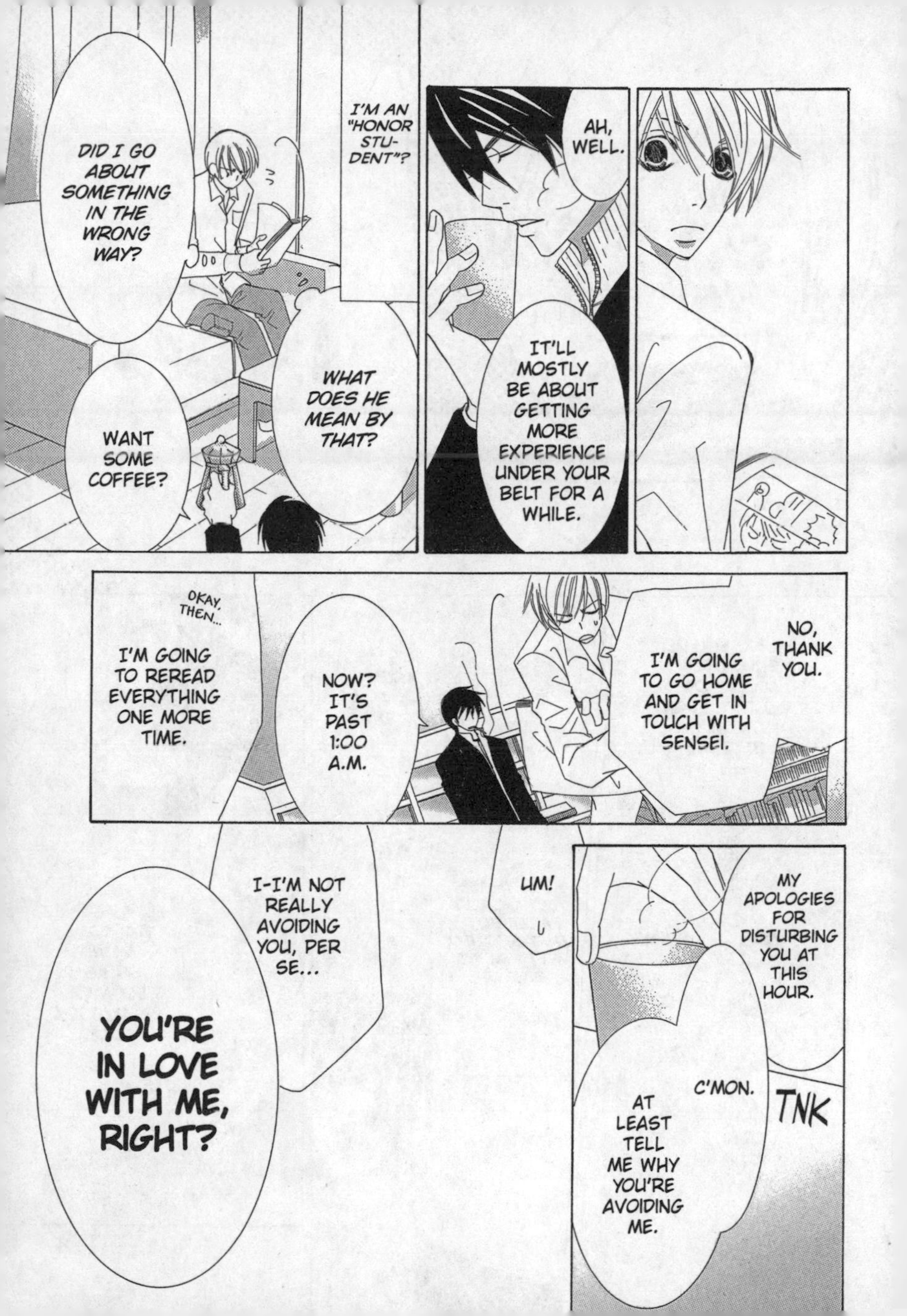
AH, WELL.
IT'LL MOSTLY BE ABOUT GETTING MORE EXPERIENCE UNDER YOUR BELT FOR A WHILE.
I'M AN "HONOR STUDENT"?
WHAT DOES HE MEAN BY THAT?
DID I GO ABOUT SOMETHING IN THE WRONG WAY?
WANT SOME COFFEE?
NO, THANK YOU.
I'M GOING TO GO HOME AND GET IN TOUCH WITH SENSEI.
NOW? IT'S PAST 1:00 A.M.
OKAY, THEN...
I'M GOING TO REREAD EVERYTHING ONE MORE TIME.
MY APOLOGIES FOR DISTURBING YOU AT THIS HOUR.
TNK
C'MON.
AT LEAST TELL ME WHY YOU'RE AVOIDING ME.
UM!
I-I'M NOT REALLY AVOIDING YOU, PER SE...
YOU'RE IN LOVE WITH ME, RIGHT?

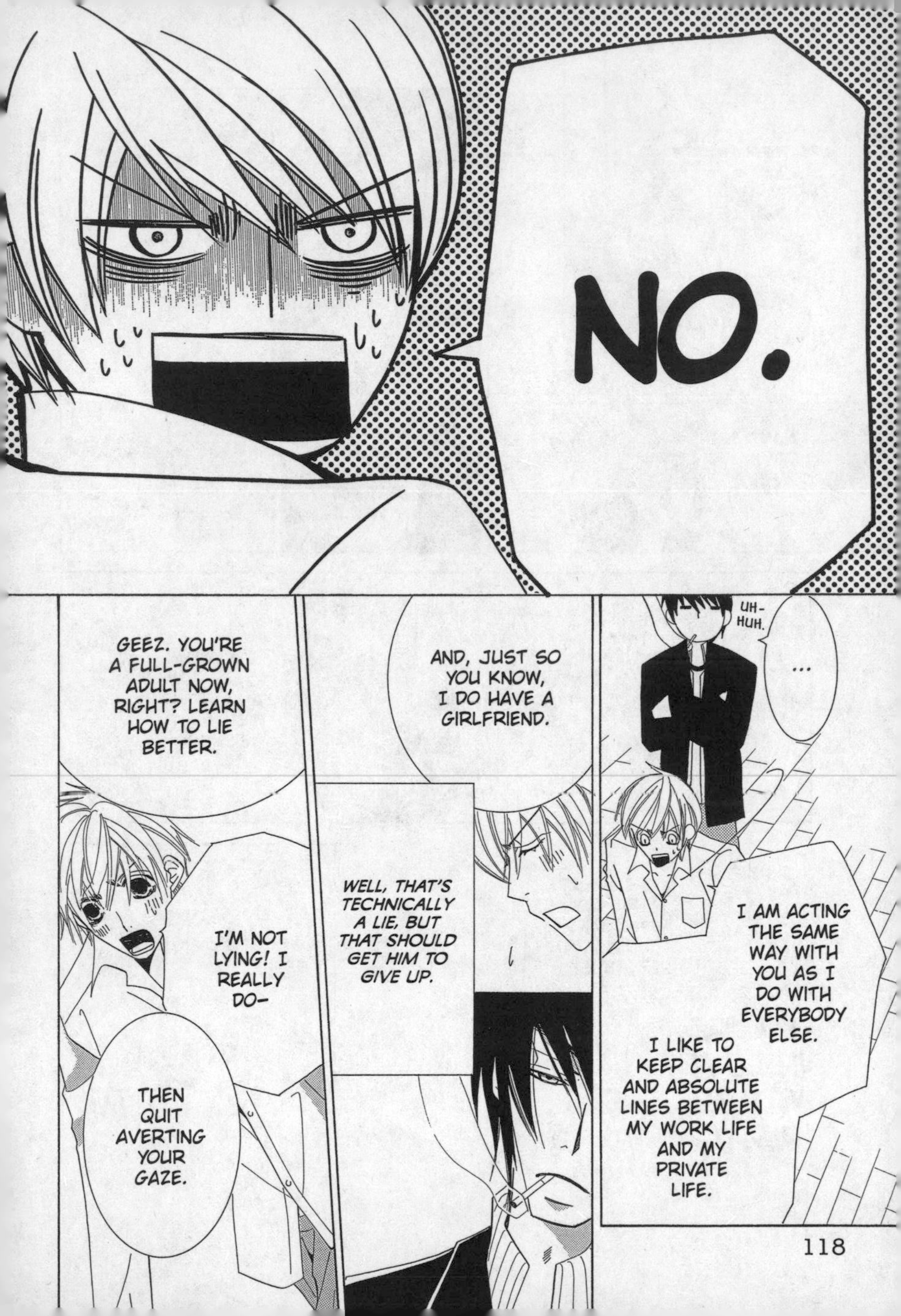
NO.
...
UH-HUH.
I AM ACTING THE SAME WAY WITH YOU AS I DO WITH EVERYBODY ELSE.
I LIKE TO KEEP CLEAR AND ABSOLUTE LINES BETWEEN MY WORK LIFE AND MY PRIVATE LIFE.
AND, JUST SO YOU KNOW, I DO HAVE A GIRLFRIEND.
WELL, THAT'S TECHNICALLY A LIE, BUT THAT SHOULD GET HIM TO GIVE UP.
GEEZ. YOU'RE A FULL-GROWN ADULT NOW, RIGHT? LEARN HOW TO LIE BETTER.
I'M NOT LYING! I REALLY DO-
THEN QUIT AVERTING YOUR GAZE.

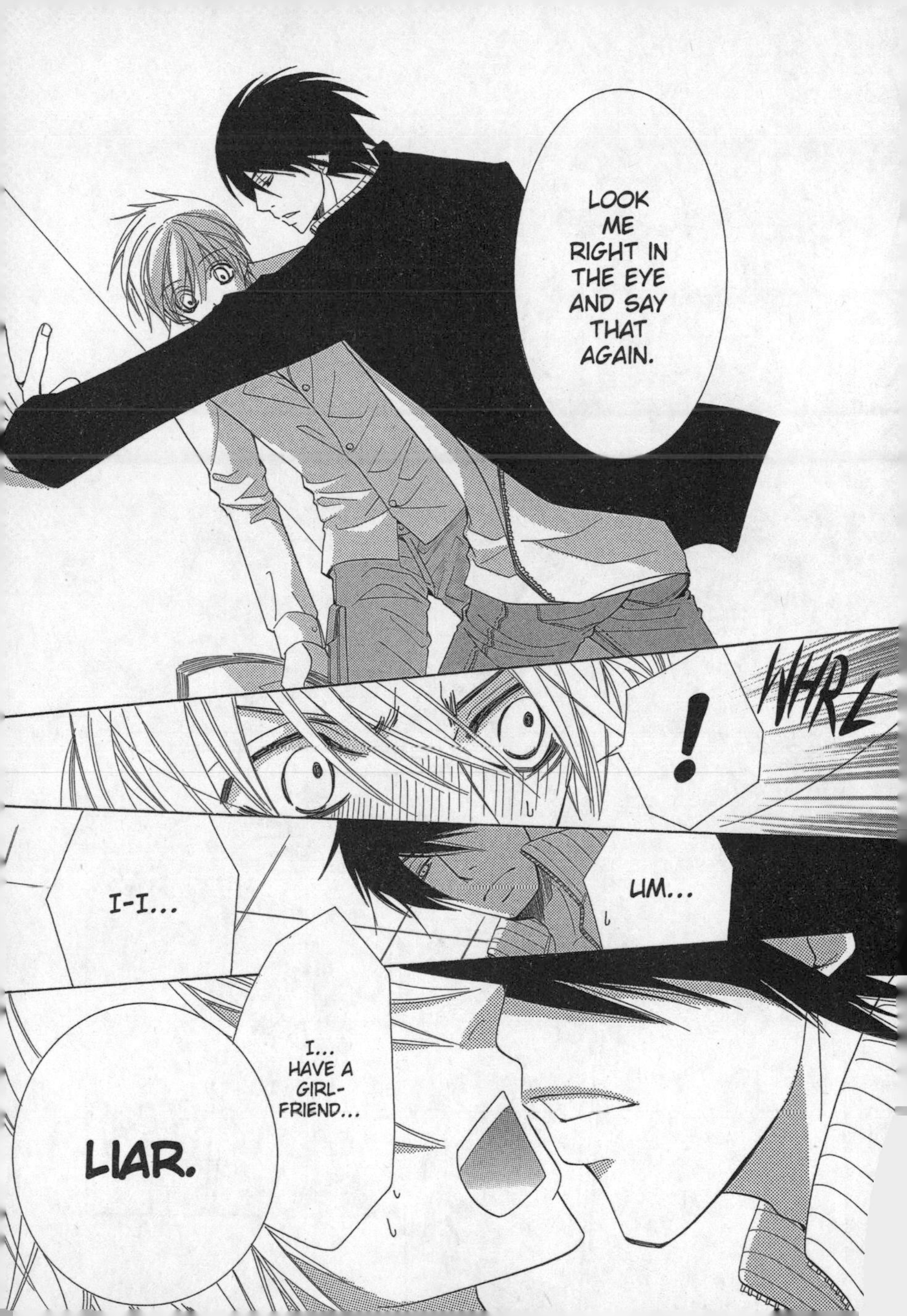
LOOK ME RIGHT IN THE EYE AND SAY THAT AGAIN.
WHRL
!
UM...
I-I...
I... HAVE A GIRL-FRIEND...
LIAR.

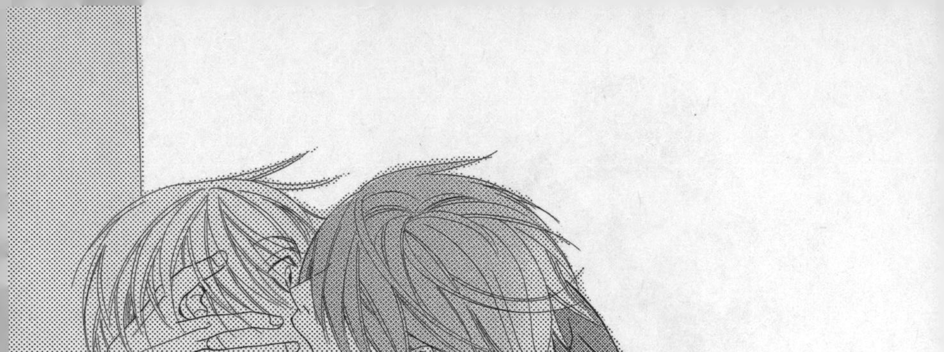
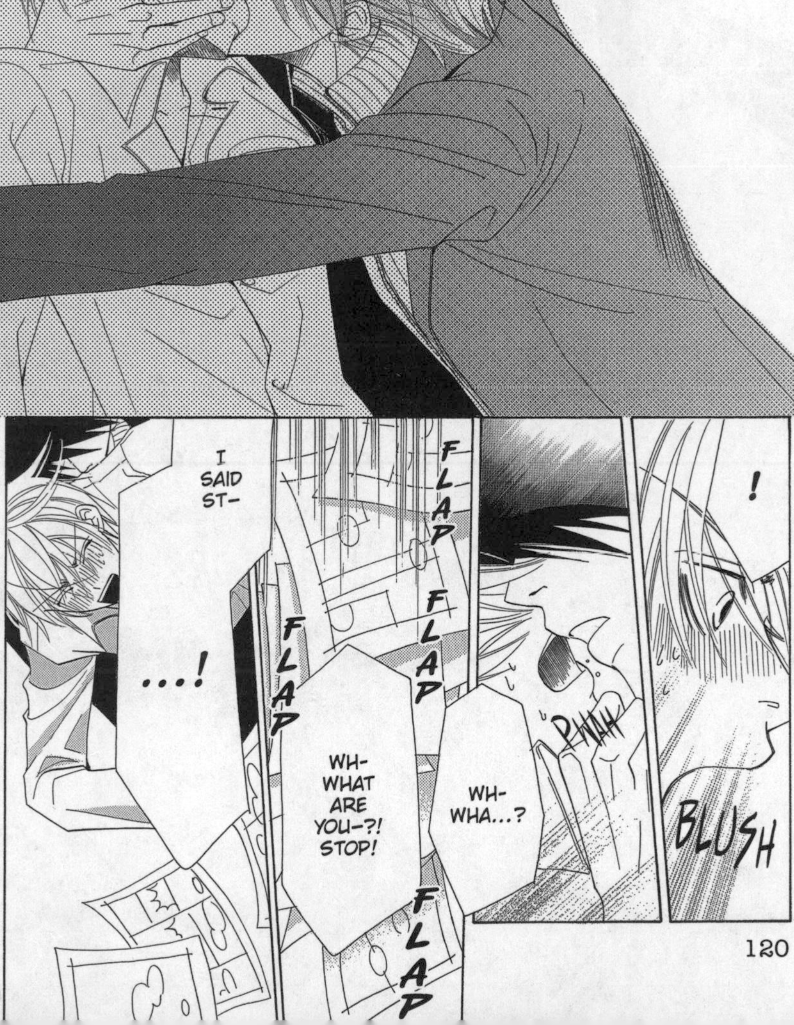
!
BLUSH
PWAH
WH-
WHA...?
FLAP
FLAP
FLAP
FLAP
WH-
WHAT
ARE
YOU-?!
STOP!
I
SAID
ST-
...!

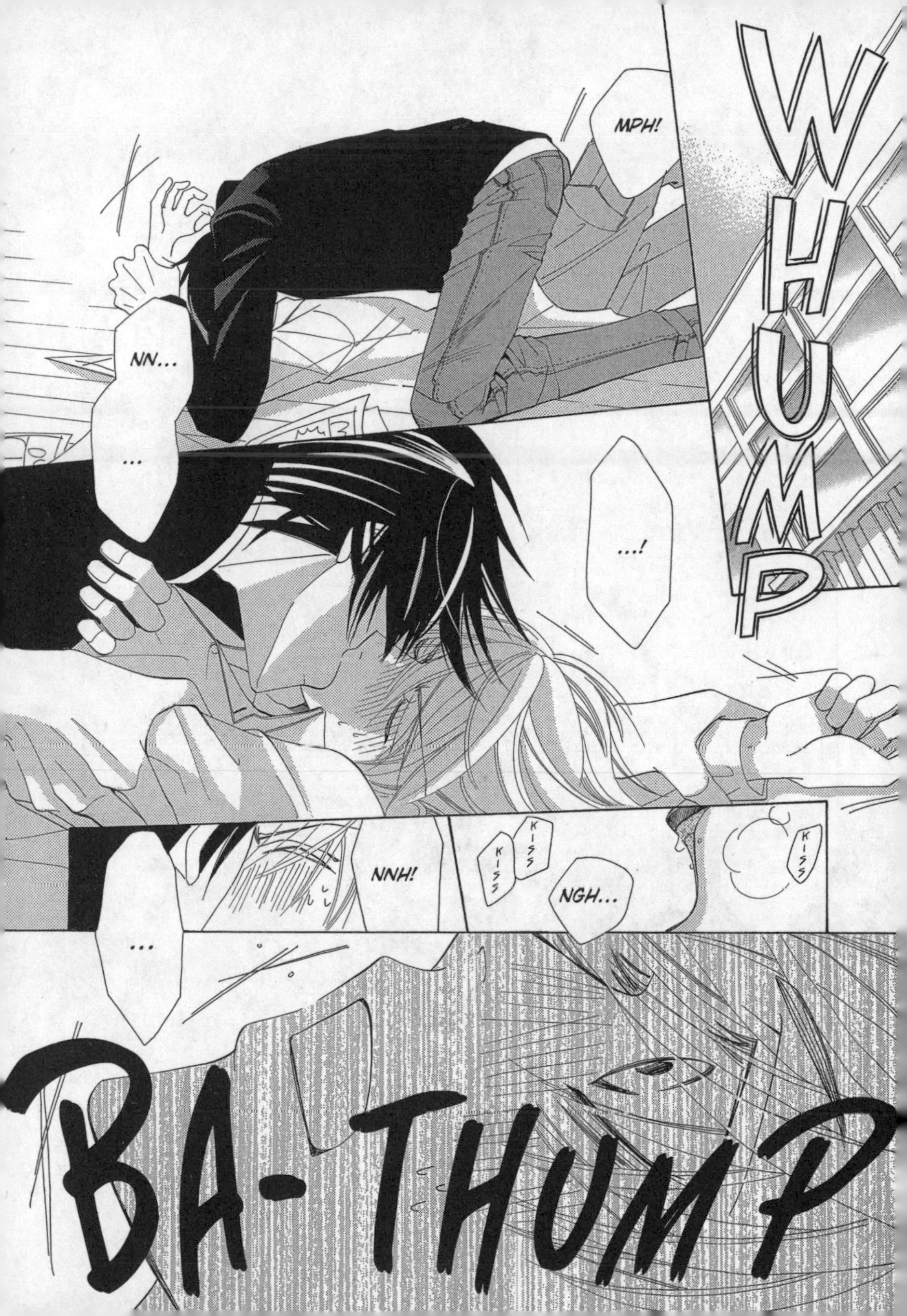
WHUMP
MPH!
NN...
...
...!
KISS
KISS
NNH!
KISS
NGH...
...
BA-THUMP

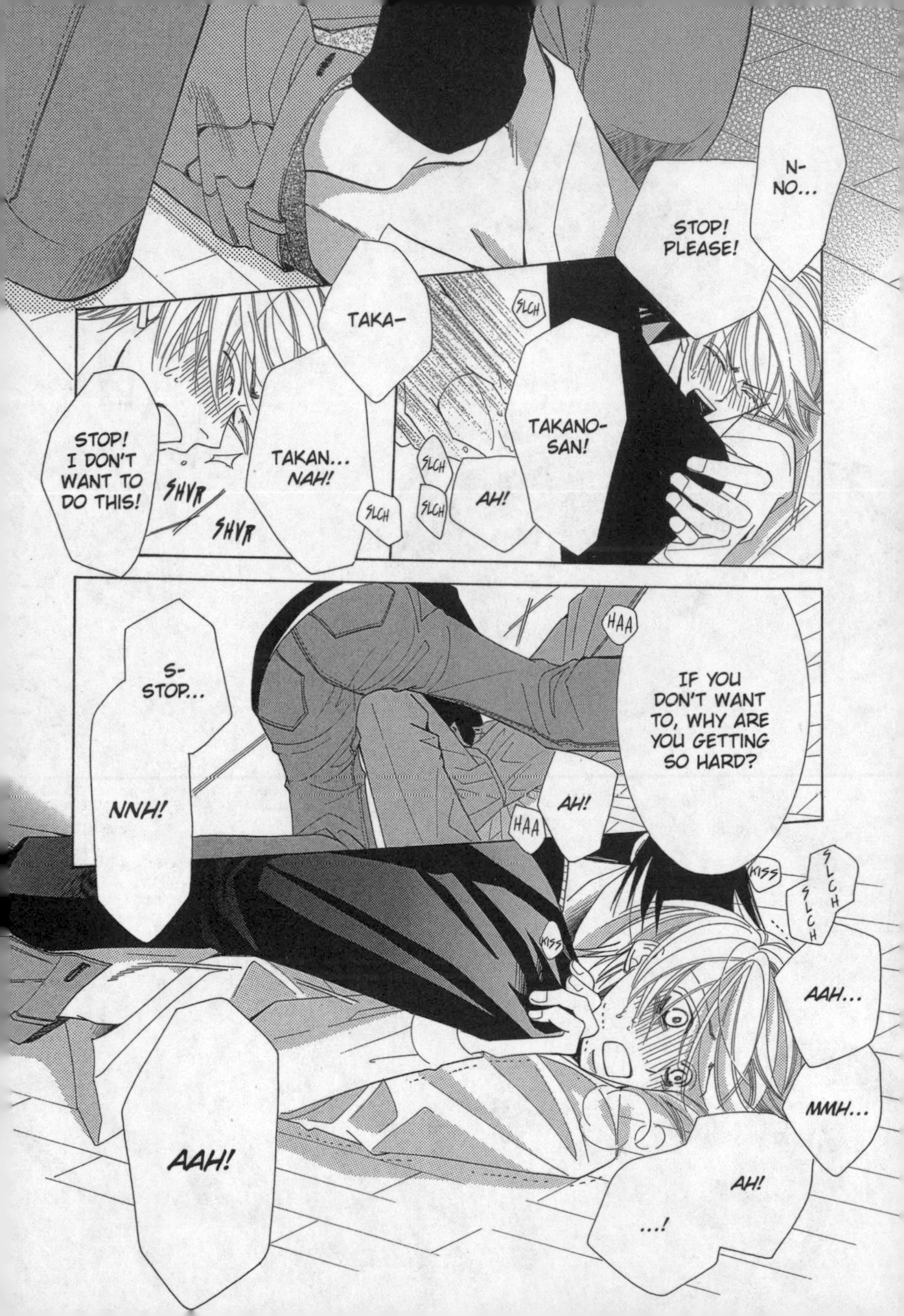
N- NO...
STOP! PLEASE!
SLCH
TAKANO-SAN!
SLCH
SLCH
AH!
TAKA-
TAKAN... NAH!
SLCH
STOP! I DON'T WANT TO DO THIS!
SHVR
SHVR
HAA
IF YOU DON'T WANT TO, WHY ARE YOU GETTING SO HARD?
AH!
HAA
S- STOP...
NNH!
KISS
SLCH
SLCH
AAH...
MMH...
AH!
...!
KISS
AAH!

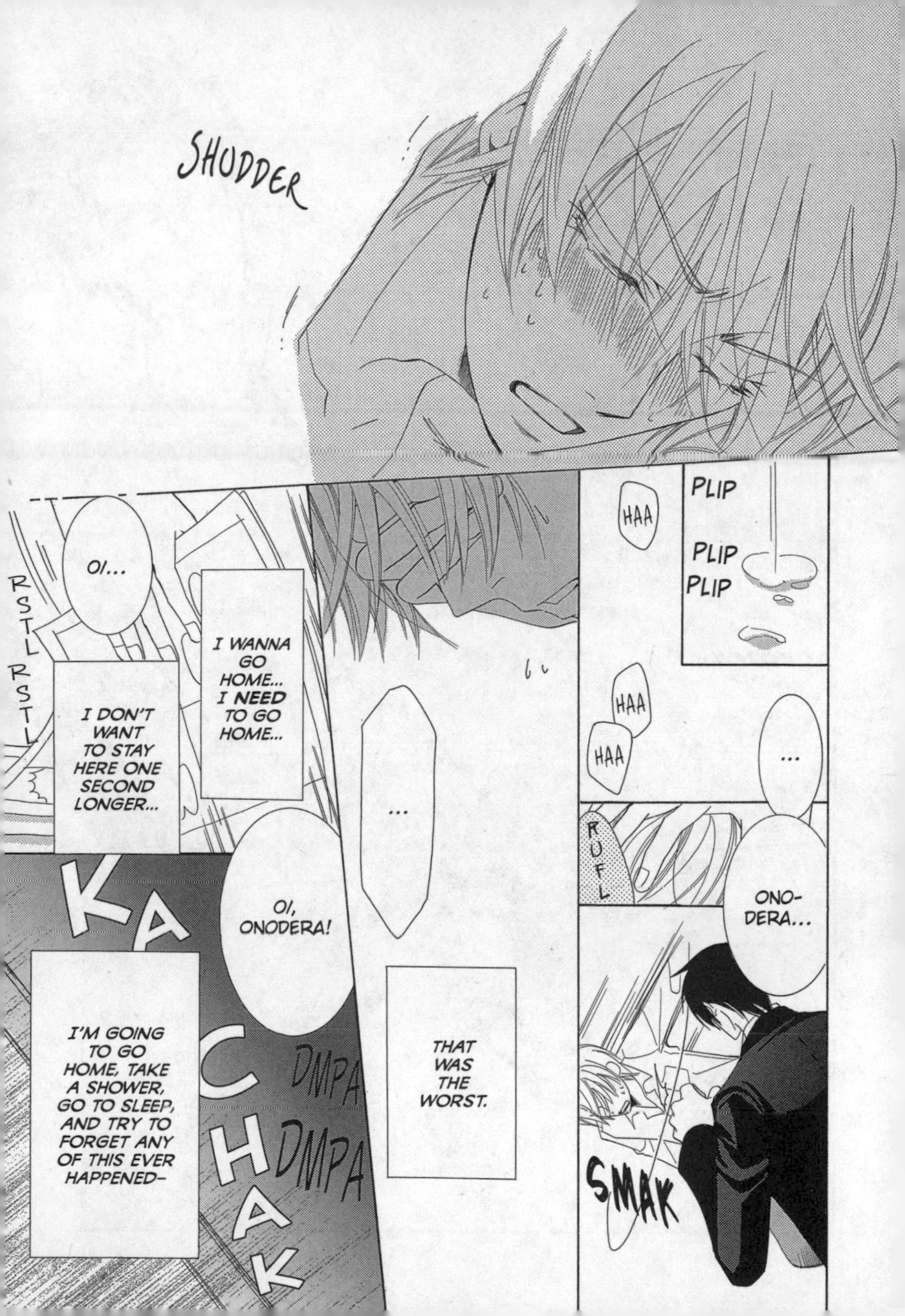
SHUDDER
PLIP
PLIP
PLIP
HAA
HAA
HAA
...
RUFL
ONO-DERA...
SMAK
...
OI, ONODERA!
THAT WAS THE WORST.
DMPA
DMPA
OI...
RSTL
RSTL
I WANNA GO HOME... I **NEED** TO GO HOME...
I DON'T WANT TO STAY HERE ONE SECOND LONGER...
KACHAK
I'M GOING TO GO HOME, TAKE A SHOWER, GO TO SLEEP, AND TRY TO FORGET ANY OF THIS EVER HAPPENED–

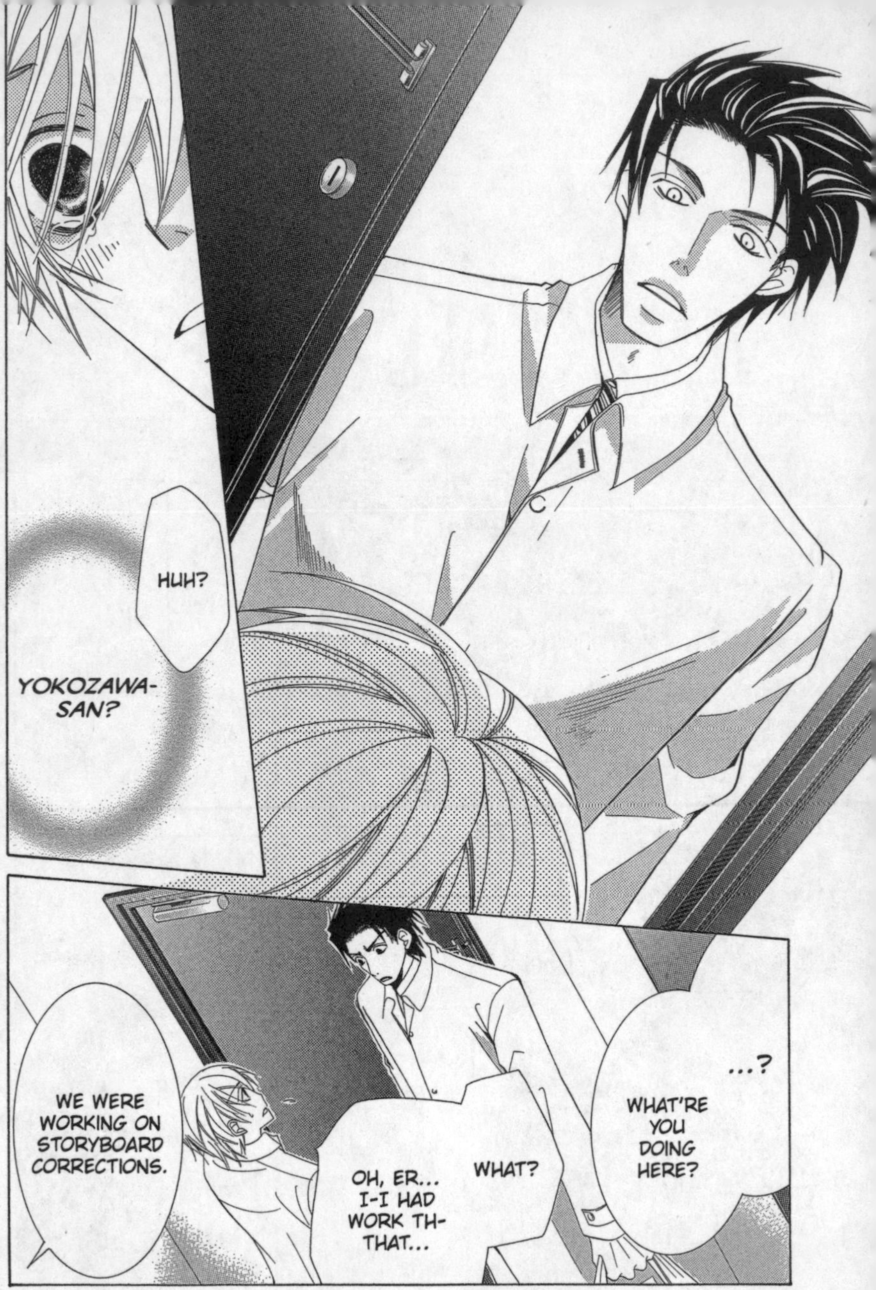
HUH?
YOKOZAWA-SAN?
...?
WHAT'RE YOU DOING HERE?
WHAT?
OH, ER... I-I HAD WORK TH-THAT...
WE WERE WORKING ON STORYBOARD CORRECTIONS.

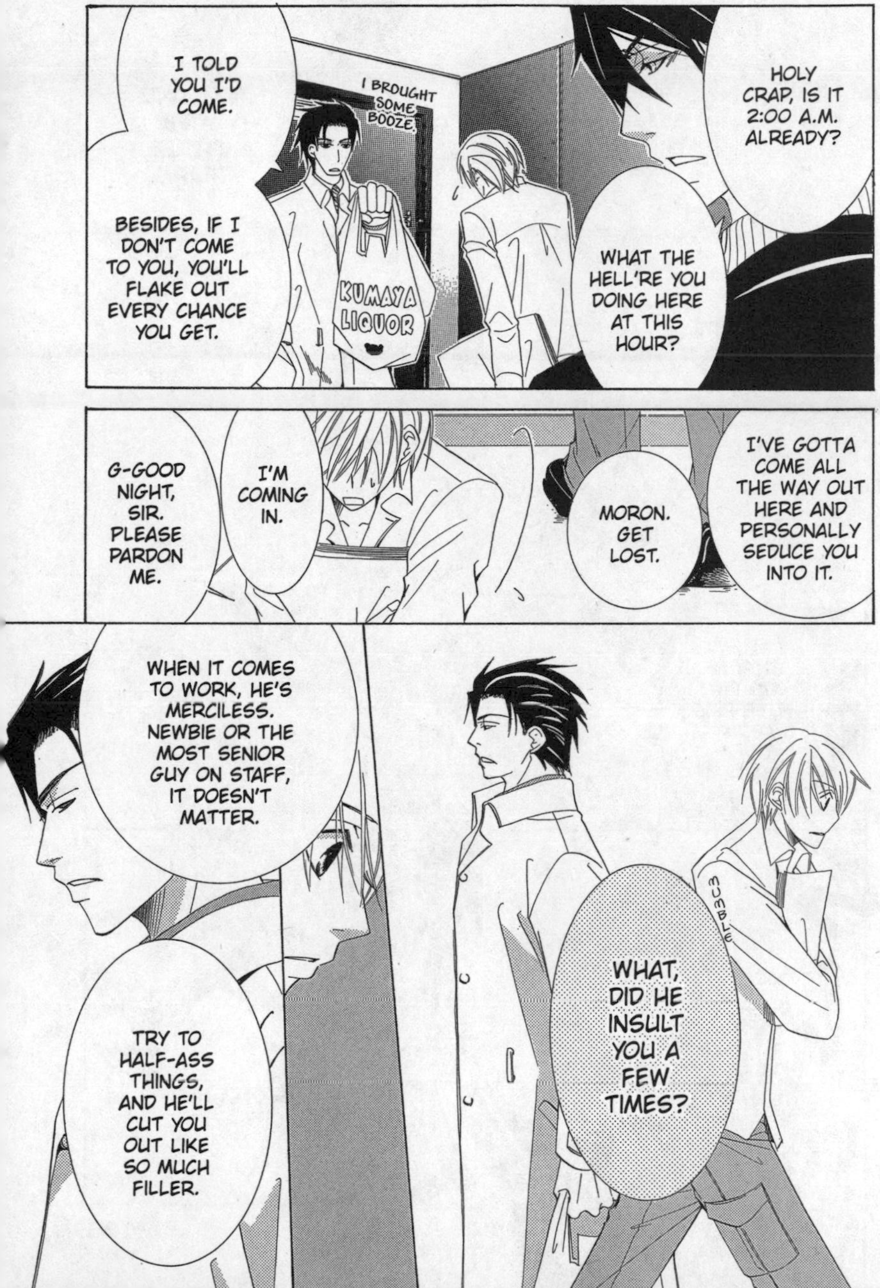
HOLY CRAP, IS IT 2:00 A.M. ALREADY?
WHAT THE HELL'RE YOU DOING HERE AT THIS HOUR?
I TOLD YOU I'D COME.
I BROUGHT SOME BOOZE.
KUMAYA LIQUOR
BESIDES, IF I DON'T COME TO YOU, YOU'LL FLAKE OUT EVERY CHANCE YOU GET.
I'VE GOTTA COME ALL THE WAY OUT HERE AND PERSONALLY SEDUCE YOU INTO IT.
MORON. GET LOST.
I'M COMING IN.
G-GOOD NIGHT, SIR. PLEASE PARDON ME.
MUMBLE
WHAT, DID HE INSULT YOU A FEW TIMES?
WHEN IT COMES TO WORK, HE'S MERCILESS. NEWBIE OR THE MOST SENIOR GUY ON STAFF, IT DOESN'T MATTER.
TRY TO HALF-ASS THINGS, AND HE'LL CUT YOU OUT LIKE SO MUCH FILLER.

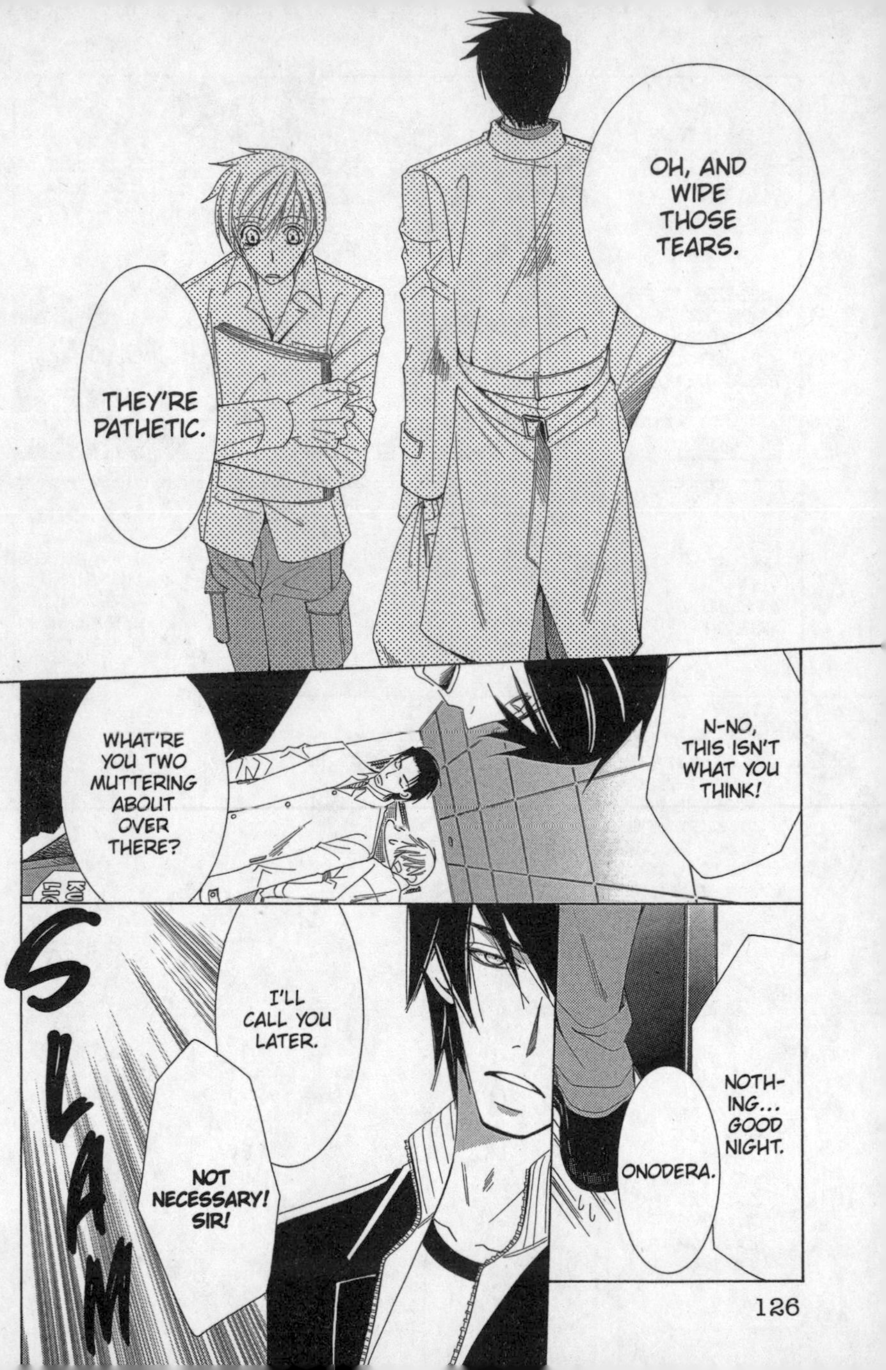
OH, AND WIPE THOSE TEARS.
THEY'RE PATHETIC.
WHAT'RE YOU TWO MUTTERING ABOUT OVER THERE?
N-NO, THIS ISN'T WHAT YOU THINK!
NOTH-ING... GOOD NIGHT.
ONODERA.
I'LL CALL YOU LATER.
NOT NECESSARY! SIR!
SLAM

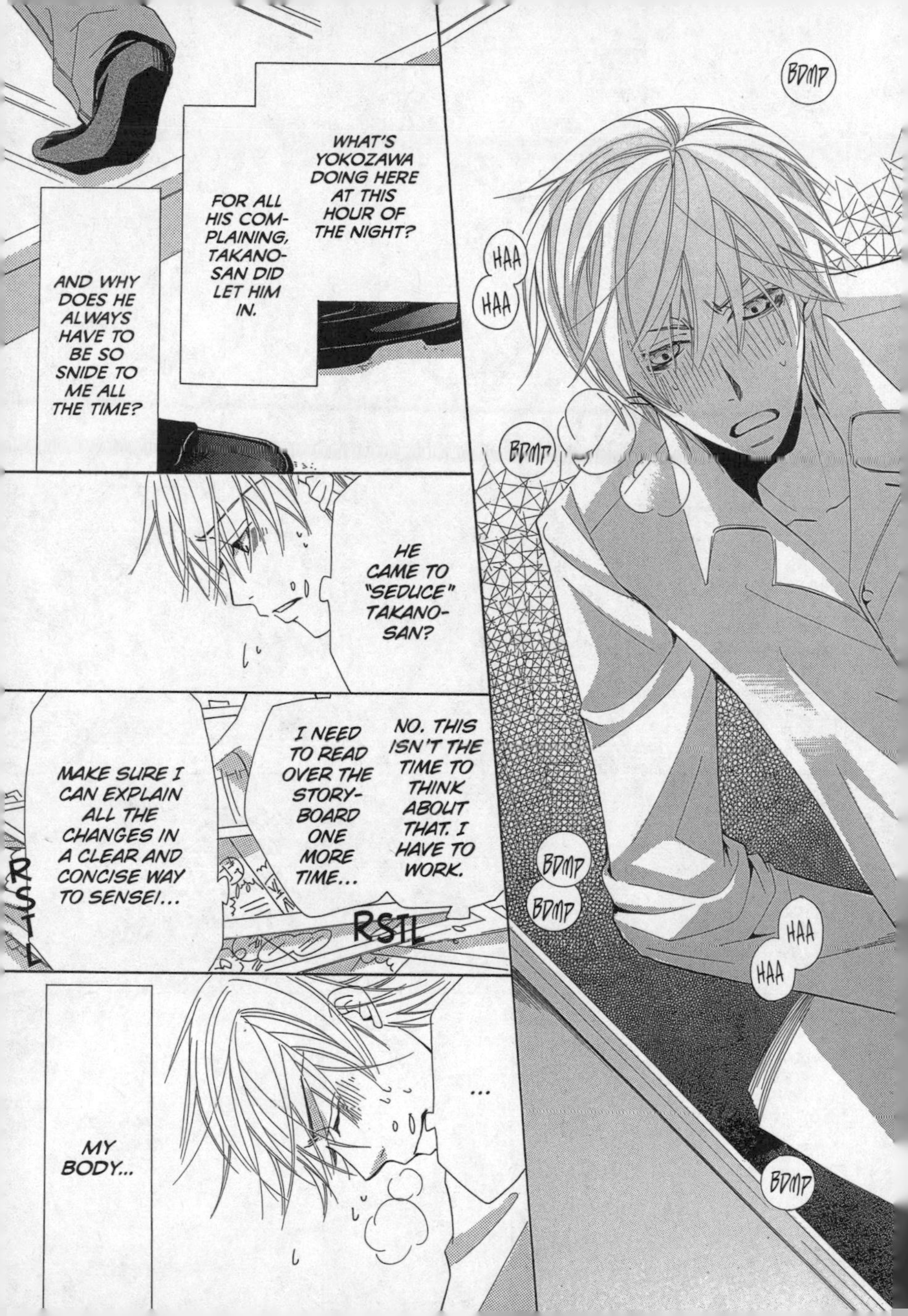
WHAT'S YOKOZAWA DOING HERE AT THIS HOUR OF THE NIGHT?
FOR ALL HIS COM-PLAINING, TAKANO-SAN DID LET HIM IN.
AND WHY DOES HE ALWAYS HAVE TO BE SO SNIDE TO ME ALL THE TIME?
HE CAME TO "SEDUCE" TAKANO-SAN?
NO. THIS ISN'T THE TIME TO THINK ABOUT THAT. I HAVE TO WORK.
I NEED TO READ OVER THE STORY-BOARD ONE MORE TIME...
MAKE SURE I CAN EXPLAIN ALL THE CHANGES IN A CLEAR AND CONCISE WAY TO SENSEI...
RSTL
RSTL
...
MY BODY...
BDMP
HAA
HAA
BDMP
BDMP
BDMP
HAA
HAA
BDMP

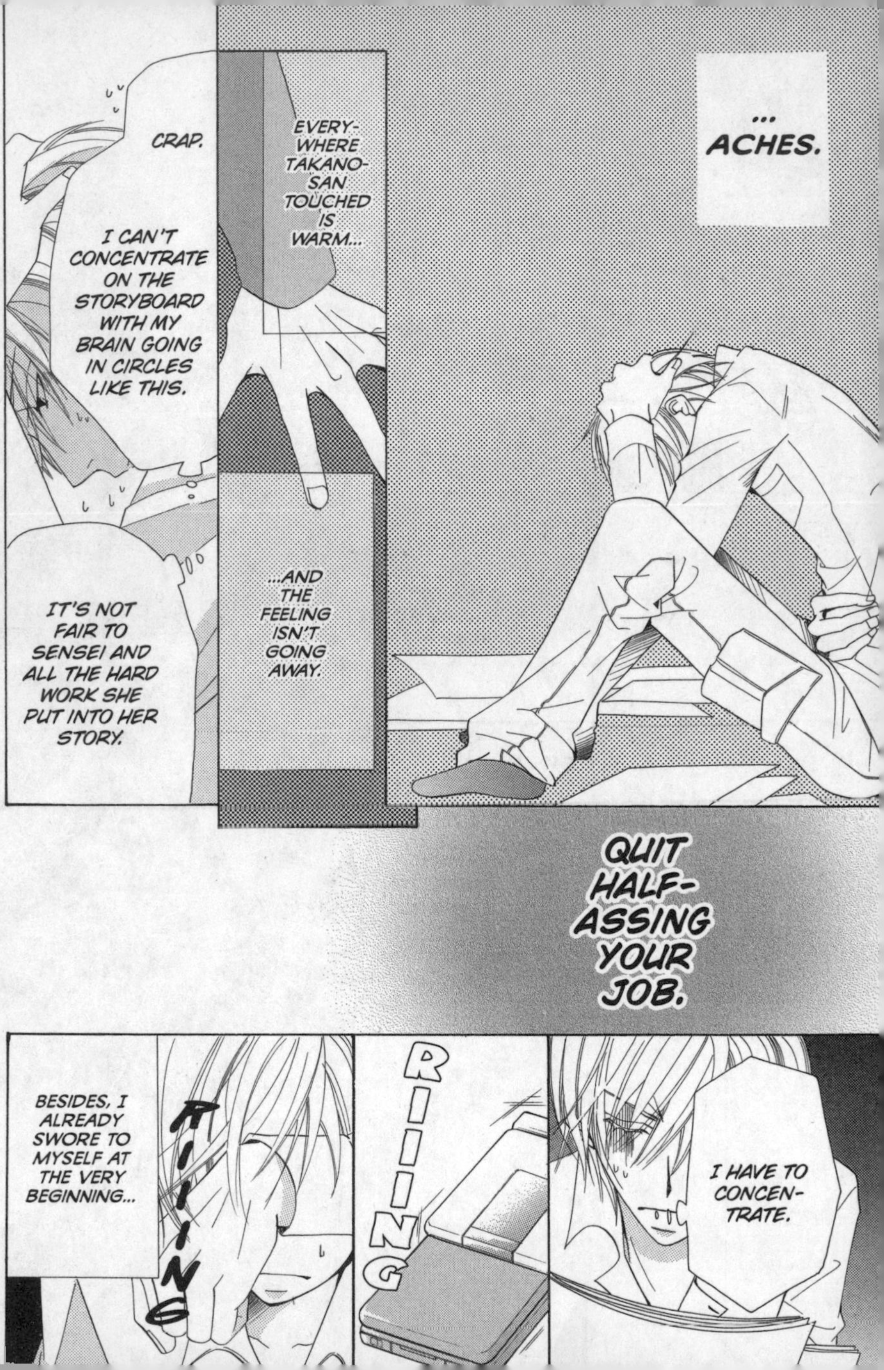

... ACHES.
EVERY-WHERE TAKANO-SAN TOUCHED IS WARM...
...AND THE FEELING ISN'T GOING AWAY.
CRAP.
I CAN'T CONCENTRATE ON THE STORYBOARD WITH MY BRAIN GOING IN CIRCLES LIKE THIS.
IT'S NOT FAIR TO SENSEI AND ALL THE HARD WORK SHE PUT INTO HER STORY.
QUIT HALF-ASSING YOUR JOB.
I HAVE TO CONCEN-TRATE.
RIIING
RIIING
BESIDES, I ALREADY SWORE TO MYSELF AT THE VERY BEGINNING...

...THAT I WILL NOT FALL IN LOVE WITH TAKANO-SAN A SECOND TIME.

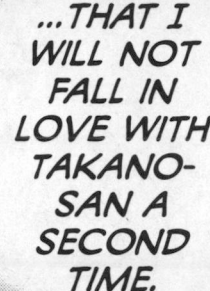

EMERALD EDITORIAL DEPARTMENT, DEADLINE DAY

EVERY LAST ONE OF YOUR ASSISTANTS IS OUT WITH THE FLU?!

WHAT?!

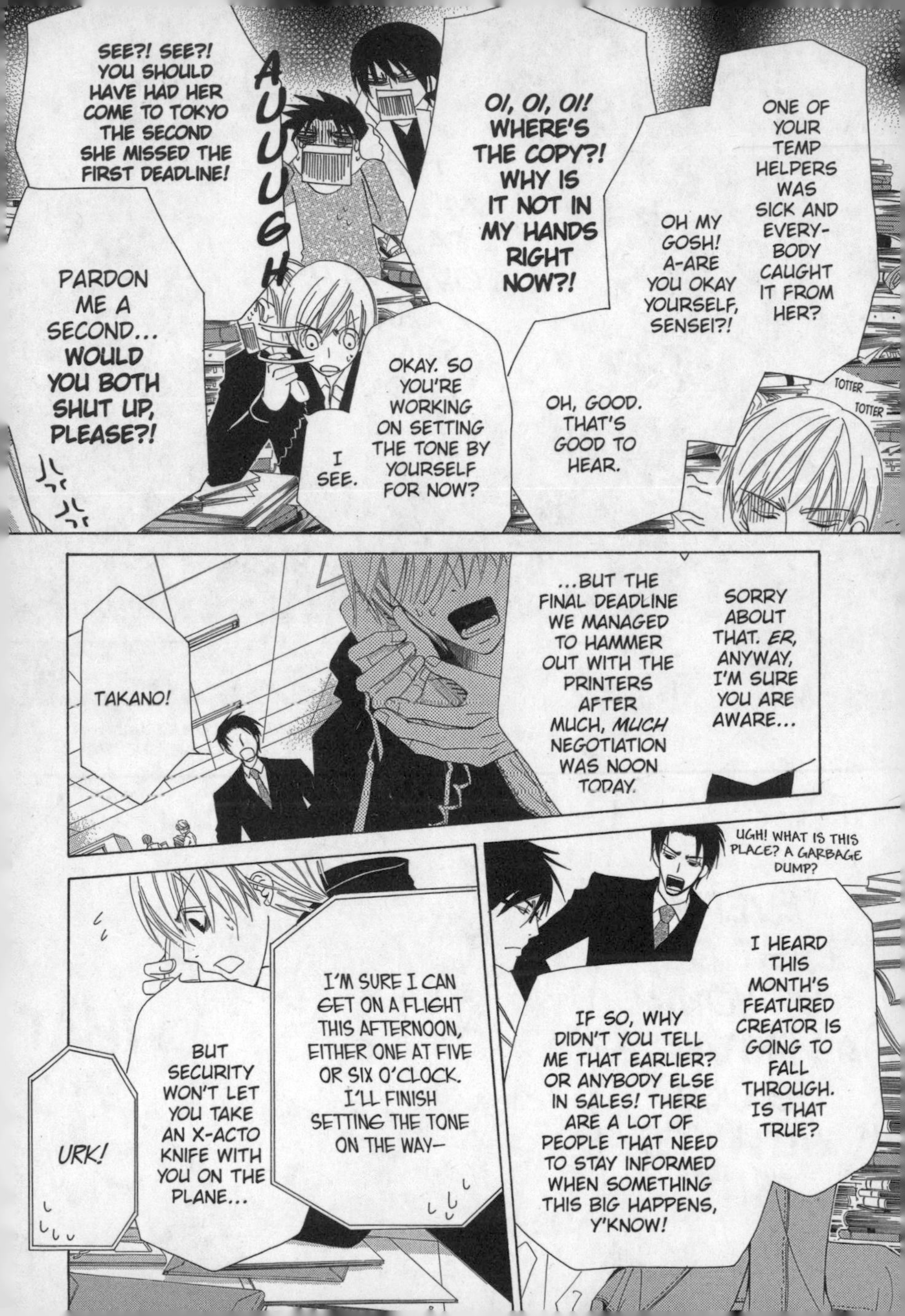
ONE OF YOUR TEMP HELPERS WAS SICK AND EVERY-BODY CAUGHT IT FROM HER?
OH MY GOSH! A-ARE YOU OKAY YOURSELF, SENSEI?!
OI, OI, OI! WHERE'S THE COPY?! WHY IS IT NOT IN MY HANDS RIGHT NOW?!
SEE?! SEE?! YOU SHOULD HAVE HAD HER COME TO TOKYO THE SECOND SHE MISSED THE FIRST DEADLINE!
AUUUGH
TOTTER
TOTTER
OH, GOOD. THAT'S GOOD TO HEAR.
OKAY. SO YOU'RE WORKING ON SETTING THE TONE BY YOURSELF FOR NOW?
I SEE.
PARDON ME A SECOND... WOULD YOU BOTH SHUT UP, PLEASE?!
SORRY ABOUT THAT. *ER*, ANYWAY, I'M SURE YOU ARE AWARE...
...BUT THE FINAL DEADLINE WE MANAGED TO HAMMER OUT WITH THE PRINTERS AFTER MUCH, *MUCH* NEGOTIATION WAS NOON TODAY.
TAKANO!
UGH! WHAT IS THIS PLACE? A GARBAGE DUMP?
I HEARD THIS MONTH'S FEATURED CREATOR IS GOING TO FALL THROUGH. IS THAT TRUE?
IF SO, WHY DIDN'T YOU TELL ME THAT EARLIER? OR ANYBODY ELSE IN SALES! THERE ARE A LOT OF PEOPLE THAT NEED TO STAY INFORMED WHEN SOMETHING THIS BIG HAPPENS, Y'KNOW!
I'M SURE I CAN GET ON A FLIGHT THIS AFTERNOON, EITHER ONE AT FIVE OR SIX O'CLOCK. I'LL FINISH SETTING THE TONE ON THE WAY–
BUT SECURITY WON'T LET YOU TAKE AN X-ACTO KNIFE WITH YOU ON THE PLANE...
URK!

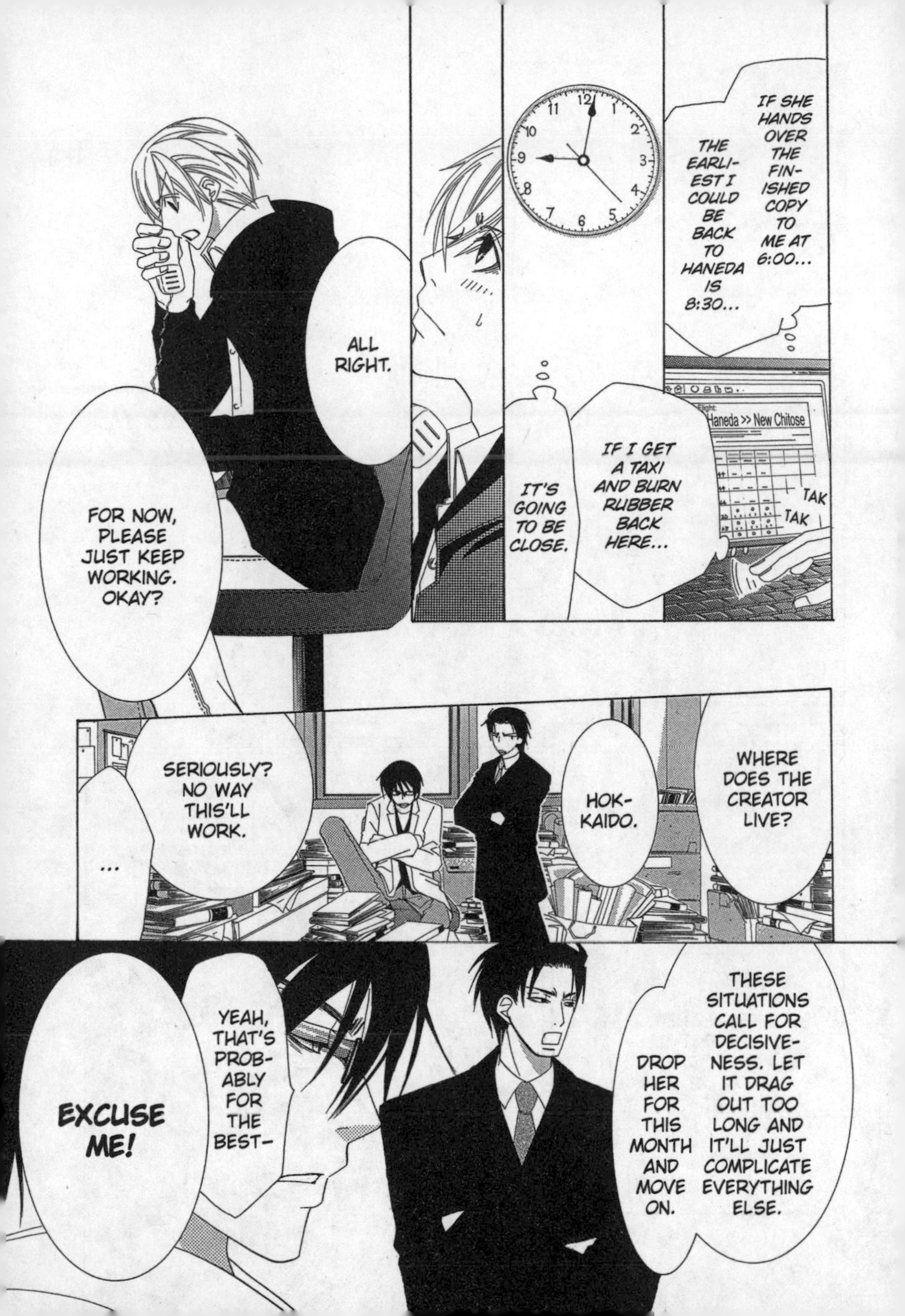
IF SHE HANDS OVER THE FINISHED COPY TO ME AT 6:00...
THE EARLIEST I COULD BE BACK TO HANEDA IS 8:30...
Flight: Haneda >> New Chitose
TAK
TAK
IF I GET A TAXI AND BURN RUBBER BACK HERE...
IT'S GOING TO BE CLOSE.
ALL RIGHT.
FOR NOW, PLEASE JUST KEEP WORKING. OKAY?
WHERE DOES THE CREATOR LIVE?
HOKKAIDO.
SERIOUSLY? NO WAY THIS'LL WORK.
...
THESE SITUATIONS CALL FOR DECISIVENESS. LET IT DRAG OUT TOO LONG AND IT'LL JUST COMPLICATE EVERYTHING ELSE.
DROP HER FOR THIS MONTH AND MOVE ON.
YEAH, THAT'S PROBABLY FOR THE BEST-
EXCUSE ME!

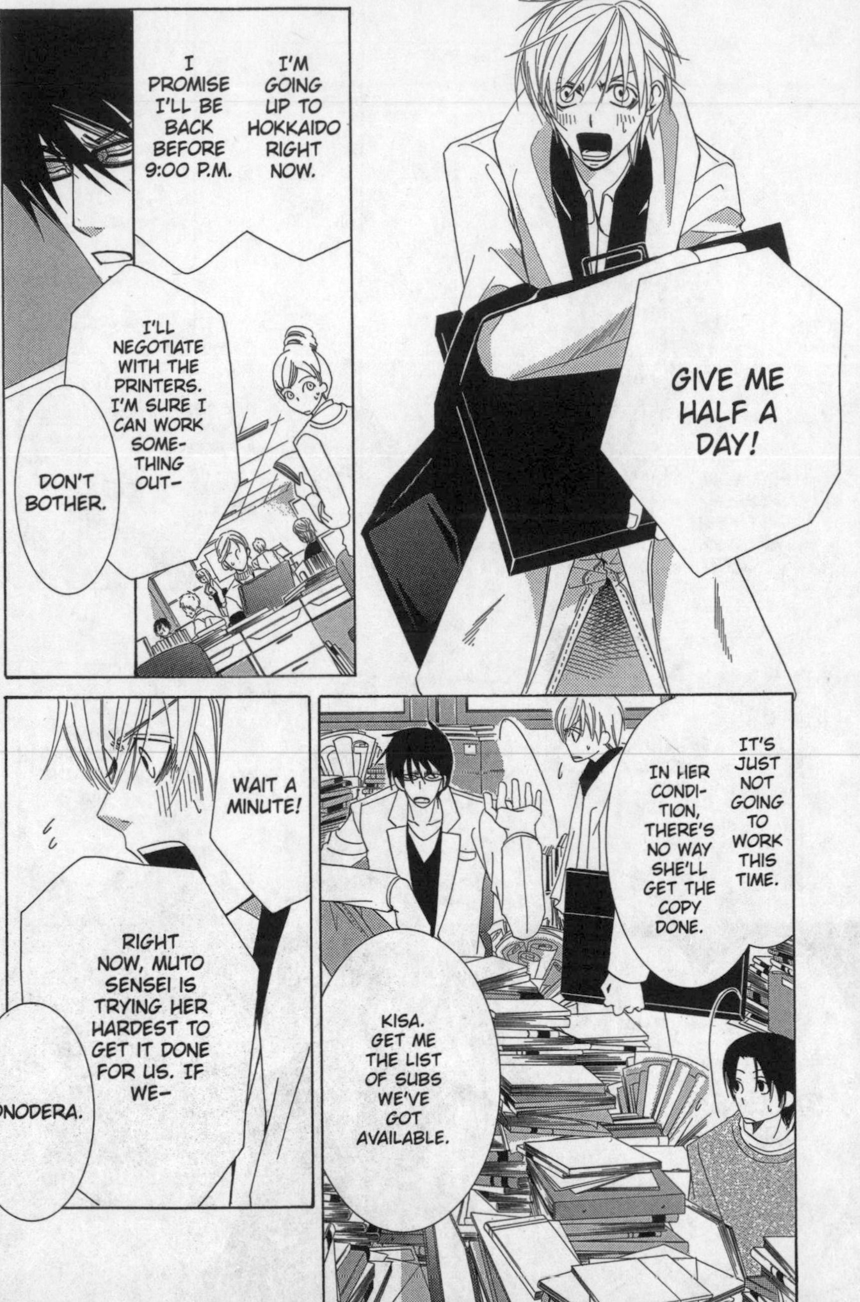
GIVE ME HALF A DAY!
I'M GOING UP TO HOKKAIDO RIGHT NOW.
I PROMISE I'LL BE BACK BEFORE 9:00 P.M.
I'LL NEGOTIATE WITH THE PRINTERS. I'M SURE I CAN WORK SOME-THING OUT–
DON'T BOTHER.
IT'S JUST NOT GOING TO WORK THIS TIME.
IN HER CONDI-TION, THERE'S NO WAY SHE'LL GET THE COPY DONE.
KISA. GET ME THE LIST OF SUBS WE'VE GOT AVAILABLE.
WAIT A MINUTE!
RIGHT NOW, MUTO SENSEI IS TRYING HER HARDEST TO GET IT DONE FOR US. IF WE–
ONODERA.

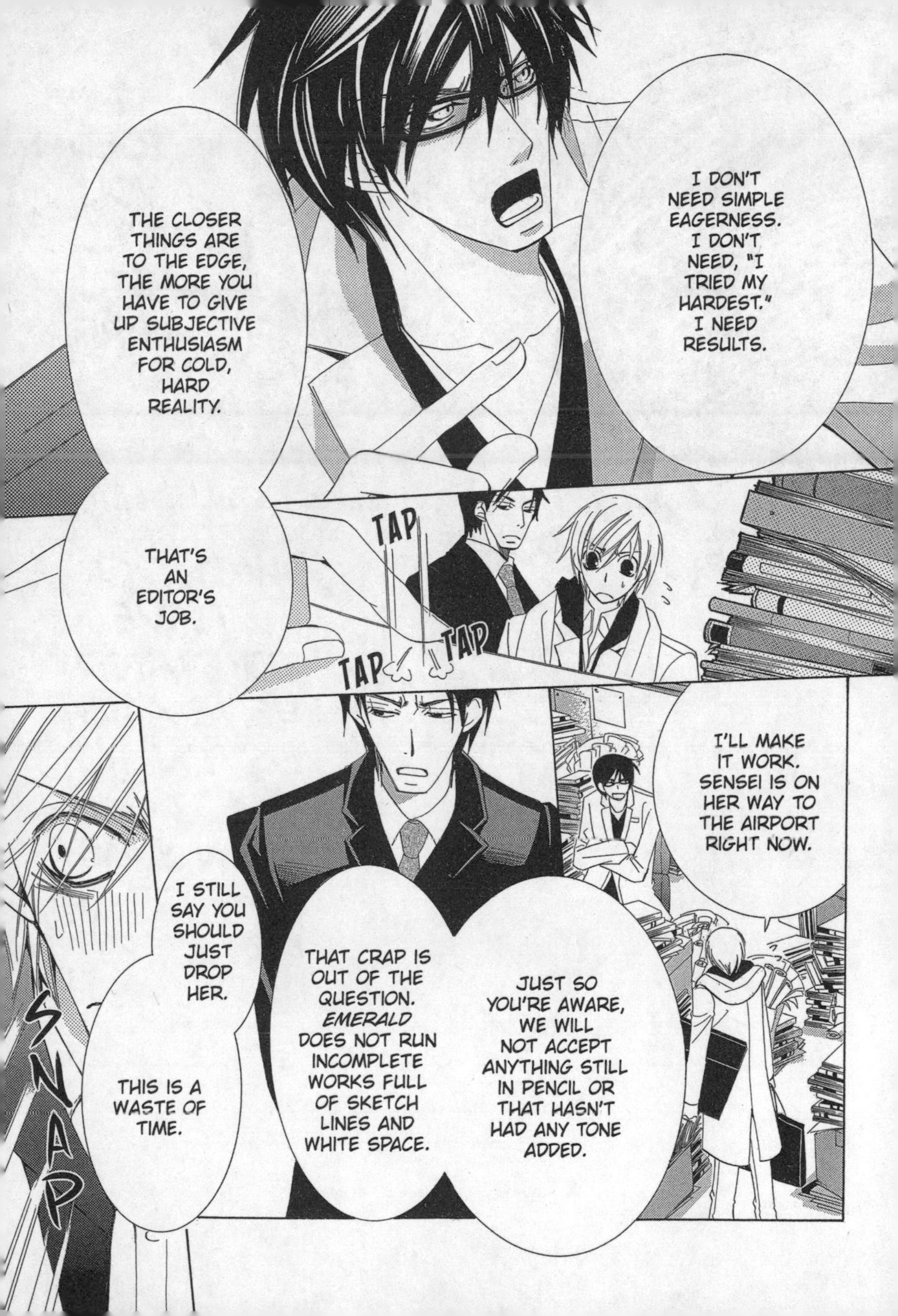
I DON'T NEED SIMPLE EAGERNESS. I DON'T NEED, "I TRIED MY HARDEST." I NEED RESULTS.
THE CLOSER THINGS ARE TO THE EDGE, THE MORE YOU HAVE TO GIVE UP SUBJECTIVE ENTHUSIASM FOR COLD, HARD REALITY.
THAT'S AN EDITOR'S JOB.
TAP
TAP
TAP
I'LL MAKE IT WORK. SENSEI IS ON HER WAY TO THE AIRPORT RIGHT NOW.
JUST SO YOU'RE AWARE, WE WILL NOT ACCEPT ANYTHING STILL IN PENCIL OR THAT HASN'T HAD ANY TONE ADDED.
THAT CRAP IS OUT OF THE QUESTION. *EMERALD* DOES NOT RUN INCOMPLETE WORKS FULL OF SKETCH LINES AND WHITE SPACE.
I STILL SAY YOU SHOULD JUST DROP HER.
THIS IS A WASTE OF TIME.
SNAP

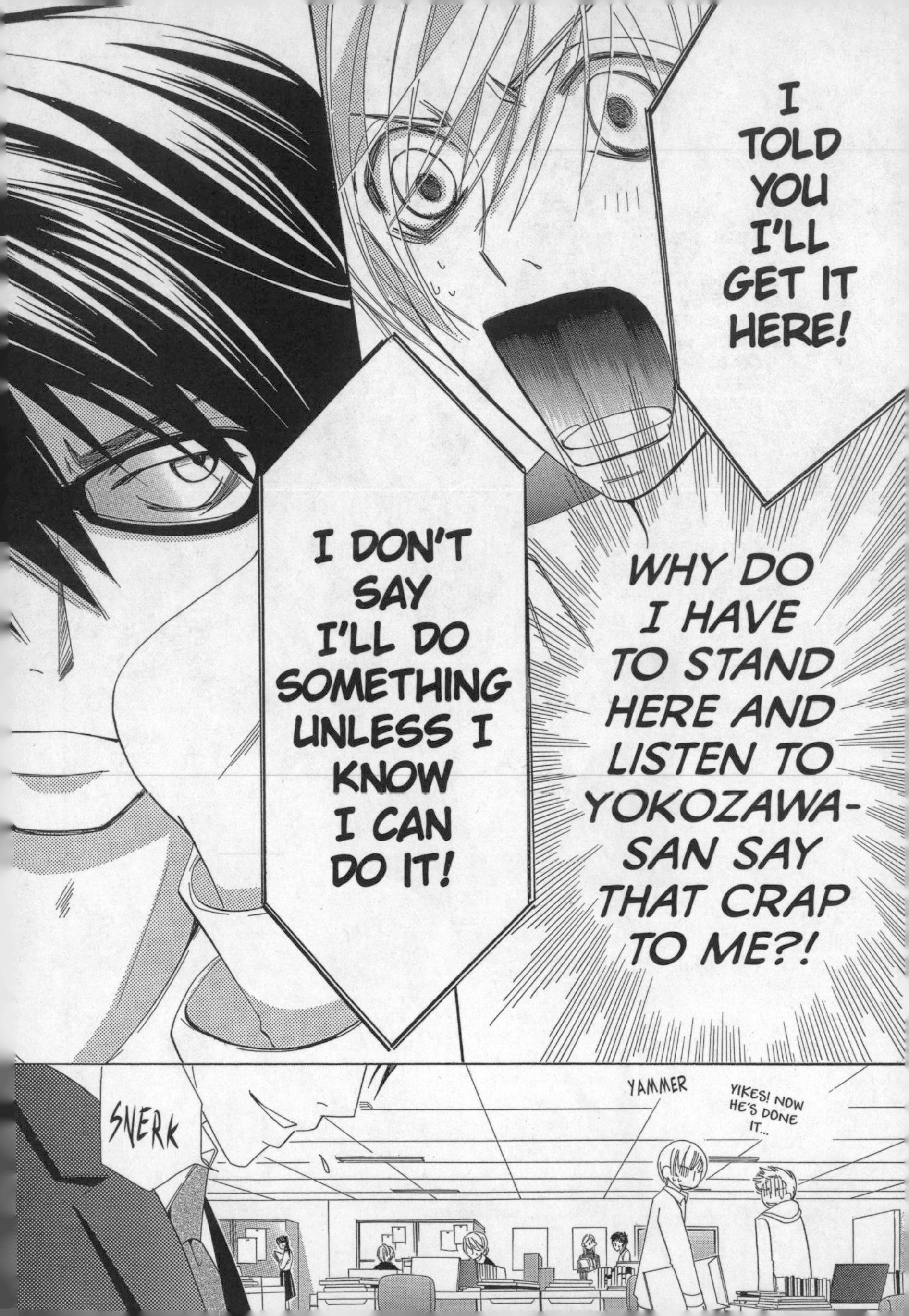
I TOLD YOU I'LL GET IT HERE!
I DON'T SAY I'LL DO SOMETHING UNLESS I KNOW I CAN DO IT!
WHY DO I HAVE TO STAND HERE AND LISTEN TO YOKOZAWA-SAN SAY THAT CRAP TO ME?!
YIKES! NOW HE'S DONE IT...
YAMMER
SNERK

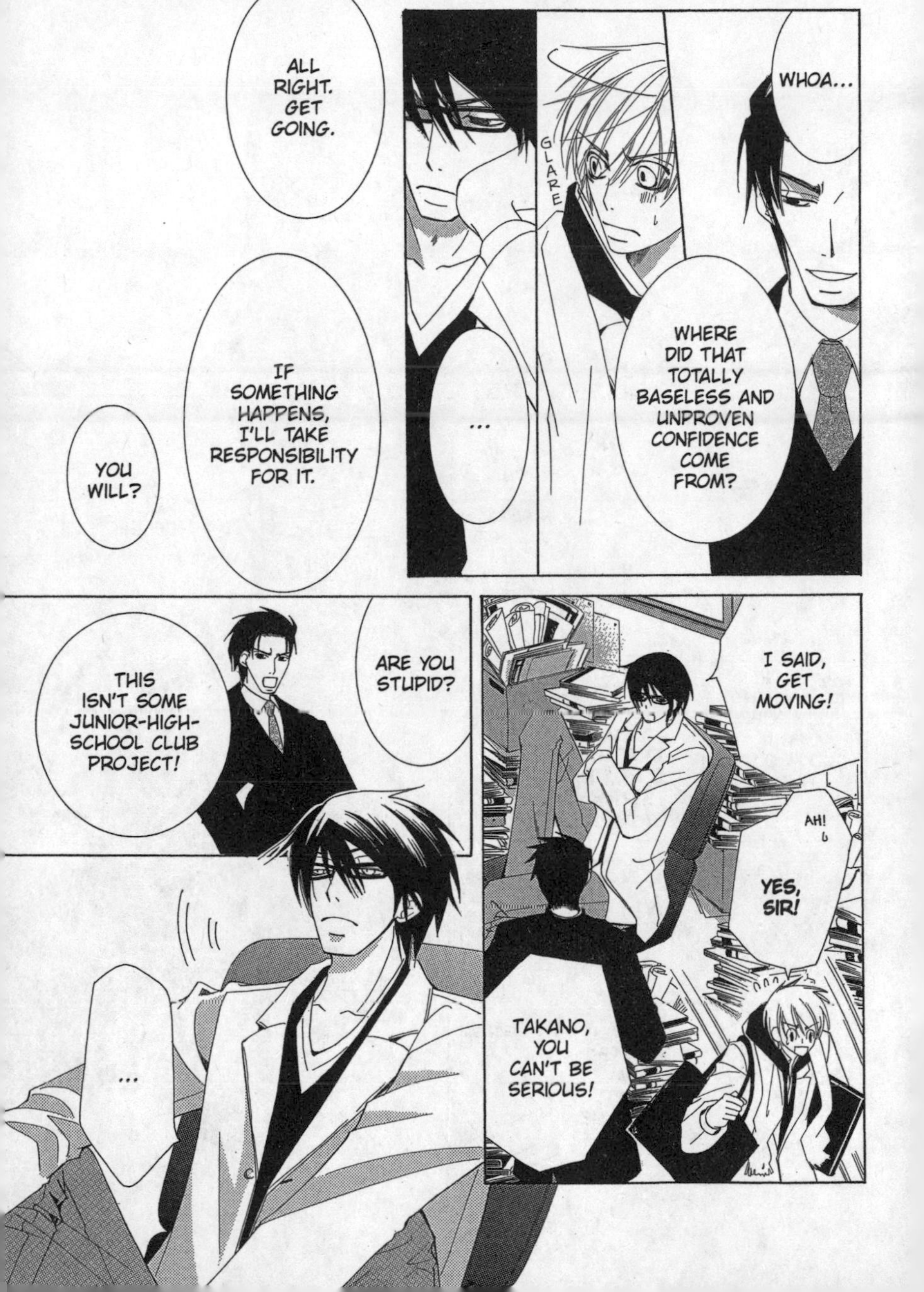
WHOA...
WHERE DID THAT TOTALLY BASELESS AND UNPROVEN CONFIDENCE COME FROM?
GLARE
...
ALL RIGHT. GET GOING.
IF SOMETHING HAPPENS, I'LL TAKE RESPONSIBILITY FOR IT.
YOU WILL?
ARE YOU STUPID?
THIS ISN'T SOME JUNIOR-HIGH-SCHOOL CLUB PROJECT!
...
I SAID, GET MOVING!
AH!
YES, SIR!
TAKANO, YOU CAN'T BE SERIOUS!

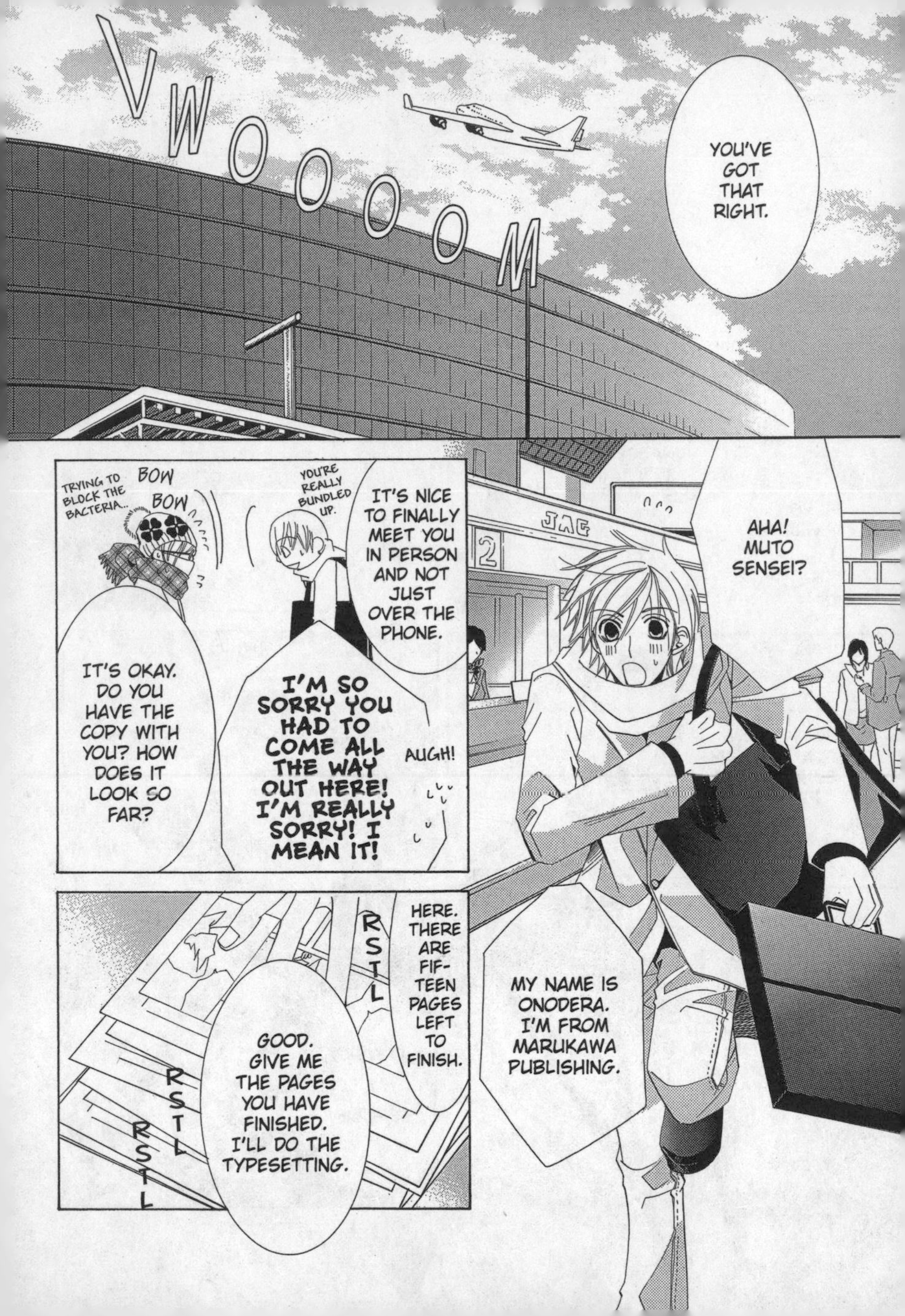
YOU'VE GOT THAT RIGHT.
VWOOOOM
AHA! MUTO SENSEI?
MY NAME IS ONODERA. I'M FROM MARUKAWA PUBLISHING.
IT'S NICE TO FINALLY MEET YOU IN PERSON AND NOT JUST OVER THE PHONE.
YOU'RE REALLY BUNDLED UP.
BOW
BOW
TRYING TO BLOCK THE BACTERIA...
AUGH!
I'M SO SORRY YOU HAD TO COME ALL THE WAY OUT HERE! I'M REALLY SORRY! I MEAN IT!
IT'S OKAY. DO YOU HAVE THE COPY WITH YOU? HOW DOES IT LOOK SO FAR?
HERE. THERE ARE FIF-TEEN PAGES LEFT TO FINISH.
RSTL
GOOD. GIVE ME THE PAGES YOU HAVE FINISHED. I'LL DO THE TYPESETTING.
RSTL
RSTL

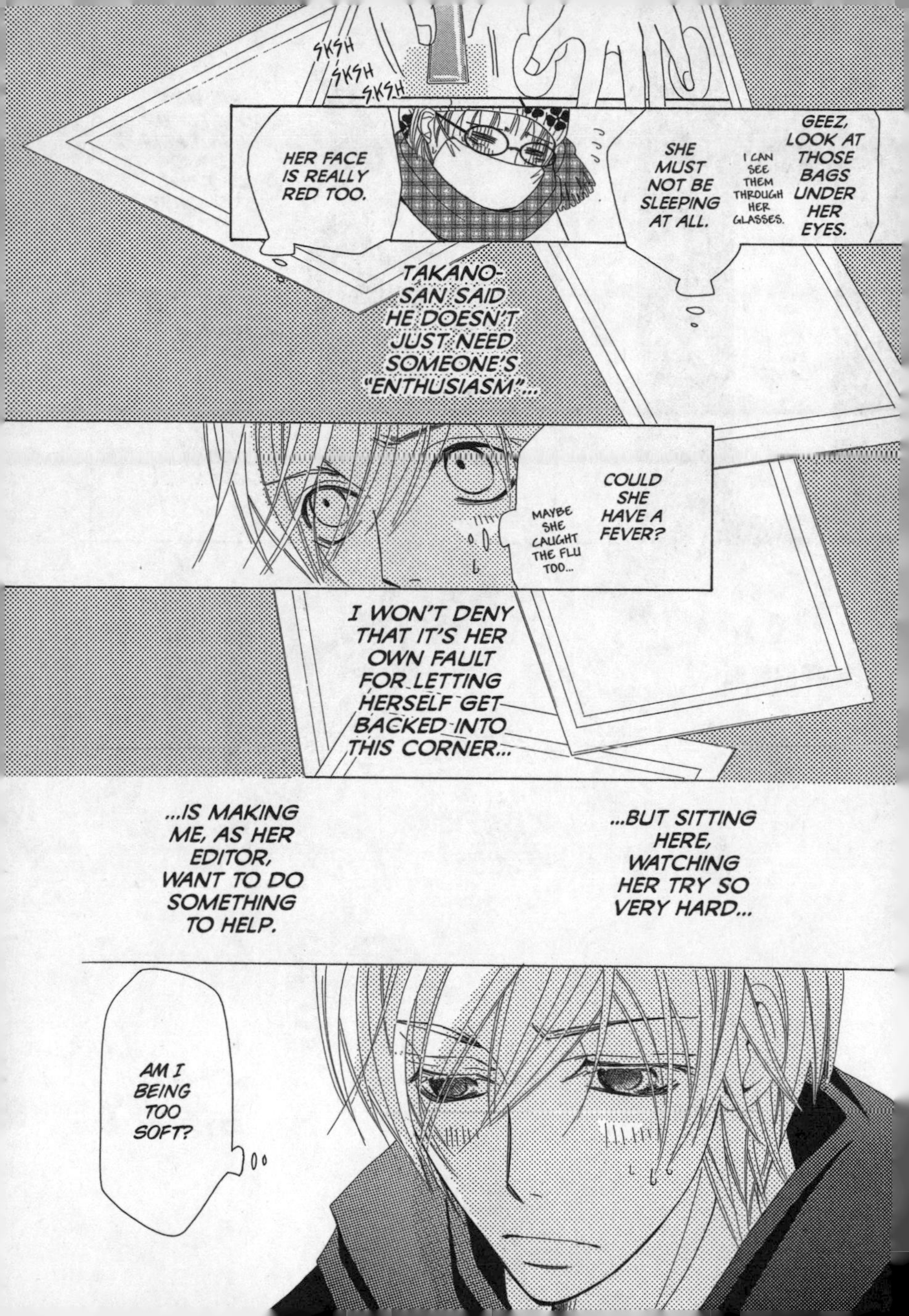
SKSH
SKSH
SKSH
GEEZ, LOOK AT THOSE BAGS UNDER HER EYES.
I CAN SEE THEM THROUGH HER GLASSES.
SHE MUST NOT BE SLEEPING AT ALL.
HER FACE IS REALLY RED TOO.
TAKANO-SAN SAID HE DOESN'T JUST NEED SOMEONE'S "ENTHUSIASM"...
COULD SHE HAVE A FEVER?
MAYBE SHE CAUGHT THE FLU TOO...
I WON'T DENY THAT IT'S HER OWN FAULT FOR LETTING HERSELF GET BACKED INTO THIS CORNER...
...BUT SITTING HERE, WATCHING HER TRY SO VERY HARD...
...IS MAKING ME, AS HER EDITOR, WANT TO DO SOMETHING TO HELP.
AM I BEING TOO SOFT?

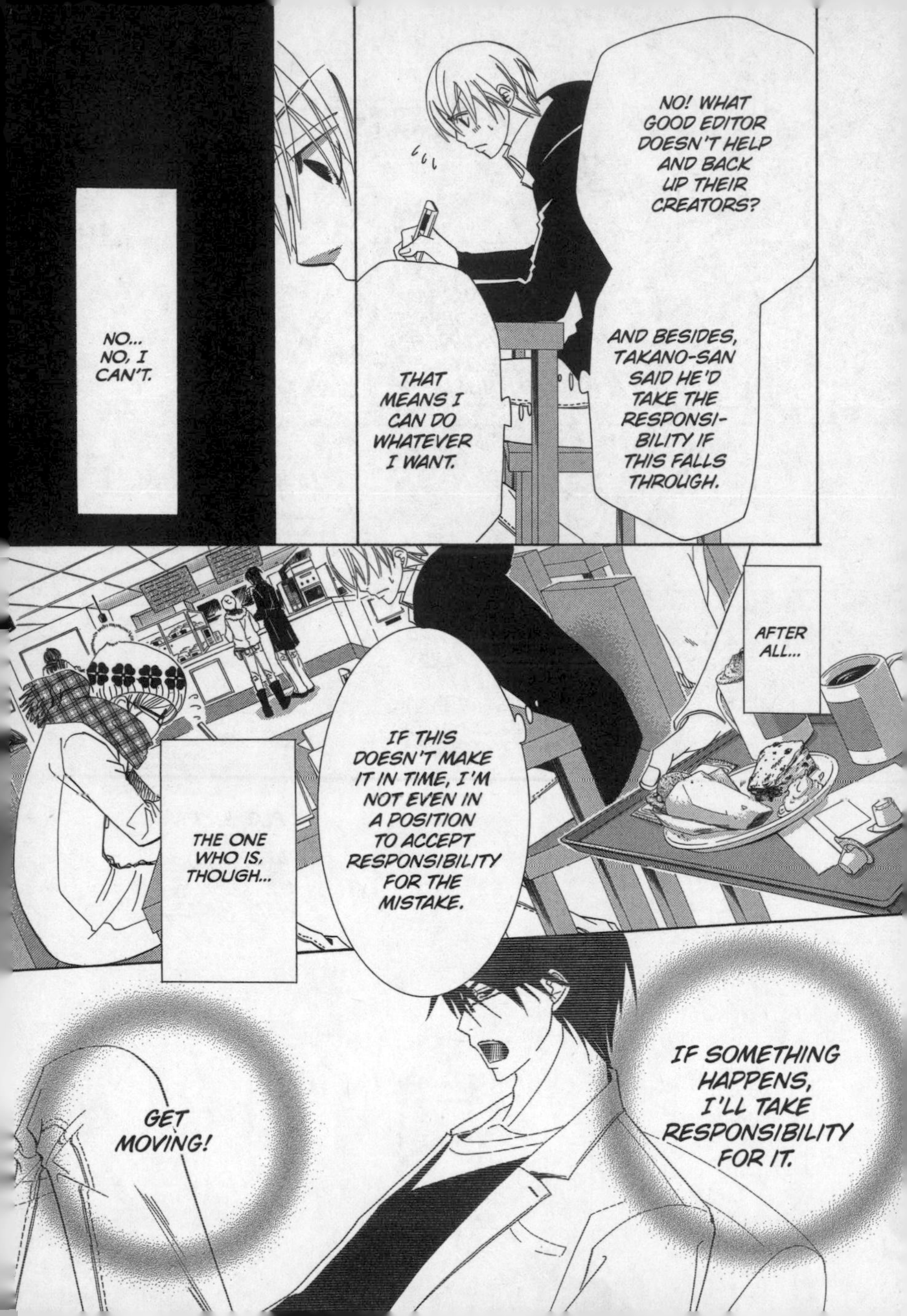
NO! WHAT GOOD EDITOR DOESN'T HELP AND BACK UP THEIR CREATORS?
AND BESIDES, TAKANO-SAN SAID HE'D TAKE THE RESPONSI-BILITY IF THIS FALLS THROUGH.
THAT MEANS I CAN DO WHATEVER I WANT.
NO... NO, I CAN'T.
AFTER ALL...
IF THIS DOESN'T MAKE IT IN TIME, I'M NOT EVEN IN A POSITION TO ACCEPT RESPONSIBILITY FOR THE MISTAKE.
THE ONE WHO IS, THOUGH...
IF SOMETHING HAPPENS, I'LL TAKE RESPONSIBILITY FOR IT.
GET MOVING!

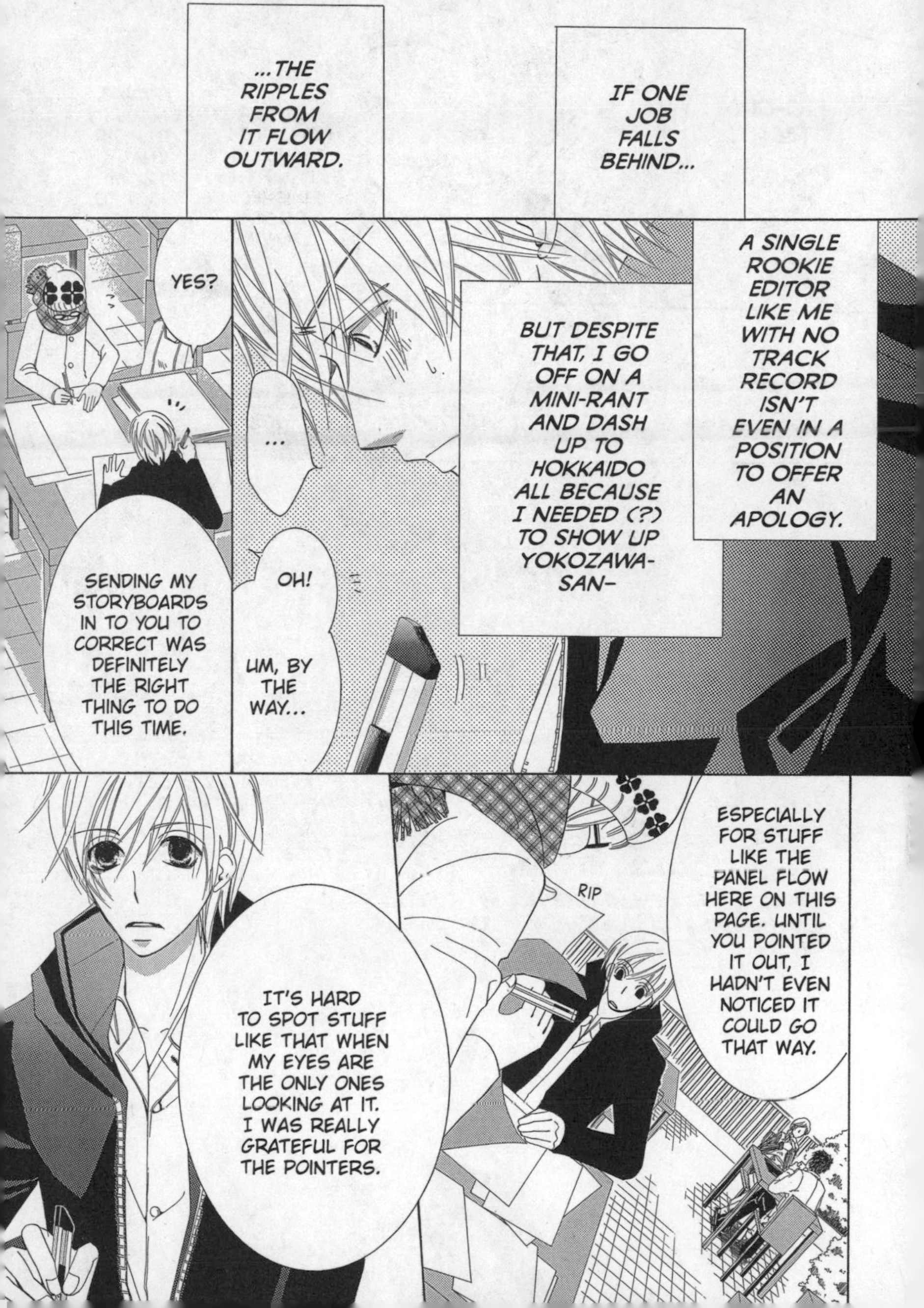
IF ONE JOB FALLS BEHIND...
...THE RIPPLES FROM IT FLOW OUTWARD.
A SINGLE ROOKIE EDITOR LIKE ME WITH NO TRACK RECORD ISN'T EVEN IN A POSITION TO OFFER AN APOLOGY.
BUT DESPITE THAT, I GO OFF ON A MINI-RANT AND DASH UP TO HOKKAIDO ALL BECAUSE I NEEDED (?) TO SHOW UP YOKOZAWA-SAN–
...
OH!
UM, BY THE WAY...
YES?
SENDING MY STORYBOARDS IN TO YOU TO CORRECT WAS DEFINITELY THE RIGHT THING TO DO THIS TIME.
ESPECIALLY FOR STUFF LIKE THE PANEL FLOW HERE ON THIS PAGE. UNTIL YOU POINTED IT OUT, I HADN'T EVEN NOTICED IT COULD GO THAT WAY.
RIP
IT'S HARD TO SPOT STUFF LIKE THAT WHEN MY EYES ARE THE ONLY ONES LOOKING AT IT. I WAS REALLY GRATEFUL FOR THE POINTERS.

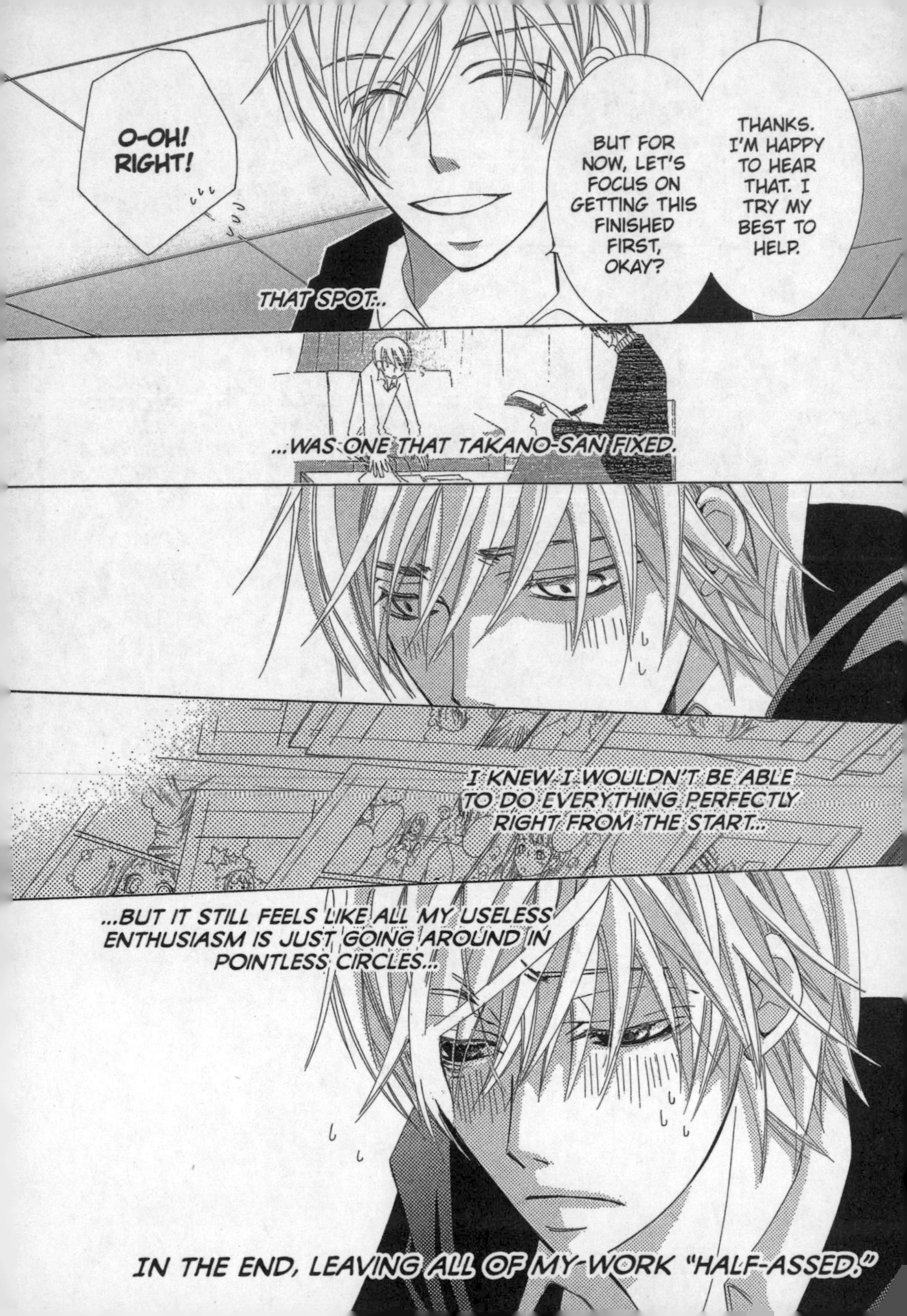
THANKS. I'M HAPPY TO HEAR THAT. I TRY MY BEST TO HELP.
BUT FOR NOW, LET'S FOCUS ON GETTING THIS FINISHED FIRST, OKAY?
O-OH! RIGHT!
THAT SPOT...
...WAS ONE THAT TAKANO-SAN FIXED.
I KNEW I WOULDN'T BE ABLE TO DO EVERYTHING PERFECTLY RIGHT FROM THE START...
...BUT IT STILL FEELS LIKE ALL MY USELESS ENTHUSIASM IS JUST GOING AROUND IN POINTLESS CIRCLES...
IN THE END, LEAVING ALL OF MY WORK "HALF-ASSED."

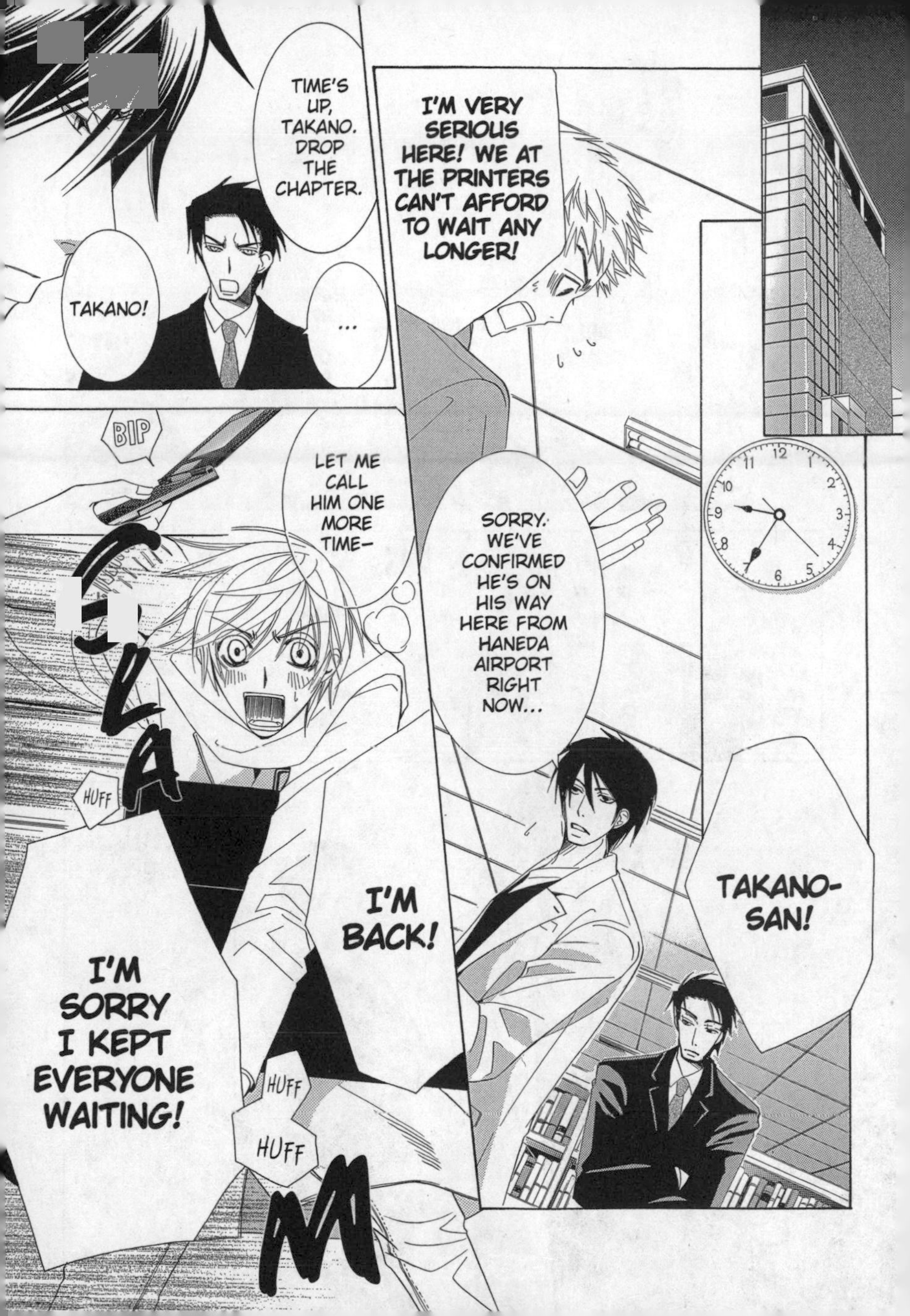
I'M VERY SERIOUS HERE! WE AT THE PRINTERS CAN'T AFFORD TO WAIT ANY LONGER!
TIME'S UP, TAKANO. DROP THE CHAPTER.
...
TAKANO!
SORRY. WE'VE CONFIRMED HE'S ON HIS WAY HERE FROM HANEDA AIRPORT RIGHT NOW...
LET ME CALL HIM ONE MORE TIME—
BIP
TAKANO-SAN!
I'M BACK!
HUFF
I'M SORRY I KEPT EVERYONE WAITING!
HUFF
HUFF

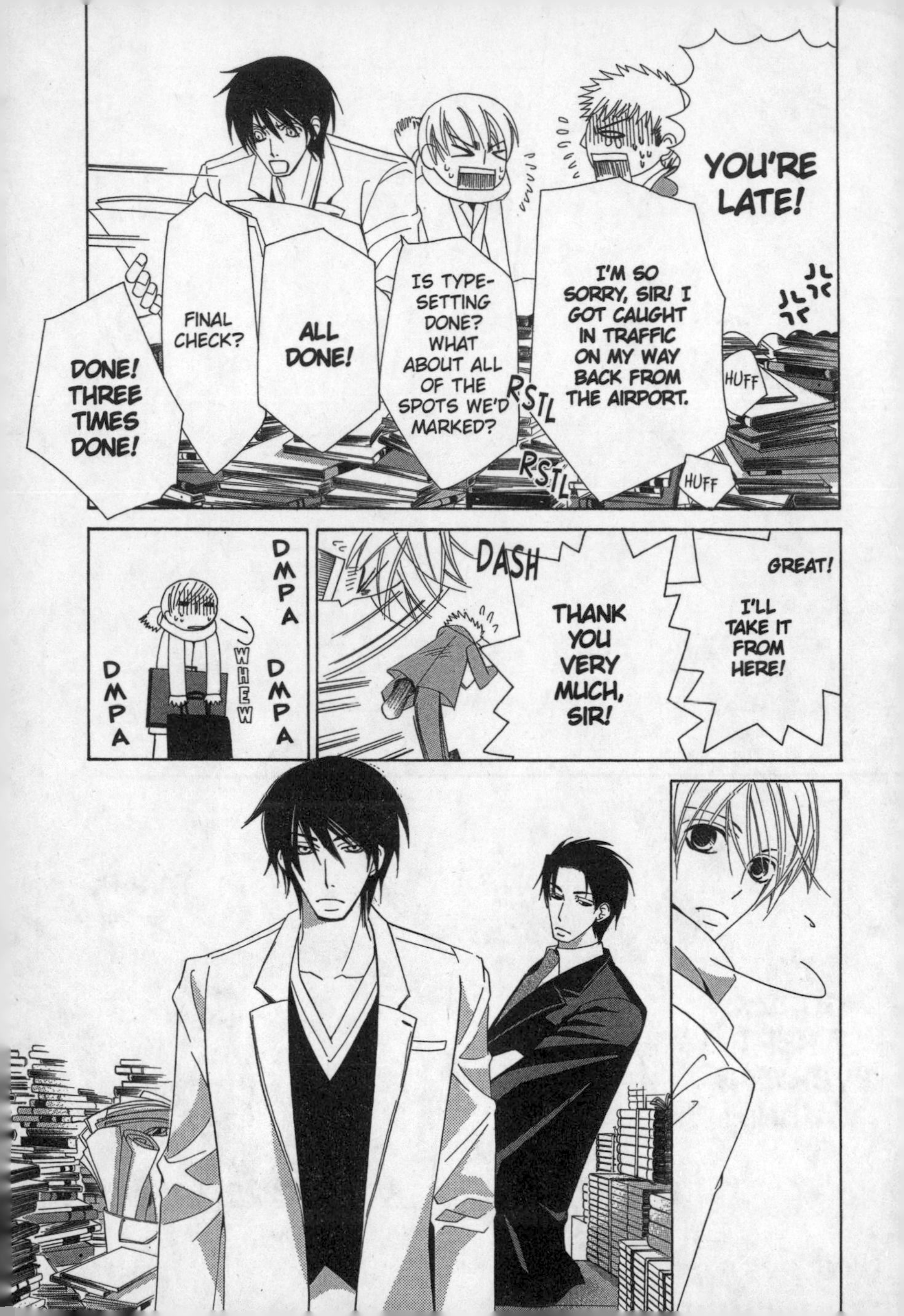
YOU'RE LATE!
I'M SO SORRY, SIR! I GOT CAUGHT IN TRAFFIC ON MY WAY BACK FROM THE AIRPORT.
HUFF
HUFF
RSTL
RSTL
IS TYPE-SETTING DONE? WHAT ABOUT ALL OF THE SPOTS WE'D MARKED?
ALL DONE!
FINAL CHECK?
DONE! THREE TIMES DONE!
GREAT!
I'LL TAKE IT FROM HERE!
THANK YOU VERY MUCH, SIR!
DASH
DMPA
DMPA
WHEW
DMPA

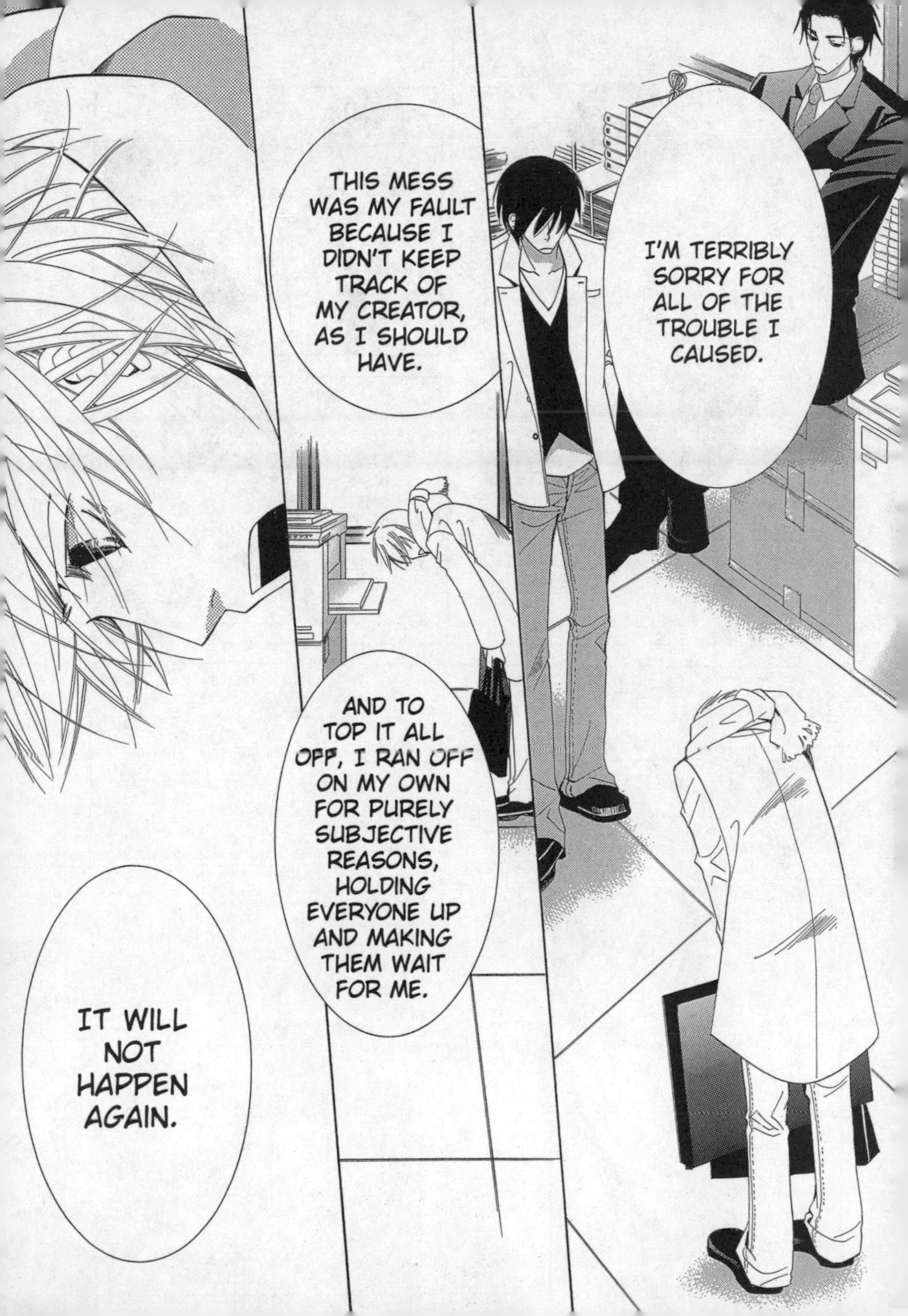
I'M TERRIBLY SORRY FOR ALL OF THE TROUBLE I CAUSED.
THIS MESS WAS MY FAULT BECAUSE I DIDN'T KEEP TRACK OF MY CREATOR, AS I SHOULD HAVE.
AND TO TOP IT ALL OFF, I RAN OFF ON MY OWN FOR PURELY SUBJECTIVE REASONS, HOLDING EVERYONE UP AND MAKING THEM WAIT FOR ME.
IT WILL NOT HAPPEN AGAIN.

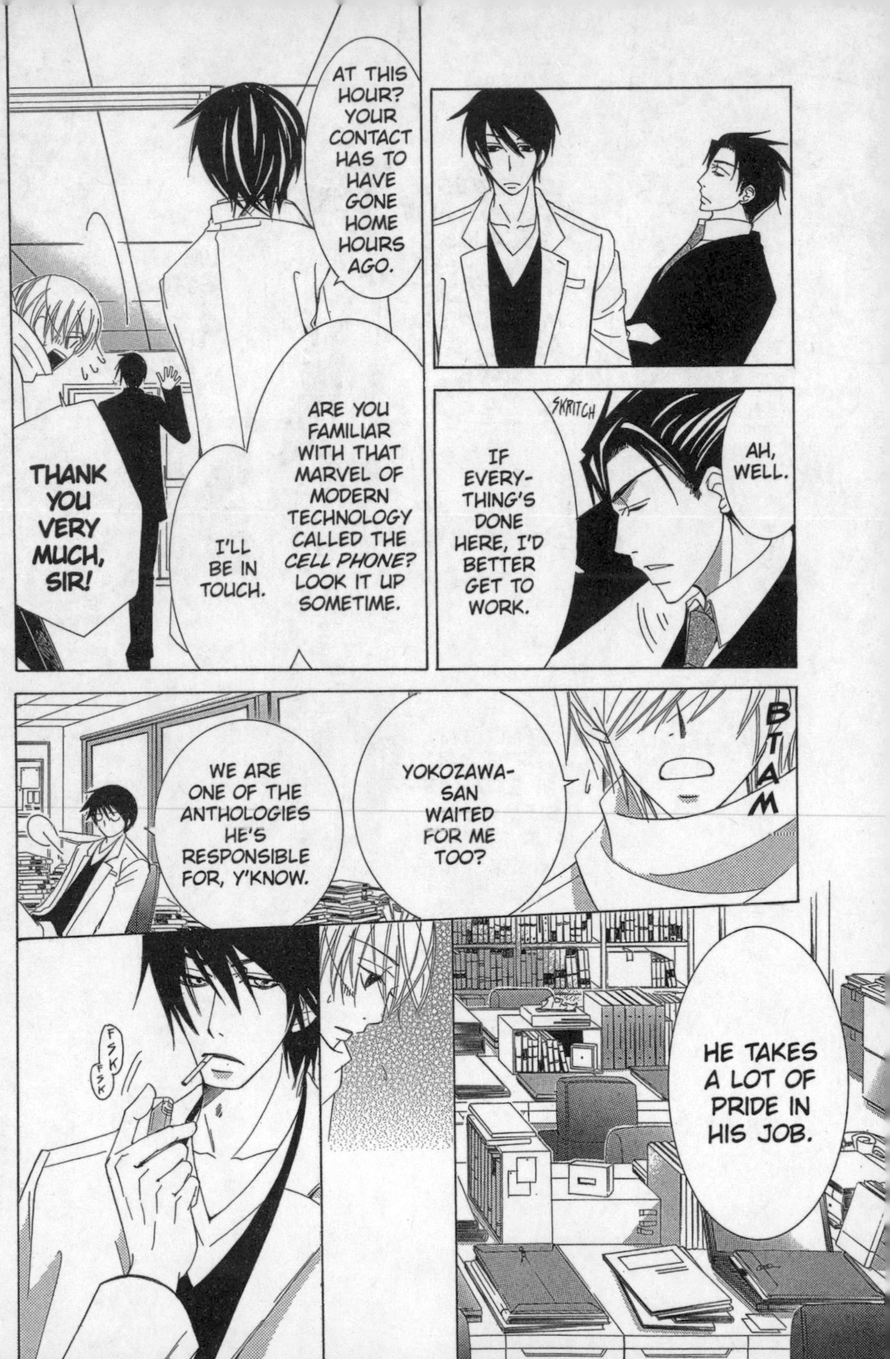
AH, WELL.
SKRITCH
IF EVERYTHING'S DONE HERE, I'D BETTER GET TO WORK.
AT THIS HOUR? YOUR CONTACT HAS TO HAVE GONE HOME HOURS AGO.
ARE YOU FAMILIAR WITH THAT MARVEL OF MODERN TECHNOLOGY CALLED THE *CELL PHONE*? LOOK IT UP SOMETIME.
I'LL BE IN TOUCH.
THANK YOU VERY MUCH, SIR!
BTAM
YOKOZAWA-SAN WAITED FOR ME TOO?
WE ARE ONE OF THE ANTHOLOGIES HE'S RESPONSIBLE FOR, Y'KNOW.
HE TAKES A LOT OF PRIDE IN HIS JOB.
FSK FSK

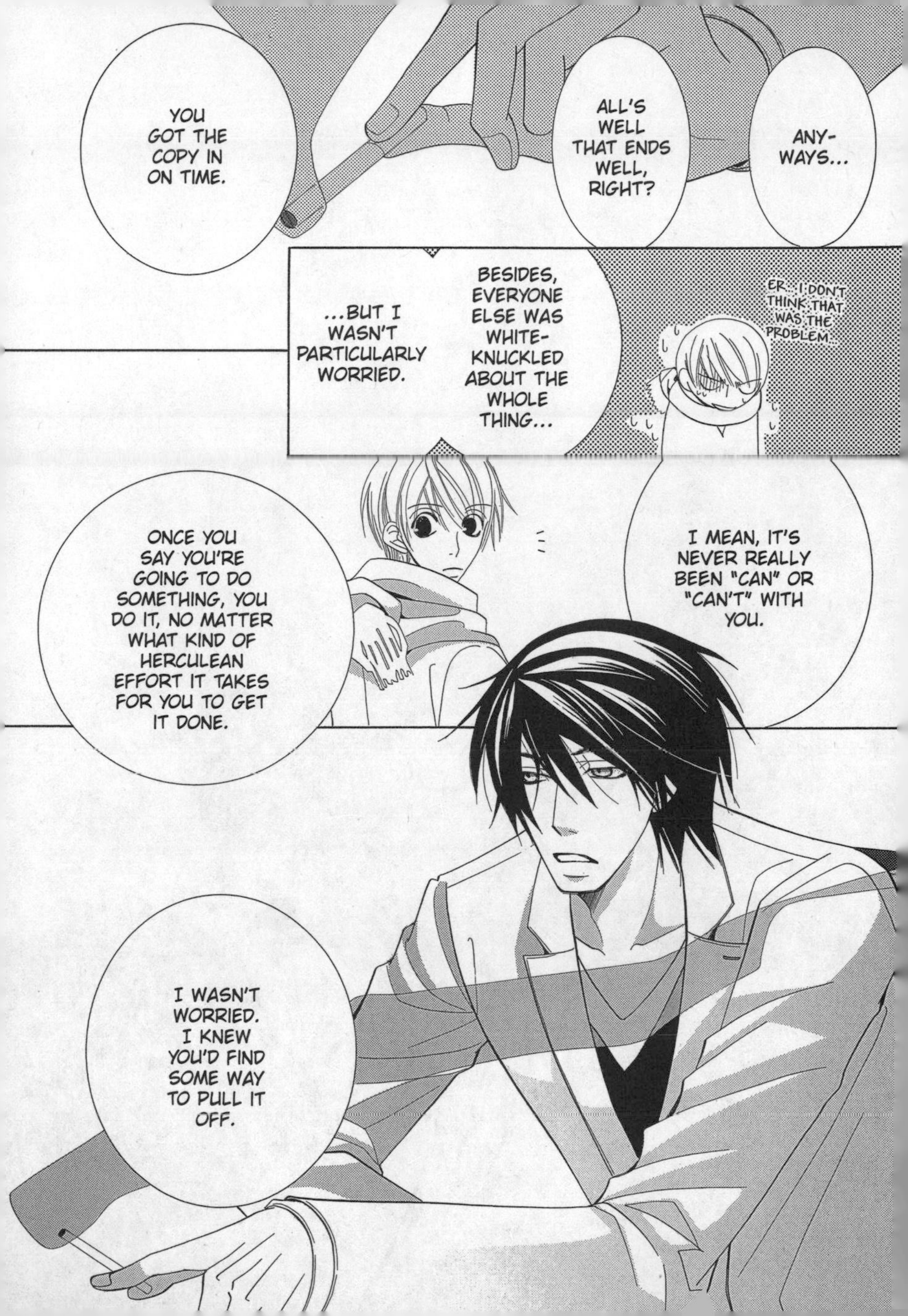
ANY-WAYS...
ALL'S WELL THAT ENDS WELL, RIGHT?
YOU GOT THE COPY IN ON TIME.
BESIDES, EVERYONE ELSE WAS WHITE-KNUCKLED ABOUT THE WHOLE THING...
...BUT I WASN'T PARTICULARLY WORRIED.
ER... I DON'T THINK THAT WAS THE PROBLEM...
I MEAN, IT'S NEVER REALLY BEEN "CAN" OR "CAN'T" WITH YOU.
ONCE YOU SAY YOU'RE GOING TO DO SOMETHING, YOU DO IT, NO MATTER WHAT KIND OF HERCULEAN EFFORT IT TAKES FOR YOU TO GET IT DONE.
I WASN'T WORRIED. I KNEW YOU'D FIND SOME WAY TO PULL IT OFF.

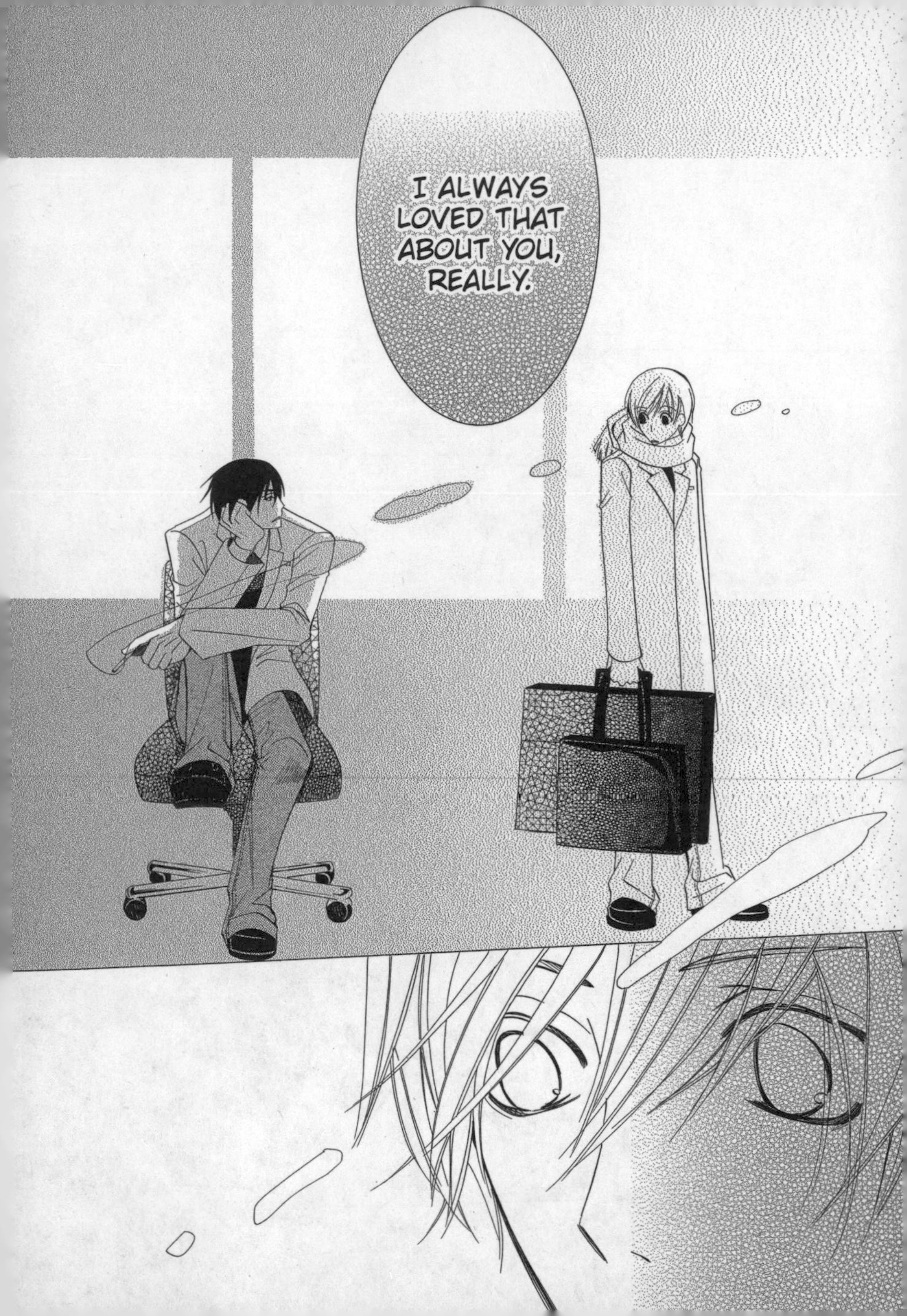
I ALWAYS LOVED THAT ABOUT YOU, REALLY.

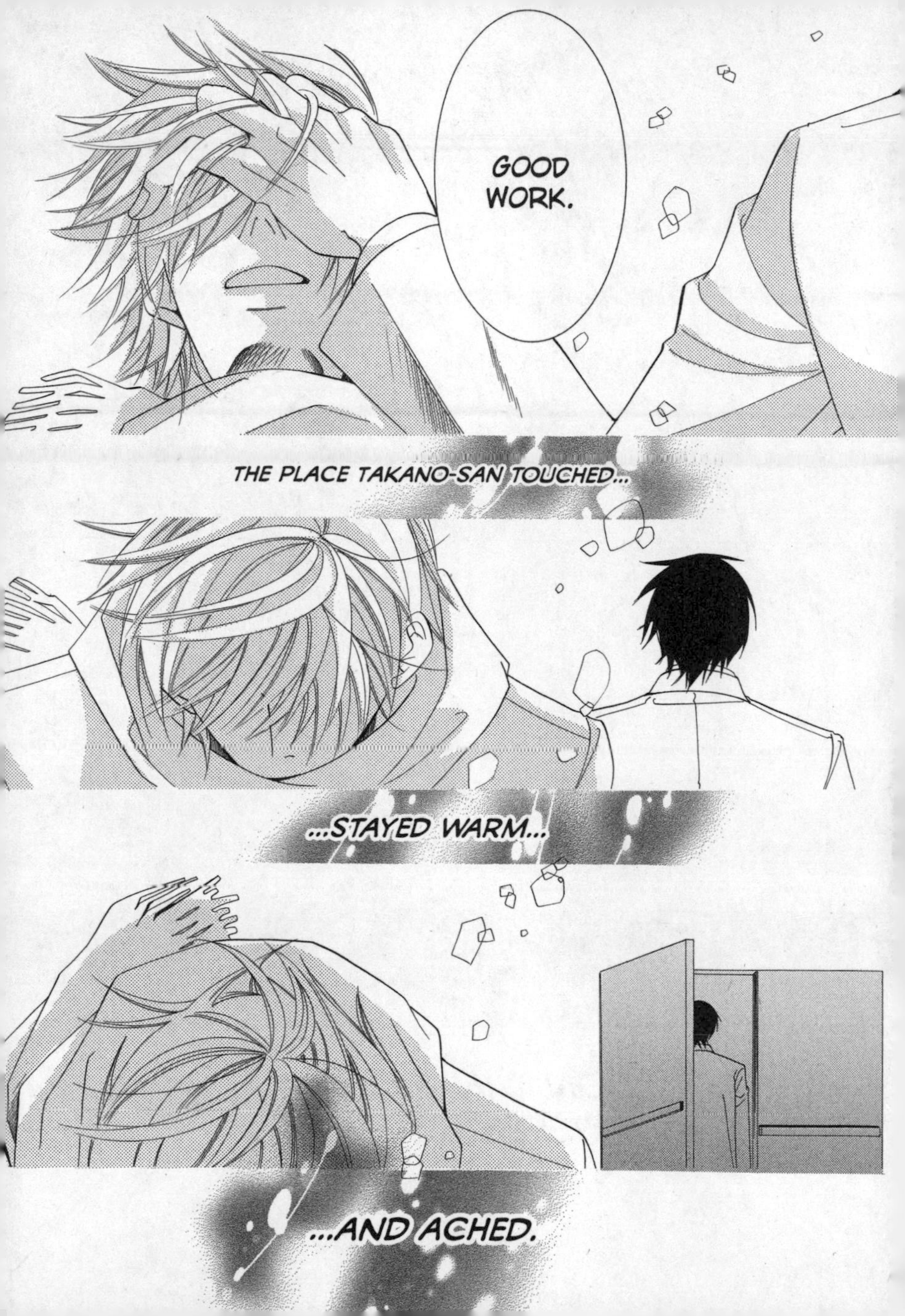
GOOD WORK.
THE PLACE TAKANO-SAN TOUCHED...
...STAYED WARM...
...AND ACHED.

PLEASE...

DON'T INVADE MY DEFENSES ANY FURTHER.

SPLSH

SPLSH

SPLSH

SPLSH

SPLSH

FSHHH

JUST BECAUSE YOU WORK IN A SHOJO MANGA DEPARTMENT DOESN'T MEAN YOU HAVE TO START THINKING LIKE A SHOJO MANGA HEROINE!

HUFF

WIPE WIPE WIPE

OI, OI, OI! GET A GRIP!

HUFF

IS THERE ANYTHING I CAN DO FOR—

AH!

YOKO-ZAWA-SAN.

I'M SORRY. I DIDN'T SEE YOU THERE.

I'M SURPRISED YOU HAD THE BALLS TO WALTZ IN AND GET A JOB HERE AFTER EVERYTHING YOU'VE DONE.

JOLT

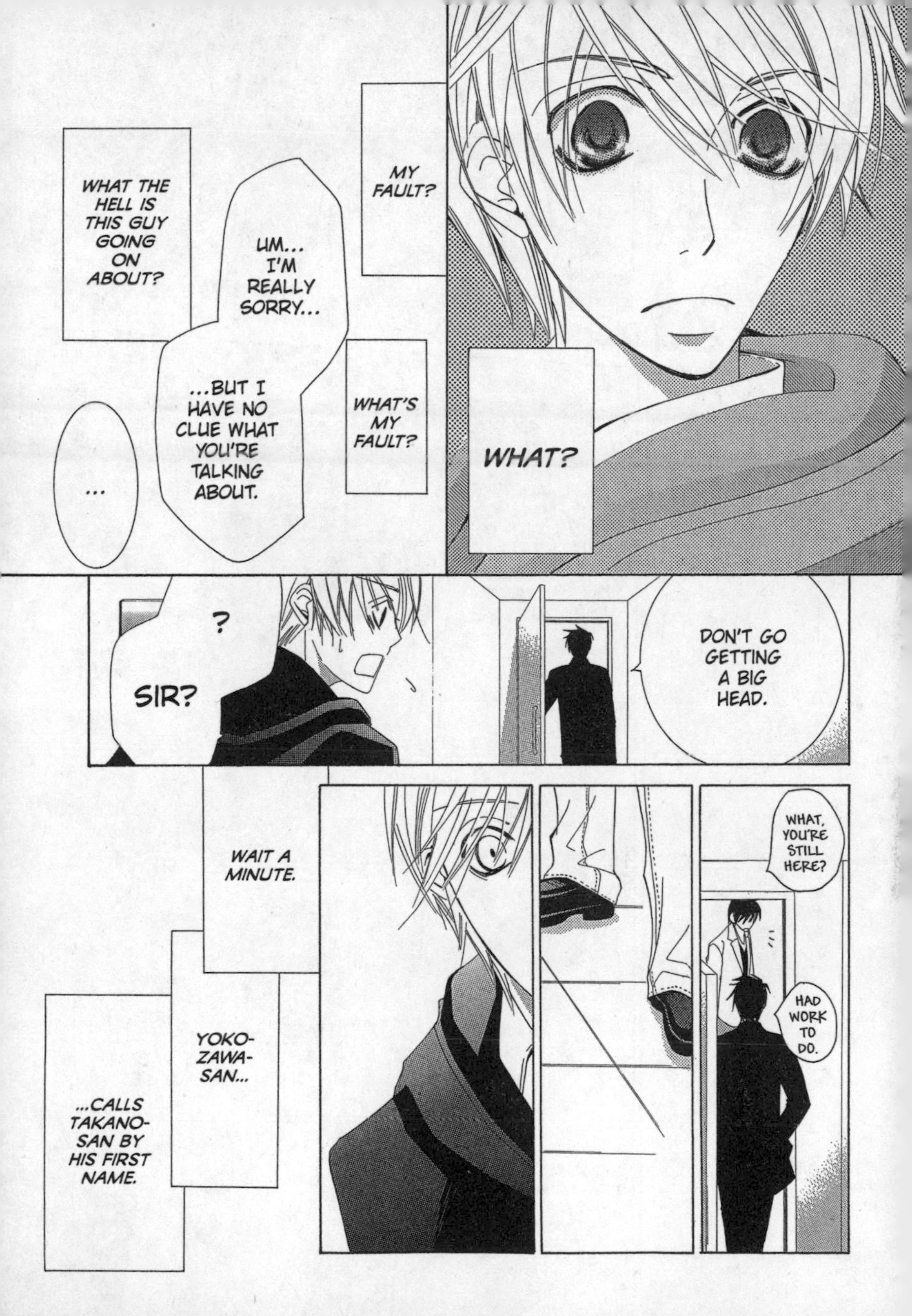
WHAT?
MY FAULT?
WHAT'S MY FAULT?
UM... I'M REALLY SORRY...
...BUT I HAVE NO CLUE WHAT YOU'RE TALKING ABOUT.
WHAT THE HELL IS THIS GUY GOING ON ABOUT?
...
DON'T GO GETTING A BIG HEAD.
?
SIR?
WHAT, YOU'RE STILL HERE?
HAD WORK TO DO.
WAIT A MINUTE.
YOKO-ZAWA-SAN...
...CALLS TAKANO-SAN BY HIS FIRST NAME.

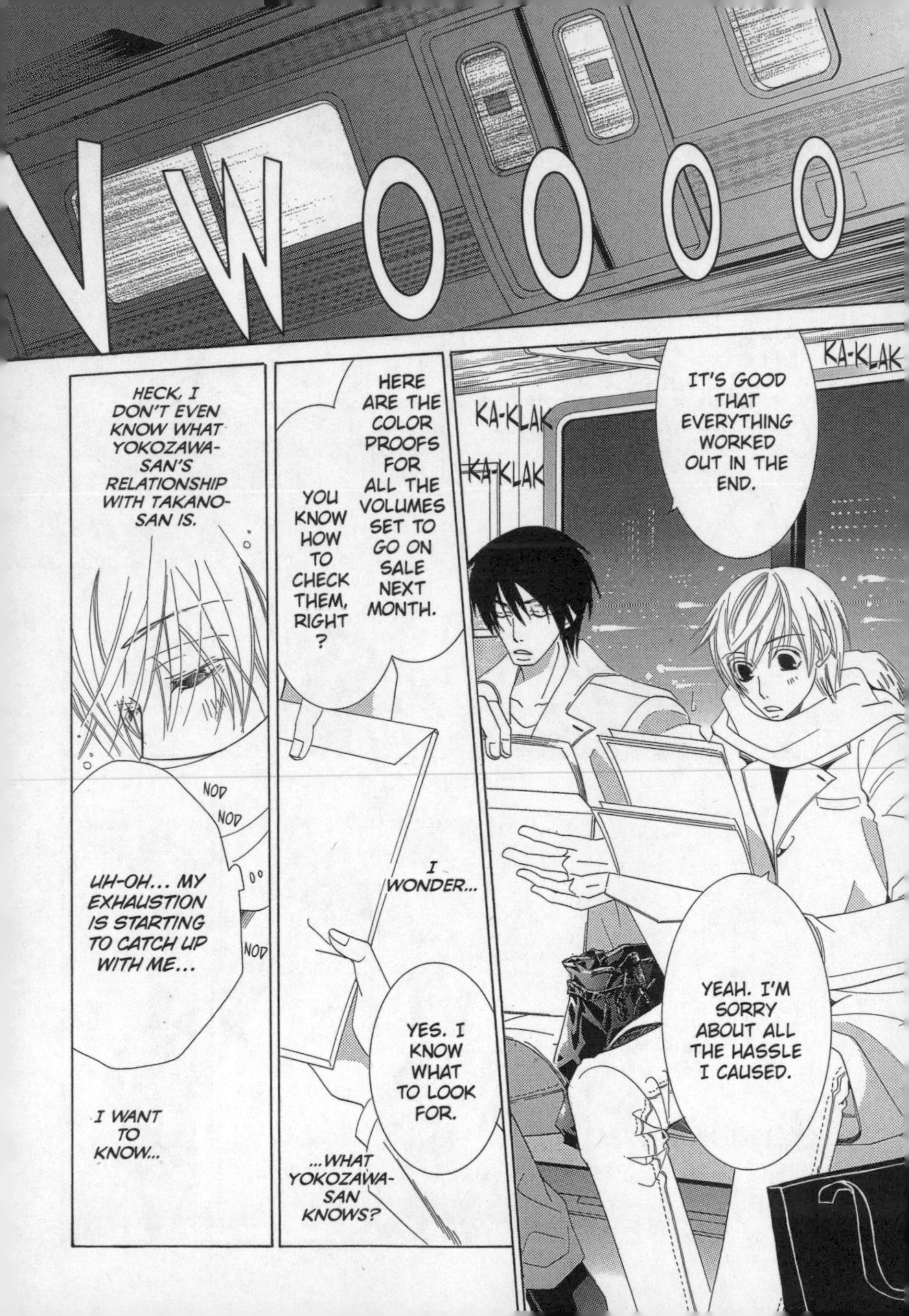
VWOOOOO
KA-KLAK
KA-KLAK
KA-KLAK
IT'S GOOD THAT EVERYTHING WORKED OUT IN THE END.
YEAH. I'M SORRY ABOUT ALL THE HASSLE I CAUSED.
HERE ARE THE COLOR PROOFS FOR ALL THE VOLUMES SET TO GO ON SALE NEXT MONTH.
YOU KNOW HOW TO CHECK THEM, RIGHT?
YES. I KNOW WHAT TO LOOK FOR.
I WONDER...
...WHAT YOKOZAWA-SAN KNOWS?
HECK, I DON'T EVEN KNOW WHAT YOKOZAWA-SAN'S RELATIONSHIP WITH TAKANO-SAN IS.
NOD
NOD
UH-OH... MY EXHAUSTION IS STARTING TO CATCH UP WITH ME...
NOD
I WANT TO KNOW...

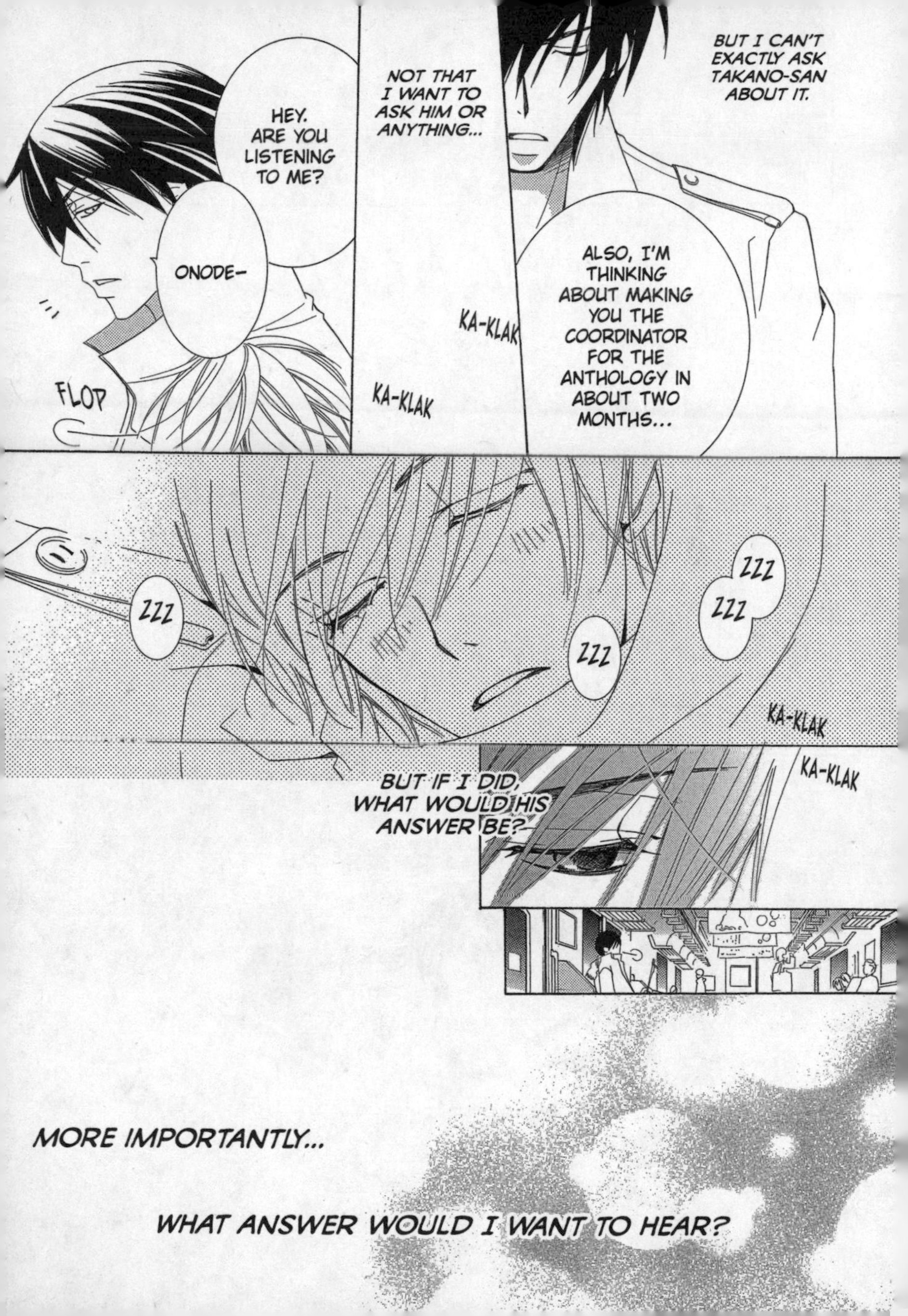
BUT I CAN'T EXACTLY ASK TAKANO-SAN ABOUT IT.
NOT THAT I WANT TO ASK HIM OR ANYTHING...
ALSO, I'M THINKING ABOUT MAKING YOU THE COORDINATOR FOR THE ANTHOLOGY IN ABOUT TWO MONTHS...
KA-KLAK
KA-KLAK
HEY. ARE YOU LISTENING TO ME?
ONODE-
FLOP
ZZZ
ZZZ
ZZZ
ZZZ
KA-KLAK
KA-KLAK
BUT IF I DID, WHAT WOULD HIS ANSWER BE?
MORE IMPORTANTLY...
WHAT ANSWER WOULD I WANT TO HEAR?

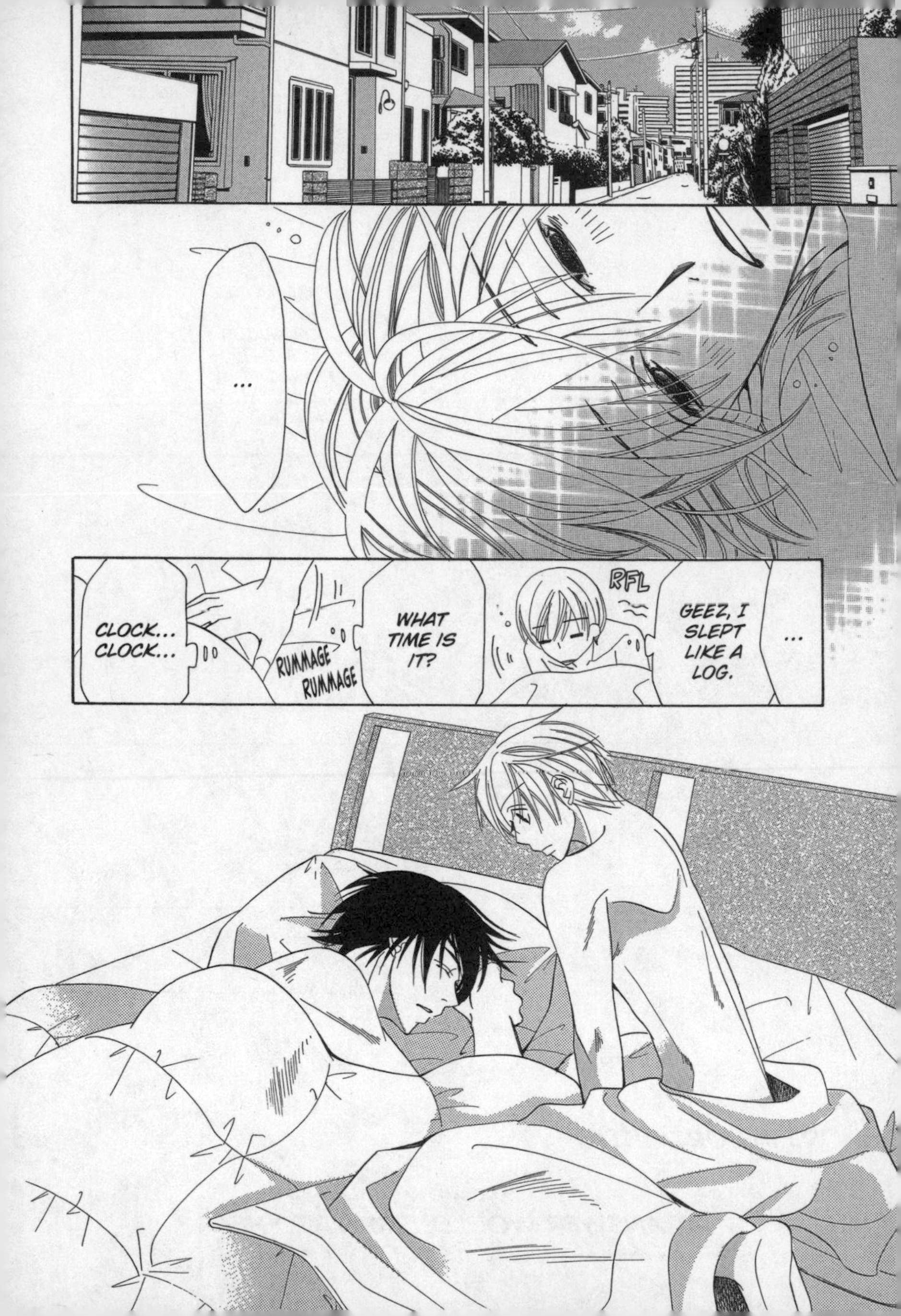
...
...
GEEZ, I SLEPT LIKE A LOG.
RFL
WHAT TIME IS IT?
RUMMAGE RUMMAGE
CLOCK... CLOCK...

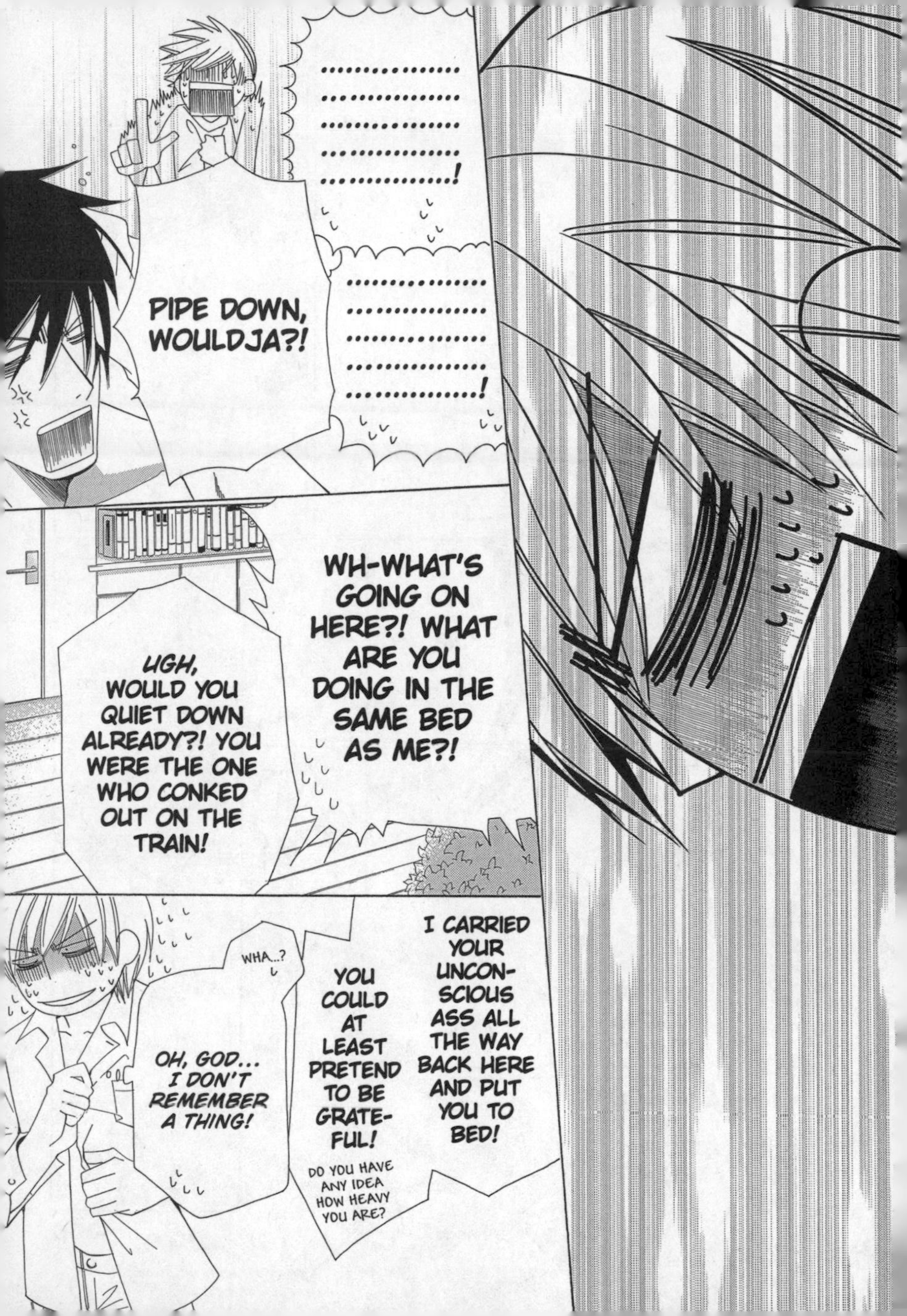

....!
....!
PIPE DOWN, WOULDJA?!
WH-WHAT'S GOING ON HERE?! WHAT ARE YOU DOING IN THE SAME BED AS ME?!
UGH, WOULD YOU QUIET DOWN ALREADY?! YOU WERE THE ONE WHO CONKED OUT ON THE TRAIN!
I CARRIED YOUR UNCON-SCIOUS ASS ALL THE WAY BACK HERE AND PUT YOU TO BED!
YOU COULD AT LEAST PRETEND TO BE GRATE-FUL!
DO YOU HAVE ANY IDEA HOW HEAVY YOU ARE?
WHA...?
OH, GOD... I DON'T REMEMBER A THING!

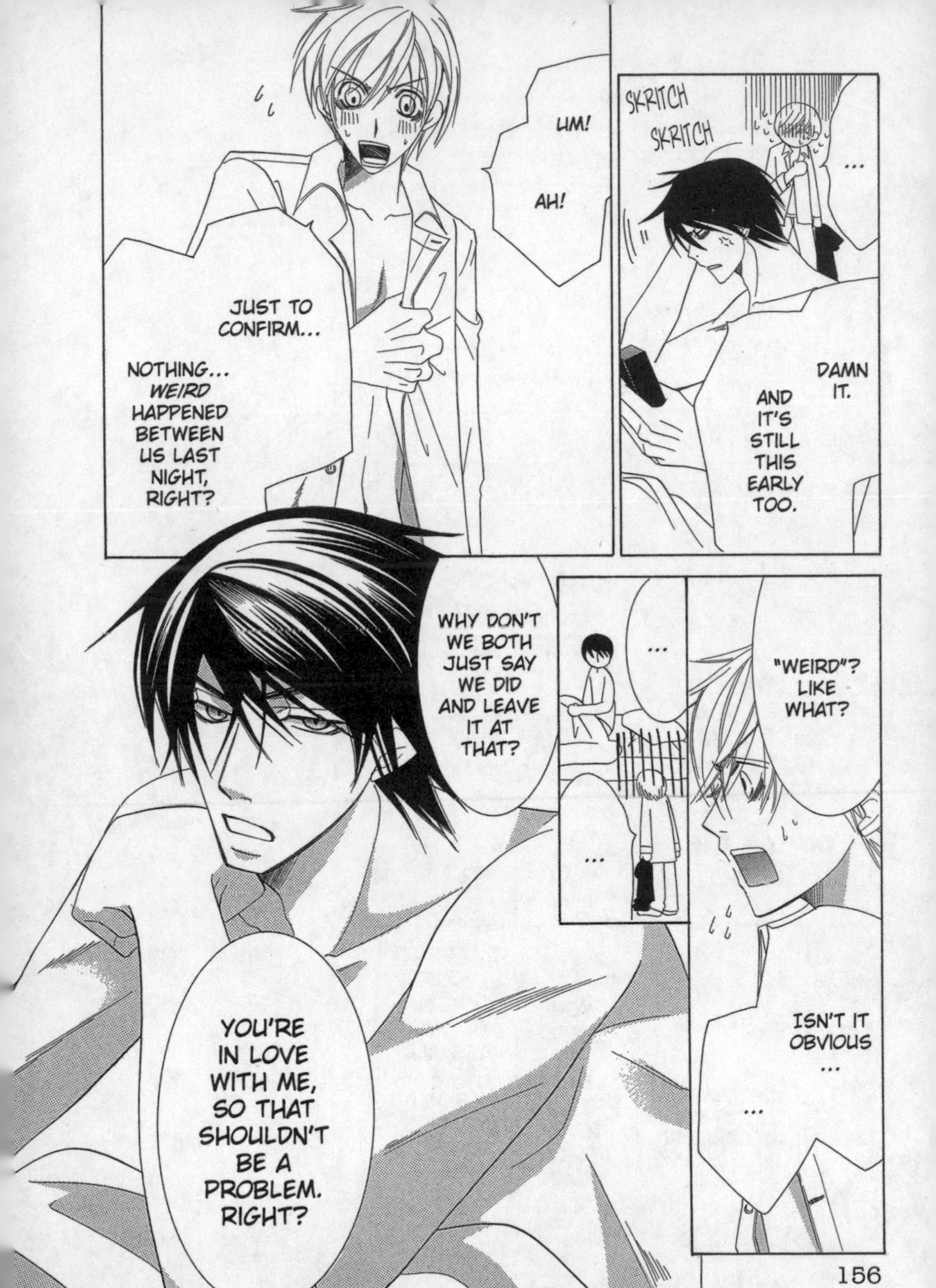
SKRITCH
SKRITCH
...
DAMN IT.
AND IT'S STILL THIS EARLY TOO.
UM!
AH!
JUST TO CONFIRM...
NOTHING... *WEIRD* HAPPENED BETWEEN US LAST NIGHT, RIGHT?
"WEIRD"? LIKE WHAT?
ISN'T IT OBVIOUS...
...
...
...
WHY DON'T WE BOTH JUST SAY WE DID AND LEAVE IT AT THAT?
YOU'RE IN LOVE WITH ME, SO THAT SHOULDN'T BE A PROBLEM. RIGHT?

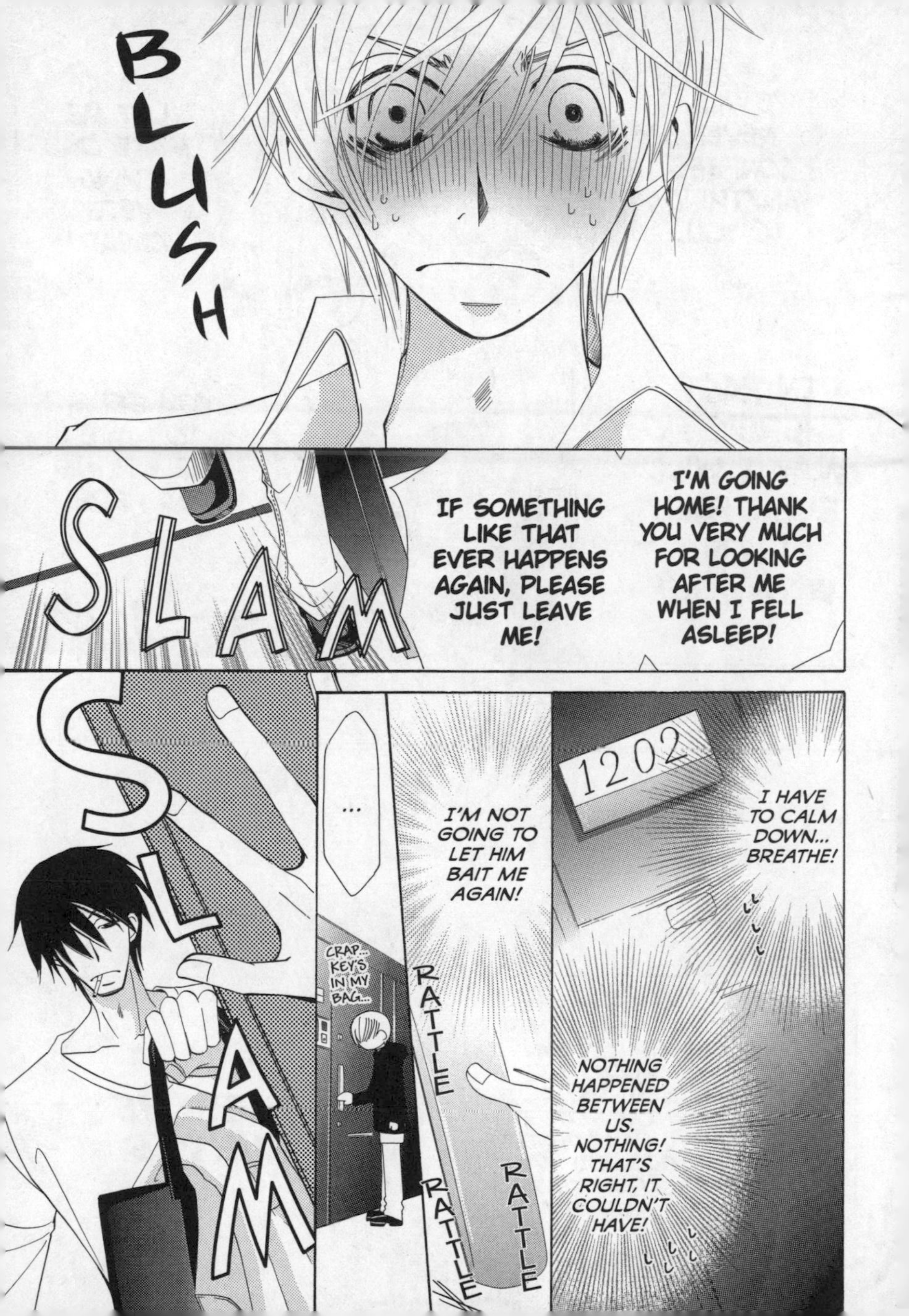
BLUSH
I'M GOING HOME! THANK YOU VERY MUCH FOR LOOKING AFTER ME WHEN I FELL ASLEEP!
IF SOMETHING LIKE THAT EVER HAPPENS AGAIN, PLEASE JUST LEAVE ME!
SLAM
1202
I HAVE TO CALM DOWN... BREATHE!
NOTHING HAPPENED BETWEEN US. NOTHING! THAT'S RIGHT, IT COULDN'T HAVE!
I'M NOT GOING TO LET HIM BAIT ME AGAIN!
...
RATTLE
RATTLE
RATTLE
CRAP... KEY'S IN MY BAG...
SLAM

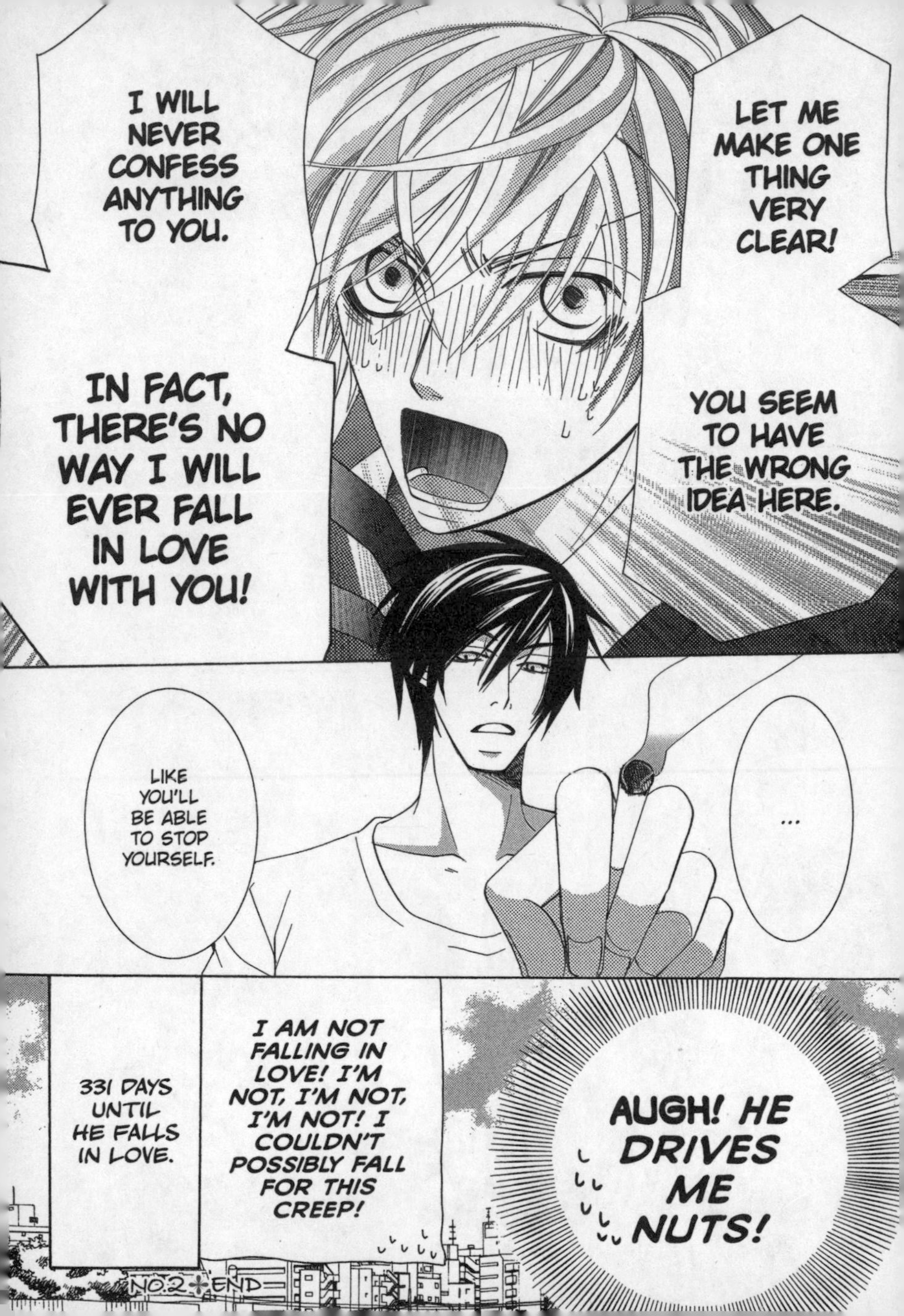
LET ME MAKE ONE THING VERY CLEAR!
YOU SEEM TO HAVE THE WRONG IDEA HERE.
I WILL NEVER CONFESS ANYTHING TO YOU.
IN FACT, THERE'S NO WAY I WILL EVER FALL IN LOVE WITH YOU!
...
LIKE YOU'LL BE ABLE TO STOP YOURSELF.
AUGH! HE DRIVES ME NUTS!
I AM NOT FALLING IN LOVE! I'M NOT, I'M NOT, I'M NOT! I COULDN'T POSSIBLY FALL FOR THIS CREEP!
331 DAYS UNTIL HE FALLS IN LOVE.
NO.2 END

MARUKAWA PUBLISHING TERMINOLOGY & JARGON (PART 3)

***NOTE:** ALL OF THE TERMINOLOGY LISTED HEREIN IS SPECIFIC TO MARUKAWA PUBLISHING AND MAY NOT BE APPLICABLE TO THE GENERAL PUBLISHING INDUSTRY.

[SUBMISSION]

FORMAL SUBMISSIONS HAPPEN WHEN EDITING DEPARTMENTS HAND EDITED COPY TO THE PRINTERS SO THAT A BOOK OR MAGAZINE CAN BE PRINTED. WHEN EDITORS FORMALLY HAND LETTER COPY OR ILLUSTRATIONS TO DESIGNERS IN ORDER FOR ARTICLES OR DESIGN PAGES TO BE PRINTED, THESE ARE CALLED "DESIGN SUBMISSIONS" OR "LAYOUT SUBMISSIONS."

[DROP-DEAD DATE]

A DROP-DEAD DATE IS THE LAST POSSIBLE DAY FOR EDITORS TO SUBMIT EDITED COPY TO PRINTERS. IT IS USUALLY WELL AFTER THE ORIGINAL DEADLINE AND OFTEN MAKES THE PRINTERS MAD. MISSING THE DROP-DEAD DATE MEANS THE COPY WON'T MAKE IT INTO THE BOOK OR MAGAZINE TO BE PRINTED. THE PRINTER CAN'T GUARANTEE THE PRINTING WON'T HAVE ANY ERRORS, AND THERE IS NO TIME TO FIX THEM.

[CYCLE END]

THE PUBLISHING CYCLE COMES TO AN END WHEN ALL COPYEDITING IS COMPLETE ON THE BLUELINES AND OTHER FINAL PROOFS AND NO MORE CHANGES NEED TO BE MADE TO THE GALLEY PROOFS. ALL SUBMISSIONS, INCLUDING THOSE "OKAY WITH CORRECTIONS" (COPY WHICH HAS PLACES TO CHANGE, BUT NO NEW GALLEY PROOF NEEDS TO BE PRINTED), ARE IN AND THE EDITING DEPARTMENT CAN RETURN TO NORMAL.

The World's Greatest First Love
The Case of Ritsu Onodera
I FEEL LIKE I'M ONLY DOING THIS JOB FOR THE FANCY TIMES.
WOW, THAT'S WRONG IN SO MANY WAYS.

MARUKAWA PUBLISHING TERMINOLOGY & JARGON (PART 4)

***NOTE:** ALL OF THE TERMINOLOGY LISTED HEREIN IS SPECIFIC TO MARUKAWA PUBLISHING AND MAY NOT BE APPLICABLE TO THE GENERAL PUBLISHING INDUSTRY.

[ANTHOLOGY COORDINATOR]

THIS IS THE DUTY RITSU ONODERA WILL UNDERTAKE IN A FEW MONTHS. THIS PERSON OVERSEES THE ANTHOLOGY CREATION CYCLE, COORDINATING SUBMISSIONS AND SERVING AS THE PRINTERS' CONTACT PERSON ON THE EDITING SIDE. OCCASIONALLY, THIS PERSON WILL ALSO NEED TO NEGOTIATE DEADLINE EXTENSIONS WITH THE PRINTERS.

[GALLEY PROOF]

GALLEYS ARE INITIAL PRINT COPIES MADE SO THAT THE TYPESETTING CAN BE CHECKED AND ANOTHER EDITING PASS MADE. GALLEYS MUST HAVE THE EXACT SAME CONTENT, BE IN THE SAME FORMAT, AND HAVE THE SAME FINISH AS THE FINAL PRODUCT.

[MANGA ASSISTANT]

MANGA ASSISTANTS SUPPORT A MANGAKA DURING THE DRAWING PROCESS. NOT ONLY DO ASSISTANTS TAKE CARE OF THINGS DIRECTLY RELATED TO THE MANGA—LIKE DRAWING BACKGROUNDS, ADDING TONE AND EFFECTS, AND ERASING OR COLORING IN LARGE AREAS—THEY ALSO OFTEN ACT AS A GENERAL "GOFER," GETTING FOOD AND SUPPLIES OR RUNNING OTHER ERRANDS.

The World's Greatest First Love
The Case of Ritsu Onodera

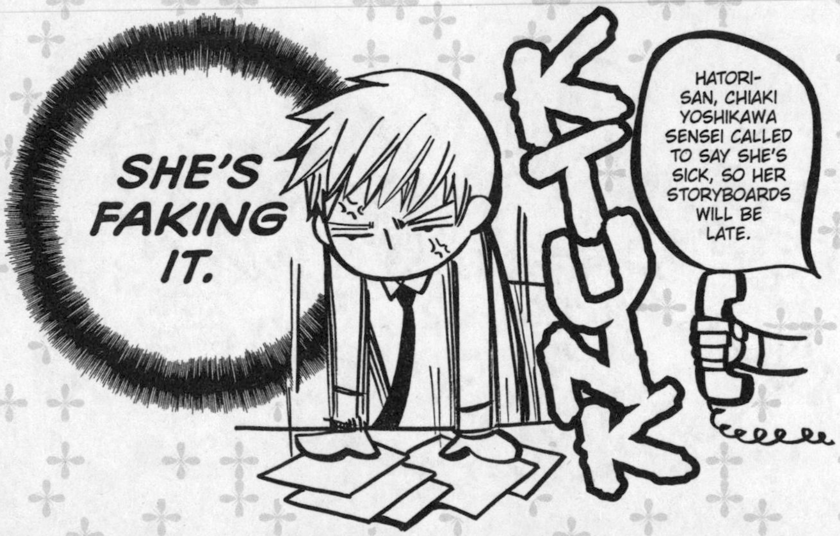
HATORI-SAN, CHIAKI YOSHIKAWA SENSEI CALLED TO SAY SHE'S SICK, SO HER STORYBOARDS WILL BE LATE.
SHE'S FAKING IT.

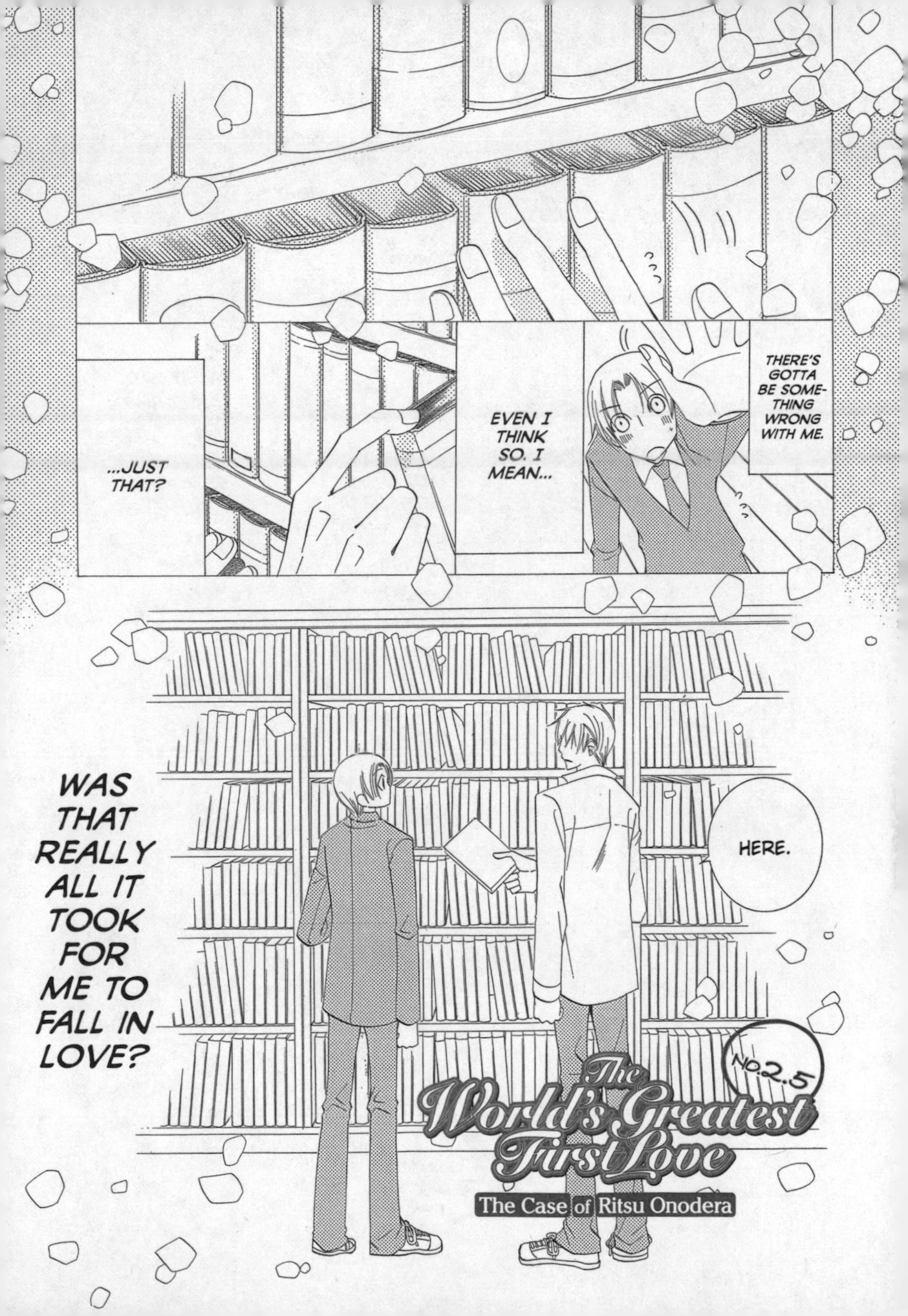
THERE'S GOTTA BE SOME-THING WRONG WITH ME.
EVEN I THINK SO. I MEAN...
...JUST THAT?
HERE.
WAS THAT REALLY ALL IT TOOK FOR ME TO FALL IN LOVE?
NO.2.5
The World's Greatest First Love
The Case of Ritsu Onodera

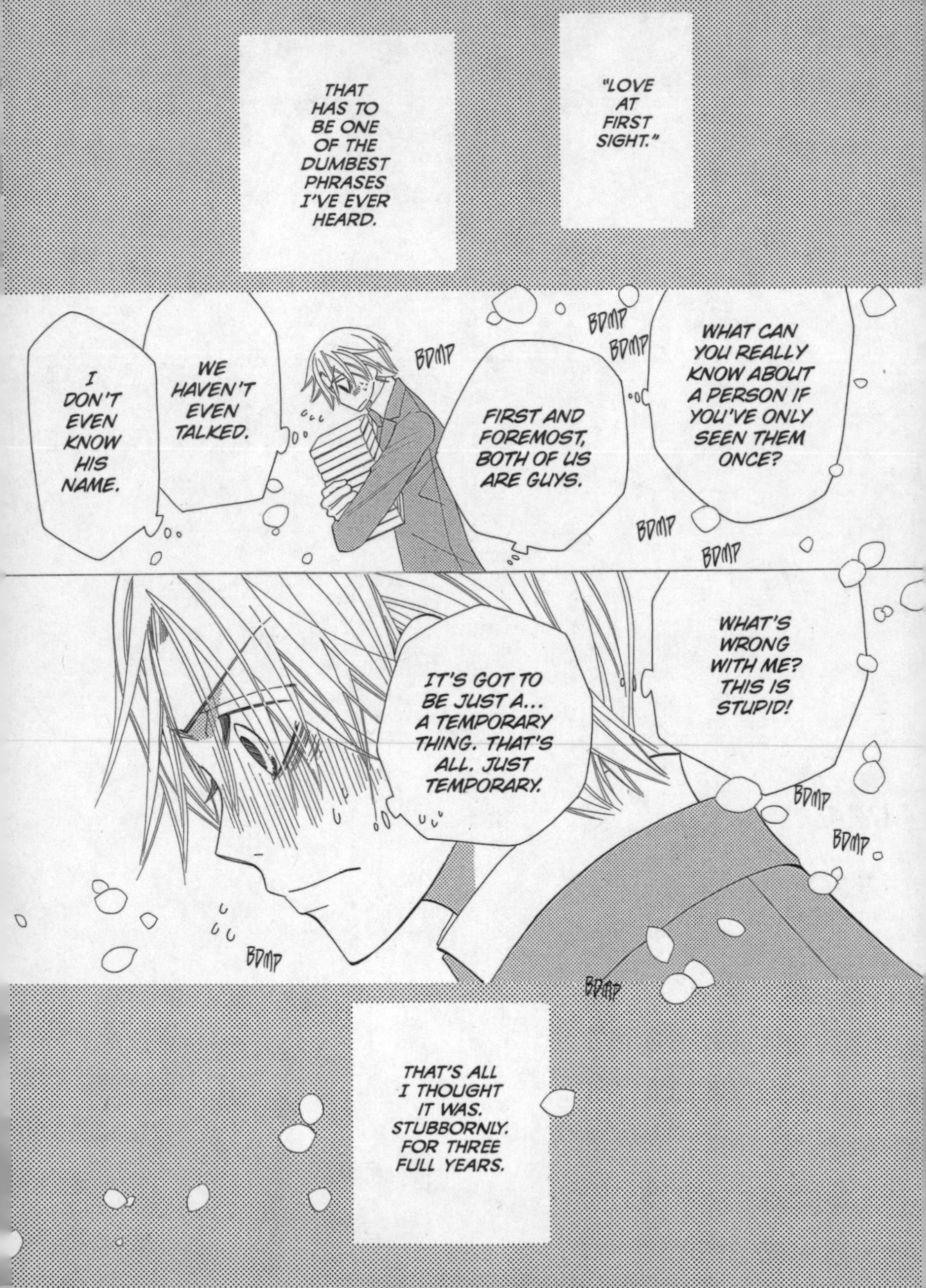
"LOVE AT FIRST SIGHT."
THAT HAS TO BE ONE OF THE DUMBEST PHRASES I'VE EVER HEARD.
BDMP
BDMP
WHAT CAN YOU REALLY KNOW ABOUT A PERSON IF YOU'VE ONLY SEEN THEM ONCE?
FIRST AND FOREMOST, BOTH OF US ARE GUYS.
BDMP
WE HAVEN'T EVEN TALKED.
I DON'T EVEN KNOW HIS NAME.
BDMP
BDMP
WHAT'S WRONG WITH ME? THIS IS STUPID!
IT'S GOT TO BE JUST A... A TEMPORARY THING. THAT'S ALL. JUST TEMPORARY.
BDMP
BDMP
BDMP
BDMP
THAT'S ALL I THOUGHT IT WAS. STUBBORNLY. FOR THREE FULL YEARS.

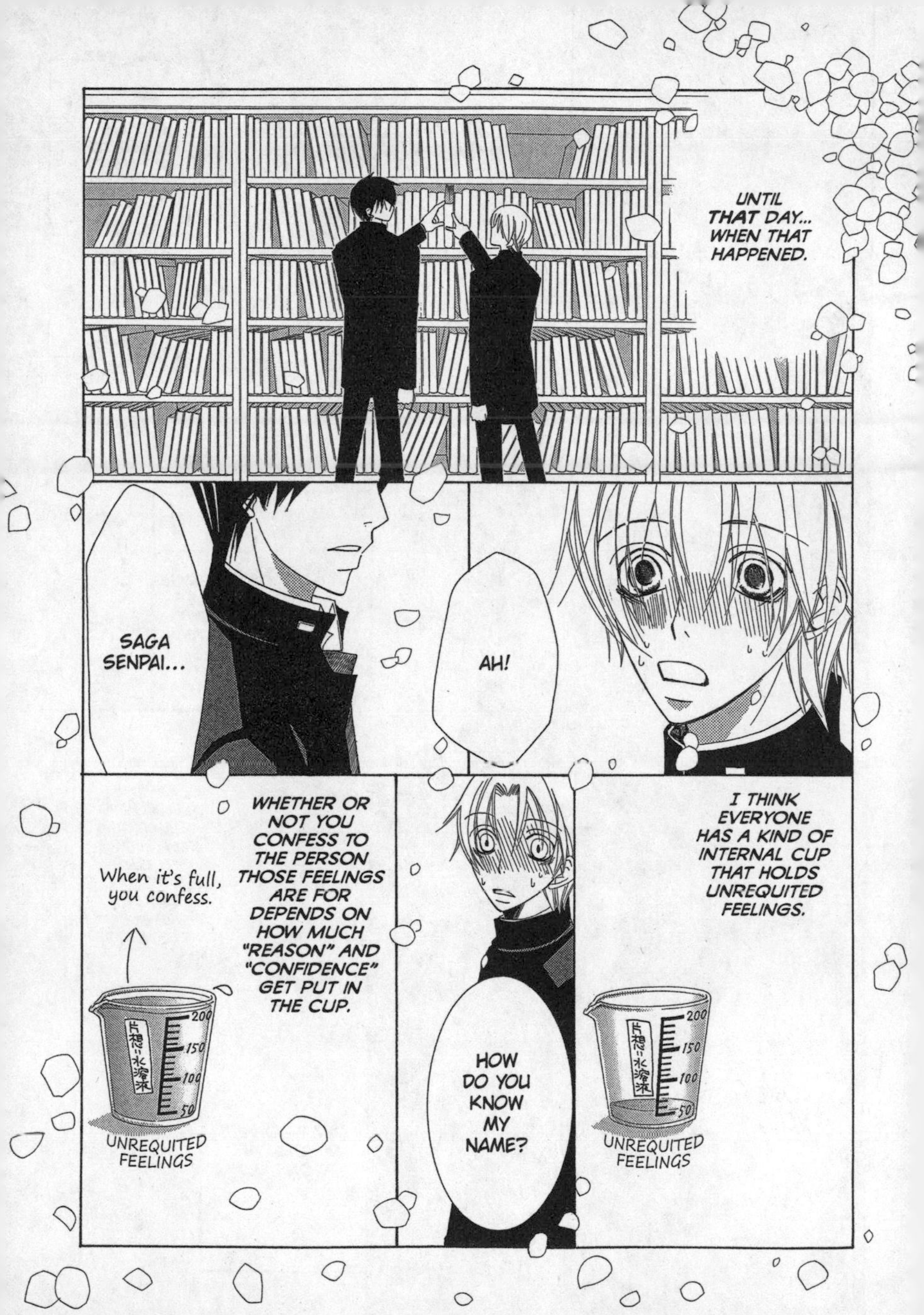
UNTIL THAT DAY... WHEN THAT HAPPENED.
AH!
SAGA SENPAI...
I THINK EVERYONE HAS A KIND OF INTERNAL CUP THAT HOLDS UNREQUITED FEELINGS.
UNREQUITED FEELINGS
HOW DO YOU KNOW MY NAME?
WHETHER OR NOT YOU CONFESS TO THE PERSON THOSE FEELINGS ARE FOR DEPENDS ON HOW MUCH "REASON" AND "CONFIDENCE" GET PUT IN THE CUP.
When it's full, you confess.
UNREQUITED FEELINGS

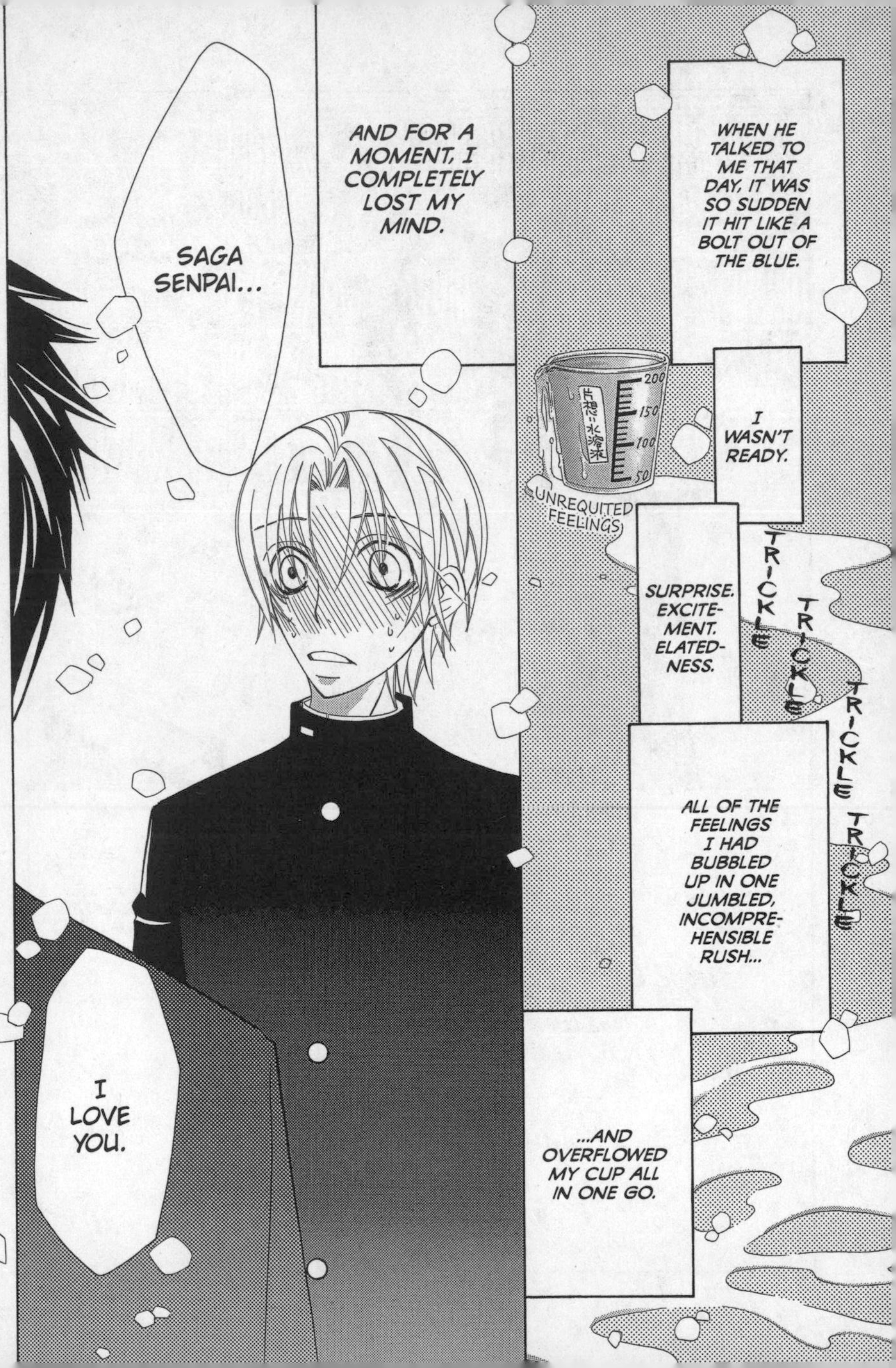
WHEN HE TALKED TO ME THAT DAY, IT WAS SO SUDDEN IT HIT LIKE A BOLT OUT OF THE BLUE.
I WASN'T READY.
UNREQUITED FEELINGS
SURPRISE. EXCITE-MENT. ELATED-NESS.
TRICKLE TRICKLE TRICKLE TRICKLE
ALL OF THE FEELINGS I HAD BUBBLED UP IN ONE JUMBLED, INCOMPRE-HENSIBLE RUSH...
...AND OVERFLOWED MY CUP ALL IN ONE GO.
AND FOR A MOMENT, I COMPLETELY LOST MY MIND.
SAGA SENPAI...
I LOVE YOU.

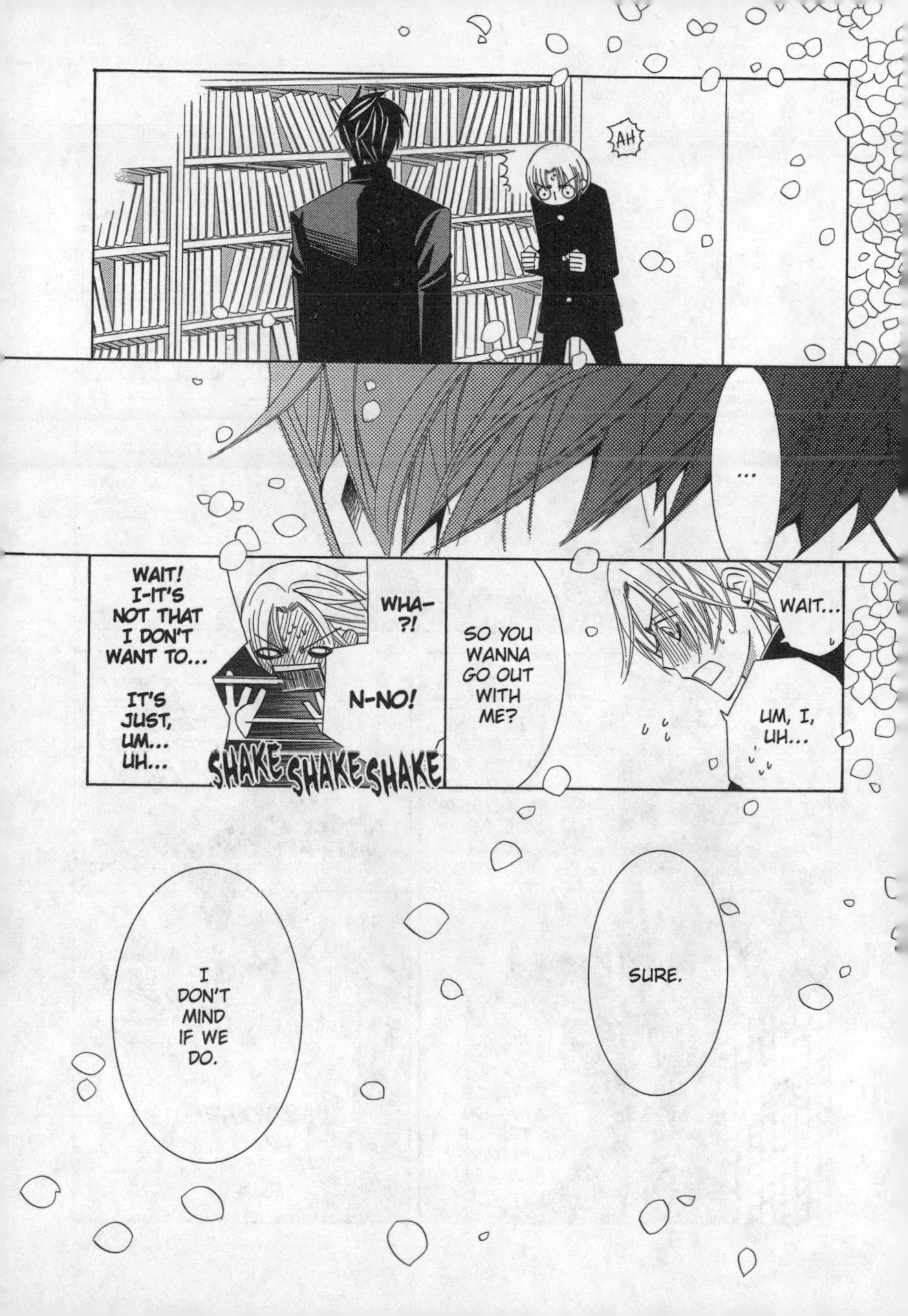
AH
...
WAIT...
UM, I, UH...
SO YOU WANNA GO OUT WITH ME?
WHA-?!
N-NO!
WAIT! I-IT'S NOT THAT I DON'T WANT TO...
IT'S JUST, UM... UH...
SHAKE SHAKE SHAKE
SURE.
I DON'T MIND IF WE DO.

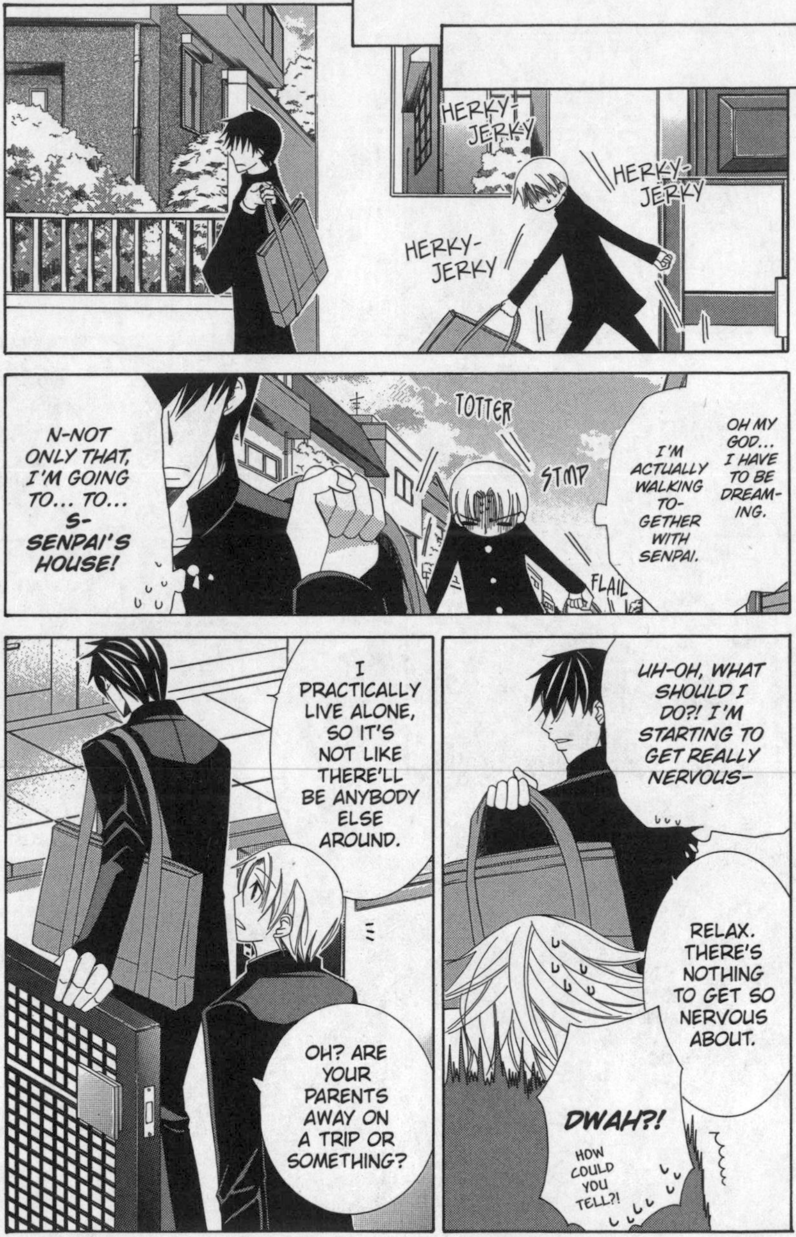
HERKY-JERKY
HERKY-JERKY
HERKY-JERKY
OH MY GOD... I HAVE TO BE DREAMING.
I'M ACTUALLY WALKING TO-GETHER WITH SENPAI.
TOTTER
STMP
FLAIL
N-NOT ONLY THAT, I'M GOING TO... TO... S-SENPAI'S HOUSE!
UH-OH, WHAT SHOULD I DO?! I'M STARTING TO GET REALLY NERVOUS-
RELAX. THERE'S NOTHING TO GET SO NERVOUS ABOUT.
DWAH?!
HOW COULD YOU TELL?!
I PRACTICALLY LIVE ALONE, SO IT'S NOT LIKE THERE'LL BE ANYBODY ELSE AROUND.
OH? ARE YOUR PARENTS AWAY ON A TRIP OR SOMETHING?

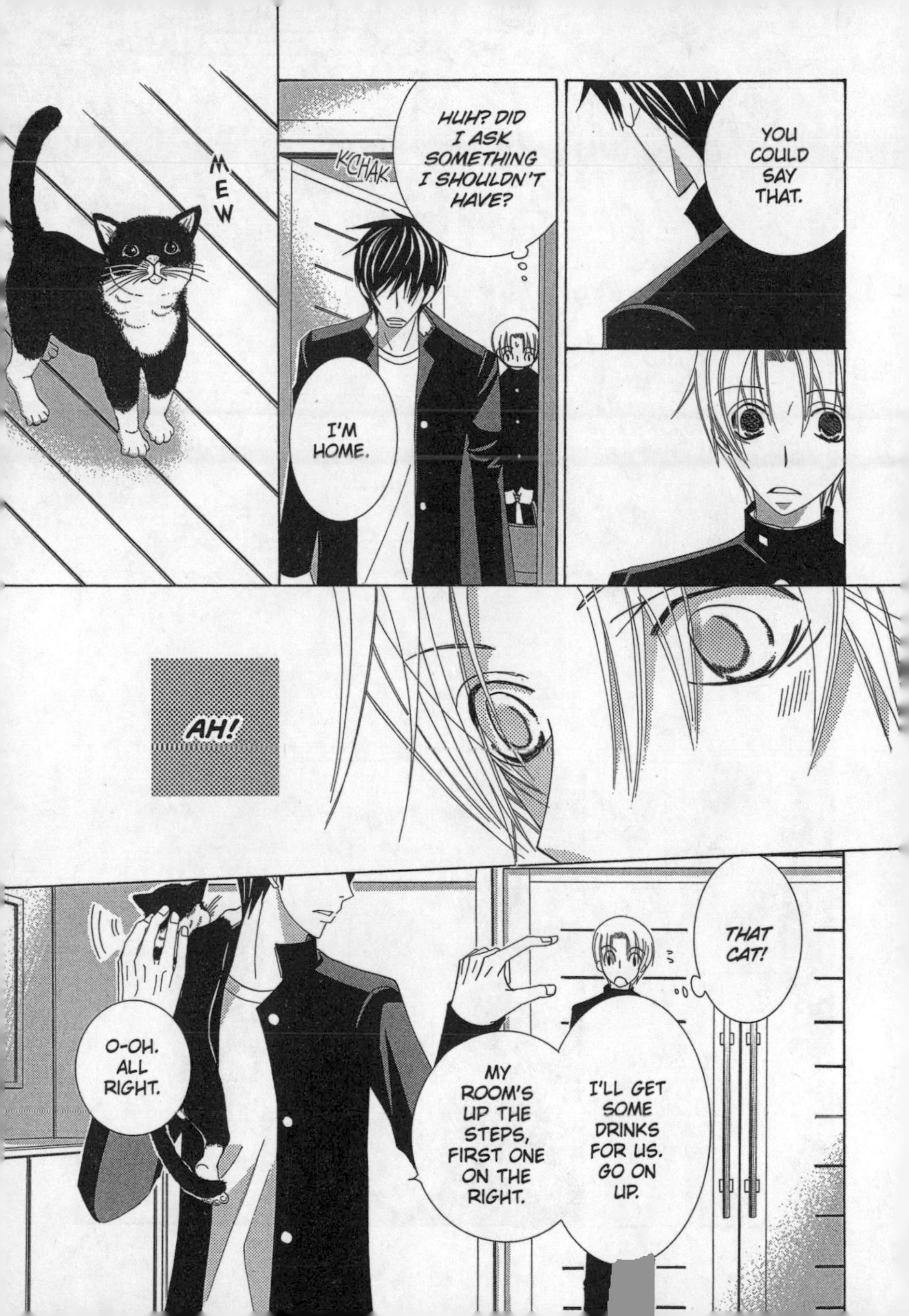
YOU COULD SAY THAT.
HUH? DID I ASK SOMETHING I SHOULDN'T HAVE?
K'CHAK
I'M HOME.
MEW
AH!
THAT CAT!
I'LL GET SOME DRINKS FOR US. GO ON UP.
MY ROOM'S UP THE STEPS, FIRST ONE ON THE RIGHT.
O-OH. ALL RIGHT.

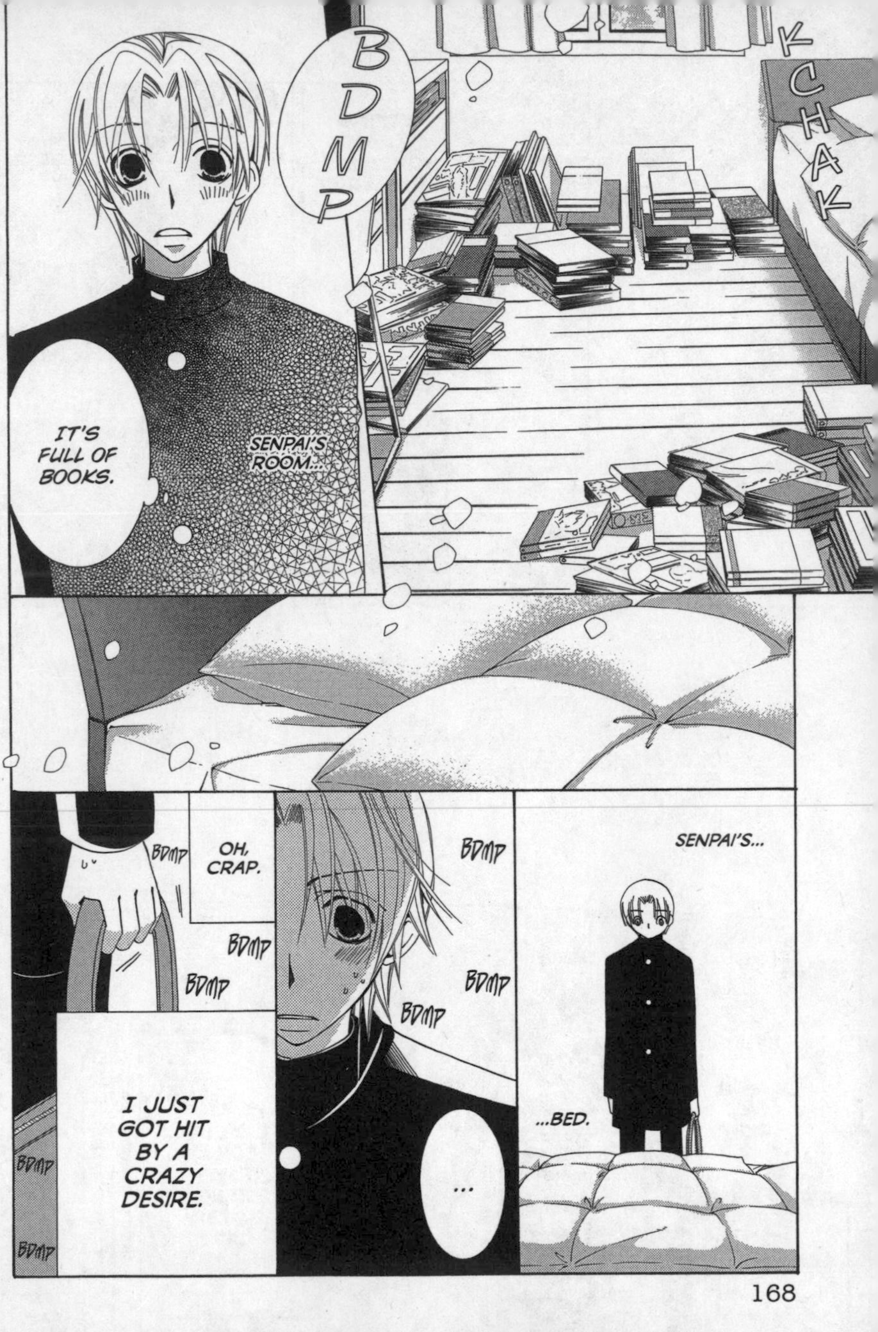
KCHAK
BDMP
SENPAI'S ROOM...
IT'S FULL OF BOOKS.
SENPAI'S...
...BED.
BDMP
BDMP
BDMP
...
OH, CRAP.
BDMP
BDMP
BDMP
I JUST GOT HIT BY A CRAZY DESIRE.
BDMP
BDMP

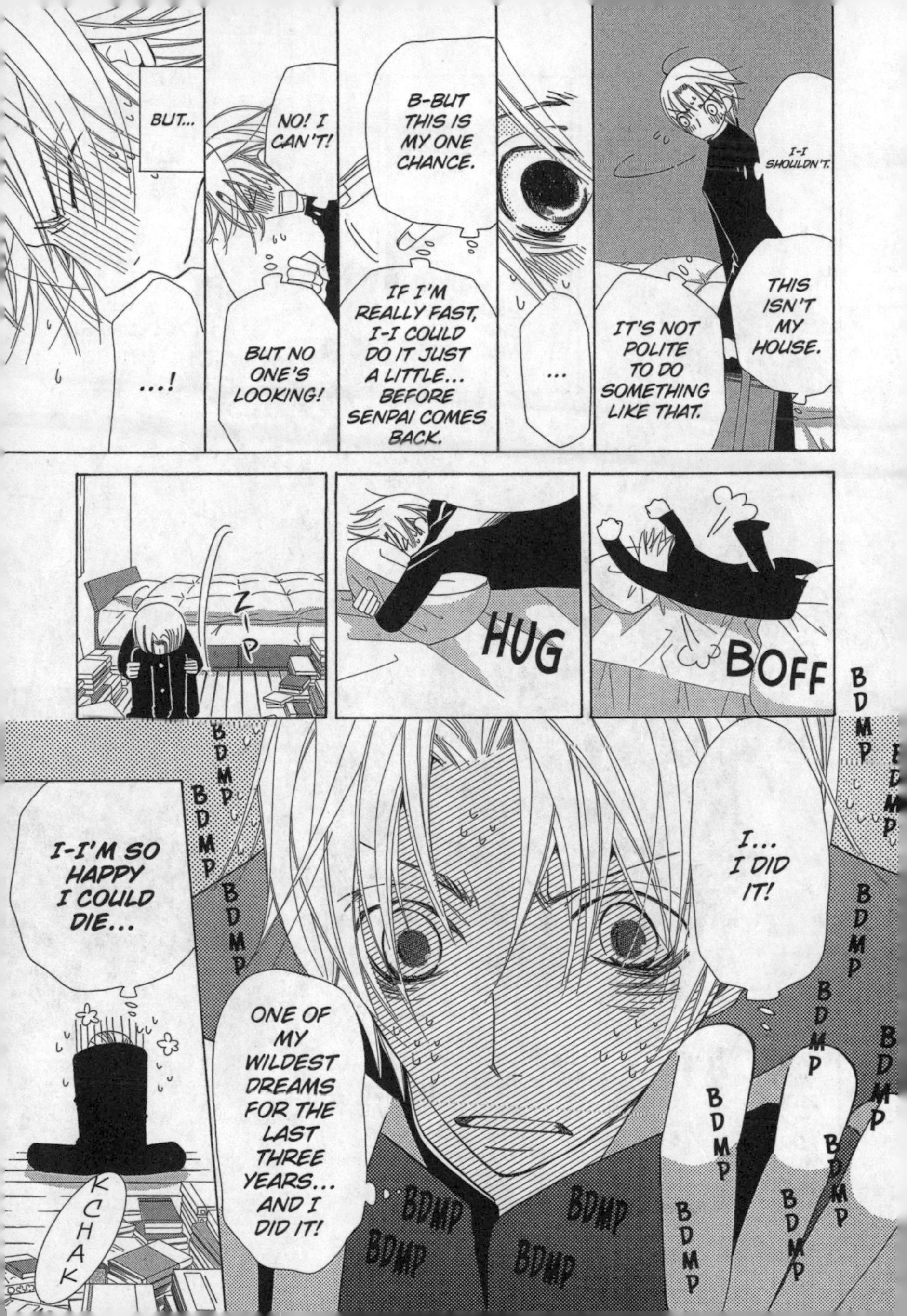
I-I SHOULDN'T.
THIS ISN'T MY HOUSE.
IT'S NOT POLITE TO DO SOMETHING LIKE THAT.
...
B-BUT THIS IS MY ONE CHANCE.
IF I'M REALLY FAST, I-I COULD DO IT JUST A LITTLE... BEFORE SENPAI COMES BACK.
NO! I CAN'T!
BUT NO ONE'S LOOKING!
BUT...
...!
BOFF
HUG
ZIP
BDMP BDMP
I... I DID IT!
BDMP BDMP BDMP BDMP BDMP BDMP
ONE OF MY WILDEST DREAMS FOR THE LAST THREE YEARS... AND I DID IT!
BDMP BDMP BDMP BDMP
BDMP BDMP BDMP BDMP
I-I'M SO HAPPY I COULD DIE...
KCHAK

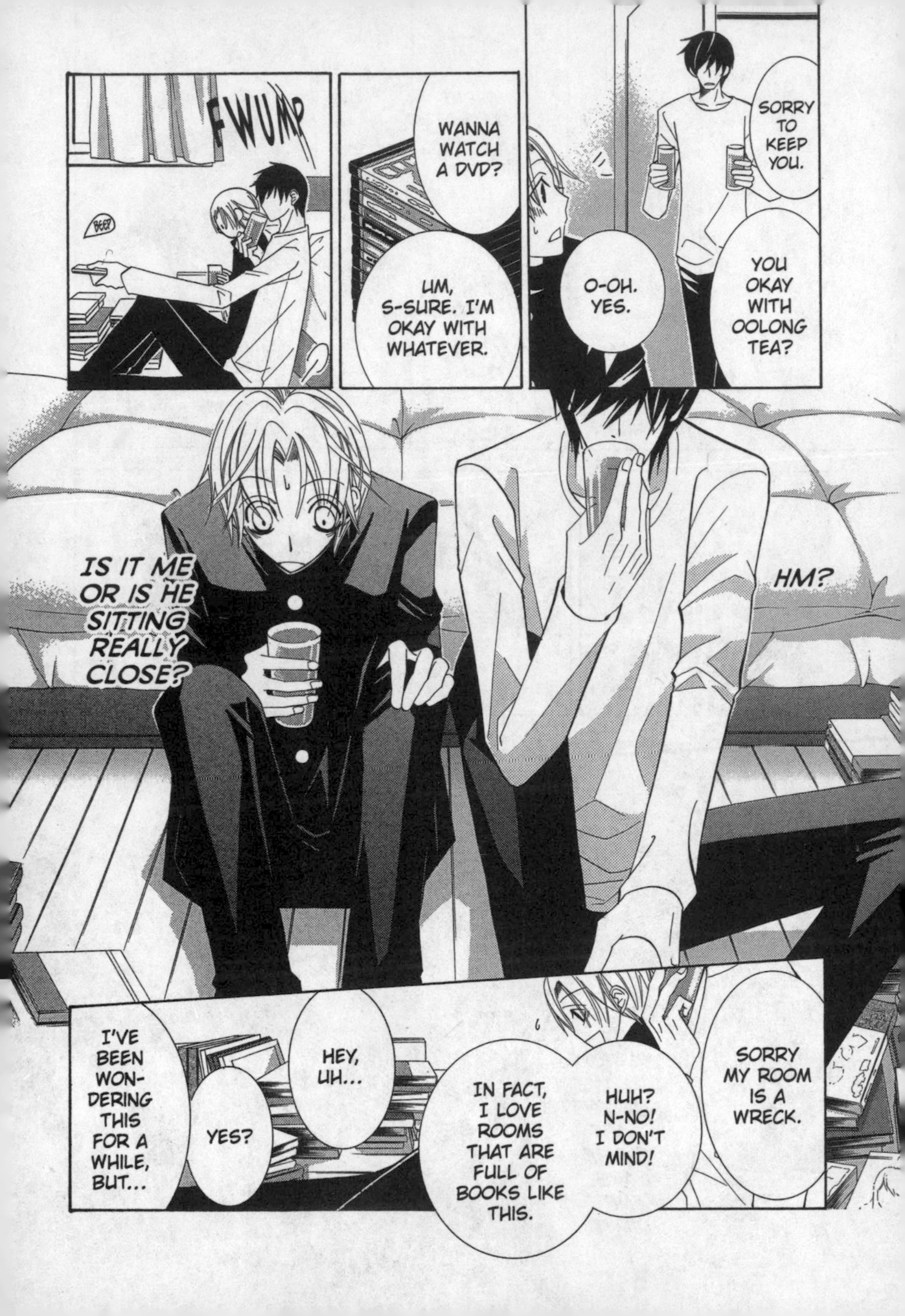
SORRY TO KEEP YOU.
YOU OKAY WITH OOLONG TEA?
O-OH. YES.
WANNA WATCH A DVD?
UM, S-SURE. I'M OKAY WITH WHATEVER.
FWUMP
BEEP
HM?
IS IT ME OR IS HE SITTING REALLY CLOSE?
SORRY MY ROOM IS A WRECK.
HUH? N-NO! I DON'T MIND!
IN FACT, I LOVE ROOMS THAT ARE FULL OF BOOKS LIKE THIS.
HEY, UH...
YES?
I'VE BEEN WONDERING THIS FOR A WHILE, BUT...

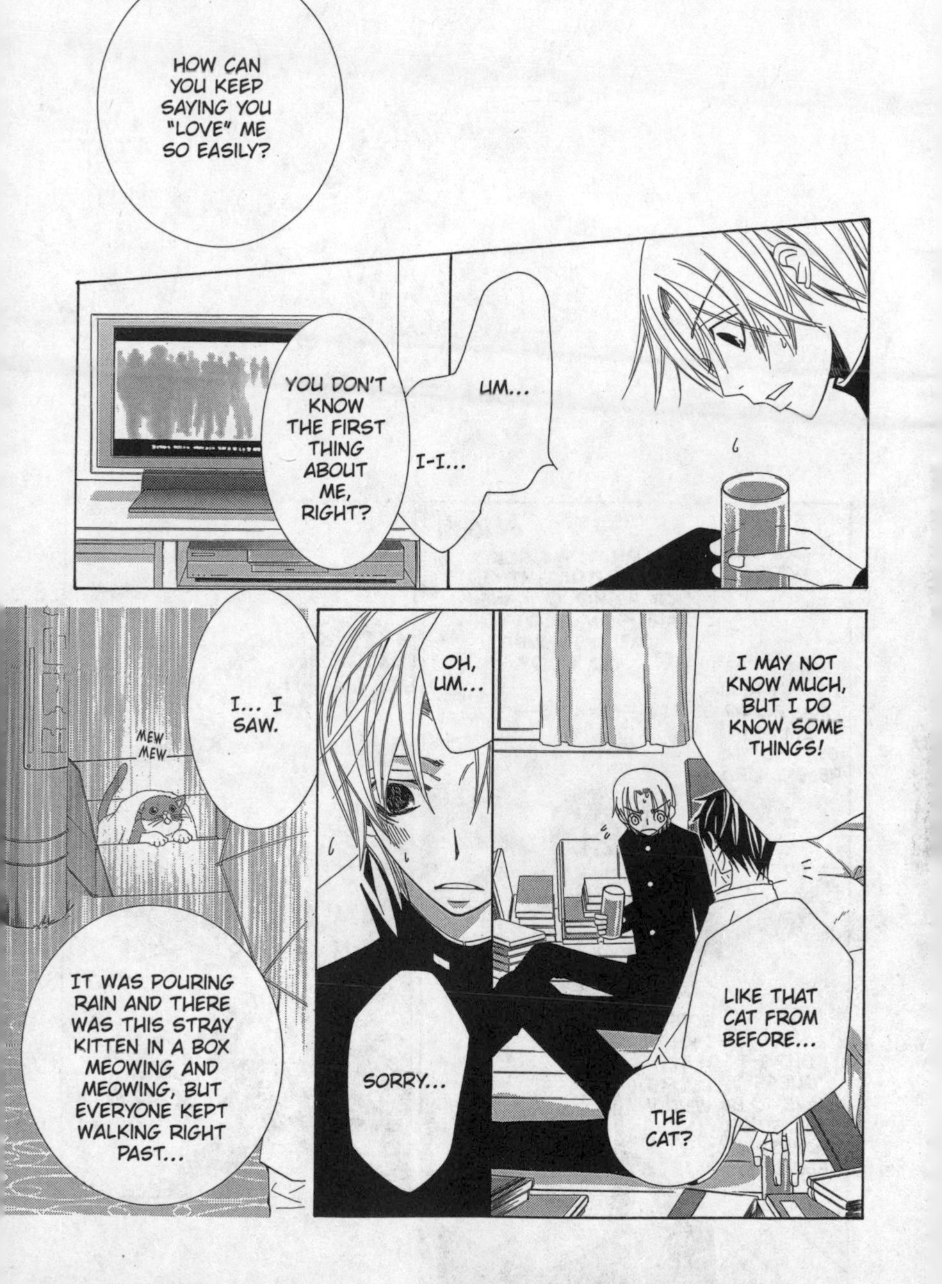
HOW CAN YOU KEEP SAYING YOU "LOVE" ME SO EASILY?
UM... I-I...
YOU DON'T KNOW THE FIRST THING ABOUT ME, RIGHT?
I MAY NOT KNOW MUCH, BUT I DO KNOW SOME THINGS!
LIKE THAT CAT FROM BEFORE...
THE CAT?
OH, UM...
SORRY...
I... I SAW.
MEW MEW
IT WAS POURING RAIN AND THERE WAS THIS STRAY KITTEN IN A BOX MEOWING AND MEOWING, BUT EVERYONE KEPT WALKING RIGHT PAST...

EVERYONE EXCEPT YOU, SENPAI.

HM? UM, I'M SORRY...

AUGH! DAMN IT! A FRICKIN' SCENE STRAIGHT OUT OF A SHOJO MANGA AND SOMEBODY SAW ME! NOW WHAT DO I DO?

I DON'T READ MANGA, SO I'M NOT GETTING THE REFERENCE...

I'M SORRY! I KNOW IT LOOKS WEIRD!

OH... THAT'S OKAY, THEN...

BUT I-I GUESS I HAVE TO BE STUPID OR SOMETHING, BECAUSE...

ANYWAYS, ARE YOU STALKING ME OR SOMETHING?

GAH!

WHAT THE HELL?! YOU SAW THAT?!

I... I'M SORRY!

172

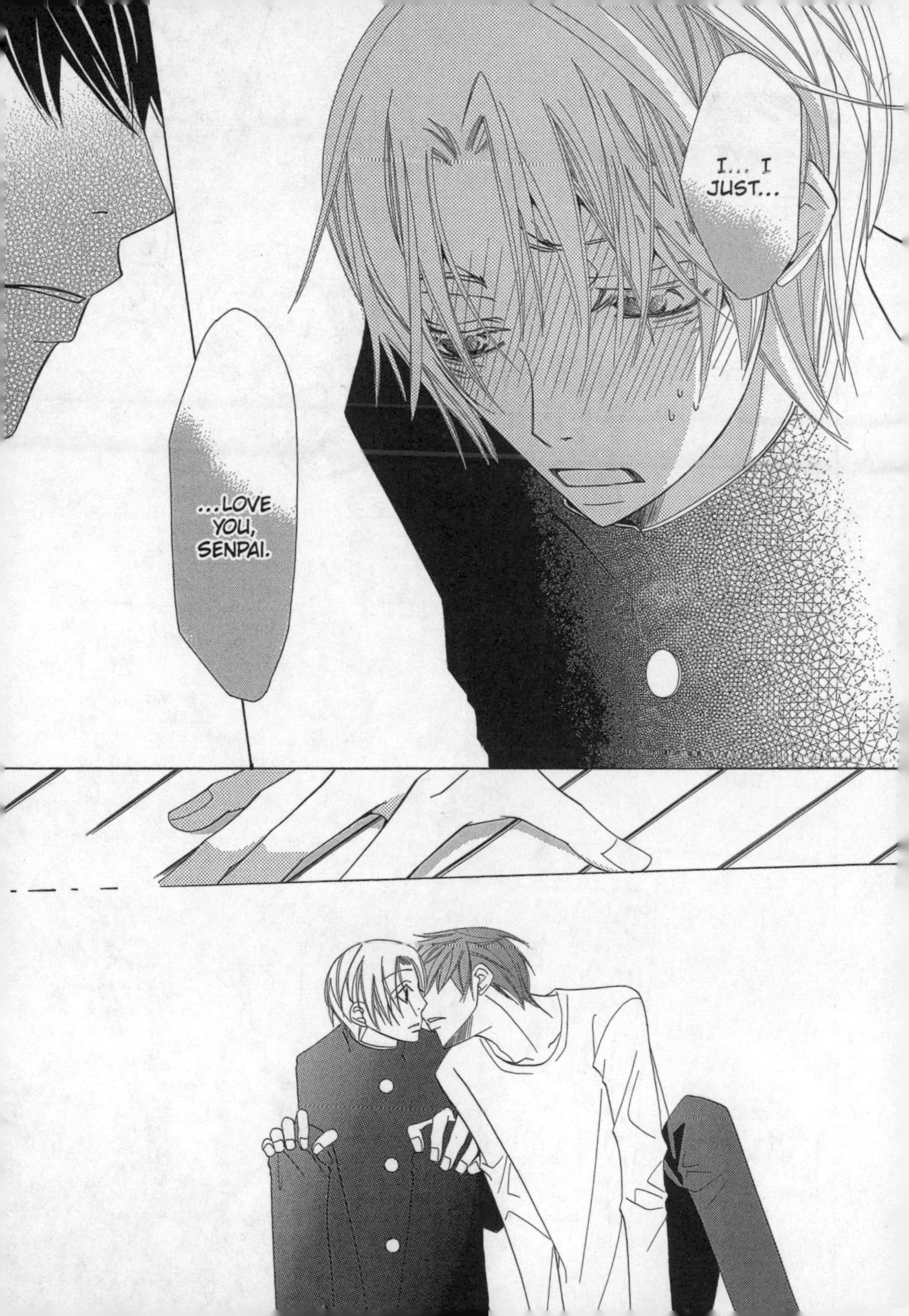
I... I JUST...
...LOVE YOU, SENPAI.

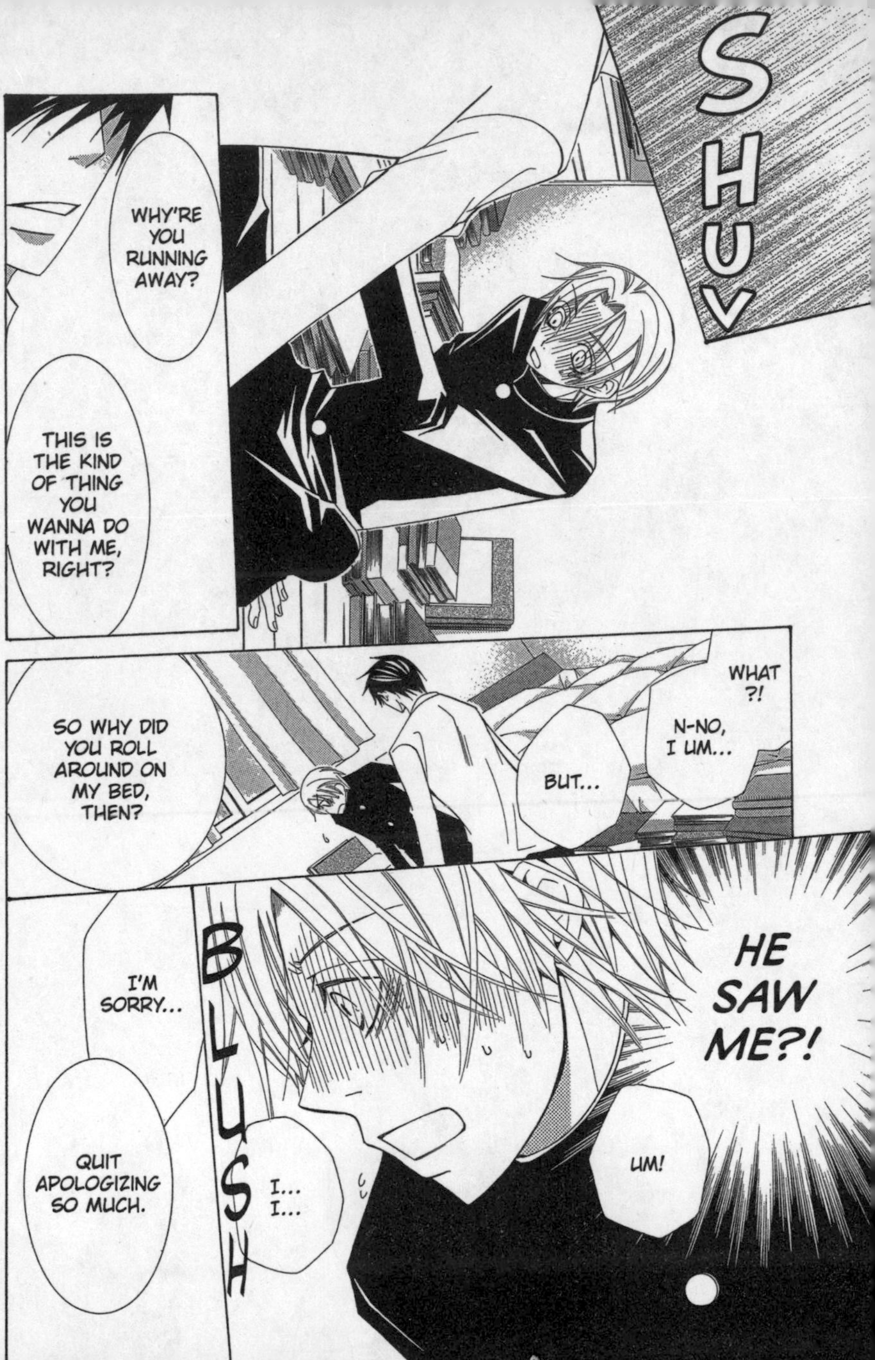
SHUV
WHY'RE YOU RUNNING AWAY?
THIS IS THE KIND OF THING YOU WANNA DO WITH ME, RIGHT?
WHAT?!
N-NO, I UM...
BUT...
SO WHY DID YOU ROLL AROUND ON MY BED, THEN?
HE SAW ME?!
UM!
BLUSH
I... I...
I'M SORRY...
QUIT APOLOGIZING SO MUCH.

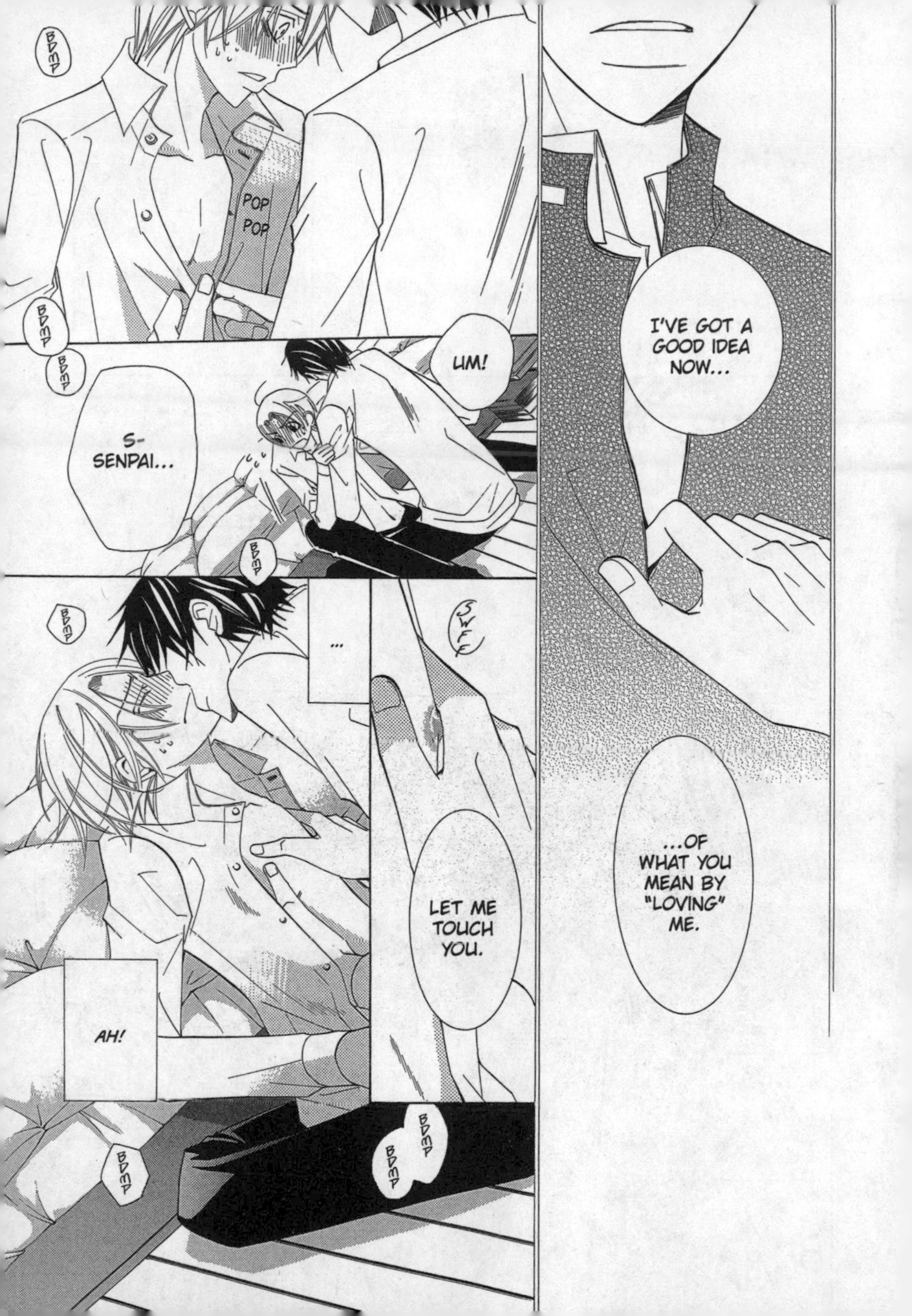
I'VE GOT A GOOD IDEA NOW...
...OF WHAT YOU MEAN BY "LOVING" ME.
BDMP
POP
POP
BDMP
BDMP
UM!
S-SENPAI...
BDMP
SWFF
LET ME TOUCH YOU.
BDMP
BDMP
...
BDMP
AH!
BDMP

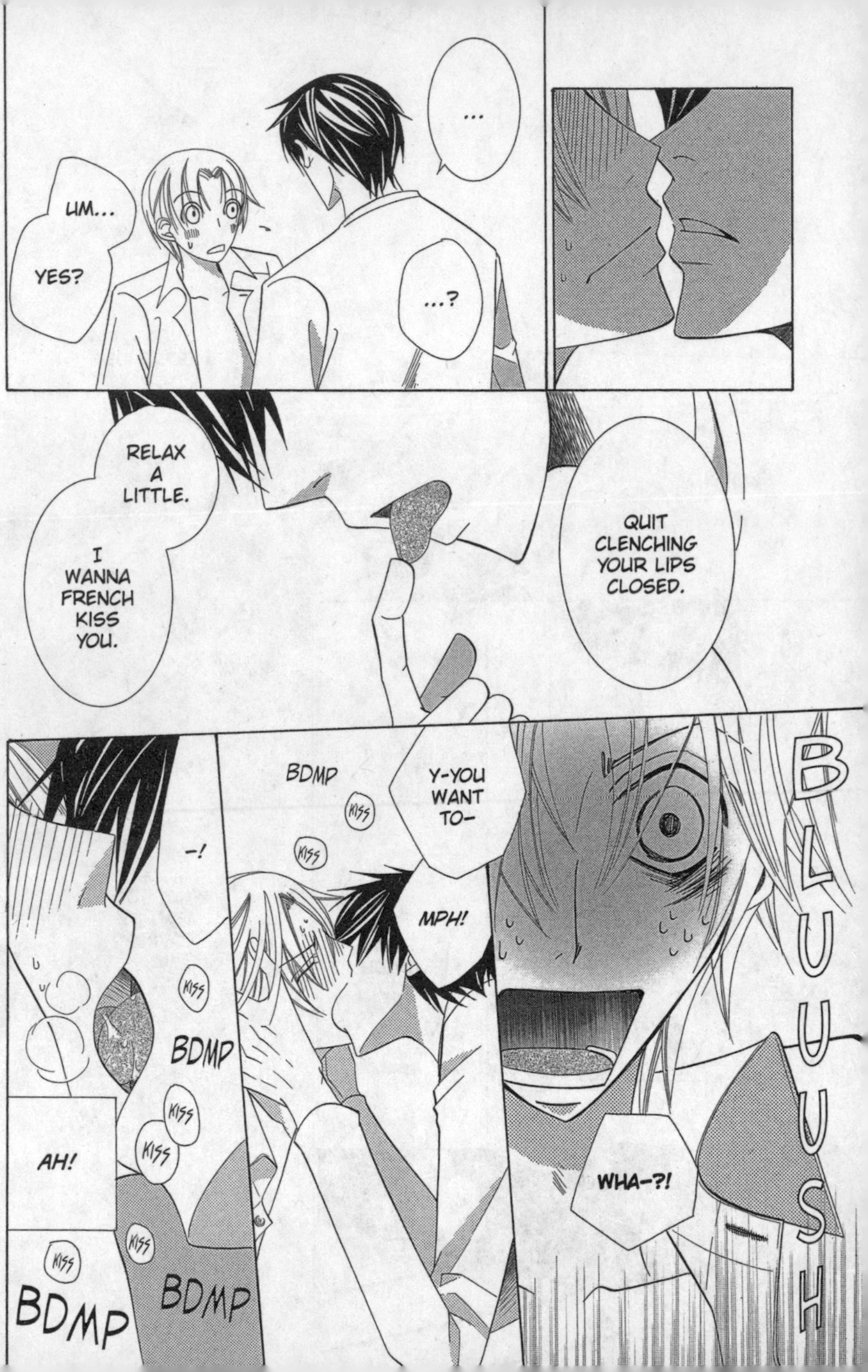
...
UM... YES?
...?
QUIT CLENCHING YOUR LIPS CLOSED.
RELAX A LITTLE.
I WANNA FRENCH KISS YOU.
BLUUUSH
Y-YOU WANT TO-
WHA-?!
BDMP
KISS
KISS
MPH!
-!
KISS
BDMP
KISS
KISS
AH!
KISS
KISS
BDMP
BDMP

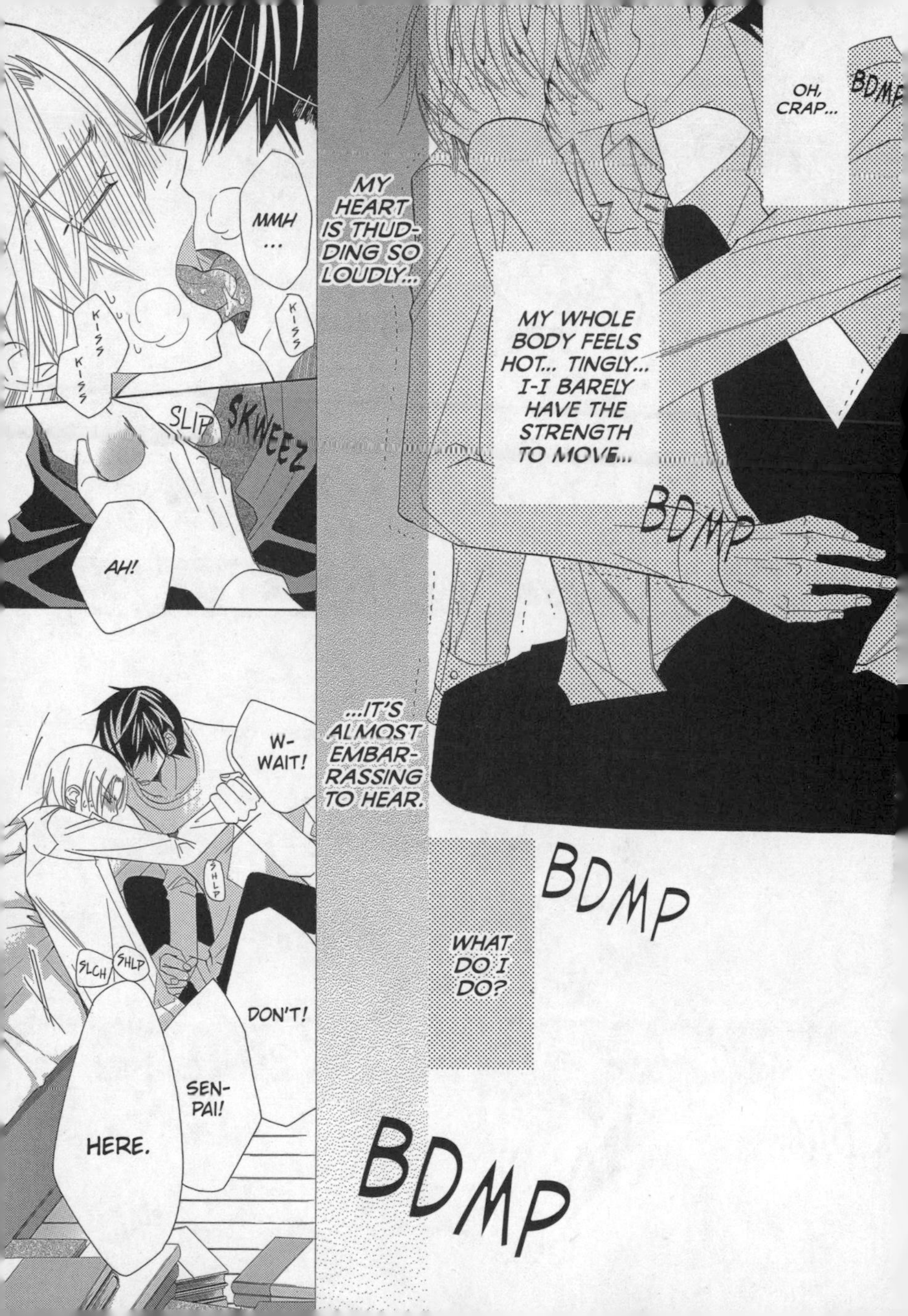
OH, CRAP...
BDMP
MY HEART IS THUD-DING SO LOUDLY...
MY WHOLE BODY FEELS HOT... TINGLY... I-I BARELY HAVE THE STRENGTH TO MOVE...
BDMP
...IT'S ALMOST EMBAR-RASSING TO HEAR.
BDMP
WHAT DO I DO?
BDMP
MMH ...
KISS
KISS
KISS
SKWEEZ
SLIP
AH!
W-WAIT!
SHLP
DON'T!
SEN-PAI!
SHLP
SLCH
HERE.

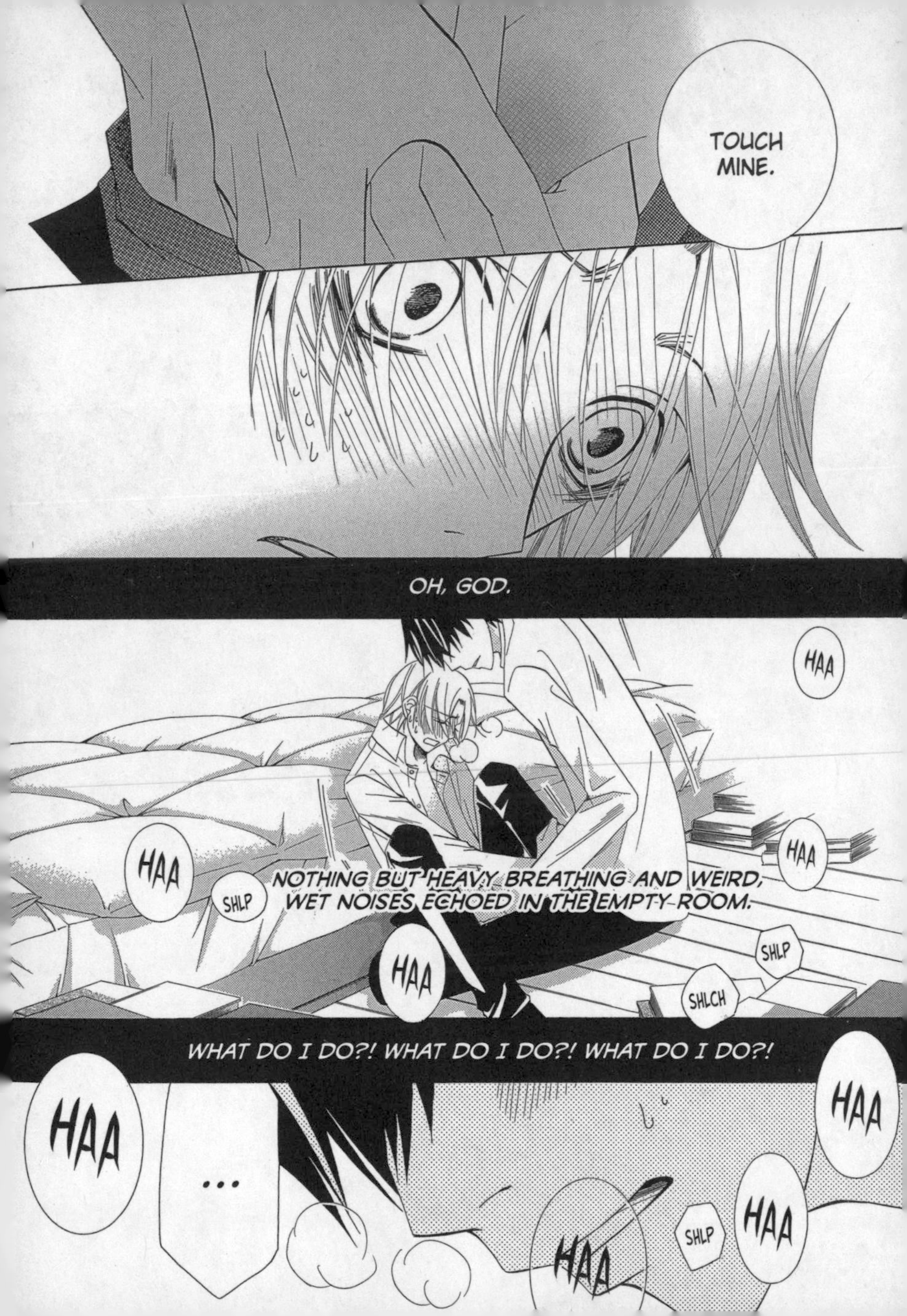
TOUCH MINE.
OH, GOD.
HAA
HAA
HAA
SHLP
NOTHING BUT HEAVY BREATHING AND WEIRD, WET NOISES ECHOED IN THE EMPTY ROOM.
SHLP
HAA
SHLCH
WHAT DO I DO?! WHAT DO I DO?! WHAT DO I DO?!
HAA
HAA
SHLP
HAA
HAA
...

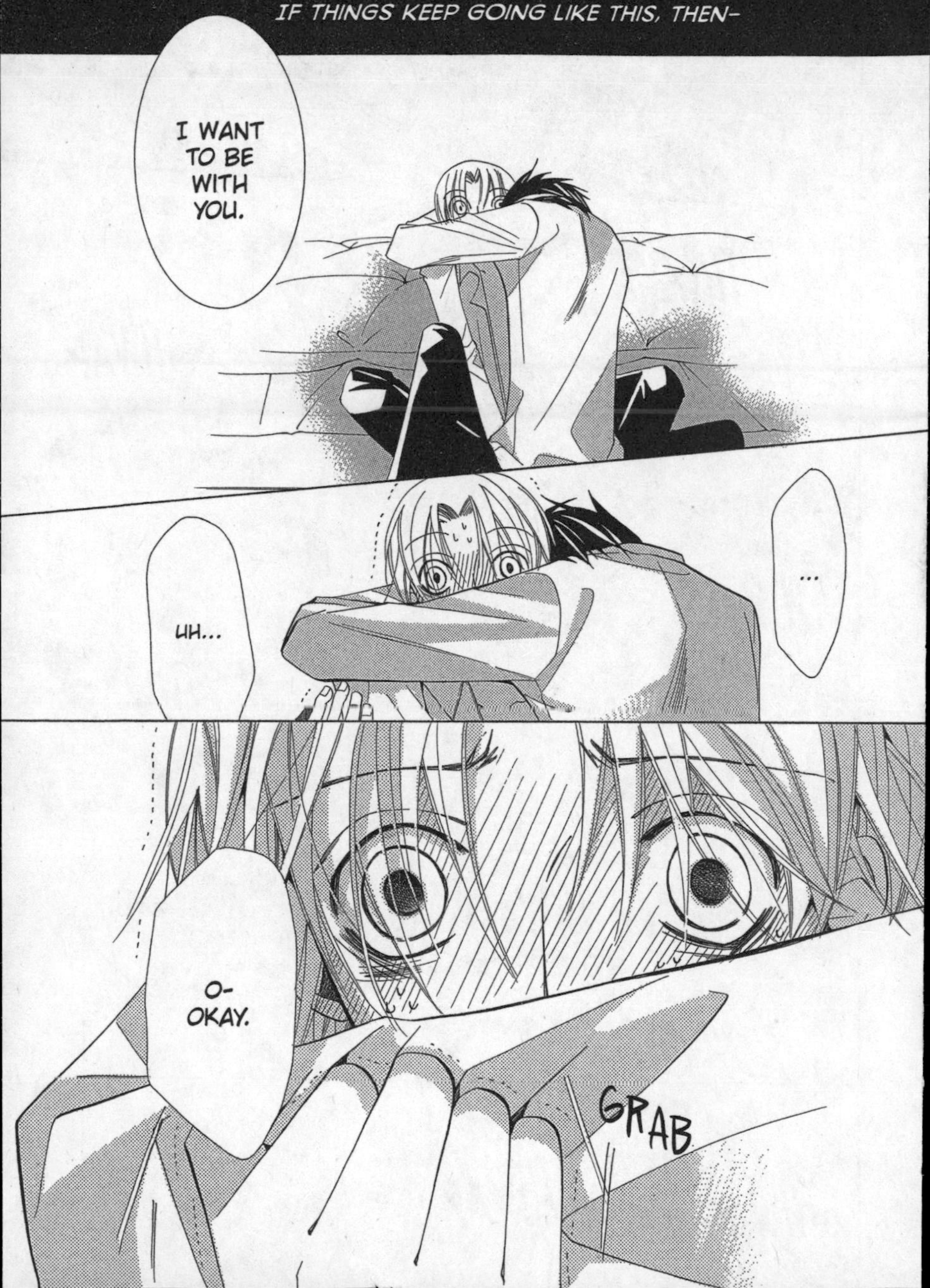
IF THINGS KEEP GOING LIKE THIS, THEN-
I WANT TO BE WITH YOU.
...
UH...
O-OKAY.
GRAB

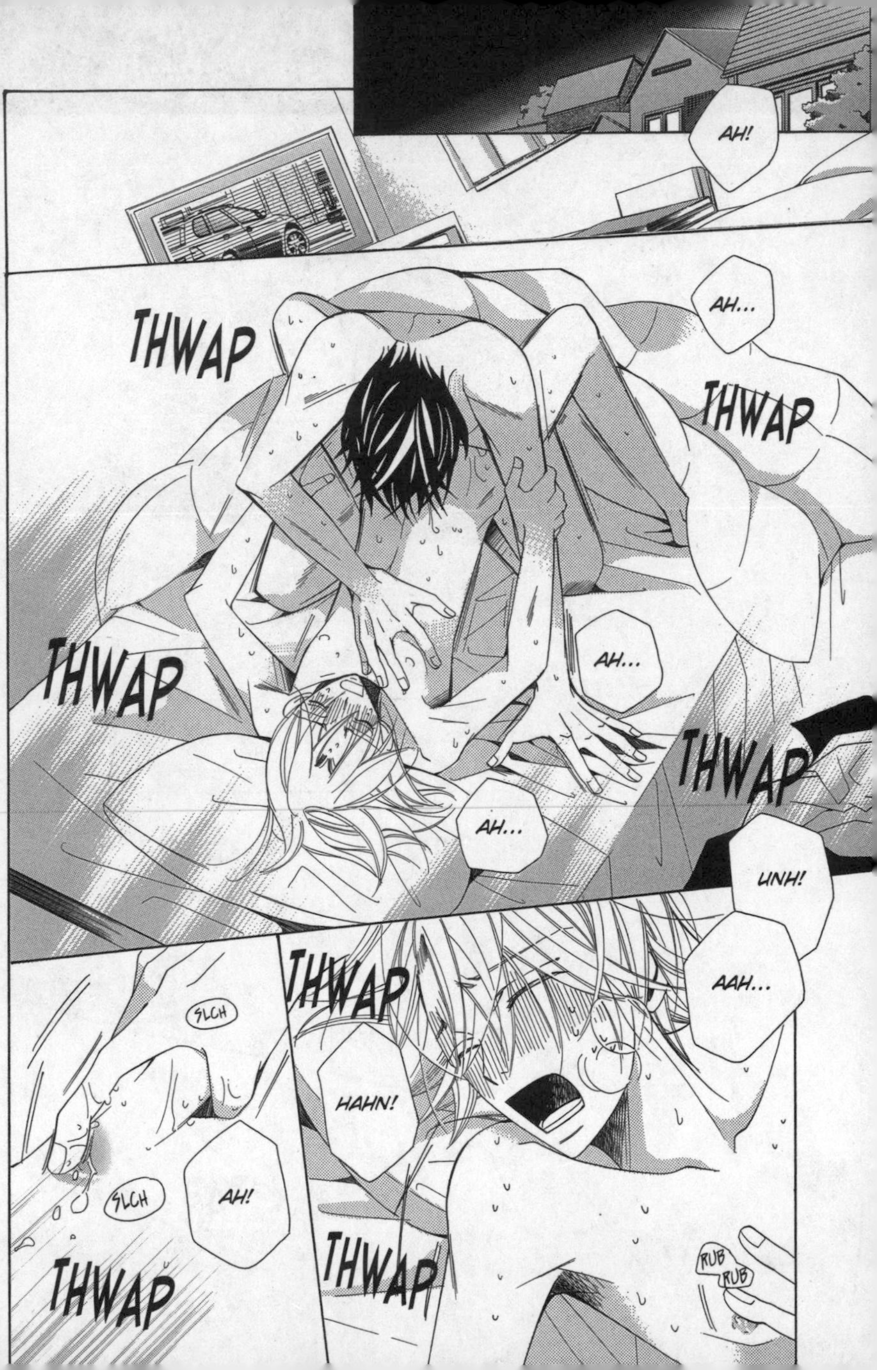
AH!
AH...
THWAP
THWAP
AH...
THWAP
THWAP
AH...
UNH!
AAH...
THWAP
HAHN!
THWAP
RUB
RUB
SLCH
AH!
SLCH
THWAP

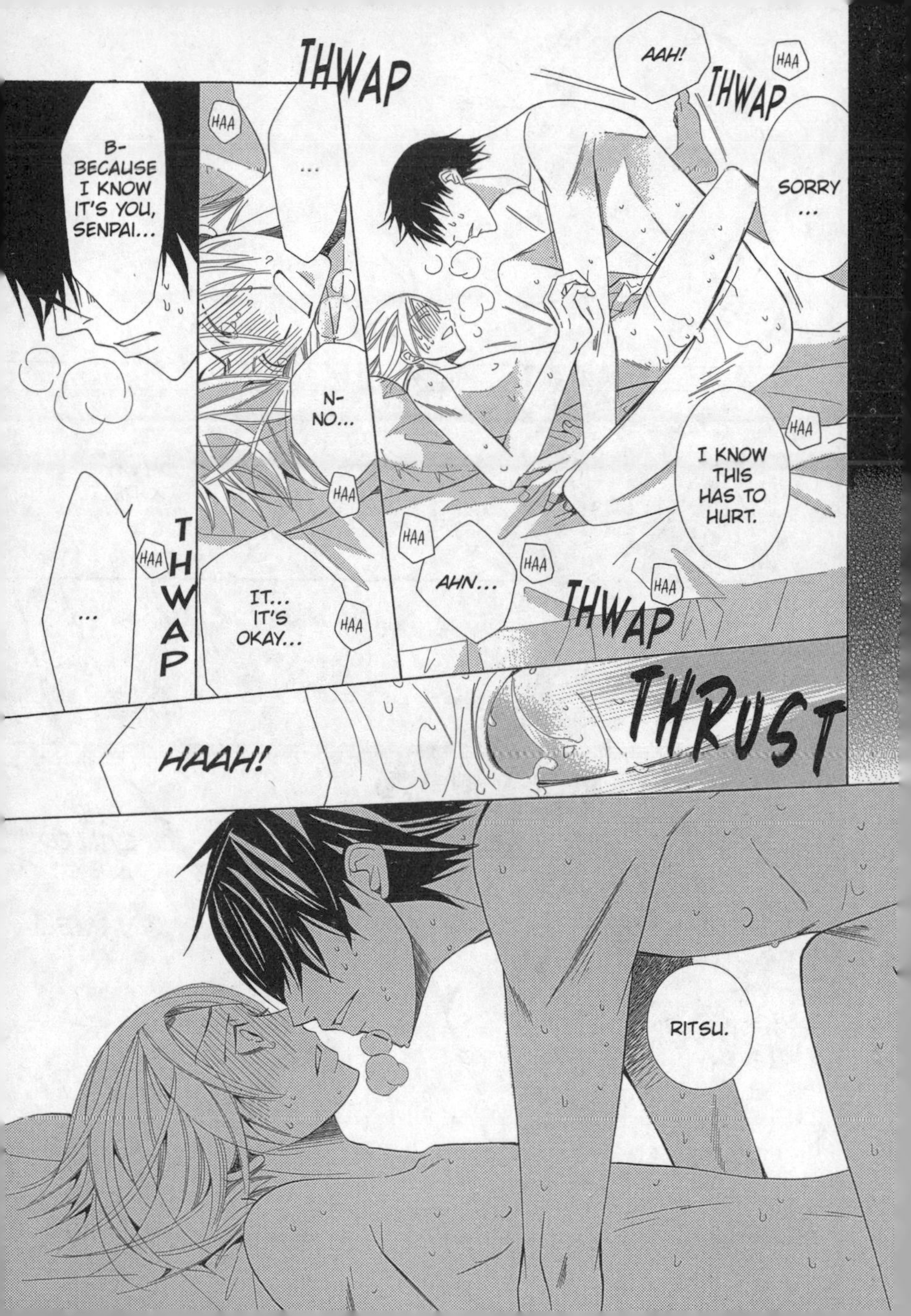
HAA
AAH!
THWAP
SORRY...
HAA
I KNOW THIS HAS TO HURT.
HAA
THWAP
HAA
AHN...
HAA
THWAP
HAA
...
N-NO...
HAA
HAA
IT... IT'S OKAY...
B-BECAUSE I KNOW IT'S YOU, SENPAI...
THWAP
HAA
...
THRUST
HAAH!
RITSU.

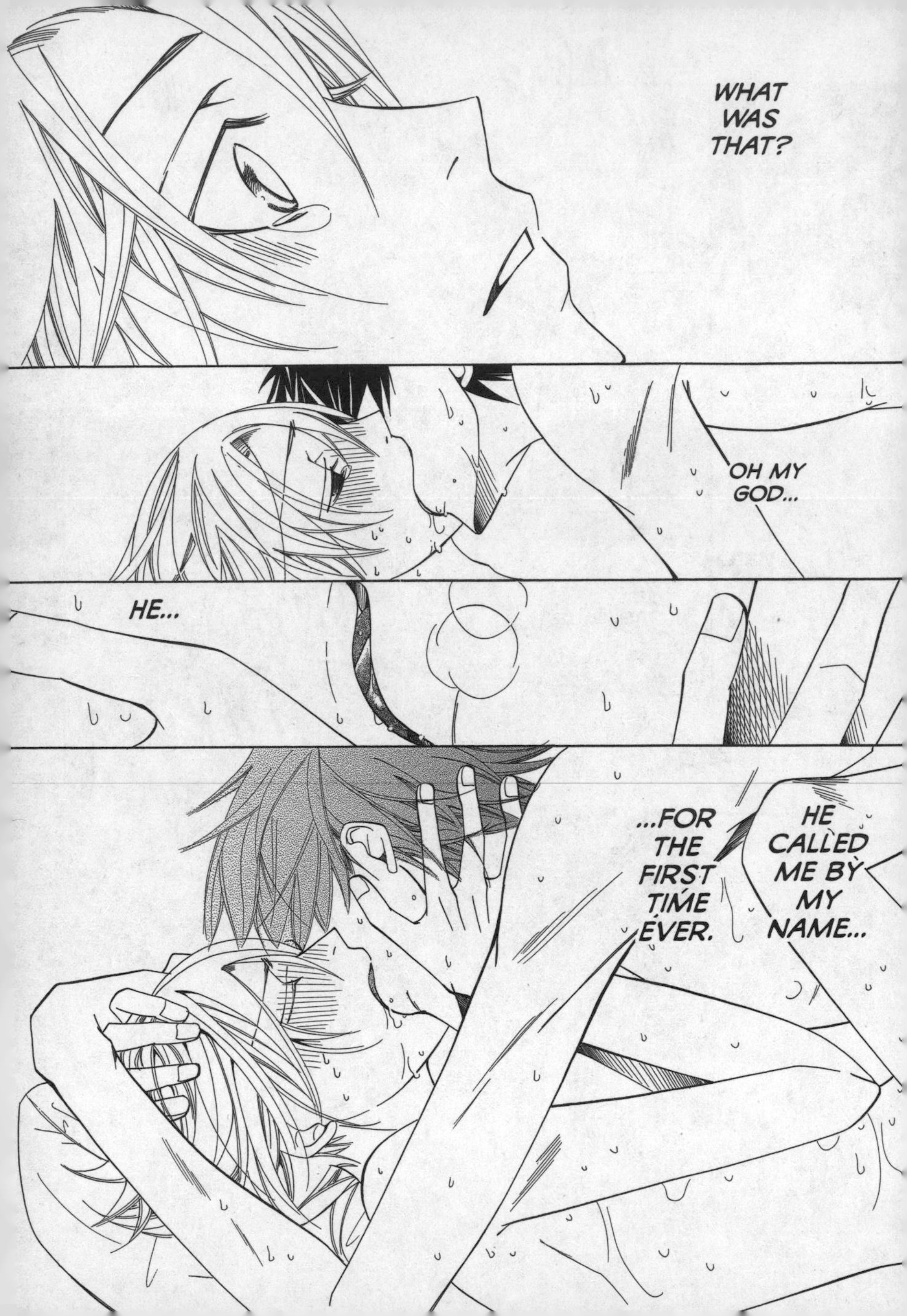
WHAT WAS THAT?
OH MY GOD...
HE...
HE CALLED ME BY MY NAME...
...FOR THE FIRST TIME EVER.

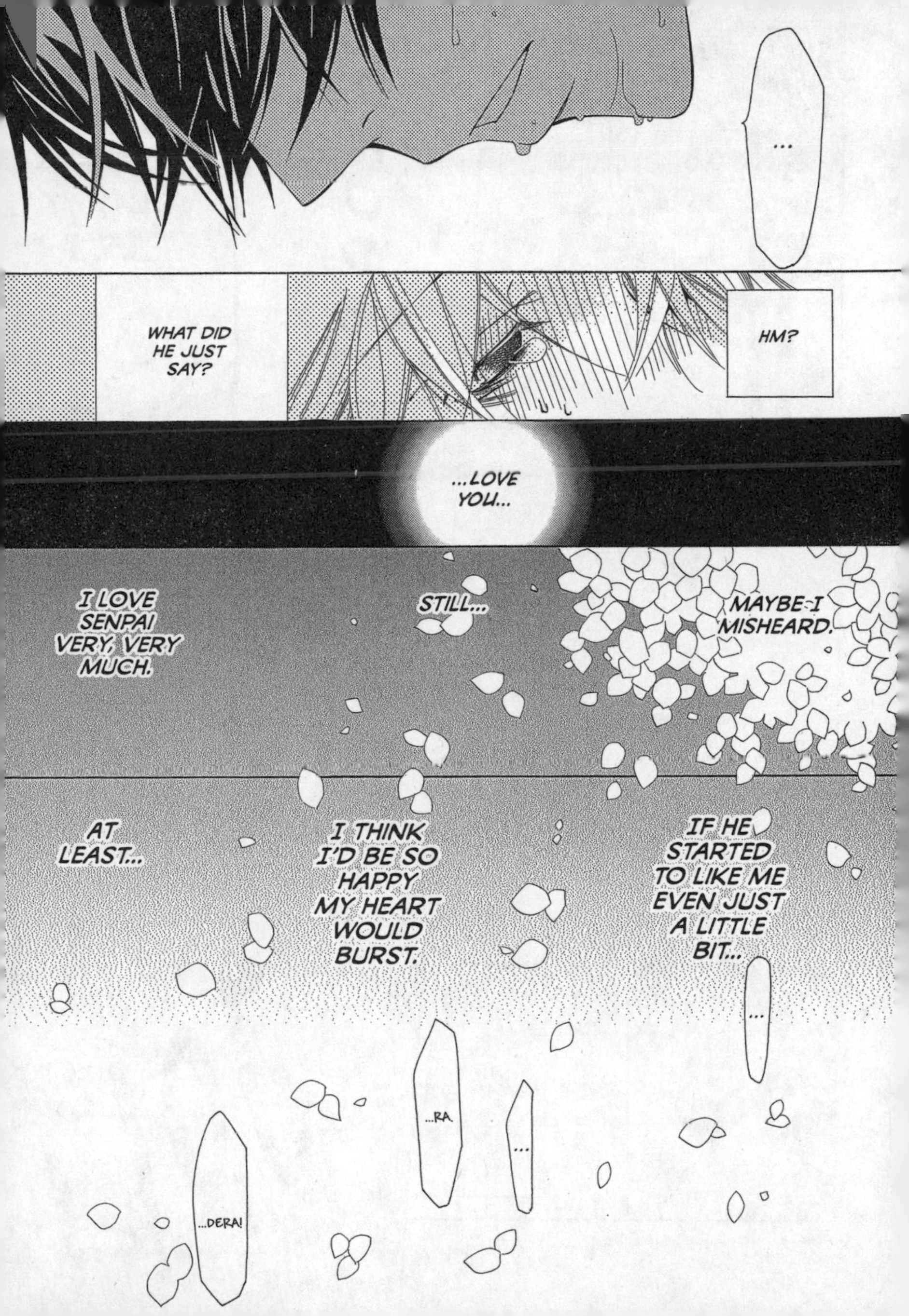
...
HM?
WHAT DID HE JUST SAY?
...LOVE YOU...
MAYBE I MISHEARD.
STILL...
I LOVE SENPAI VERY, VERY MUCH.
IF HE STARTED TO LIKE ME EVEN JUST A LITTLE BIT...
I THINK I'D BE SO HAPPY MY HEART WOULD BURST.
AT LEAST...
...
...
...RA
...DERA!

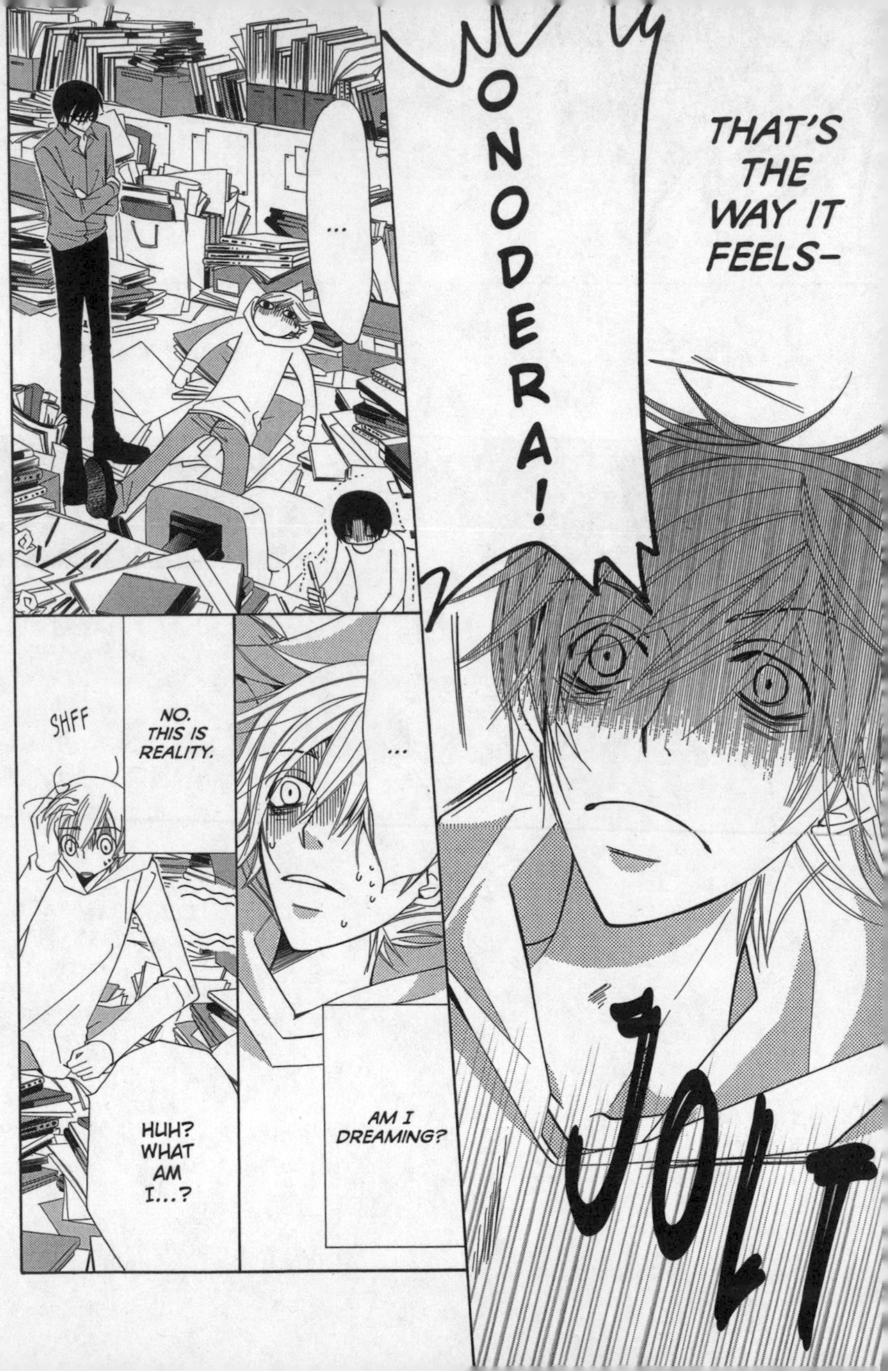
THAT'S THE WAY IT FEELS-
ONODERA!
JOLT
...
...
AM I DREAMING?
NO. THIS IS REALITY.
SHFF
HUH? WHAT AM I...?

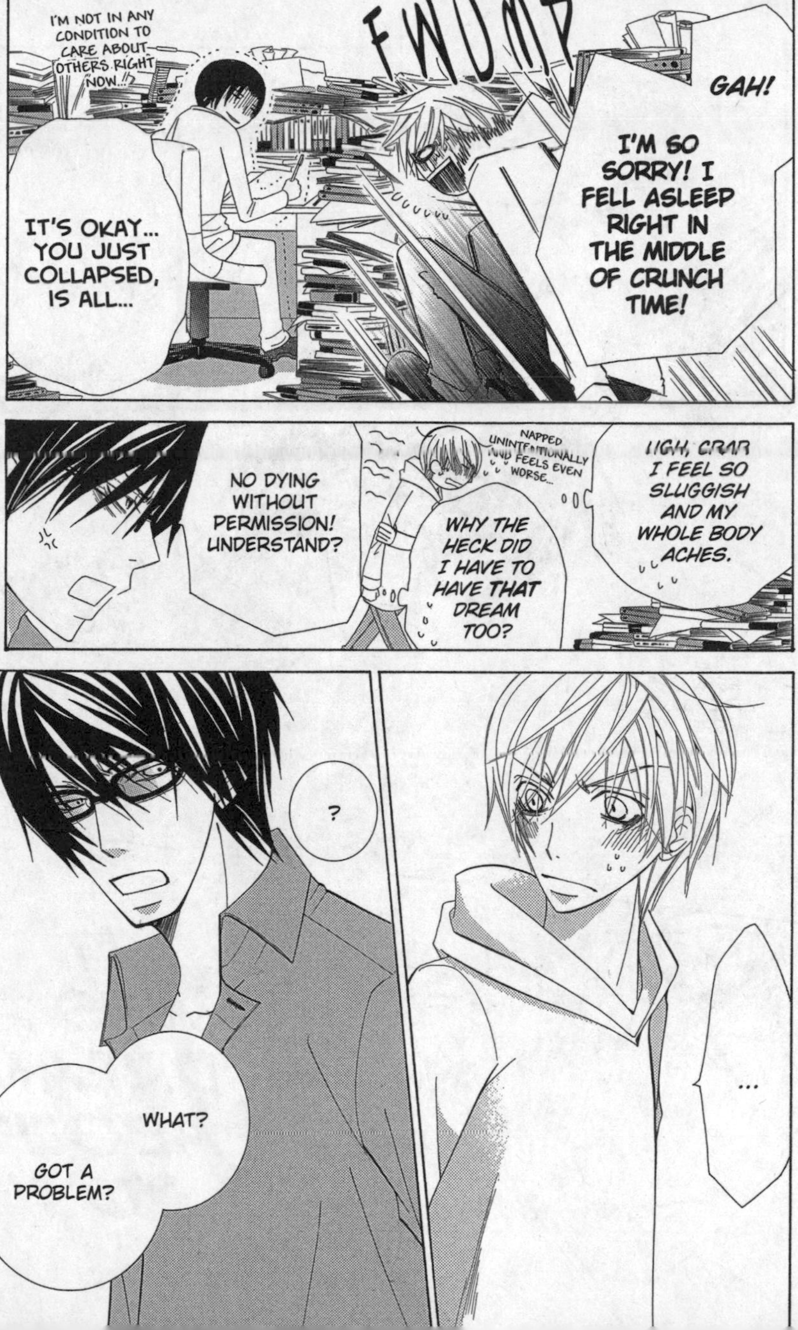
GAH!
I'M SO SORRY! I FELL ASLEEP RIGHT IN THE MIDDLE OF CRUNCH TIME!
FWUMP
I'M NOT IN ANY CONDITION TO CARE ABOUT OTHERS RIGHT NOW...!!
IT'S OKAY... YOU JUST COLLAPSED, IS ALL...
UGH, CRAP I FEEL SO SLUGGISH AND MY WHOLE BODY ACHES.
NAPPED UNINTENTIONALLY AND FEELS EVEN WORSE...
WHY THE HECK DID I HAVE TO HAVE THAT DREAM TOO?
NO DYING WITHOUT PERMISSION! UNDERSTAND?
...
?
WHAT?
GOT A PROBLEM?

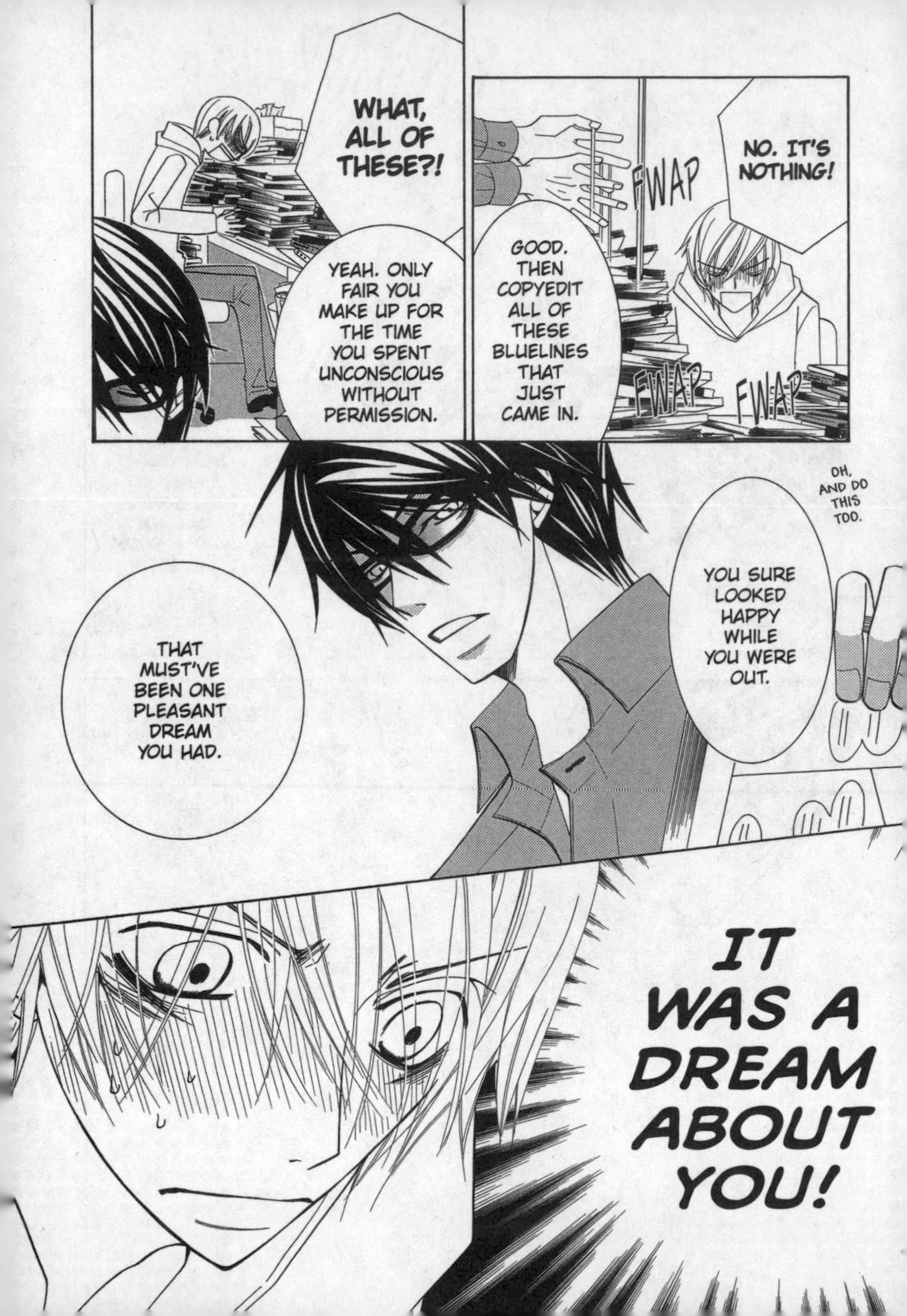
NO. IT'S NOTHING!
FWAP
GOOD. THEN COPYEDIT ALL OF THESE BLUELINES THAT JUST CAME IN.
FWAP
FWAP
WHAT, ALL OF THESE?!
YEAH. ONLY FAIR YOU MAKE UP FOR THE TIME YOU SPENT UNCONSCIOUS WITHOUT PERMISSION.
OH, AND DO THIS TOO.
YOU SURE LOOKED HAPPY WHILE YOU WERE OUT.
THAT MUST'VE BEEN ONE PLEASANT DREAM YOU HAD.
IT WAS A DREAM ABOUT YOU!

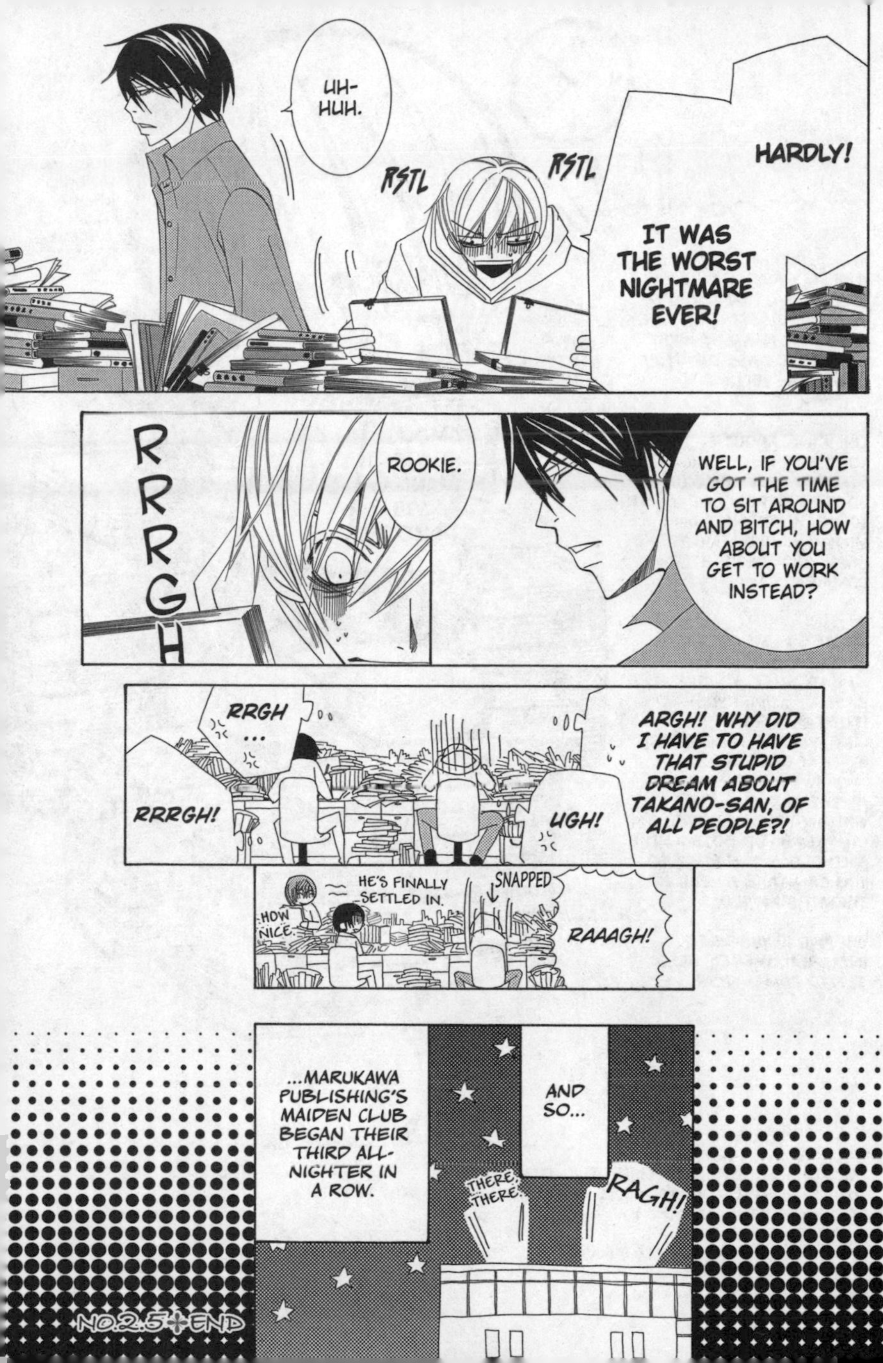
HARDLY!
IT WAS THE WORST NIGHTMARE EVER!
RSTL
RSTL
UH-HUH.
WELL, IF YOU'VE GOT THE TIME TO SIT AROUND AND BITCH, HOW ABOUT YOU GET TO WORK INSTEAD?
ROOKIE.
RRRGH
ARGH! WHY DID I HAVE TO HAVE THAT STUPID DREAM ABOUT TAKANO-SAN, OF ALL PEOPLE?!
UGH!
RRGH...
RRRGH!
RAAAGH!
SNAPPED
HE'S FINALLY SETTLED IN.
HOW NICE.
AND SO...
...MARUKAWA PUBLISHING'S MAIDEN CLUB BEGAN THEIR THIRD ALL-NIGHTER IN A ROW.
RAGH!
THERE, THERE.
NO.2.5 END

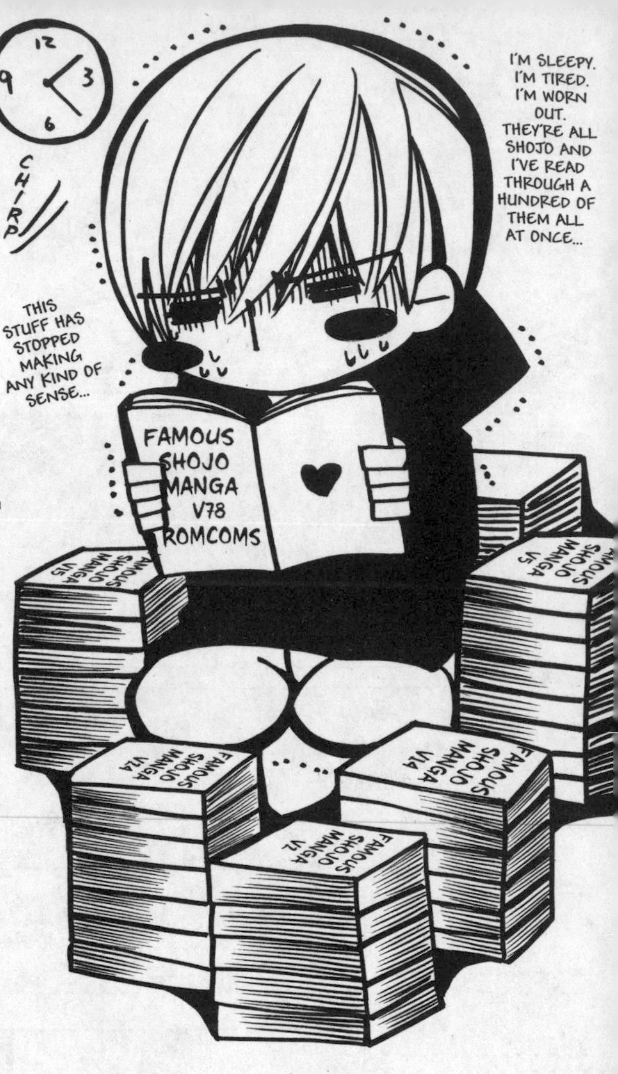
CHIRP CHIRP
I'M SLEEPY. I'M TIRED. I'M WORN OUT. THEY'RE ALL SHOJO AND I'VE READ THROUGH A HUNDRED OF THEM ALL AT ONCE...
THIS STUFF HAS STOPPED MAKING ANY KIND OF SENSE...
FAMOUS SHOJO MANGA V78 ROMCOMS
FAMOUS SHOJO MANGA V15
FAMOUS SHOJO MANGA V5
FAMOUS SHOJO MANGA V14
FAMOUS SHOJO MANGA V14
FAMOUS SHOJO MANGA V2

HELLO. IT'S NICE TO MEET YOU! MY NAME IS SHUNGIKU NAKAMURA. THANK YOU SO MUCH FOR PICKING UP THE WORLD'S GREATEST FIRST LOVE ~THE CASE OF RITSU ONODERA~ VOLUME 1!

THINKING ABOUT IT, THIS IS THE FIRST NEW SERIES I'VE STARTED IN A WHILE (OOH!), SO IT'S ALL REALLY EXCITING TO ME. IF YOU WOULDN'T MIND, I WOULD LOVE TO HEAR YOUR THOUGHTS AND COMMENTS ON IT.

THERE'S ALSO THE NOVEL SIDE, *THE WORLD'S GREATEST FIRST LOVE ~THE CASE OF CHIAKI YOSHINO~* (RUBY BUNKO). IF YOU'D LIKE, PLEASE TAKE A LOOK AT THAT ONE.

AT THE MOMENT, I'M WRITING THE MOST RECENT CHAPTERS FOR BOTH IN THE ANTHOLOGY *THE RUBY*, SO YOU CAN TAKE A LOOK AT THEM THERE TOO.

OH! AND IF YOU'RE SO INCLINED, THERE'S ALSO *JUNJO ROMANTICA*!

CURRENT SITUATION: I'D LOVE TO KNOCK DOWN MY "TO READ" MANGA STACK (BY READING IT). I'VE ADDED SO MUCH STUFF TO IT NOW THAT IT'S FALLING OVER ON ITS OWN...

UNTIL WE SEE EACH OTHER AGAIN~

SHUNGIKU NAKAMURA 2008 ★

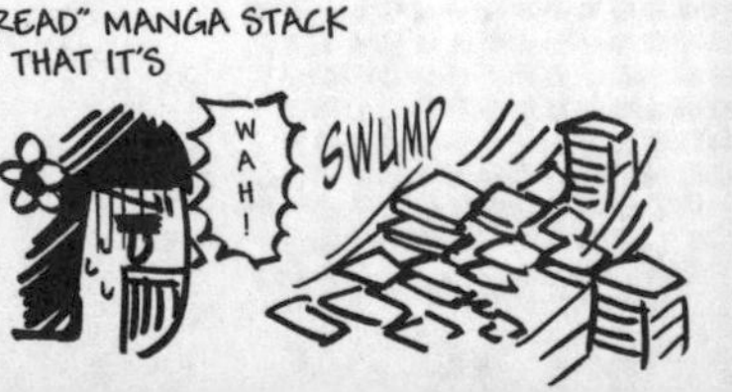
WAH!
SWUMP

For the first time in a while, I decided to write a brand-new story. I hope you enjoy it. This picture is my pen-nib jar and the nibs it holds. I lined up all my pen nibs by type once. They covered my whole desktop.

About the Author

Shungiku Nakamura is one of the most popular yaoi creators worldwide. She is best known for her series *Junjo Romantica*, which has been adapted into both an anime and drama CD. Her other English-language title, *Hybrid Child*, is also being adapted into an anime. Her current series, *The World's Greatest First Love*, is running in *Emerald* magazine. Born on December 13, she's a Sagittarius with an O blood type.

The World's Greatest
First Love:
The Case of Ritsu Onodera

Volume 1
SuBLime Manga Edition

Story and Art by **Shungiku Nakamura**

Translation—**Adrienne Beck**
Touch-up Art and Lettering—**NRP Studios**
Cover and Graphic Design—**Fawn Lau**
Editor—**Jennifer LeBlanc**

SEKAIICHI HATSUKOI ~ONODERA RITSU NO BAAI~ Volume 1
© Shungiku NAKAMURA 2008
First published in Japan in 2008 by KADOKAWA CORPORATION, Tokyo.
English translation rights arranged with KADOKAWA CORPORATION, Tokyo.

ASUKA
COMICS
CL D X

Printed in the U.S.A.

Published by SuBLime Manga
P.O. Box 77010
San Francisco, CA 94107

10 9 8 7 6 5
First printing, April 2015
Fifth printing, November 2021

 PARENTAL ADVISORY
THE WORLD'S GREATEST FIRST LOVE is rated M for Mature and is
recommended for mature readers. This volume contains graphic
MATURE imagery and mature themes.

www.SuBLimeManga.com

For more information

on all our products, along with the most up-to-date news on releases, series announcements, and contests, please visit us at:

 SuBLimeManga.com

 twitter.com/**SuBLimeManga**

 facebook.com/**SuBLimeManga**

 SuBLimeManga.tumblr.com

Downloading is as easy as:

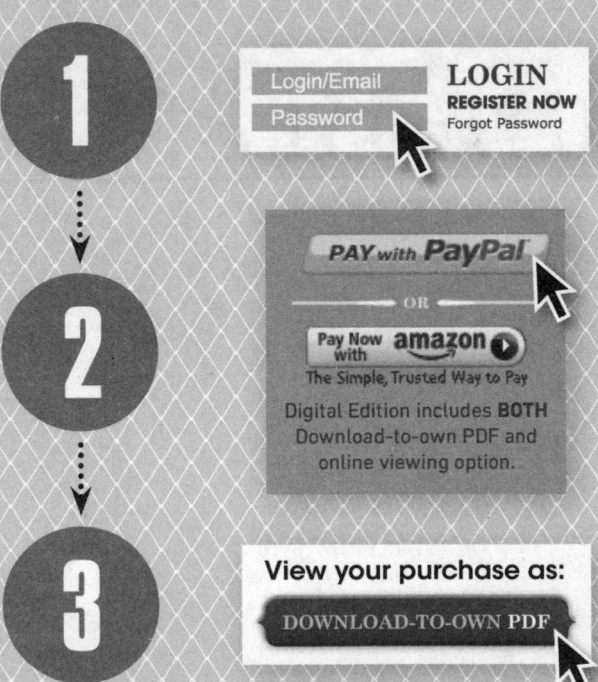

SuBLime

Your Toys Love Boys' Love

Own your SuBLime book as a convenient PDF document that is downloadable to the following devices:

- ♥ Computer
- ♥ Kindle™
- ♥ NOOK™
- ♥ iPad™, iPhone™, and iPod Touch™
- ♥ Any device capable of reading a PDF document

The Scent of Apple Blossoms
BLOG
How's Your Ex?
The Night Before the Wedding
Punch Up!
Bond of Dreams, Bond of Love
Honey Darling
Do You Like Me?
Three Wolves Mountain

SuBLime

www.SuBLimeManga.com

More of the best digital BL manga from

SUBLIME

Sweet Monster
by Tsubaki Mikage

Pretty Men Fighting Dirty
by Sakira

Perfect Training
by Yuiji Aniya

Available **Worldwide** in
Download-To-Own Format

Get them now for only **$5.99** each at **SuBLimeManga.com!**